New World Orders

M000026798

EARLY AMERICAN STUDIES

Daniel K. Richter and Kathleen M. Brown, Series Editors

Exploring neglected aspects of our colonial, revolutionary, and early
national history and culture, Early American Studies reinterprets familiar
themes and events in fresh ways. Interdisciplinary in character, and with
a special emphasis on the period from about 1600 to 1850, the series
is published in partnership with the McNeil Center
for Early American Studies.

A complete list of books in the series is available from the publisher.

New World Orders

Violence, Sanction, and Authority
in the Colonial Americas

Edited by
John Smolenski and
Thomas J. Humphrey

PENN

University of Pennsylvania Press
Philadelphia

Copyright © 2005 University of Pennsylvania Press
All rights reserved
Printed in the United States of America on acid-free paper

10   9   8   7   6   5   4   3   2   1

Published by
University of Pennsylvania Press
Philadelphia, Pennsylvania 19104-4112

Library of Congress Cataloging-in-Publication Data

New World orders : violence, sanction, and authority in the colonial Americas /
edited by John Smolenski and Thomas J. Humphrey.
    p. cm. — (Early American studies)
    Includes bibliographical references and index.
    ISBN-13: 978-0-8122-3895-2
    ISBN-10: 0-8122-3895-8 (cloth : alk. paper)
    1. America—History—To 1810. 2. Violence—America—History.
I. Smolenski, John. II. Humphrey, Thomas J., 1965–. III. Series.
E18.82.N485 2005
973.2—dc22

                                                    2005042306

Contents

Introduction

The Ordering of Authority in the Colonial Americas

John Smolenski

In 1720, Experience Mayhew published an account of the state of the Wampanoag Indians living on Martha's Vineyard, off the coast of Massachusetts.[1] Mayhew's text celebrated the missionaries' success at improving the Indians' spiritual and material conditions. Although the island's native population was "very much diminished," Mayhew noted the increasing number of Wampanoags who "have Houses of the *English* fashion" and had adopted English modes of husbandry.[2] He also predicted that island Indians would adopt English principles of governance as readily as they had adopted English religion, dress, shelter, and farming. His hopes were not entirely misplaced; by 1720, most Indian settlements had replaced the sachemship with a form of government that was "more akin to a town meeting"—the fabled institution at the center of colonial New England.[3]

At first glance, Mayhew's account epitomizes the dramatic success of colonial Anglo-American "ceremonies of possession." The spread of English housing and husbandry was part of a larger transformation of the landscape. Patricia Seed has argued that English colonists, alone among Europeans in America, viewed the enclosure and development of "waste" land as the only legitimate means of taking possession of territory.[4] The erection of houses and fences thus reflected and effected the spread of colonial authority. Certainly, in Mayhew's mind, the remaking of physical space was an assertion of English cultural and legal mastery: space, culture, and sovereignty were isomorphic.[5] Fences, farms, and livestock were only the most visible signs of a colonial project that included the reformation of the Natives' political and spiritual worlds as well. His account thus embodied the prototypical "planting" discourse in which claims to sovereignty were rooted not merely in English law but also in assumptions about race, identity, and superiority that provided the ideological foundation for Anglo-American colonization.

But treating these changes in landscape and authority merely as manifestations of a colonizing discourse would be misleading. As David Silverman has recently shown, some of these changes resulted from Native choices. Island Wampanoags benefited from selective adoption of English farming and herding practices, which provided an important source of food and an economic boost. But incorporating animal husbandry into their communities offered Vineyard Indians more than "protein and profit": establishing claims to the land through signs and practices that colonists recognized as legitimate helped some keep their land in the face of English expansion.[6] "The Wampanoags," Silverman writes, "had adopted the colonists' animals, but most of them had not embraced the colonists' values. The fence and the animals it enclosed were no longer only symbols of English expansion, but now, also, of the Wampanoags' commitment to the land, one another, and their communal traditions."[7] Similarly, the decline of the sachemship at Christiantown and Chappaquiddick allowed these communities to prevent individual sachems from selling communal land to settlers. Thus, the move toward town-meeting governance helped some communities to resist pressures that had forced other Native communities in New England off their lands.

Faced with a colonial project that drew sharp boundaries between "civilized" and "savage" practices, Vineyard Indians crafted a third option. More than simply a technique of "resistance," the evolution of their farming practices and political institutions challenged the system of legality through which colonists defined and took control of their world.[8] The colonists' response reveals the seriousness of the challenge; having justified their claim to "waste" lands on the grounds that Indians had done nothing to improve (and thus possess) them, some colonists threatened violence when faced with Indian fences marking the boundaries of native lands.[9] Thus, what Mayhew saw as a process of acculturation—Wampanoag Indians' evolutionary transition from a lower to a higher stage of civilization—was really part of a process of transculturation in which Vineyard Indians integrated aspects of English life into their own society, but with Native meanings, for Native ends.[10]

The disjuncture between Mayhew's narrative and the Wampanoags' experience is instructive. The Indians' continued presence on the land belied Mayhew's assumption that the boundaries of colonial sovereignty were coterminous with the limits of English cultural space; mastery in one realm did not automatically follow in the other. Nor were the links between legal claims to sovereignty and extralegal claims to cultural authority as natural as Mayhew assumed. English settlers may well have believed that their agricultural improvements had transformed *vacuum domicilium*—legally vacant land outside any civil jurisdiction—into property under provincial authority.[11] But their resistance to Wampanoag efforts to develop their own farms and herds suggests that colonizers found these practices legitimate only when performed by English subjects; the Wampanoags, understandably, disagreed. Thus, the meaning of legal rules emerged through debate, not simply from rote application. Finally, it is unlikely that the Wampanoags would have ignored the role of violence—actual or threatened—in defining colonial authority, as Mayhew had. Threats to resolve debates over the cultural and legal meanings of particular practices through force revealed that violence was never absent from assertions of sovereignty.

That the critique of Mayhew's account as a colonizing discourse seems so familiar to historians of the colonial Americas and yet fails to account for the lived experience of the Wampanoags under colonization should caution us to be cognizant of the gap between the assertion and achievement of colonial sovereignty and of that between legal and extralegal claims to rule. It highlights the difficulties that historians have had in understanding the operation of colonial power, their difficulty in crafting narratives of colonization flexible enough to incorporate analysis of ideologies with accounts of Native resistance and adaptation. The chapters in this collection address that conceptual gap by reexamining the relationship between violence, sanction, and authority in the colonial Americas. The authors explore a number of themes, including the wide variety of legal and extralegal means through which social order was secured, with a particular emphasis on how extralegal behavioral norms were defined and used; the relationship between legal and extralegal efforts to create colonial authority; the problem of containing violence within structures of colonial legality or illegality; and how these attempts to construct authority, embedded within other forms of colonialism, created cultural, legal, social, or imperial "spaces" in the Americas. Eschewing a narrowly regional analysis, these chapters collectively cut across imperial boundaries, exploring the dimensions of colonial rule throughout the hemisphere.

Uniting these case studies is a common interest in understanding the role of sanction in constituting colonial power. The term "sanction" carries multiple—and seemingly contradictory—meanings. It can mean to permit, authorize, ratify, countenance, encourage, or make legal—or it can mean to

penalize for the violation of a legal rule or norm. It can refer to the imposition of a punishment itself or to the recognition (implicit or explicit) of a
practice as valid. But sanction's multiple meanings—as prohibition and permission, as the judgment and its enforcement—are only seemingly contradictory.
The notion that the expression of power has productive and repressive effects
is certainly familiar to scholars in the wake of Michel Foucault's work,
but it was likewise familiar to earlier legal authorities.[12] The jurist William
Blackstone noted that "human legislators have for the most part chosen to
make the sanction of their laws rather *vindicatory* than *remunatory*," demonstrating an awareness of the fact that the encouragement of legality and the
punishment of illegality went hand in hand.[13] But sanctioning, in both its
senses of permission and prohibition, is more than the simple application of
legal (or extralegal) norms. Sanction has an evaluative, interpretive dimension: it defines norms in the process of enforcing them. Sanction, then,
encapsulates the process through which order is produced through the distribution of punishments and rewards. Through their examination of sanction in its multiple dimensions, the authors in this volume demonstrate that
colonial authority—be it cultural, legal, or political—did not exist in inert
form; it was constituted through its expression.

Through their examination of authority emerging through practice
rather than in principle, these authors extend Christopher Tomlins's recent
call for legal historians to shift the object of their inquiry from an analysis
of law in history to an examination of the history of legality. Legality, as
Tomlins defines it, is the process through which legal power is expressed.
"Legalities," he writes, "are the symbols, signs, and instantiations of formal
law's classificatory impulse, the outcomes of its specialized practices, the
products of its institutions. They are the means of effecting law's discourses,
the mechanisms through which law names, blames, and claims."[14] If the
law's authority is often grounded in its claims to reason and timelessness—
as the legal scholar Paul Kahn has argued in his critical inquiry into the "culture of rule of law" in the Euro-American tradition[15]—then exploring legality is a tool for grounding legal analysis in a social and historical context.
Similarly, Tomlins suggests that the concept of legality can also include unofficial practices, customs, and traditions that carry the sanction of social
authority—practices which themselves should be seen as historical products
rather than timeless. In examining histories of sanctioning—the points at
which actions are interpreted, evaluated, debated, and defined—the chapters in this volume provide a means of understanding how legalities, official
and unofficial, were produced in the colonial Americas.

This volume builds upon an already well-established literature addressing the process of colonization in the Americas. It is by now commonplace to point out that historical narratives such as Mayhew's—triumphalist master narratives of the colonial Americas that render Natives either passive receptors of a superior European culture or a swiftly vanishing vestige of the precolonial past—represented colonizers' fantasies rather than historical fact. Scholars have attempted to write against these master narratives by foregrounding the development and operation of colonial authority in the Americas as an object of historical analysis rather than a providential inevitability; these efforts have generally followed one of three tracks. First, many historians and anthropologists have examined the processes through which indigenous peoples resisted and adapted to colonial rule. These studies—often, but not always, focused on the colonial experience of a specific people—have emphasized the role Native agency played in shaping colonial rule, casting Native peoples as subjects in a contest for power and not simply objects of colonial power.[16] Second, historians and literary critics have interrogated the imperial ideologies of the various European colonial powers in the Americas. Through their critiques of the cultural underpinnings of the colonial project, these scholars have shown how European discourses of law, religion, and civilization naturalized and legitimated colonization; indeed, some of these authors would seem to suggest that the colonial discourses that legitimated European rule were among the colonizers' most powerful tools of domination.[17] And third, many historians have shown how interactions between colonizers and colonized created hybrid cultures in the Americas.[18]

These three strands of scholarship have done much to further our understanding of colonial power in the Americas. At the same time, however, each has, in its own way, hindered greater understanding of the establishment and maintenance of colonial authority. Studies focused on Native agency, for example, have defined colonial authority as something acted against, obscuring it as a topic of analysis in its own right. Meanwhile, studies of colonial ideology have, in making their critique, often assumed the dominance of colonial sovereignty. By treating colonization as a discursive or performative project, this approach ignores the ongoing process through which colonial rule was secured. As Lauren Benton has pointed out, such critiques have tended to focus on the moments of taking possession or justifications for conquest, missing the fact that the exigencies of exercising colonial jurisdiction frequently transformed the culture of colonial legality.[19] In addition, some critics have charged that scholars foregrounding the significance of "middle grounds" in colonial history have exaggerated the significance and durability of these hybrid cultural spaces. Admitting that a localized balance of power might facilitate the temporary emergence of communities of interest marked by a rough harmony, critics note, does little to mitigate the overall level of violence and conflict that marked colonial-Indian relations.[20]

In any case, synthesizing these different approaches has been problematic. It is in some ways difficult to see how one can reconcile John Locke's intellectual justifications for dispossessing Indians of their land—so central in David Armitage's and Anthony Pagden's discussions of the English conception of empire—with the actual course of colonial settlement on the eastern coast of North America in which colonizers and Indians frequently lived side by side. Despite frequent outbreaks of violence, in practice the tenor of Anglo-Native relations was dictated more by extralegal customs governing social and economic exchange than by the formal justifications for English power.[21] And while colonists may have in theory denied Indians' legal title to land, in practice they recognized Native title when doing so expedited land purchases.[22] Thus, historians have struggled, often unsuccessfully, to integrate insights gleaned from these burgeoning historiographic traditions into a more coherent account of the linkages between assertions of sovereignty and expressions of authority in other social and cultural domains in the development of the colonial Americas.

This problem has been exacerbated by a historiographic division between scholars interested in studying relations of power between natives and colonizers and those studying relations of power—legal and extralegal—within colonial communities themselves. While historians of indigenous peoples have not always incorporated insights gleaned from colonial legal history into their studies, legal historians have largely failed to integrate narratives of colonization into their case studies.[23] Historians of both colonial British and Spanish America have grounded legal history in a social context by examining legal culture—that is, the values and attitudes that govern the functioning of legal institutions and processes.[24] By approaching their subject through the lens of legal culture, historians have been able to delineate how various legal practices—assertions of jurisdiction, displays of legitimacy, enforcement of criminal sanctions, regulation of economic life—structured and were structured by concepts of gender, race, and identity or broader patterns of community, hierarchy, and social structure.[25] They have also revealed the importance of extralegal power relations in shaping emerging hierarchies, particularly with respect to the construction of gender and race.[26] This holistic approach has been consistent with the dominant trends in early American social history, where authors of community studies have drawn heavily on the anthropological "culture concept" in their efforts to discern patterns within colonial society; the most significant studies exploring the relations between legal and extralegal power relations have focused on a particular community.[27]

But this holistic approach toward understanding the relationship between law and culture has been problematic as well. Indeed, the concept of legal culture suffers from many of the same problems as the anthropological culture concept itself. [28] Critics of the culture concept have argued that anthropologists and historians have essentialized culture as an object with determinate boundaries and features, often operating with what Akhil Gupta and James Ferguson have called an "assumed isomorphism of space, place, and culture."[29] This logic of cultural sameness and difference has led scholars to overemphasize homogeneity within particular societies or "cultures" and to presume sharp boundaries between cultures. In response to this criticism, cultural anthropologists and historians have altered the scope and emphasis of their work. Both have expanded the boundaries of their inquiry; for colonial historians this has involved looking at borderlands at the edges of imperial rule or the Atlantic dimensions of colonial history, all the while paying closer attention to the cultural diversity and hybridity within American societies more generally.[30] In a similar vein, historians studying the legal dynamics of European colonization have had to come to terms with the very real tensions between local and imperial governance and conflict over the meaning of legal authority. In their analysis of the overlapping and competing layers of authority within colonial societies, however, legal historians have been relatively slow to analyze the legal pluralism within the colonial Americas, particularly within colonial British America.[31]

Tellingly, most Anglo-American historians who have engaged the question of competing legal orders have focused, somewhat narrowly, on conflicts surrounding property rights, most often among Euro-American colonists themselves.[32] The history of this struggle within colonial settlements, however, is infrequently examined in the context of ongoing competition over the definition of property between Anglo-Americans and others. While these studies have made an extremely significant contribution to our broader understanding of the social and economic aspects of legality in early American history, their cumulative effect has been to limit the range of scholarly examination of the interactions between unofficial notions and procedures and official definitions and processes of justice, subsuming it within narratives of popular opposition to capitalism. Institutional efforts to quash plural

legal regimes in colonial settings were part of an effort to impose a particular Western conception of property and did advance both colonial and
capitalist projects, but the scope of conflict over legal pluralism and property in colonial contexts was far broader than the history of capitalism's rise
(and resistance to that rise).[33]

Patricia Seed's comparative history of the means by which various
European imperial powers created political authority over the Americas
illustrates the potentials and pitfalls of incorporating the insights of the historical study of legal culture with the cultural dimensions of European colonization.[34] Attempting to understand how law influenced the conquest of
the Americas, Seed examines the pains Europeans took to render conquest
legal. Colonizers secured their authority in the Americas, she argues, "by
deploying symbolically significant words and gestures made sometimes preceding, sometimes following, sometimes simultaneously with military conquest." These ritual enactments, in effect, made the conquest legal, at least in
the eyes of the colonizing powers.[35] Treating the "rationales and legitimation
of the exercise of imperial power as cultural constructions," Seed locates these
justifications of rule not in legal theories but in quotidian practices that
each power saw as legitimating possession: Spanish legal protocol, French
processions, English planting, Dutch mapmaking, Portuguese astronomy.[36]
Because each relied on different rituals to establish authority, the various
European powers found each other's claims to power mutually incompre-
hensible and criticized their rivals' colonial projects as arbitrary, unjust, and
illegal. Ultimately, Seed suggests that this anthropological perspective on the
cultural roots of colonial power offers a way to move beyond historians'
tendency to treat the history of colonialism either "as [the] intellectual cultures of dominant peoples, on the one hand, or as the history of resisting
peoples, on the other hand." [37]

At the same time, Seed's analysis of the cultural roots of colonial legal
authority replicates many of the elements that critics of the culture concept
have raised. Seed successfully undermines the notion that there was a single
cultural logic of imperialism, showing sharp distinctions between national
colonial projects, but in doing so she renders these imperial cultures of
power internally homogeneous over time and space.[38] Her treatment of the
question of colonial dissent is revealing of this approach. Seed's claim that
internal critics of colonization never proffered alternative conceptions of
colonial legality describes the positions of critics such as Roger Williams or
Bartolomé de las Casas too narrowly.[39] Williams's writings on authority in
early New England, for example, drew on an eclectic range of discourses,

including his legal and religious background and his pioneering ethno-graphic work on Indian languages. His work epitomizes the fallacy of re-ducing imperial efforts to theorize and project authority to a single national idiom.[40] In rendering European rituals of power as relatively fixed "ideal types," Seed ignores the fluidity of colonial negotiations on the ground. French colonizers recognized the value of hybrid "middle grounds" in secur-ing commerce and amity with Natives. English colonial authorities who insisted on their sovereignty over Natives redefined certain crimes as polit-ical disputes to recognize Native sovereignty in practice, if not in theory. And Spanish officials affirmed the independence of Indian nations living on the frontiers of Spain's American empire after it became clear that impos-ing *imperium* over all the Americas was futile.[41] In other words, the prac-tical difficulties of imperial management frequently prompted a revision of the legal underpinnings of European colonial power. Ignoring this fact dehistoricizes the construction of colonial authority. In the end, Seed bril-liantly reconstructs the meaning of these various systems of symbolic authority at moments of conquest without addressing the fact that symbolic systems—in their meaning, their application, and their relationship to soci-ety as a whole—change over time.[42]

What the chapters collected here reveal, however, is that in many re-spects, the methodological difficulties inherent in Seed's ambitious attempt to explain the instantiation of authority in the Americas stem from contra-dictions in the colonial project itself. European colonialism involved, almost from the beginning, both the description and the production of colonial spaces: explorers, missionaries, settlers, and imperial representatives gener-ated extensive scientific accounts of the Americas. This project involved the creation of maps detailing the region's topographical features and locating major indigenous polities and tribes;[43] the writing of ethnographic accounts of Indian religion, language, politics, and technology;[44] histories of the Americas, based in various degrees on both colonial and native sources;[45] and extensive studies of American plants and wildlife. Moreover, this scien-tific mapping of the Americas—in both a geographic and a cultural sense—played a crucial political role in colonization. The collection of ethno-graphic data on the governmental structure and spatial ordering of Indian societies, for example, was not simply part of the articulation of European cultural superiority but was deeply related to European attempts to secure Native allies in their struggles against other indigenous groups and rival colo-nial powers.[46] Maps also played a crucial role in European colonial rivalries in America: since European states offered maps of their New World territories as evidence of their sovereignty in the region, detailed maps frequently became valuable as these states fought over competing colonial claims. At other times, governments allowed the circulation only of vague, seemingly primitive maps of the Americas, the better to prevent rivals from locating and poaching valuable colonial possessions.[47] Relying in varying degrees on all of these techniques, European colonial powers asserted their sovereignty over the Americas, transforming land into territory—producing it, in effect, as colonial space.

Just as the creation of a colonial space implied a single sovereign, it also implied a kind of cultural unity among colonial subjects, at least in theory. The intensification of colonial states' claims over subjects within their jurisdiction had the effect of sharpening legal distinctions between members of the dominant culture and cultural "others." While this process entailed at various times the equation of nationality and citizenship (as Tamar Herzog has suggested for Spain and Spanish America) or the reduction of civic status to a question of race (as Gene Ogle has observed in Hilliard D'Auberteuil's proposed "Enlightened" reforms in Saint Domingue), the ultimate result was the same: "foreignness" came to mark both cultural and legal boundaries simultaneously.[48] The "legal cartography" of the Atlantic world presumed that the "uncivilized" lived outside the rules of law that governed European nations.[49] In practice, colonization greatly increased the diversity of peoples under European rule, creating new jurisdictional problems. Thus, colonization also involved the construction of colonial space in the Americas through what Pierre Bourdieu has called the mapping of social topologies—the delineation of relationships between individuals within a hierarchical social setting.[50] Government officials throughout the New World were involved in classifying different groups and defining the nature of their relationship to institutions of authority, whether legal, religious, or political: defining colonial jurisdiction involved generating and enforcing legal and social identities along—most prominently but not exclusively—the lines of race, gender, religion, nationality, and free or unfree status. Colonial governments found the problem of defining boundaries within colonial societies exacerbated by the presence of indigenous peoples and diversity caused by the migration, voluntary or involuntary, of Europeans and Africans to the Americas—in other words, by the very diversity of colonial societies. Metropolitan authorities likewise found their efforts to maintain these boundaries in conflict with the wishes of American communities, which often insisted on defining ethnic and racial boundary lines themselves, as Ann Twinam suggests.[51]

Thus, assertions of European sovereignty in the Americas involved the creation of colonial spaces through the mapping of internal and external boundaries demarcating lines of colonial jurisdiction. While colonial officials may have intended their proclamations of authority over the peoples and places as monologue—a performative display that effected the instantiation of rule it announced—their ceremonies of possession turned out in fact to be the opening of ongoing colonial dialogues in which the nature of imperial powers in the Americas was defined through negotiation. European claims to sovereignty in the Americas, despite their pretenses of establishing a single legitimate authority within colonial territory, never extinguished legal pluralism in colonial societies. In fact, by opening up spaces in which definitions and practices of rules could be asserted and contested, these claims to eliminate legal pluralism generated novel pluralisms, a plethora of cultural and social spaces in which alternative conceptions of authority could be articulated. Efforts to create jurisdiction over people and places inevitably created zones of jurisdictional conflict, a fact of which colonial officials were quite painfully aware. Those living under colonial rule, meanwhile, frequently found negotiating these zones of intrainstitutional conflict strategically useful in securing some relative autonomy from one or more sources of colonial power.[52] What Benton has noted about the borderlands of northern New Spain was true throughout the colonial Americas: "[T]he indeterminacy of power on the borderlands reflected a larger structural condition. The border itself—the line between imperial control populated by Christian subjects of the crown and hazardous lands of the 'wild' Indians—was simply a more visible example of the many 'borders' separating groups with different legal and cultural status within the empire."[53]

It would be tempting to dismiss this border trouble as peripheral to the "main" story of the development of authority in colonial societies in much the same way that the historiography on the development of legal cultures in Anglo-America has remained separate from the historiography on colonial-Native relations. But European claims to have achieved sovereignty through rituals of possession cannot be taken at face value, and the efforts of those subject to colonization to shape the nature of authority in the Americas cannot simply be subsumed under the category of "resistance" to an already constituted colonial rule. Indians in the Americas, for example, played an active role in shaping the evolution of colonial legal structures, through their efforts either to remain outside of or to work within imperial legal systems. Even within the brutal slave systems of the Americas the expression and meaning of power was negotiated.[54] This conflict over jurisdiction and the construction of authority was not an anomaly within colonial cultures, an exception to European rule; these contests over the expression and limits of authority were what constituted colonial culture. Greg Urban's analysis of how cultural authority is produced is instructive in this regard. There is nothing inherent in any culture, Urban argues, that allows it to claim superiority over any other culture. Culture, he writes, "is inert. It contains no force that would cause it to spread, to perpetuate itself, in the face of resistance or in the form of alternatives."[55] This motive force, the claim to authority over other cultures or peoples, he continues, can come only from arguing *about* culture; it is, in a word, metacultural. Thus, all legal authority is inherently metacultural; declarations of sovereignty always involve the assertion— sometimes implicit, sometimes explicit—that competing assertions of sovereignty are inferior and therefore null and void. Urban's discussion reveals the fallacy of separating the study of legal cultures in a "core" from the negotiation of authority on the periphery or of drawing too sharp an analytical line between jurisdictional disputes along internal and those along external boundary lines.

The construction of colonial authority also involved conflicts over sanction—the defining and expression of violence. Violence in the colonial Americas—like violence everywhere, was often "a vivid expression of cultural values," freighted with symbolic meaning. Conceptions of which forms of violence were appropriate (and when) and of who were appropriate objects of violence were culturally bounded. And the colonial encounter in the Americas was, from the beginning, a conflict between cultures of violence. Conflicts between Spaniards and Nahua during the conquest of Mexico, between Dutch and several Indian groups in New Netherlands during Kieft's War, and between English and Wampanoag and Narragansett Indians in King Philip's War in New England witnessed similar phenomena: revulsion at Indian styles of warfare—and the resultant belief that this kind of unrestrained violence placed Natives outside the bounds of civilized society—encouraged European and Creole soldiers to resort to early modern variations of "total war."[56] Conceptions of violence thus helped reinforce boundaries of culture and law through the construction of what Michael Taussig has called "the colonial mirror which reflects back onto the colonists the barbarity of their own social relations, but as imputed to the savage or evil figures they wish to colonize."[57]

Symbolic displays of violence encoded and enforced power relations. Plantation owners and overseers maintained order through theatrics of power incorporating ritualized threats of power as much as through the infliction of violent punishment itself.[58] And among colonials themselves, provincial officials were cognizant of the fact that much of their authority rested not on maintaining a monopoly of violence—one of the traditional definitions of state authority—but on maintaining a monopoly on defining the meaning of violence. The ritualized rebellion William Prendergast led against New York land barons in 1766 provides a case in point. Prendergast's actions symbolized popular justice to provincial tenants but treason to landowners and magistrates, leading to his arrest. After Prendergast's trial and conviction for treason, provincial officials pardoned his sentence of death by beheading and quartering.[59] The incident thus encapsulates the significance of sanction in its multiple dimensions. Just as Prendergast's actions articulated both an alternative conception of property rights and the tenants' legitimate authority to enforce these rights, so too was his trial and pardon a theatrical display of state authority; far from a sign of its weakness, the state's expression of generosity in letting a popular rebel live highlighted its discretionary authority in enforcing punishment.

At the same time, violence was more than a reflection of colonial culture—it was one of its constituent elements. The generative relationship between colonialism and culture, and particularly between colonialism and identity, has been well established. Writing on Anglo-American colonization, Tomlins has written that legalities play an essential role in "defining who is who: who is a British subject, who is not, and how the resources and terms of interaction given to each arise from that initial point of difference."[60] And Benton has noted that under the legal pluralism that so often characterized colonial rule, identity, in as much as it defined legal status vis-à-vis colonial authorities, was "often logically viewed . . . itself as a *form of property.*"[61] But scholars have been more hesitant to explore violence as a foundational element in colonial culture. Urban's assertion that cultural authority emerges only through metacultural arguments about culture leads to a disturbing conclusion: "Violence," he notes, "is metacultural and, indeed, may be a fundamental manifestation of metaculture."[62] Culture, in other words, is at its root a product of violence of some form or another—even more so, perhaps, in a situation in which the definitions and boundaries of cultural authority are unclear, as was the case in the colonization of the Americas. Describing the colonial encounter in Venezuela as a "space of death," Taussig has argued that colonial violence created a culture of terror that was integral to European rule, enjoining scholars to realize that "terror . . . as well as being a psychological state is also a social fact and a cultural construction whose baroque dimensions allow it to serve as the mediator *par excellence* of colonial hegemony. The space of death is one of the crucial spaces where Indian, African, and white gave birth to the New World."[63]

As the authors in this volume demonstrate, colonial identities emerged in the Americas through the relationship between sanction and violence. On both an individual and a social level, colonial communities worked to establish a common repertoire of ways of violence among their members. Colonial identities were created in some degree through economies of violence—the range of permissible exchanges of violence in colonial society that defined who could inflict violence against whom and under what conditions.[64] As Ogle, Block, Vidal, and Gauderman show, the meaning of race and gender in everyday life was defined by sanctioned expressions of violence. As colonial authorities struggled to define specific acts of violence—such as determining the limits of a slave owner's authority when it conflicted with either the king's authority or racial regimes of violence in Louisiana and Saint Domingue, respectively—they affirmed the notion that the legitimate use of violence in the colonies was increasingly a generalized prerogative available to all white men, especially with respect to violence against African Americans. Likewise, Richard Price shows that the contest to define the meaning of colonial violence created a space within which alternative identities and communities could be created, as the objects of colonial violence—enslaved African Americans and their descendents—crafted their own narratives of plantation violence in which masters' and magistrates' claims to power were held up to ridicule and censure. Discussions over what forms of violence would be sanctioned—in both senses of the term—were crucial in defining colonial space and culture, whether such debates took place in courtrooms, through networks of community gossip, or in hybrid colonial-Native settlements along the colonial periphery.

These studies hardly exhaust the possibilities for the further exploration of the myriad strategies used to establish power in the Americas or how the nature of colonial authority changed through its enforcement. Indeed, they collectively offer two things about the future study of colonialism in the Americas. First, they suggest that we focus less on social and cultural order in the colonies, and instead on ordering—the practices through which authority was maintained. Through their focus on sanction—the evaluative process through which punishments or permissions were distributed—the authors demonstrate how thoroughly entwined conceptions of colonial legality and sovereignty were with extralegal discourses of race, gender, and civilization. They likewise amplify the historical dimensions of colonial power by tracing its emergence not merely through assertion of conquest but through constant creation and re-creation, revealing the colonial origins of contemporary notions of sovereignty and power. Their findings that the application of colonial "rules" was at times fluid—that governments and communities sometimes chose to sanction behaviors that they ordinarily might not have—do not mitigate the severity of American colonialism but instead uncover a flexibility that both helped colonial governments maintain control when they could not unilaterally enforce their will and created a space in which colonial rules might be challenged and rewritten. Interrogating the space between the discourse and the experience of colonization, they show how narratives of colonial sanction might themselves provide new ways of evaluating the legitimacy of colonial authority in the past as well as its historical resonance in the present.

Second, these chapters demonstrate the necessity of examining the questions of violence, sanction, and authority in hemispheric perspective. Organized not by political (imperial) boundaries but thematically, they reveal significant commonalities as well as differences throughout the colonial Americas. This thematic unity and geographic diversity reflect the volume's origins. The chapters in *New World Orders* are drawn from a conference of the same name, held in Philadelphia in October 2001. In organizing the conference the program committee—two historians of British North America and one historian of colonial Mexico—believed that local histories of violence and colonial power could fruitfully be analyzed as examples of a larger phenomenon of American colonization. Bringing together scholars of different regions, the conference forced participants to resituate their work in a wider context, to productive effect. The individual case studies presented challenged participants' assumptions about the larger contours of colonial authority in the Americas, while placing their own work within the history of the Americas writ large allowed authors to see local or regional histories in a new light.[65]

Of course, it may be, in practical terms, impossible for any book, any scholar, or even any collection such as this to offer a truly comprehensive analysis of the various ways in which colonial authority was defined, established, and challenged or through which colonial spaces and identities were created. But in their common efforts to trace the threads of this process in a variety of times and places these authors begin to outline, at least, what such a project might look like. As Experience Mayhew's narrative of the history of the Vineyard Indians shows, the ordering of the colonial Americas was a multifaceted affair; both his account and the Wampanoags' actions in the face of this transforming colonial project involved a mapping and remapping of social, cultural, political, religious, and physical landscapes. By juxtaposing case studies of this process from Brazil, Venezuela, New York, and California with treatments of broader trends within Anglo-America or Spanish America more generally, the studies in this volume collectively render Mayhew's narrative more and less familiar to historians of the colonial Americas. They are less familiar, perhaps, in that they erode the sense of singular mission—of exceptionalism—that informed his Puritan historiography and has too often divided Anglo-American ("US-onion") historiography from the rest of American history; but more familiar, hopefully, to the extent that the story of that colonial encounter can now be seen as one aspect of a common history of the Americas. By rendering the histories of the colonial Americas simultaneously more and less familiar, these authors reveal hidden linkages within a broader story as well as the conceptual and historiographical gaps that need to be bridged for that common American history to be written more fully.

PART I

Narrating Violence and Legality

I t is by now commonplace for scholars to note that the formation of collective identities requires, as Benedict Anderson has shown, a curious
process of remembering and forgetting. Nations, he notes, need narratives
of identity replete with triumphs and sacrifices that must be remembered
and traumas its members were "'obliged already to have forgotten.'"[1] Violence, Anderson writes, plays a curious role in the construction of these stories—sometimes excised, sometimes exaggerated. In both cases, what matters
is how storytellers employ incidents of violence to cultivate a common identity. "To serve the narrative purpose," he argues, "these violent deaths must
be remembered/forgotten as 'our own.'"[2] This recuperation of violence is, in
turn, essential to history's role in legitimating particular forms of authority.
And if the process Anderson describes holds true in the creation of national
narratives it also holds equally true in the construction of colonial histories.
The chapters in Part I, entitled "Narrating Violence and Legality," explore the
stories that sanctioned colonial rule and their role in constructing American
histories.

Christopher Tomlins uses *Titus Andronicus* as a lens through which to
explore the literary, cartographic, and legal texts that provided the discursive frames for English colonization of the Americas. Tomlins argues that
Andronicus embodied the process through which the early modern English
created boundaries between territory and wasteland, civility and barbarism,
and law and violence. Through the construction of these antimonies, he
writes, the English not only justified their own appropriation of America, by
positioning their actions as legal, they also allowed Anglo-Americans during the colonial and post-colonial periods to evade the violence inherent in
English colonialism. Richard Price, meanwhile, examines "three emblematic
moments of Caribbean rimland history, three linked narratives of death and
creation." Analyzing these instances of exemplary violence, Price demonstrates the centrality of stories of life and death in the creation of Sarama-
kan histories—not simply in their relation of particular events, people, and
places, but by shaping the meaning of that violence. Rejecting the notion
that the past can be seen only as a historians' discursive construct, he nonetheless shows that, to the extent that histories of colonial violence exercise

legitimating force in the present, these narratives matter and must be examined with care.

Both Tomlins's and Price's chapters show that neither expressions of violence—especially at moments of cultural interaction or formation—nor the execution of legal authority can be understood outside of the histories that relate, and interpret, them. They exemplify Michel-Rolph Trouillot's assessment of the relationship between power and history: "Power does not enter the story once and for all, but at different times and from different angles. It precedes the narrative proper, contributes to its creation and to its interpretation."[3] But through their identification and interrogation of particular examples of historical memory or forgetting in American history—moments in which the colonial authority was legitimated, contested, or silenced—these authors reveal the possibility and the necessity of developing alternative histories that address the violence of colonization directly.

Chapter 1

Law's Wilderness: The Discourse of English Colonizing, the Violence of Intrusion, and the Failures of American History

Christopher Tomlins

Prologue

> Titus: *Dost thou not perceive*
> *That Rome is but a wilderness of tigers?*
> —William Shakespeare, Titus Andronicus, *III.i.54 (c. 1591)*

This chapter grapples with two subjects, one a subject in history, the other history itself. The first is the opening of North America to the violent intrusions of early occidental modernity; that is, the first century of transoceanic English colonizing of the North Atlantic seaboard. I investigate the terms on which colonizing created America by inquiring into conjoined discourses, literary and legal, in which the meanings of those terms were first put on display. The second is the failure, upon which modern American history's liberal metanarrative is founded, to acknowledge the realities of origins. I argue that failure subordinates history to myth, making historical inquiry a means more to forgetfulness than critique.

The violence I address in this chapter is in its largest part textual, enduring in words spoken or written rather than in behavior. The texts are literary, legal, cartographic, and historical. I start with an attempt to characterize the relationship of texts to violence—how they authorize violence, narrate its display, and represent, or efface, its effects. Then I move to an examination of texts' relationship to the English colonizing project, and to each other. I conclude by assessing how American history has dealt with its "origins" question, concentrating in particular on the founding metanarrative of modern American legal history.

Recent work by Joyce Chaplin and Karen Kupperman has addressed the origins of English North America by tracing the discursive processes by which colonists attempted to understand and eventually to claim "bodily and cultural superiority" over the indigenous population. Far from an enterprise grounded in foundational assumptions of ascendancy over a primitive "other," their work suggests, English colonists "did not come to these confrontations with set, preconceived categories for describing others." Confident ascendancy was produced only gradually, over the course of a century's experiential interaction between colonists, Indians, and environment.[1]

The metropolitan texts discussed in this essay suggest that other discursive frames for success in colonizing existed than those generated by experience over time in America. From the outset, metropolitan law proved to be a technology of description and definition integral to the process of realizing colonization as a practice and colonists as its agents. English and European theories of rightful occupation, exclusive possession, sovereign authority, and just war fueled and expressed the colonizer's violent ideology of possession, differentiation, and exclusion.

Violence and the Word

> *Enter Aron, Chiron and Demetrius at one door, and at the other door Young Lucius and another, with a bundle of weapons, and verses writ upon them.*
> —Titus Andronicus *(stage direction, opening IV.ii.)*

Titus Andronicus (c. 1591) was one of Shakespeare's earliest plays.[2] From its first performance until the closing of the theaters in 1642, it retained an extraordinary following. Throughout, it is suffused with elaborate discourses of legality and injustice, of innocence and evil, and of civility and barbarity. It is also grotesquely violent.

Titus Andronicus conforms broadly to the genre of revenge tragedy found in the classical Roman work of Seneca and reestablished in the later 1580s by Thomas Kyd. Revenge tragedy has a particular plot form: an introductory assertion of a prior foundational injustice, followed by unremitting and often fantastic violence in the service of injustice's resolution.[3] Once critics had wrested Shakespeare from audiences, *Titus Andronicus*'s excursion into the "rough theater" of revenge tragedy was thought reason enough to cast it out of the canon, and until the 1950s the play languished, mocked and reviled.[4]

Dismissing *Titus Andronicus* as mere youthful excess, critics failed to reflect upon the manner and media by which the violence they abhorred was narrated in the play, in particular the attention Shakespeare devoted to relationships among text, law, and violence. Legal and quasi-legal texts that do violence figure in the play's most consequential moments. Aron the Moor, servant and lover of the Goth queen Tamora whom Titus has brought to Rome a captive, initiates Tamora's cycle of vengeance upon the Andronici with a "fatal-plotted scroll"—a forged letter—that results immediately in the condemnation and subsequent execution of Quintus and Martius, two of Titus's three surviving sons. Tamora gleefully calls the letter a "fatal writ," which indeed it is, for on its dubious authority alone the emperor Saturninus (who has meantime made Tamora his empress) dispenses with trial, plea, and testimony: "Let them not speak a word; the guilt is plain."[5] In his turn, Titus makes texts the instrumentalities of *his* revenge. To Tamora's sons Chiron and Demetrius, who at Aron's instigation have raped and mutilated his daughter Lavinia, Titus sends an odd gift—"the goodliest weapons of his armory" wound about with words from the first verse of an ode from Horace: *Integer vitae scelerisque purus / Non eget Mauri iaculis nec arcu* [one of upright life and free of villainy needs no Moorish javelins nor bow]. The boys, dull-witted, shrug. But Aron understands Titus' indictment: "the old man hath found their guilt, / And sends them weapons wrapped about with lines / That wound, beyond their feeling, to the quick."[6] In the next scene, apparently deranged, Titus has his kinsmen shoot arrows into the air wrapped in petitions that "will solicit heaven, and move the gods / To send down Justice for to wreak our wrongs." His brother Marcus directs the others to aim at the palace of Saturninus to afflict not the emperor's body but his pride with "scrolls to fly about the streets of Rome!" that, by "blazoning [his] unjustice," will arouse the populace. Whether directed to gods or men, the petitions, not the arrows, are the point. Immediately thereafter, the Andronici hatch a third text that does violence: they trick a "clown" into delivering a "supplication," wrapped around a knife, that accuses Saturninus of conspiring to procure the unlawful execution of Titus's sons. Saturninus has the unwitting messenger hung. As with Aron's letter, in each of these moves in Titus's pattern of vengeance the text effects an outcome on its own, unmediated.[7]

Shakespeare parses the relationship of text to violence throughout the play. Titus tells Lavinia that her mutilated, silenced body—hands chopped off, tongue cut out—is a text that will allow him knowledge of the violence inflicted upon her. "Thou shalt not sigh, nor hold thy stumps to heaven, /

Nor wink, nor nod, nor kneel, nor make a sign, / But I of these will wrest an alphabet / And by still practice learn to know thy meaning." Her body becomes testimony as well as evidence, a means to abet the subsequent slaughter of her rapists.[8] Lavinia herself creates texts to narrate her story. First, she draws Titus's attention to Ovid's account of the rape of Philomela in a handy copy of the *Metamorphoses.* Then she names her assailants and their crime by scratching words in a patch of sand. Finally, with Chiron and Demetrius gagged and their throats slit, their heads baked in a pie served to Tamora and Saturninus, Titus kills Lavinia in one more silent death decreed by a text—the customary law ("pattern, precedent, and *lively warrant*") that a Roman's daughter shall not shame him by surviving her own shame.[9]

Although *Titus Andronicus* is an extraordinarily violent play, the actual weapons with which it is replete are subordinated in the parts they play to the texts that enclose them. Weapons are mute, just like their victims. Texts speak and deal the violence. The play also gives these texts legal connotations, naming them as writs, petitions and warrants and setting them in sequences of legal proceedings—accusations, trials, executions—that purport to deliver justice but never do. In a genre (revenge tragedy) whose narrative structure is linear—the bloody redress of a pre-existing injustice—*Titus Andronicus* is anything but. Instead, competing original injustices result in multiple feuding claims to legality. Far from imposing order on the play's willful confusion, the legal texts and processes it repeatedly invokes are key participants in sustaining confusion itself.

Writing at the dawn of English modernity, Shakespeare calls to our attention intimacies of law and violence that render fanciful any notion of "the rule of law." Four hundred years later, at the high tide of late modernity, we encounter a lawyer, Robert Cover, interrogating precisely the same intimacies. What, if anything, had changed?

Cover's haunting soliloquy, "Violence and the Word," is a late twentieth-century reflection on the achievements of liberal jurisprudence, the jurisprudence of modernity. Its beginning is not flattering. "Legal interpretation takes place in a field of pain and death." It always had, "from John Winthrop through Warren Burger." Its violence was "utterly real—a naïve but immediate reality, in need of no interpretation, no critic to reveal it." That law could have violent consequences was not the issue; there was an "*unseverable* connection between legal interpretation and violence." The observation denied liberalism's fondest claim, that history told of legality's relentless strangulation of violence and of the creation of a rule of law that celebrated civility's ascendancy.[10]

Cover, however, hedged. "Connection" implied not seamless sameness but essential separation. Moreover, the connection Cover pursued was not one between violence and law per se but between legal interpretation undertaken by judges and the violence constituted in the "pyramid" atop which the judge sat—the bureaucracies and practices of social control; the state. Finding that law had a "violent side," Cover blamed the irresponsible separations and lethal recombinations of word and deed that were created in the alchemy of bureaucratic hierarchy.[11]

In an earlier work, Cover had sought to cleanse "law" of its association with state violence by granting "all collective behavior entailing systematic understandings of our commitments to future worlds equal claim to the word." Law, separated and cleansed, became "a bridge in normative space connecting . . . the 'world-that-is' . . . with our projections of alternative 'worlds-that-might-be.'" And even deep in the belly of the state, Cover detected "narratives of judicial resistance" that he termed "sacred narratives of jurisdiction," which legal interpreters—judges, officials—could invoke to make and defend honorable choices.[12]

In Cover's jurisprudence, then, legal interpretation took place in a field of pain and death, but neither wholly nor necessarily so. What was inherent in the word was not violence at all, but choice. The exercise of choice was the means to recognize law as "the committed social behavior which constitutes the way a group of people will attempt to get from here to there . . . [from] 'reality' to alternity." Violence killed choice: "pain and death destroy the world that 'interpretation' calls up."[13] Indeed, violence destroyed language itself. It was inarticulate, not part of "the word" at all.[14] Evading the history with which he had begun, Cover relapsed into the classic liberal evolutionary separation of word and action, of text and force, of law as a "categorical advancement over force," which his indignation, momentarily, had challenged.[15]

Cover's rehabilitation of the liberal rule of law, outside the state and outside history, should not surprise us. He wrote in a long and respectable tradition of severance, which his own account of law's myths—its "sacred narratives of jurisdiction"—celebrated. Prominent in that account we find the classic Anglo-American narrative, the confrontation in November 1608 between Lord Chief Justice Edward Coke and James I over the authority of the king to decide the jurisdiction of courts, both common law and ecclesiastical. Coke's account, published after his death as the *Prohibitions del Roy*, describes a scene in which calm, courageous reason prevails in the face of kingly power. "It was answered by me . . . that the Law was the golden

Metawand and Measure to try Causes of the Subjects, which protected his Majesty in safety and Peace: With which the King was greatly offended, and said that then he should be under the Law, which was treason to affirm (as he said). To which I said, that Bracton saith, *Quod Rex non debet esse sub homine, sed sub Deo et Lege*—that the King should not be under man, but under God and the Laws."[16]

Witnesses saw something rather different: "his Majestie fell into that high indignation as the like was never knowne in him, looking and speaking fiercely with a bended fist, offering to strike him &c. Which the Lo. Cooke perceiving fell flat on all fower; humbly beseeching his Majestie to take compassion on him and to pardon him if he thought zeale had gone beyond his duty and allegiance."[17] Cover nonetheless canonizes Coke's text. "The gesture of courage is the aspiration," no matter that it is fabricated.[18]

So little separated from *Titus Andronicus* in historical time, Coke's *Prohibitions* is an ocean apart in its representation of law. But if Coke was writing myth, might Shakespeare have been writing history? Cover knew the difference. "Myth is the part of reality we create and choose to remember in order to *reenact* . . . History corrects for the scale of heroics that we would otherwise project upon the past." As history, what does a text like *Titus Andronicus* have to tell us about law's gestures of courage? Do we encounter law as "a bridge in normative space" that will connect reality to "alternity?"[19] What sort of committed social behavior did English law encourage to bridge the gap between ambitious colonizers and North American alternity?

Speaking Law to Power?

> *With the passage from the sociologist's bland world of ceremonial flag-planting in an empty landscape to violent displacement and insidious death, we have already moved toward Shakespeare's tragedy.*
>
> —Stephen Greenblatt, Renaissance Self-Fashioning (1980)

Titus Andronicus was, I have noted, an extraordinarily popular play. Its impact during the 1590s was "overwhelming," demand for the text in print continuous for the next thirty years. Ballads were sung of its fame. Ben Jonson's own *Bartholomew Fair* (1614) paid tribute to its mass following.[20]

No doubt much of the play's appeal for Tudor-Stuart audiences came from the familiarity of its dramatic form. Contemporary political analogies were no less important.[21] But immediate political resonances fail as an explanation of enduring popularity. In any case, Shakespeare's historical drama "is much more 'sociological' or 'anthropological' than moral or political." The play was "the first sustained attempt to put a consistent foreign world upon the stage."[22] What was the sociology and anthropology of foreignness in *Titus Andronicus*?

Begin with the plot. Vanquished by Titus, Tamora, queen of the Goths, barbarian "other" to Rome, enters the city a helpless captive, accompanied by her three sons and her attendant, Aron. What awaits them is not the serene nobility of a civitas but ferocious fratricidal factionalism[23] and, abruptly, shocking brutal slaughter—the sacrificial disemboweling and burning of Alarbus, Tamora's first-born, by the Andronici.[24] As abruptly, the new emperor, Saturninus, claims Titus's daughter Lavinia for his wife, then spurns her and makes Tamora his empress instead.[25] Helpless captives are suddenly incorporated in the civitas and its ruling circle. The once-powerful Andronici become "prey," to be entrapped and dispatched. The Goths meanwhile are cleft in two: within the civitas, renamed Romans, Tamora, her remaining sons (Chiron and Demetrius), and Aron all become murderous conspirators; outside, where they were barbarians, Tamora's former subjects ally themselves with the few remaining Andronici against the city that their queen now rules. When the Goths enter Rome with Titus's last living son, Lucius at their head, they guard his coup, then hurl the body of their former queen "forth to beasts and birds to prey" in the wilderness beyond the walls whence they themselves had come. "That ravenous tiger, Tamora," says Lucius, "Her life was beastly." But here is no final restorative justice: who was the beast when Lucius at the outset had demanded "the proudest prisoner of the Goths, / That we may hew his limbs and . . . sacrifice his flesh"? Throughout, Rome consumes itself, dismembering the Andronici just as they had dismembered Alarbus, at the end cynically manipulated by the last of the Andronici, Marcus and Lucius, who—surrounded by Goth bodyguards—promise to "knit again" those limbs "by uproar severed."[26] At the play's end, as at the beginning, Rome, the ultimate civitas, remains simultaneously the ultimate wilderness.[27]

In *Worlds Apart: The Market and the Theater in Anglo-American Thought*, Jean-Christophe Agnew addressed the intricate sociology of looming modernity presented by the Tudor-Stuart theater. For Agnew, modernity meant a new society of unbounded market exchange. His subject was the interrelationship of theater and market as spheres for the performance of social transformation—the disintegration of social unity and traditional ways of life and the emergence of new unfixed identities. Like the unbounded market, the theater of the Renaissance was subversive, no longer

confined to "the deliberate representation of common ideals in the negotiated relations between the individual and God" but instead offering endless
"*mis*representation of private meanings in the negotiated relations among
men and women." The collapse of cultural fixedness rendered identity cor-
rosively problematic, producing "the plastic, polymorphous, performative
figure that is both the ideal and the nightmare of modernity"—artificial
person, social and economic actor.[28]

Agnew read the Tudor-Stuart theater as an institution, seeking its
material subtext, finding, convincingly, an emerging sociology of the market. To read the theater's performed texts is, however, to find an anthropology as well as a sociology, and on the surface too, where audiences could
participate directly in the experience of discovery and recognition. It is an
anthropology that begins with the ostensibly familiar—the body. It ends
with the unfamiliar—the bodies of distant others. In between it establishes
the terms of their differentiation.

The body, Robert Blair St. George has written, was "a pivotal metaphor
of the English nation-state" in the late sixteenth and seventeenth centuries.
"England's imperial expansion overseas occurred alongside a dramatic intensification of domestic inequality, social alienation and political unrest that
accompanied the uneven cultural impact of commercial capitalism." Fears of
"dismemberment," whether as a result of domestic disintegration or foreign
threat, called forth an intensified discourse of "hierarchic embodiment."[29]

As the state's discourse became ever more saturated by the body's corporate metaphor, "Elizabethan dramatists found in the body a convenient
target for their literary play."[30] *Titus Andronicus* provides an early and intense immersion. The play targeted primal Elizabethan fears unerringly,
smashing bodies to pieces in a vicious, unending loop of dismemberment,
rape, and death.[31] But dismemberment is only one of the play's texts, back-
drop to a broader interrogation of one of modernity's earliest and most
important themes—its contrapuntal anthropology of civility and savagery,
refinement and barbarism, law and violence, "our" bodies and theirs.[32] An
anthropology in formation from "the moment of first contact with 'America,'" in England the theater was one of its main media of mass distribution,
consumption, and debate.[33] In this highly strategic moment, what was on
display in *Titus* fundamentally challenged the dyadic polarities that colonizing's anthropology so conveniently imagined. Rome is simultaneously law
and violence, culture *and* barbarity, civitas *and* wilderness. The most loaded
signifiers of savagery that the sixteenth-century Occidental colonizer could
conjure—human sacrifice, incest, child murder, and cannibalism—are all
perpetrated by the Andronici.[34]

Tudor-Stuart drama sustained its interrogation of modernity well beyond *Titus Andronicus*. Francis Barker's deep excavation of the discourse of Shakespearian tragedy has shown how it articulates a common structure of comprehension, intention, and representation—a "project" of cultural formation—centered on the first manifestations of the problematic of self and other (identity) in discourses of economy, of social and political relations, of body and mind, and above all of boundaries and their violent penetration.[35] Text and performance meet on the same ground where we have already encountered the beginnings of modernity in Agnew's unboundedness—dissolving boundaries (between market and world), dissolving institutions (ruined monasteries), dissolving bodies, plasticity, dislocation.[36]

The discourse of the tragic project suffused the Tudor-Stuart world. The commonalities that Barker's excavation reveals in Shakespeare's tragedies were homologous with, and complicit in, contemporaneous discourses of English transoceanic colonizing, as represented in the works of such as Walter Raleigh, George Peckham, Samuel Purchas, and the two Richard Hakluyts, elder and younger, and in the legal texts in which the process of colonizing was formulated. Tragedy, colonizing, and the contrapuntal trajectory of law and violence all directly implicate each other.

Discourses of sovereignty and invasion, of territory and its occupation, of the city and barbarity, and of violence extravagantly expressed and silently concealed are everywhere in the tragedies. They are everywhere in the texts of early modern colonizing. Take for example the city, the *civitas*, the epitome of civil association and civilization, the seat of sovereignty, the center of commerce, the source of empire (of armies and authority). For the elder Hakluyt, setting the city down in the transatlantic wilderness was perhaps *the* essential condition for success in colonizing, the most reliable signification of barbarism's displacement. Colonizing meant the creation of actual "cities"—physical emplacements of Englishness. But it also meant the establishment of all those other "thinges without which no Citie may bee made nor people in civill sorte be kept together"—legalities, revenues, arms, authority, relations of power and acquiescence. In all these ways the city was the plantation of Occidental ways in the colonized locale and the means of achieving dominion over it.[37]

The city was also the signifier of sovereignty's effects. Shakespearean discourse represents land within the domain of a secured sovereignty as fecund, peaceful, "settled" (enclosed and improved), the source of abundance precisely because it is constituted by sovereignty's authority and legality. The space beyond is really not land at all but an arbitrary emptiness—"heath" or "wilderness" or "waste," terms signifying the absence of ordered existence. It is "unsettled" space, by presumption uninhabited and unimproved, a site only for licentious self-indulgence.[38] So too, for colonizers, that which lay beyond familiar civil association was a space of deprivation and savagery, occupied only by barbarism's profound disorder. "Being thus passed ye vast ocean," wrote William Bradford in his extraordinary history of the settlement of Plymouth Plantation, "they had no freinds to wellcome them, nor inns to entertaine or refresh their weatherbeaten bodys, no houses or much less townes to repaire too, to seeke for succoure." The "savage barbarians" were "readier to fill their sids full of arrows then otherwise." Surrounding the newcomers was "a hidious and desolate wildernes, full of wild beasts and willd men," the whole untamed, "woods and thickets . . . wild and savage."[39]

As such, in Occidental perception, this was space at once appallingly dangerous but also up for grabs. "'God did not create the world to be empty.' And therefore the seizure of vacant places is regarded as a law of nature."[40] America was *vacuum domicilium*—space awaiting jurisdiction.[41] In Plymouth's case, the legal void was filled on arrival by those "whose names are underwriten," who now did "covenant and combine our selves togeather in a civill body politick, for our better ordering & preservation & furtherance of ye ends aforesaid."[42]

English colonizing's official legal texts employed identical tropes to narrate similar conjectural histories, then used those narratives to constitute similar altered spaces. The New England charter (1620) invoked a history of chaos and absence as both reason and opportunity for colonizing. The charter cited the recent "wonderfull Plague, together with many horrible Slaugthers and Murthers, committed amongst the Sauages and brutish People there, heeretofore inhabiting, in a manner to the utter Destruction, Deuastacion, and Depopulacion of that whole Territorye," wherefore "those large and goodly Territoryes, deserted as it were by their naturall Inhabitants, should be possessed and enjoyed by . . . our Subjects."[43] The phrase "deserted as it were" is a key discursive move, proclaiming the land both physically and jurisdictionally forfeit.[44] Such moves can be observed in all the English texts chartering mainland colonies. Virginia's charter glances briefly at "the Infidels and Savages living in those parts" and denominates theirs an existence of "Darkness and miserable Inorance," signifying the absence of the "human civility," the "settled and quiet government," that colonizing would supply.[45] Barbarians manifested no capacity for human sociability; they were "outside normal morality." More's Utopians thought it "perfectly justifiable to make war on people who leave their land idle and waste yet forbid the use and possession of it to others." As John Donne told the Virginia Company in 1622, "In the Law of Nature and of Nations, a Land never inhabited, by any, or utterly derelicted and immemorially abandoned by the former Inhabitants, becomes theirs that will possess it. So also is it, if the inhabitants doe not in some measure fill the Land, so as the Land may bring forth her increase for the use of men."[46] At the far end of the century, the Pennsylvania charter, so different in so many ways from the Virginia charter, was at one in its sidelong glance at the existing indigenous population and its accompanying denial that their actual presence carried any significance as an obstacle to European standing. In the Georgia Charter (1732), the land is "waste and desolate," the indigenous population simply a marauding enemy.[47]

Sovereignty's claims to possess and control wound the colonizing project in violence in much the same way that Titus used Horace to narrate the real deadliness of his gift to Chiron and Demetrius, and on a far grander scale. Colonizing did not *have* to imply violence. Prominent among the early motivations of English colonizers, for example, were evangelism and commerce. Richard Hakluyt the Younger's *Discourse of Western Planting* (1584) took as its opening proposition "That this westerne discoverie will be greately for thinlargement of the gospell of Christe."[48] Both Hakluyts also extolled commerce. The younger embraced the possibilities of "marchandize" with "people goodd and of a gentle and amyable nature;" his cousin spoke of opportunities for "trafficke and change of commodities," for "iust and lawfull trafficke."[49]

Morally, one might argue, evangelism and commerce were indeed the "goodliest weapons" in the English armory, hinting at possibilities of enlightened purpose and mutuality in dealings with indigenous populations. Certainly, historians have found sufficient complexity and reciprocity in European evangelical and commercial interactions with the indigenous peoples of North America to belie their simple instrumentality as tools of invasion.[50]

Yet, in each case, the possibility of reciprocity was deeply compromised by the overall design in which the interaction was encased. Hakluyt's *Discourse* segued seamlessly from transcendent moral end (evangelism) to necessary practicalities (planting colonies "of our nation").[51] His cousin followed a similar trajectory in the matter of commerce. As his focus shifted from east to west, from the Mediterranean and the Baltic to the American Atlantic coast, commerce ceased to describe bilateral exchanges of commodities across trading frontiers between peoples, becoming instead an activity predicated upon the colonizer's appropriation of productive resources for his own use to which the indigenous population was irrelevant: "how the natu-rall people of the countrey may be made skilfull to plant . . . is a matter of small consideration: but to conquer a countrey . . . to man it, to plant it, and to keepe it . . . were a matter of great importance."[52]

It was the colonial charters that licensed England's appropriation of American space and designed both the manner and the process that appro-priation would follow—the manning, the planting, and the keeping. In a scrupulously legal discourse, the charters elaborated the precise statements of relationships between places and people, existing and desired, crucial to success. Law provided not simply the means for design and implementation of those relationships, and thus of actually realizing plantations, but also the medium by which meaning was imposed on the activities thus engendered. Considered as parsable documents, the charters in the detail of their legali-ties largely occluded the violence of the processes they configured. Consid-ered as a sustained discursive act, however, the charters themselves did the very violence they occluded. First, they produced empty space by discur-sively cleansing America of what was, empirically, there. Second, they con-verted empty space to English "territory" by an assertion of jurisdiction. Having thus produced territory, the charters then enabled it to be made "productive"—bought, sold, farmed, exploited, surveyed, defended, valued, and taxed—through the very detail of their jurisdictional impositions: the division of lands; the construction of fortifications, churches, and manors; the establishment of towns and markets; the management of revenues, arms, and people; and the making of "All Manner of wholesome and rea-sonable Orders, Lawes, Statutes, and Ordiñnces, Direccôns and Instruccôns not contrairie to the Lawes of this our Realme of England."[53] The charters, that is, became the point of origin of the law that constructed the new ob-jects of English attention—a law of property, of commercialized exchange, and of just war in their defense. All became subjects of elaborated legal record, creating an authoritative inventory of the human activities that would constitute what "America" was to be henceforth.[54]

The Unbound Economy

> Barabbas: *And thus methinks should men of judgment frame*
> *Their means of traffic from the vulgar trade,*
> *And as their wealth increaseth, so enclose*
> *Infinite riches in a little room*
>
> —Richard Marlowe, The Jew of Malta *(c. 1589)*

Going Outside: Boundaries in a Boundless World

Both in the project of early modern colonizers and in Shakespeare's tragic project, one encounters the absolute importance of boundaries and definition to identity.[55] How else could colonizers construct their project except by imagining both what lay inside their own civitas and what lay beyond it? Hence the plenitude they planned was defined against the waste they encountered, champion against heath. Once inserted into that other savage space, how could colonizers remain necessarily separated from it except by conceptually bounding themselves off from the others they encountered? Hence civility fended off barbarity, humanity savagery. Theirs was a mighty struggle, for they were deep within the other—as Bradford had it, separated "from all ye civill parts of ye world."[56]

William Bradford's narrative constructed a *nomos*—"a normative universe . . . of right and wrong, of lawful and unlawful, of valid and void"[57]— that tied the colonized world tightly to its formative anthropology. Its boundaries were historical no less than physical. Boundaries defined and protected appropriated space, but boundaries also segregated the English from an anxious awareness of their own past incivility and America's invitation to return to it. "Studies of early modern Europe have emphasized the significance of binary contrasts and the horror of inversion to conceptualization of cultural difference."[58] By inhabiting a normative world of rightness, lawfulness, and validity, colonizers would be protected from temptation and backsliding. Violence, should it transpire, would always be in their own, or civility's, defense.[59]

In fact, boundaries proved brittle and porous, transgression a constant. "Lament for the primitive virtues . . . a species of nostalgia, [was] an essential element of English colonization."[60] Nostalgia could be accommodated— it was, after all, merely civility's own romantic self-indulgence. But when men actually went native, transgression became a deep threat to rule.[61] As in Shakespeare, so in Virginia: how easily in *Macbeth* and *Hamlet* and *Lear* authority turns into powerlessness, alliance to betrayal, civility to savagery, goodly champion to alien heath. *Lear*, no doubt, is the most famous example, but *Andronicus* is the best. Here distinction collapses completely, the one constantly in the process of becoming its framing other.

As the homologies of tragedy and colonization accumulate, they reinforce the argument that these texts address the passage from premodernity to modernity, from a Europe turned inward to navigation's frightening ascendancy over a boundless world, and with it from a constraining physical exterior to the newly invented, deeply disciplined, unbound interiority of accumulation, ambition, and self-reproduction to which Marlowe's Barabbas alludes and which *Hamlet* more famously examines.[62] It was a passage from which the Shakespearean exploration recoiled in dismay at the epistemological crisis it signified. It was a passage that, in contrast, the promoters of colonization pursued relentlessly. Their single-minded appropriations and commodifications placed colonizers squarely in the vanguard of the modernity that the tragic project fended off, pushing outward to breach the "known" spatial and temporal capsule in which the Old World had lived, constantly constructing their own new fences, but only to push beyond them too. Frontiers moved incessantly; space and time became plastic, constantly subject to redefinition. Colonizers reached for new disciplines—the spirit of capitalism, the rule of law—to justify their transgressions and to mark their progress.[63]

Whether ambivalent or aggressive, the texts of law, of literature, and of colonizing reveal that the historical passage to modernity and progress is not one in which violence becomes in any sense at all the antithesis of civility. Rather, it is one of which violence is a necessary condition and an integral component. The fearsome violence of the tragic project's confrontations helps suggest the depth of Shakespearian unease at modernity. But that isn't quite the point. In its displays of violence *against* barbarism, on behalf of sovereignty threatened or invaded from without; in its displays of sovereignty's *own* assured, ordered, routine violence within (the interior violence of its legality), the tragic project proclaims that violence is of a piece with sovereignty and law. Here premodernity and modernity are, like other spurious oppositions, of a piece. Carol Greenhouse observes that "the roots of sociolegal scholars' concerns with law have been consistently nourished by the distinction they draw between social orders based on personal power and force, and those 'superior,' 'more advanced,' or 'more rational' orders based on the authority of words."[64] Liberal law, we have seen, proclaims the distinction by awarding itself the authority of words, but the words it chooses undermine the boundary it proclaims by in their turn awarding themselves a monopoly of force. Violence is not a negation of the legality of the civitas, pre– or post–Enlightenment, but a condition of its existence, its jural order, its political economy. As Weber long ago realized, liberal modernity's achievement is to have gathered words, power, and force all into one grasp.[65]

Documenting Space: Putting Maps in Their Place

In *Shakespeare and the Geography of Difference,* John Gillies reproduces the unease of the Tudor-Stuart encounter with modernity through an examination of Shakespeare's cartography. According to Gillies, Shakespeare's cartographic imagination embraces both the classical and the "new." It is classical in its sense of what is mapped—the comfort of sovereignty, the plenitude of order—and in what this places beyond the map's edge—chaos and barbarity, the exterior of order. This is precisely the purpose and representational discourse of pre-Renaissance cartographic depiction of the world. Vico "derives the archaic origins of the 'world' from that of the city . . . The order of city and world is constituted by their violent differentiation from 'the infamous promiscuity of people and things in the bestial state.'"[66]

In the sixteenth century, however, a new geography began to countermand the old: "in place of the comfort of the medieval map we find restlessness[;] in place of stasis, dynamism . . . For perhaps the first time in the history of world cartography, world maps post-1492 began to privilege the unknown and unpossessed over the known and possessed."[67] Early modernity meant a political economy of increasingly unbounded markets and unbounded voyaging, of possession of all that lay beyond old boundaries of market and map. It meant a political economy whose significance was situated in an established Occidental explanatory discourse of civitas and barbarity, but one that no longer recoiled from the boundary but deliberately encountered and penetrated it.

Elizabethan drama explored the new cartographic world as avidly as the old.[68] The result was a cartography of legality and violence. In *Lear*, the map that divides the realm is simultaneously legality (sovereignty) and violence (dismemberment, tension, conflict). The map provides the play's "focus of power and danger" where the tragedy will be fought out.[69] A hint of something similar, though less developed, can be found in *Titus Andronicus*. Gazing upon Lavinia after her rape and mutilation, Titus calls her a "map of woe." Her body, says Titus, "dost talk in signs."[70]

In an important sense, all maps of colonized lands are maps of woe. As the late J. B. Harley put it, one hundred fifty years after the first English intrusions upon the American mainland the mid-eighteenth century's maps of the interior showed "how successfully a European colonial society had reproduced itself in the New World." Their depictions of place names, settlements, roads, and local administrative boundaries were a constant reminder of the "European geography" and the European economy that English colonization had created.[71]

For Harley, the map facilitated "spatial understanding" of what had actually occurred on the ground—"things, concepts, conditions, processes, or events in the human world."[72] But maps are as much "ideal models, in whose image an inadequate reality had to be fashioned." That is, they could represent anticipation (or wishful thinking). "In presenting space as politically and economically manageable, in promising imaginary control through ocular access, cartographic investments *prefigured* material exploits and the act of beholding 'the whole world at one view' *anticipated* the imperial gaze of spatial desire."[73]

A map that purported to record a present colonized reality might thus, in reality, be imagining its future. But this made it no less potent a text, particularly in the metropolis, where, as we have seen, "as it were" counted as what was. Who was to say that metropolitan meanings did not comport with reality, if not the reality of the ground at that moment then the reality of intention for that ground? Like the charters, cartographic texts appropriated their objects mentally and politically, producing "a depopulated and empty, dispossessed and conquered space that could be . . . subjected to new, politically charged, topographical visions."[74] Maps gave intention its own materiality. Early modern cartographers could thrust metropolitan desires upon a precolonial reality and make it disappear.

The locale of desire is important here, for it provides another measure of the significance of metropolitan texts. It is the metropolis that desires the world "at one view" and where the means actually to realize desire—knowledge, capital, labor, force—are generated. Voyagers travel outward with the intention of *returning* with the information from which metropolitan projects will be constituted. In the metropolis, information—narratives, inscriptions, texts—meets and melds: it is "mobile . . . immutable, presentable, readable and combinable." The metropolis receives, combines, and calculates. "[T]otally new phenomena emerge, hidden from the other people from whom all these inscriptions have been exacted."[75]

Here then is the discursive context for the political economy—or, better, the *legal* economy—of colonizing. The charters by which patentees laid claim to American space and designed jurisdictions for their claims were texts amongst others. Their instrumental capacities were enhanced by the layers of knowledge—legal, cartographic—to which they were bound. And all these texts were organized by the same anthropology of civility and barbarism, the same sociology of markets, the same politics of sovereignty and violence, displayed in the tragedies.

From these discursive resources appeared a new *geography* for sovereignty, an unbounded sovereignty of jurisdiction and inhabitation. Both figuratively and literally, as we have seen, the charters rendered space beyond the borders of the Christian European civitas empty so as to claim it for the metropolis. As texts, the charters occluded the violence of the extinguishment that they licensed while justifying extinguishment itself by the imputed violence and savagery of those upon whom it was visited, and whose removal from the scene was a condition precedent for the achievement of English plenitude.[76] Jurisdiction—the implementation of sovereignty—was the condition of possession, possession the condition of improvement, improvement the condition of "gain." The promise of improvement and gain was what would make "English" land appear beyond the defunct boundary of the old map. Locke confirmed it, explicitly and repeatedly, in the Second Treatise,[77] but Locke was merely one in a long line who had already confirmed that "vacant places" might always be appropriated by those who could use them.[78]

The map itself, meanwhile, became boundless. Abraham Ortelius's massive 1570 atlas, the aptly named *Theatrum Orbis Terrarum*, represented a claim to "absolute spatial control: the world . . . taken home to rest on a shelf."[79] A few years earlier the ever–resourceful elder Hakluyt had written to Ortelius to suggest a variation that would better serve the practical needs of metropolitan projectors. "For as much as men usually live in houses which are neither spacious enough nor light enough within for them to be able to place or spread out conveniently a large world map in them, it will be most gratifying to many to have a map thought out on the following lines: namely that when spread out to its full extent it is quite fit and suitable for a hall or other spacious place of that kind, and also when rolled up at each end on two smooth revolving rods it lies conveniently on a table about three or four feet square." All over the metropolis, a new documentary economy was emerging in map rooms, treasure rooms, muniment rooms—each a "little room" built to contain the information (charters, patents, lists of subscribers, accounts, notes, maps, hydrographical tables, bills of lading, indentures) that was the means to manage and control infinite riches the world over. "In this way you will perform a most acceptable service to a number of English lawyers, to the students of both Oxford and Cambridge Universities, to the citizens of London."[80]

Assigning People: Aron's Fury

The anthropology of civility and barbarism embedded in the legal economy of English colonizing was, we have seen, simultaneously a sociology of markets—markets in land, markets in labor, brought into being and managed by means of metropolitan plans, projects, voyages. Transoceanic colonizing commodified American land in a radical extension of processes that had dominated first English and then Irish life during the sixteenth century. The mapping and surveying of land in England and Ireland had "gradually naturalize[d] a perspective on agrarian space which foregrounded its status not as social realm but as marketable commodity."[81] With the transformation of land came transformation of social relations on the land. In its mind's eye, Spenser's *View of the Present State of Ireland* (1596) was centered on the promise of a "transformative cartography generat[ing] a new spatial order and annihilat[ing] a landscape of custom and use" and the complete submission of the Irish to that order "lyke captives trembling at the victors sight."[82] John Norden's *Surveyor's Dialogue* (1607) acknowledged how, to many Englishmen, the new spatial order constructed by land surveyors supplied "the cords whereby poore men are drawne into seruitude and slauery." As Bernhard Klein notes, surveyor and overseer share the same etymological root.[83]

Labor was essential to English colonizing: "keeping" required "planting," and planting "manning." Englishmen drawn into indentured servitude made their way to the newly commodified lands of the Atlantic seaboard as commodified labor, as did Irish captives. But in the legal economy of colonizing, barbarians were the best of commodified migrants. Barbarians were savages and infidels—"natural slaves" whom, according to sixteenth century humanist legal doctrine, Christians might "justly" enslave in wars.[84]

In *Titus Andronicus*, Aron the Moor is the quintessential barbarian. For his infidel atheism and his catalog of sins—"adultery, forgery, planting evidence, incitement to rape, slander leading to decapitation of the innocent, dismemberment, promise-breaking, and outright murder"—Aron is usually taken as Shakespeare's attempt to portray "pure evil."[85] But this is to turn Aron into a cartoon. He is on stage for most of the first act but silent throughout, simply attending upon Tamora and her sons. The audience has no reason to think him significant. Aron speaks for the first time only when he is alone. His words exult in Tamora's betrothal to Saturninus and abrupt elevation to rule but reveal that in fact Tamora is besotted with him. Her elevation is thus also his opportunity. But why is Aron's rejoicing so fierce? Because, simultaneously, he lets slip that he is Tamora's slave. "Then, Aron, arm thy heart and fit thy thoughts / To mount aloft with thy imperial mistress . . . / Away with slavish weeds and servile thoughts."[86] The opportunity is not simply to rise with her but in rising to leave slavery behind.

Throughout, Aron is driven by scorching, barely-repressed rage. He tells Lucius near the end, "O, why should wrath be mute, and fury dumb? /

I am no baby, I, that with base prayers / I should repent the evils I have done: / Ten thousand worse than ever yet I did / Would I perform, if I might have my will."[87] Critics have concentrated on the evils, not their cause. Why is Aron furious? His fury is his own—he is no cipher obediently pursuing his mistress's desire to destroy the Andronici. Indeed, when Tamora's attention wanders from the task at hand to lust for him, Aron stays completely focused on vengeance and death.[88] Why is his fury so consuming? Can it be that he is furious at a foundational injustice of his own—the enslavement earned by the very blackness of which he is so proud?

Tamora hates the Andronici, but Aron hates them more. His hatred is given particular edge by their racist contempt for him. Sweet Lavinia thoroughly enjoys racial banter with Bassianus at Aron's expense: "swart Cimmerian . . . Spotted, detested and abominable . . . barbarous Moor . . . raven-colored love." Lucius later renews the barrage: "inhuman dog! unhallow'd slave!"[89] But Aron encounters the same from all sides, and it leaves him with few loyalties to Tamora's sons or even Tamora herself. His infant son, whom Tamora bears, is described to his face as "loathsome as a toad / Amongst the fair-faced breeders of our clime." Tamora (who is of course "fair") orders the child destroyed immediately, not because it is a bastard but because it is black. Demetrius, snarling that Aron is "hellish . . . loathèd . . . foul," attempts to skewer the baby. "I'll broach the tadpole on my rapier's point." Aron spirits the child away but they fall captive to Lucius and the same lascivious threats. "Too like the sire for ever being good. / First hang the child, that he may see it *sprawl*."[90]

Whether against Tamora's sons or against Lucius, Aron defends the child fiercely. Looking at it he sees himself: "Look how the black slave smiles upon the father, / As who should say 'Old lad, I am thine own' . . . thick-lipped slave . . . tawny slave . . . villain." In Aron's mouth these are terms of endearment. In Lucius's mouth they are racist invective: "Say, wall-eyed slave, whither wouldst thou convey / This growing image of thy fiend-like face?"[91]

Aron's métier is deception and trickery, not direct action. He exploits the stupidity of Chiron and Demetrius, manipulates Saturninus, fools Titus into begging him to chop off Titus's own hand. Each is an unwitting accomplice, for until his final outburst Aron is always obsequious, always the attendant, the servant, the assistant. Berthoud argues that he is the epitome of self-sufficient autonomy, but Aron's reliance on deception and manipulation suggests little capacity to act autonomously, particularly when contrasted with the brutal direct force of Lucius. Instead, he lets men's cattle stray to their destruction; he burns their barns and haystacks in the night.[92] As Berthoud rightly observes, "Every moment of his life represents a nullification of those collaborations that build up and preserve human communities."[93] But why should a slave seek "human community" with slaveholders? Only when alone with the one thing like him in the play—his son— does Aron have any community of his own. It hardly needs observing that, as befits a rebellious slave, Aron's death is the cruelest, the most exotic, the most public of all.[94]

Violence and Silence

> *The thirst of a tiger for blood is the fittest emblem of the rapacity with which the members of all the new states fly at the public lands.*
> —*John Quincy Adams, in Brooks Adams, ed.,* The Degradation of the Democratic Dogma *(1920)*

> *Lavinia: When did the tiger's young ones teach the dam?*
> —*William Shakespeare,* Titus Andronicus *(II.iii.142)*

Appropriative colonizing was the empirical point of origin for the Anglo-America that is the stuff of formative historical experience: spatial, temporal, jurisdictional, geographic, human. Simultaneously, early modern colonization's constitutive texts reached beyond the processes that, as technologies, they had facilitated, to construct and maintain the nomos—the normative universe—that lent those processes validity and, hence, justification. The structure of the nomos "is no less fundamental" than the structure of the physical world.[95] In our case, the homology between normative order and the cultural organization of colonized space starkly underlines the absence of separation.

The nomos of English colonizing obtained its philosophical coherence from the contrapuntal anthropology of Christian, European civility and New World barbarism that had informed the whole project of New World contact since Columbus.[96] In his *De Iure Belli* (1588), Alberico Gentili, Regius Professor of Civil Law at Oxford, held that "nature has established among men kinship, love, kindliness, and a bond of fellowship." Those who violated nature—"who practiced abominable lewdness . . . who ate human flesh"— were outside humanity, brutes, upon whom war might justly be made. So also might brutes' vacant lands be appropriated; so also might they be enslaved. In the better-known *De Iure Belli Ac Pacis* (1625), Hugo Grotius followed Gentili's example: "War is lawful against those who offend against Nature." Grotius also insisted on a right to occupy vacant land.[97]

Whether in its academic or its mythopoeic metanarratives, however, American history has largely insisted on locating America's nomos elsewhere than in the originating discourses of colonization, appropriation, and enslavement.[98] American history has done so in the representation of the routines of seventeenth- and eighteenth-century migration and settlement as virtually autonomous processes that, in Bernard Bailyn's words, "peopled" the Eastern seaboard and built its economy.[99] It has done so in its denials of significance to colonizing's founding texts, its insistence that the reality of America was made by its migrants.[100] It has done so in the more general notion, at once epic and anodyne, of a later "westward movement" across an "unopened" landscape.[101] It has done so, finally, at the elevated level of America's dual foundation myths—of an initiating pious journey into a desolate wilderness;[102] and, some 150 years after, of self-creation in a confabulation of fathers.

Each of these historical narratives, from piecemeal routine to elevated myth, participates in the maintenance of a different American nomos—not the nomos of colonization but its antithesis, the nomos of freedom. But this is a nomos created by forgetting origins, not by remembering them. The founding myths of Plymouth and Philadelphia exemplify this, in their discursive occlusion of colonizing's violence, theft, exploitation, and enslavement. Both take their stand instead on Anglo-America's supervening modernity and individualism, as epochal representations of social formation as contractual choice. Both stand for a nomos of right intent and self-fashioning through law, hence for the essential truth of original emptiness and the essential rightness of proprietorship conferred upon Englishmen by the activities of improvement (the two components of Locke's theory of property).[103] Both are singular but disguised acts of appropriation—of space, obviously, but also, like all forms of social contractualism, of universal generative capacity to their highly particularized participants.[104] Both are sacred narratives of jurisdiction, for both produce a people living the rule of law.

It is interesting to note that it is nevertheless quite difficult for Plymouth and Philadelphia to coexist politically as "national" origin myths. The second necessarily displaces the first as the point of "American" departure. The difficulty is deeply embedded in the conceptual structure of American history itself, for that history has proven thus far unable to articulate a narrative that is not always fractured by the revolutionary climacteric of the late eighteenth century and its accompanying and uniquely constitutive legalities. Discontinuity is shown to be false once America is relocated in the nomos of colonization. We can understand both as acts of appropriation. But in fact the discontinuity imputed to American history by the assertion of a late eighteenth-century self-invention is crucial to subsequent American self-understanding, for it is the chief means of removing of what we know as "America" from the violence done by colonizing.

Removal is manifest in the metanarratives of American history and its essential constituent histories.[105] Of those constituents, the history of law is particularly crucial in sustaining America's nomos of freedom. Cover points out that "no set of legal institutions or prescriptions exists apart from the narratives that locate it and give it meaning . . . Every prescription is insistent in its demand to be located in discourse—to be supplied with history and destiny, beginning and end, explanation and purpose."[106]

American legal history's founding father, Willard Hurst, situated American law within a problematic beyond colonization simply by ignoring the whole history of colonizing's violent intrusion on the continent.[107] For Hurst and the generations of scholars that he influenced—which means the vast majority of American legal historians of the past fifty years—nothing that happened in America much before the beginning of the nineteenth century really had any relevance to the meaning of America per se, except as the point from which the America "we" know, liberal and modernizing, had departed. Simply excising the violence of early American colonization from American history in this fashion is startling. What is even more startling about Hurst's project, however, is that in crafting his representation of *American* law as a generative "release of middle-class energy" and of the early nineteenth century as its point of origin, Hurst seized upon a scenario that was in fact utterly continuous with the primal motive force—relentless expansion—of the first two centuries, thus completely contradicting the excision in which he was participating.[108]

For Hurst, what made American law *American* was its purposive dedication to the realization of human creativity through freedom of choice.[109] Hurst figured this unique American legal culture precisely in an emblematic instance of westward movement—that is, in an instance of the legal economy of colonizing. But he failed to recognize it as such, notwithstanding unanswerable evidence. Hurst's legendary figuration of the release of energy is his narrative of the establishment in 1836 of a Claimants' Union on the newly settled banks of the Pike River, in the southeast corner of what is now the state of Wisconsin. The documents that he used to construct the narrative show that the settlers had originally joined together in a "Western

Emigration Company" to remove from Oswego County in New York to what they described as a "new country." Their effort of removal itself gave them entitlement to reward, they said, because it was a transforming journey, conducted on behalf of civilization, into a void, where human sociability did not exist. Their civilizing mission was to transform that space, through their improving labor, from open prairie hunted by Indians to enclosed agricultural smallholdings.

They considered their place of settlement fruitful but perilous, "a state of nature," prone to "anarchy" and "confusion." Their "protective union" was constituted to resolve disputes among themselves and to guard their claims against threats from other migrants, described variously as "malignant . . . avaricious" or simply the "mob;" from speculators; and also from Indians, whose presence challenged possession, whose competing practices—they "fired the prairies . . . for hunting purposes"—endangered the settlers' farms, and whose brutishness was manifest in thieving and drunkenness.[110]

The continuity of the discourse of these emblematic settlers with that which animated English colonizing from its outset is difficult to miss. Yet it was missed. Emphatically, we are not observing here an obtuse or narrow mind.[111] Hurst acknowledged that the claimants' intimations of moral superiority masked their own illegality. They were trespassers, "ahead of official survey, without color of title." But theirs was illegality within a delimited Occidental consciousness: their trespass was on lands declared "public." So, inevitably, Hurst resolved the matter decisively in the claimants' favor, approving their impatient determination to meet "the challenge of the unexploited continent," approving their seizure of law as an instrumentality to be put to work in that service. Here were historical inevitabilities that dwarfed the detail of behavior, prescriptions that Hurst had "located in discourse . . . supplied with history and destiny, beginning and end, explanation and purpose."[112] By enabling and then regulating transactional behavior, law and the state would assist in the generation of material benefits that would tame the mob and actually put the speculator to good use. Law would civilize. In that same service it would also remove the Indian, although that was not a story that Hurst told at all, except by its very elision. In what was a brilliant observation, Hurst wrote of contract's "capture of the land" as its "first and most dramatic victory." He was ready, it seems, to acknowledge that law was capable of waging war. It could have been a more telling insight yet had he remarked on whom its war was waged. Instead, Hurst rested his meaning entirely on the victory of one intra-European principle—market exchange—over another, a "feudal type of tenure."[113]

What was the nature of the space that Hurst selected to stage the opening scene of his epic of American law? His Pike Creek is dug deep in the rich sod of the Upper Mississippi Valley, pastoral and pristine, tremblingly fecund. It is yeoman space, safely divorced from the coastal colonies and their compromised histories, far from the pitiless warfare and removals of the South's western frontier, fully a part of the old Northwest Territory where America's founding fathers supposedly got slavery right (as they did not in their first birthing of the nation), by freeing at least that part of the continent from commodified humans.[114] Unfortunately for them—and also for Hurst, who misplaced slaves as well as Indians[115]—slavery was alive and well in the Northwest Territory, taken there by the federal army sent to police the line of European settlement.[116] The political economies of colonizing and slavery are, we have seen, intimately related—the one an instrument of the other. It is no surprise to find both so intimately related and conveniently forgotten in the construction of a metanarrative of how American law came to be.

What is the significance of these elisions and occlusions in a history? "If the land is a place of fulsomeness and abundance, it is at the same moment one of ideal emptiness, a depopulated landscape . . . [F]rom the point of view of those for whom there is space and validity, emptiness . . . may even be a definition of the ideal."[117] As for earlier colonizers, so for Hurst: America was an empty place, a void. It could safely be appropriated and organized by law and a few squatters.

Afterword: A Wilderness of Tigers

> *You know I am not as you are. I am of a quite different*
> *Nature from you.*
>
> —*Saghughsuniunt, of the Susquehanna Oneida, Lancaster Treaty*
> *Council, Pennsylvania (1762)*

In Hurstian discourse, law's abiding purpose is the release of "energy." The word has an interesting etymology, for it leads us back four centuries to *energia*, the term adopted by Shakespeare's contemporaries to describe the "stir to the mind" imparted to audiences by the extraordinary capacity of the language of Elizabethan drama "to produce, shape, and organize collective physical and mental experiences."[118]

In *Titus Andronicus*, Shakespeare created a brutally intense stir in the minds of Tudor-Stuart audiences by exposing them to a representation of

Rome that was simultaneously a representation of their own encounter with the sociology and anthropology of modernity and its formative discourses —commodification, colonization, appropriation, and enslavement.

Willard Hurst's metanarrative builds modernity on the countervailing nomos of freedom – opportunity to release creative energy, liberty to exercise choice – uniquely embodied in the United States, where "unclaimed natural abundance" and "technical command of nature" combined to create "conditions of freedom" for all. Pike Creek is Hurst's metaphor for the originating moment, the moment, as Stephen Greenblatt notes, "in which the master hand shapes the concentrated social energy into the sublime aesthetic object."[119] Sublime indeed. Here, in this obscure corner of the American Midwest, "we" articulated ideas of "special significance for the future of mankind."[120]

Writ large, as Hurst clearly intended, Pike Creek indulges the claim to "an original political right . . . to fill the empty vessel," to appropriate reproductive power and give birth to new political life. But there are no originating moments, no "pure acts of untrammeled creation." To create their appearance for some, one must displace others. Here, others were displaced by Hurst's acceptance of the Occidental claim to an all-enveloping proprietorship of America, his emphatic occlusion of intrusion, the 250-year story of how his settlers came to be where they were.[121]

What was the historical expression of the nomos of freedom? What, once arrived from elsewhere, did Hurst's settlers use their energetic freedom to create? They created a modernizing political economy in territory expropriated from its enervated inhabitants under the watchful eye of an army serviced by slaves:[122] a reasonable enough representation, one might suggest, of the reality of the early American republic.[123] These were the "conditions of freedom" in the creation of which American law was so thoroughly implicated. They had been the conditions of Anglo-American freedom from the outset. As Locke wrote in the *Second Treatise*, American land was for the "use of the Industrious and Rational." Anyone who interfered with Europeans' appropriation of that land might, for the protection of human sociability, "be destroyed as a *Lyon* or a *Tyger*, one of those wild Savage Beasts, with whom men can have no Society nor Security."[124]

In establishing the conditions of their own sociability and freedom on the American continent, European settlers created savagery and violence for others.[125] There was nothing new in this, either historically, as we have seen, or indeed spatially. It was the reason Saghughsuniunt, of the Susquehanna Oneida, declared his own independence from the very nature of those who had intruded themselves upon the indigenous inhabitants of the Susque-hanna country. It was the reason the Tswana-speaking peoples of Southern Africa, when undergoing *their* nineteenth-century colonization, called law in its varied manifestations "the English mode of warfare."[126]

It was also the reason that on his arrival at the Port of San Francisco in the early twentieth century a Chinese migrant named Xu, from Xiangshan, found oppression, not freedom, residing in America's nomos. "With laws harsh as tigers," he wrote, "I had a taste of all the barbarities."[127] Enigmatically, Xu intended his poem to "encourag[e] the traveler." To persevere? To go home? To revolt? We don't know. All we know is that on his arrival in America Xu encountered laws "harsh as tigers." America, like Rome, was a wilderness of tigers. Failure to acknowledge this does violence to history.

Chapter 2
Dialogical Encounters in a Space of Death

Richard Price

But who in the New World does not have a horror of the past, whether his ancestor was torturer or victim? Who, in the depth of conscience, is not silently screaming for pardon or revenge?

—Derek Walcott

For twenty-first-century historians, any attempt to interpret the systematic use of torture and terror in eighteenth-century plantation societies begs two theoretical/methodological questions. Can we understand, much less re-present, such phenomena given that, as Michael Taussig puts it, "terror makes mockery of sense making"?[1] And can we, in the current epistemological and moral climate of postcolonialism, legitimately explore and re-present the African American past at all?

Jamaican anthropologist David Scott has been raising the latter question with insistence.[2] Singling out the work of Melville Herskovits and me, he argues that "both turn on a distinctive attempt to place the 'cultures' of the ex-African/ex-slave in relation to what we might call an authentic past, that is, an anthropologically identifiable, ethnologically recoverable, and textually re-presentable past."[3] And he recommends against such futile and perhaps even morally suspect efforts to represent or verify or corroborate "authentic Afro-American pasts" ("what really happened"), instead suggesting that scholars focus on "discourse"—how African Americans in various parts of the hemisphere envision and talk about and act in terms of their pasts and, presumably, how others write and speak about them.[4] In a similar postcolonial spirit, Marcus Wood reads eighteenth-century representations of slaves under torture, by John Gabriel Stedman and William Blake, as if all that matters (or all that interests him, or all that is legitimately recoverable) is, once again, discourse—deconstructing the eighteenth-century author's or artist's intent, intellectual influences, audience reactions, and so forth.[5]

I, on the other hand, wish to explore the world of the eighteenth-century "victims"—the people depicted by Stedman, Blake, and others—and attempt to "read through" available discourses (eighteenth-century accounts and images, twentieth-century oral testimonies and folktales) to try to understand and re-present something of what they might have been thinking and feeling, and to explore the broader implications. In other words, fully accepting the problematic nature (the inevitable constructedness and perspectivality and incompleteness) of available historical and ethnological "sources," I will try (like most historians) to read through them to arrive at partial understandings of a past and distant world.

The post-Columbian Caribbean rimland constituted a tumultuous stage for an unlikely and varied set of actors—from European pirates and buccaneers through African and Afro-American maroons to Caribs deported from the islands and large numbers of Native Indian groups. In this colonial arena, unspeakable greed, lust, and conquest rubbed shoulders with heroic acts of resistance and solidarity. Millions of human beings were killed outright—by enslavement, forced labor, and disease. Yet in many parts of the region, vibrant new societies and cultures emerged from the ashes. Within this prototypical space of death (to borrow Taussig's felicitous metaphor)[6]—indeed, often within the complex interstices that divided it internally—displaced Africans, a motley crew of Europeans, and what remained of Native American populations forged new, distinctively American modes of human interaction. And through the complex processes of negotiation between such groups, whole new cultures and societies were born.

Recent work in the emerging field of ethnographic history makes clear that, as Greg Dening has written, "Ethnographic moments are never so piquant for a poetics of histories as they are in the contact of Natives and Strangers. The compounded nature of histories, the self-images in the cartoons of the other, the processes of culture and expressed structures are simply writ large in circumstances of extravagant ambiguity."[7]

A focus on new kinds of sources and on readings of them that stress dialogics and intersubjectivity has begun to enrich our understandings of these ambiguous encounters. We are beginning, at last, to unravel the tightly woven threads that bind destruction and invention, death and creation, in the wake of the Columbian moment.

This chapter takes the form of a triptych: three emblematic moments of Caribbean rimland history, three linked narratives of death and creation. Through these colonial encounters, which we read in the inscriptions of the colonizers and listen to in the voices of the colonized—the words of slaves and their masters, the words of Afro-American maroons and the missionaries sent out to convert them—we are privileged to witness the birth of new cultures, precious moments in the forging of what was becoming truly a New World.

Death Defied: Neptune and the (Failed) Totalization of the Plantation World

In the idealized slaveocracy, planter hegemony left little room for slave response or maneuver. As Sidney Mintz and I have pointed out elsewhere, "The often unquestioning acceptance by the masters of their right to treat the slaves [who were defined legally as property] as if they were not human rationalized the system of control." But it is equally clear that in practice, throughout the Americas, "the masters did recognize that they were dealing with fellow humans, even if they did not want to concede as much . . . A literature produced over centuries, in a dozen European languages, attests throughout to the implicit recognition by the masters of the humanity of the slaves, even in instances where the authors seem most bent upon proving the opposite."[8] As is well known, the planter class, in spite of itself, remained dependent in countless ways upon the slaves. And in such a society, deeply cleft by status divisions yet unified by the theoretically unlimited power of the masters, it was this "core contradiction" that was the motor for much of the creative institution-building that characterized the plantation regions of the New World.

In the exercise of totalizing power, capital punishment constitutes a limiting case. Yet for this very reason, it may be a good place to begin, if we are interested in the ultimate capacities of the oppressed to respond, resist, and create. For an examination of the ways that condemned slaves throughout the Caribbean rimland went to their deaths reveals much about the limits of planter power and about the spirit that allowed slaves to create, within the spaces available to them (which varied sharply by place and time), a world of their own, one that influenced not only every aspect of their own descendants' lives but also that of the descendants of their oppressors.

The theatrical public torture and execution of slaves who had transgressed one or another plantation rule was a ubiquitous feature of societies throughout the Caribbean and its rimlands, from early colonial days until well into the nineteenth century. Both planters and the colonial judiciary strongly believed that such gruesome spectacles would act as a disincentive to other slaves; a formal sentence involving public torture was characteristically preceded by a justification that it was being handed down "in the hope that it would provide an Example and deterrent to the [victims'] associates, and reduce the propensity of slaves to escape."[9] But such ceremonies of order and discipline differed in one crucial respect from the public executions that were commonplace in contemporary metropoles. To the surprise of European visitors, these victims consistently *refused to acknowledge that the executioners could cause them pain.* Indeed, it was the calm and dignity (never resignation!), and even the sense of irony, with which these African and Afro-American men and women went to their deaths that prompted comment by European observers. Even while submitting to the most excruciating tortures, these victims were refusing to acknowledge the whitefolks' ultimate sanction. And, in so refusing, they managed—within the very limited range of action available to them—to render it strangely impotent.[10]

Let us begin with a narrative that illustrates these generalizations and permits some further elaborations. Early one morning in 1776, John Gabriel Stedman, a young Scotsman then living in the capital of the Dutch colony of Suriname, was

musing on all the different Dangers and Chastisements that the Lower Class of People are Subjected to[11]/ [when] I heard a Crow'd pass under my Window—Curiosity made me Start up, Dress in a hurry, & Follow them When I discovered 3 Negroes in chains Surrounded by a Guard going to be Executed in the Savannah—their Undaunted look however Averse to Cruelty's fassinated my Attention and determined me to see the Result, Which was Viz, that the Sentence being Read /in Low dutch which they did not understand/ one was Condemned to have his head Chop'd Off With an Ax for having Shot a Slave who had Come to steal Plantains on the Estate of his Mistress, While his Accomplice was Flogg'd below the Gallows—the Truth Was However that this had been done by the mistresses Absolute Command, but who being detected & Preferring the Loss of the Negro to the Penalty of 500 Florins, Allow'd the Poor man to be Sacrificed; he laid down his Head on the Block With uncommon Deliberation & even Streached out his Neck when with one blow it was Severed from his Body—

The third negro whose name was *Neptune* was no Slave, but his own Master, & a Carpenter by Trade, he was Young and handsome—But having kill'd the Overseer of the Estate Altona in the Para Creek in Consequence of some Despute he Justly Lost his Life with his Liberty.—However, the *particulars* are Worth Relating, which Briefly were that he having Stole a Sheep to Entertain some Favourite Women, the Overseer had Determined to See him Hang'd, Which to Prevent he Shot him dead Amongst the Sugar Canes—this man being Sentenced to be brook *Alive* upon the Rack, without the benefit of the *Coup de Grace,* or mercy Stroke, laid himself down Deliberately on his Back upon a Strong Cross, on which with Arms & Legs Expanded he was Fastned by Ropes—The Executioner /also a Black/ having now with a Hatchet Chop'd off his Left hand, next took up a heavy Iron Crow or Bar, with Which Blow After Blow he Broke to Shivers every Bone in his Body till the Splinters Blood and Marrow Flew About the Field, but the Prisoner never Uttered a Groan, or a Sigh—the Roaps being now Unlashed I imagined him dead & Felt happy till the Magistrates moving to Depart he Wreathed from the Cross till he Fell in the Grass, and Damn'd them all for a Pack of Barbarous Rascals, at the Same time Removing his Right hand by the help of his Teeth, he Rested his Head on Part of the timber and ask'd the by Standers for a Pipe of Tobacco Which was infamously Answered by kicking & Spitting on him, till I with some Americans thought Proper to Prevent it—

he then begg'd that his head might be Chopt off, but to no Purpose, at Last Seeing no end to his Misery, he declared that though he had Deserved death, he had not Expected to die So many Deaths, "However you Christians /Said he/ have mis'd your Aim, and I now Care not were I to lay here alive a month Longer," After Which he Sung two Extempore Songs, With a Clear Voice taking leave from his Living Friends & Acquainting his Deceased Relations that in a Little time more he Should be with them to enjoy their Company for ever—this done he Entered in Conversation With two Gentlemen Concerning his Process Relating every one Particular with Uncommon tranquillity, but Said he Abruptly, "by the Sun it must be Eight OClock, & by any Longer discourse I Should be Sorry to be the Cause of your Loosing y^r. Breakfast" then turning his Eyes to a Jew Whose name was *De Vries*, "Appropo Sir said he Won't you please to pay me the 5 Shillings you owe me"—*for what to do*— "to buy meat & Drink to be Sure: don't you perceive that I am to be kept Alive" Which /Seeing the Jew look like a Fool/ he Accompanied With a Loud and Hearty Laugh—Next Observing the Soldier Who stood Sentinel over him biting Occasionally on a piece of Dry Bread he asked him, "how it Came that he a *White Man* Should have no meat to eat along with it" *Because I am not So rich* said the Soldier. "then I will make you a Present first pick my Hand that was Chopt of[f] Clean to the Bones Sir—Next begin to myself till you be Glutted & you'l have both Bread and Meat which best becomes you" & Which piece of Humour was Followed by a 2^d. Laugh & thus he Continued when I left him which was about 3 Hours After the Execution but to dwelt more on this Subject my Heart

—Disdains

> Lo! tortures, Racks, whips, Famine, Gibbets, Chains
> Rise on my mind, Appall my Tear Stain'd Eye
> Attract my Rage, & Draw a Soul felt Sigh,
> I Blush, I Shudder, at the Bloody theme,[12]

In the Adjoyning Plate see the above Dreadfull Chastisment.[13]

Figure 2.1. "The Execution of Breaking on the Rack." Engraving by William Blake after a drawing by John Gabriel Stedman. From John Gabriel Stedman, *Narrative of a Five Years Expedition against the Revolted Negroes of Surinam*, transcribed from the original 1790 manuscript, ed. Richard Price and Sally Price (Baltimore: Johns Hopkins University Press, 1998), 548.

Stedman speculated, with awe, about the way that Neptune, and other condemned slaves or freedmen, confronted their torturers: "Now How in the name of Heaven Human nature Can go through so much Torture, With So much Fortitude, is truly Astonishing, Without it be a mixture of Rage, Contempt, pride, And hopes of Going to a Better place or at Least to be Relieved from this, & Worse than Which I Verrily Believe Some Africans know no Other Hell—."[14]

A mixture of rage, contempt, and pride seems pretty much on the mark. These final, dignified gestures of resistance helped lend meaning to the lives of slaves and maroons and gave their fellows the courage to continue building. In the mid-nineteenth century, Suriname slaves were still using the bitterly ironic proverb "Tangi vo spansi boko mi si binfoto" [Thanks to the Spanish bok (a devastating torture/punishment administered to slaves and recaptured maroons in Fort Zeelandia), I got to see the inside of the fort].[15] And a favorite Suriname slave folk tale turned the tables quite completely: in various versions, situated on many different plantations, a rebellious slave manages to prepare himself ritually so that every lash of the whip delivered on his back in public by the master's "executioners" finds its mark, instead, on (variously or serially) the master's back, his daughter's back, his wife's back, or the overseer's back.[16]

Neptune's story, recounted in the words of a foreign observer, reveals much about the degree of totalization of the local plantation world. The protagonist, a freedman/artisan—already a liminal category in a society in which 99 percent of the population was either black and slave or white and free—ran a very human risk (stealing a sheep to entertain some [potential?] lovers), had the misfortune to be caught by an overseer, seems to have been the victim either of specific (personal) jealousy or simply of the widespread hatred of overseers for all blacks who were not slaves or "toms,"[17] and—knowing he was condemned to die—was left with precious little room to maneuver. Yet, if we listen closely to Stedman's words, maneuver Neptune did, unctuously excusing himself for making two gentlemen observers miss their breakfast, publicly exposing the money-grubbing Jew as a fool, and, while ridiculing the sentry's poverty, making a final comment about the local articulation of color and class. Like those other Afro-Americans who suffered "the discipline," Neptune went to the land of his ancestors (with a characteristic song) leaving bystanders with little doubt that—whatever the character of his persecutors or the moral bankruptcy of the slaveocracy—this was a man.[18]

Death Endured: Kwakú and the (Successful) Institutionalization of the Maroon World

If the first panel of our triptych represents the ultimate failure of the slave-ocracy to be fully totalizing, the second reveals the relative success of con-temporaneous maroon societies in attaining internal control, in creating new and vibrant Afro-American institutions of their own. Our emblematic narrative, which we hear in the voices of the Saramaka Maroon descendants of the protagonists as well as through the diaries of German Moravian eye witnesses, touches on certain themes already encountered in Neptune's story: love, jealousy, murder, and, ultimately, public torture and execution. But, while slave control and the fear of property loss provided the rational-ization for the theatrical executions in the first case, fear of betrayal—a cen-tral practical concern of early maroons, which becomes the linchpin of their ideology—is the driving force behind the gruesome execution in the second narrative. Within the world of maroons, new social and cultural forms had been created and institutionalized, building on diverse African precedents. In this context, public executions for heinous crimes, ordered and carried out by maroons themselves, may be seen as a sign of the triumph of societas and civitas. Lacking the irony or the class conflict of the plantation world executions, those in contemporaneous Saramaka reveal a society dealing with everyday problems of disorder in a fully communitarian way.

For early maroon societies throughout the Caribbean and its rimland, internal security and discipline were paramount concerns. Whether orga-nized as centralized states (like Palmares in northeast Brazil), loose and shifting federations (like the Windward Maroons of Jamaica), or isolated bands (like that of André in French Guiana), these were communities at war, fighting for their very existence.[19] Spies and counterspies were ubiquitous on the plantation-maroon periphery, and new recruits from slavery were put through complex and lengthy trials before being accepted into maroon communities. "Kwasímukámba's Gambit," a narrative that forms the center-piece of Saramaka Maroon historiography, makes clear that betrayal by out-siders was a core ideological concern.[20]

But a second area of danger lay within. The internal peace of maroon societies was severely threatened by disputes over men's rights to women. And here again the issues of betrayal and deception came to the fore. Dur-ing the early colonial period throughout the Americas, there was a severe imbalance of male to female slaves, and this proportion was even greater among the original bands of runaways because a disproportionately large number of men escaped from plantation life. Moreover, polygyny was the prerogative of important maroon men in many areas (for example, in Jamaica, French Guiana, and Palmares, as well as Suriname), further reducing the number of wives available for the rest of the community. Many maroon groups tried to solve this problem by capturing Indian women. But until they were able to raise their own children to maturity, almost all groups had to live with a severe shortage of women. Maroon men were well aware that fights over women could have the most serious consequences; where we have information on the penalty for adultery in early maroon communities, such as in Palmares or among the Windward Maroons of Jamaica, it is commonly death. Saramakas preserve a number of stories regarding early fights over women, and the avenging spirits-ghosts of newly runaway slave men, whose wives were "stolen" away from them by Saramaka men soon after their arrival in Saramaka territory, continue to haunt, sicken, and kill Saramakas even today.

The second panel of our triptych dates from 1781 (two decades after Saramakas made final Peace with the Dutch crown), when one of the most venerated Saramaka war heroes, the elderly chief Kwakú Kwádjaní, died suddenly and divination revealed that a Ndyuka man (from the neighboring maroon society) was responsible, by witchcraft. The Moravians, who were then living in Saramaka territory, report that

On the twenty-fifth [July 1781] we heard the news that a chief of a village two hours from here had died suddenly. All the negroes [from the Moravian village of Bambey] went there in order to take part in the funeral. The negroes there believed that the deceased had died because of poison [sorcery],[21] and the corpse was examined [through divination], revealing—according to them—that a certain Auka [Ndyuka] Negro was the perpetrator. A canoe was immediately dispatched with deputies in order to capture him and bring him here . . . As it turns out, the poor man was burned to death on the 15th of September.[22]

The Moravians report further that the execution was attended by several Ndyuka Maroons, as official witnesses. On the day following the burning at the stake, "Four Ndyukas visited us, one of whom was a captain. They were very friendly and humble and recommended that we . . . help see to it that the peace between them and the whites not be broken."[23]

Saramakas, more than two centuries later, retain yet more detailed memories of what happened.

Kwakú [Kwádjaní] and the Ndyuka were *máti* [formal friends]. The Ndyuka came here [to Saramaka] simply to visit. But [after a while] he began to want Kwakú's wife! The Ndyuka dug a spot under the woman's hearthstones, right where she cooked for Kwádjaní, and he buried something there. That's what killed him! When they raised his coffin [in divination] that's what it indicated.[24] It [the coffin] went right to that spot and "knocked" it. They dug and everyone saw it. "Who put it there?" they asked the coffin. "His *máti* from Ndyuka who came to visit," was the reply. [Tribal Chief] Kwakú Étja [the brother of Kwádjaní] left there and went all the way to Ndyuka! To get the person. to bring him to Kambalóa [their village]. Then they held a council meeting. But suddenly, they didn't see Étja any more. No sign of him. Until . . . at dusk he returned to the council meeting. And then, until morning, they didn't see him again. He had been going off to cut firewood across the river! He cut it until there was really a lot, and he piled it into a great heap. Then in the morning, he took fire and kerosene[25] and poured it all over until the fire was roaring. Well, when he disappeared from the council meeting, it was to see if the fire was really blazing. At last, the fire was just as he wanted it. He came back to the council meeting, went up to the Ndyuka man, and tied him up. He dragged him along, shrieking all the way to the fire. And they burned him. Right there at Puumá Sándu [behind Kambalóa].[26]

A German Moravian who spent some months in Saramaka in 1779–80 left a generalized description of such executions, which may help round out the current narrative.[27]

The relatives of the deceased, with the help of some associates, take the criminal by canoe to a distant place where they had already constructed a funeral pyre the previous day. Here, they bind him to a prickly [*awara* palm] tree right next to the pyre, and first cut off his nose and ears which they fry over the fire and then force him to eat. They then cut open his back and rub the wounds with hot pepper and salt, and then rub his open back up and down against the prickly tree, during which his cries of misery can be heard at a great distance. In addition, they carry out many other kinds of barbaric acts from which human nature shrinks, and which decency prevents me from describing. Finally, they light up the funeral pyre near him, and allow him to burn little by little, and the victim, who is bound to the tree, suffers greatly before the fire fully reaches the tree. All this takes place without in the least bit moving the observers or the executioners to show the slightest bit of pity.[28]

The account of Kwakú's death and the Ndyuka's execution bespeak much about the ongoing institutionalization of the Maroon world. First, there is the primacy of the *máti* relationship itself (and its susceptibility to betrayal). This highly charged volitional relationship between men dates back to the Middle Passage—*máti* were originally "shipmates," those who had sailed out from Africa and survived the journey together; by the eighteenth century, *máti* was a lifelong relationship entered into only with great caution and in the case of very strong mutual affection and admiration. Today, an oft-cited Saramaka proverb holds that *máti ganyá i, án o láfu* (if your *máti* betrays you, he won't be smiling—that is, he'll be dead serious).

Figure 2.2. "Execution of the Sorcerer." From Johann Andreus Riemer, *Missions-Reise nach Suriname und Barbice* (Zittau and Leipzig, 1801).

And for a man, perhaps the most strongly forbidden of all sexual partners is the wife of a *máti*, since between *máti*s there should be absolute trust. In this respect, then, the narrative of Kwádjaní's death serves as a cautionary tale for Saramakas, a tale with the same general message as "Kwasímu-kámba's Gambit." And it is this same message, inscribed in the folktale of *nóuna*, that Saramakas allude to, elliptically, when they wish to caution one another against what in less tropical metaphorical language we call a wolf in sheep's clothing.[29] Second, we see the complex development, by the eighteenth century, of a panoply of formal judicial procedures: divination with coffins to determine the cause of death and the identity of a "murderer," the *kangáa* ordeal (in which a medicated feather was thrust through a suspect's tongue to confirm guilt or innocence), the *gaán kuútu*s (tribal council) meetings at which sentences were meted out, and the formal "witnesses" from the tribe of the accused (who participated in a "humble" manner). And finally, there is the execution itself, carefully and publicly orchestrated, with the victim—unlike the proud, defiant slaves who underwent whitefolks' tortures—"shrieking all the way" and otherwise playing the guilty victim's role precisely as the society had defined it for this ultimate rite or ceremony.

Death Averted: Étja's Sister's Husband and the Creation of a New Negotiated Order

If our first panel was devoted to the plantation world and the second to the nearly separate world created by Saramaka Maroons, the final panel of our triptych depicts their interaction, the ambiguous negotiations that took place across the divide that separated these two realities. And, once again, we choose an emblematic narrative—this time recorded in the words of a Dutch administrative official sent out to negotiate with the Free Saramakas—that reveals something of the stakes and strategies in the circumscribed interactions between these two worlds, interactions that continue with much the same tone and content up to the present day.

After the 1762 treaty between the Saramaka Maroons and the Dutch, two issues (like others, sealed in blood—"à l'africaine"—by both parties at the treaty signing) emerged as paramount in their ongoing relations. The first involved intense pressure from the whites on the Saramakas to return "slaves." The plantation system, to perdure, could not tolerate any open door, any way out for the massive labor force that supported the foundations of the colony. The colonists now depended on the Saramakas to turn in all slaves who escaped after the treaty date. Yet, as the whites themselves dimly perceived, in the years following the treaty the Saramakas were in fact very actively, if clandestinely, working to assimilate large numbers of such people into their families and villages.[30]

The second issue concerned the "tribute" that the Saramakas demanded from the whites. Now that wartime plantation raiding was a thing of the past, Saramakas were dependent on the colonial government to provide them with material goods of various sorts—guns, tools, pots, and cloth.[31] But the colonists, then fighting wars against new maroon groups and suffering from severe financial difficulties of their own, were reluctant both to spend the money for these goods and, more important, to admit to any obligation to the Maroons. The symbolic meaning of these goods clearly differed for colonists and Saramakas. Were they to be conceptualized as presents, freely given by the whites to needy subjects, or were they in fact tribute, exacted from the whites by the victorious Saramakas as a kind of war damages? The whites understood very well what was at stake in these contrasting definitions: one planter wrote, with considerable discomfort, of "the weakness of the government of Suriname when they offered them [the Saramakas] freedom...and submitted to conditions so humiliating for us and so glorious for them . . . It is they who demand and receive our homage in the form of annual presents . . . a kind of annual tribute under the name of presents which, at base, is nothing less than the public recognition of their superiority."[32]

The periodic transfer of these goods became, along with the transfer of the whites' "slaves" in the other direction, the pivot upon which the whole issue of political dependence was symbolically balanced. Indeed, the colonial government consistently tried to link the granting of presents to the returning of "slaves." The colonial official sent out to distribute the first set of tribute clearly believed that it was his prerogative to try to trick the "childlike" Saramakas, and he described with apparent glee how "I arranged all the shares [of goods] in such an attractive way that they [the Saramakas] would think that there was three times as much as there actually was"; yet he seemed indignant and angry when these same Saramakas showed that they were not fooled and subjected him to some characteristic rhetorical whiplashing.[33] During this post treaty period, each relevant negotiation, no matter how small, came to balance on issues of symbolic dependency and autonomy, on each side's assumptions about themselves and the "other." A whole new political relationship was being forged, and both sides were involved in a complicated dance of threats and retreats, demands and acceptances, posturing, flattery, and self-effacement. And through these complex negotiations of meaning and power—these very particular circumscribed interactions that nonetheless may stand for thousands of others taking place throughout the Caribbean rimland—a new order was being created, an order that in many places continues to retain its force today.

The eighteenth-century Caribbean rimland was a thoroughly colonial arena. Unlike the more "pristine" European-Indian encounters of earlier centuries (which Todorov framed as Columbus treating Indians as animals, while the Aztecs treated the Spaniards as Gods),[34] the Dutch now saw Saramakas as "vermin," "pernicious scum," "a crowd of monsters," or "a Hydra,"[35] while the Saramakas, in turn, considered their former slavemasters too low to be called human—*ná sèmbè* (not people), they called them. Their circumscribed encounters involved subtle new processes of interaction, something like what Taussig, writing of the confrontation between Indians and colonists near the headwaters of the Amazon, has glossed as "new rituals, rites of conquest and colony formation, mystiques of race and power, little dramas of civilization tailoring savagery which did not mix or homogenize ingredients from the two sides of the colonial divide but instead bound Indian understandings of white understandings to white understandings of Indian understandings of whites."[36]

Our third emblematic narrative, roughly contemporaneous with the other two, dates from 1774. The Dutch colonists, frustrated by two decades of difficulties in getting the Saramakas to comply with their treaty obligation to return new runaways from the plantations, had decided to get tough, and they instructed Postholder Daunitz, their military administrative official in Saramaka, not to compromise any longer. The postholder's negotiations with the Saramakas, marked by dramatic posturing and threats, give some hint of what was at stake. Daunitz's opponent in this interchange is Captain Kwakú Étja (whom Moravian eyewitnesses described as "one of the most respected captains and most famous Gado- and Obia-men in the entire land"). As Daunitz wrote in his diary,

30 May [1774] ... Étja said "Am I the only one who has 'slaves' that you always complain about this to me? I will not hand them over now." Then I said to him, "Then I shall not come live near you." [N.B. Kwakú Étja, to reinforce his claims on the office of tribal chief, very much wanted Daunitz to establish his permanent post across from his new village.] At which the boy [Étja was then in his eighties!] became so fresh that he slapped me and said "If you utter another word, I'll kill you on the spot." And he ordered me off exactly as if I were a mad dog. I also became angry but I didn't back down. I stood right up to him while he was threatening me with death

and I said "Here I am. Kill me if you have the guts. I won't flee from you!" But he didn't carry it any further and I said to Alábi [the Saramaka captain and convert to Christianity] . . . "Let's go home and let this crazy keep railing as long as he wants."

Daunitz, after exchanging further threats with Étja, went to wait at the riverbank for Alábi, who remained in Étja's village to complete some other business. There he mused that he had been sorely tempted to fight Étja "as I would have bested him because he is not very strong. [Then,] Étja came to me by the riverbank . . . and said, 'Daunitz, do you really want the 'slave' Kodjo? Then go to my sister, who is his wife, and argue the matter with her.' I answered that I had no orders to argue with women."

But Daunitz did go back into the village and entered Étja's house.

Étja had his sister summoned. [Kodjo] brought his wife, that is Étja's sister, on his shoulder because she is lame in one leg and cannot walk without being carried . . . Étja said to his brother-in-law, "Kodjo, this is the white man who is so hungry to turn you in. Take a knife and fight him. If he is stronger and beats you, that is all right. But if you succeed in killing him, that is also good. He deserves it." When I heard this, I was truly despairing but at the same time I thought of God who helps me with all my needs .... When Étja saw that the slave Kodjo was not coming after me with a knife, Étja went right up to him and hit him, saying "You bastard! Why don't you ever do as I tell you?" The slave began to cry and came to me weeping, saying, "Massa, if the whites want to kill me, it's their money [they are wasting], but if they let me live, I'd accept that too." When I heard this from the slave, I gave him my hand and said, "Kodjo, as long as you don't withdraw your hand from mine, you have no need to fear. I shall ask the Court to spare your life." But the obscenities that his wife then uttered I cannot write down. This slave then put his wife on his back and carried her back to her house.[37]

Other Saramakas soon came carrying muskets, hearing that there was a fight, and threatened Daunitz. Étja finally offered him a conciliatory drink but he refused, fearing poison.

During this same period, Étja used various arguments to justify not returning the two (some documents say three) whitefolks' slaves he was allegedly harboring. For example, he once asked, "Why should I give up my three 'slaves' when Samsám [a rival captain] still has a whole village full?" At other times he claimed that the two slaves were a substitute for the original husband of his crippled sister, who had been killed by the whites. On still other occasions, he stressed that one of the slaves was married to his sister.[38] To my knowledge, neither Kodjo nor the other(s) were ever returned.

The negotiations of 1774–75, intended by Postholder Daunitz and the court in Paramaribo to be final, in fact led to very few new slave returns.[39]

Indeed, during this period and after, Saramakas never turned back more than a handful of such newcomers, successfully practicing vis-à-vis the whites what might be characterized as a politics of mass confusion. And during these circumscribed interactions, the Saramaka chiefs relentlessly demanded (and often received) goods of the most diverse kinds—which the whites consistently tried to tie to the return of runaways. On balance, the negotiations that took place in 1774–75 are best seen as a remarkably successful smoke screen, set up by the Saramakas, which permitted them finally to assimilate a group of 100-odd "slaves" who had arrived in their territory some five years before. After 1775, pressures form the colonial government and its postholders on this score waned markedly: Saramakas clearly maintained the upper hand, in part by making sure that the colonial government never understood that such was the case. A close reading of the historical records reveals that the postholders—arrogant, condescending, and confident of their racial superiority—remained largely unaware of their ultimate powerlessness and ignorance regarding the shell game Saramakas had been playing with the new runaways. In the early nineteenth century, one postholder illustrated this mystification when he summed up decades of administrative experience on this issue with the assertion that "[t]he [Saramaka] Bush Negroes are exceptionally jealous, hateful, and vengeful, which is why they are unable to protect many new runaways—since one of them will easily betray the next in return for a small gift from the postholder."[40]

Given the situation of grossly unequal power, and considering the means at their disposal—guile, wit, and the full Afro-American cultural repertoire they had developed on the plantations and in the forests—the Saramakas had the whites just where they wanted. Using cleverness, and playing on the ambiguities of their respective negotiating positions, Saramakas consistently had learned to avert the return of whitefolks' "slaves" to almost certain death and, at the same time, to extract many of the material goods they needed.

Envoi

A Saramaka Maroon folk tale provides a fitting coda, for it links the final panel of the triptych with the first.[41] In this tale, plantation slavery and wage slavery are poetically merged, and the secret to slaves' or maroons' survival in these contexts is clearly spelled out: never accept the whiteman's definition of the situation. Taking to heart the lessons that Neptune and his fellows taught, Saramakas have learned to survive and even triumph in situations of gross inequality. And "play" is one of the means that permits them to assure that the whiteman consistently gets his comeuppance.[42]

It used to be there was plenty of wage-labor work. You'd go off to look for work, and there would always be some job available. There was one guy and you'd just go ask him for work, a white man. He was the one in charge of it. Now when you went to ask him for work, You'd say, "Well, Brother, I've come to ask you for a job." Then he'd say to you, "Well, look. I've got some." He has a gigantic rice field. He's got a cacao field. He's got all kinds of fields spread out all around. He's got pigs. He's got cows. He's got chickens. He's got ducks. So you just appear out of nowhere, and ask him for a job, and he says to you, "Well, Brother, I've got some cacao over there. You could go gather the pods and bring them back to me. I'll give you a bag." So off you'd go. But when you went to touch it, one of the cacao pods would break off, and all the beans would fall down and run all over the place. The plant would be absolutely stripped. So you walk back to the king. (That's the white man who has the jobs. He's just like a king.) You'd talk to him and say, "Well, king. Here I am. I went and touched one of the cacao plants to harvest it, and all the beans fell on the ground." So you told him about how everything fell down to the ground. The man says, "Really? Well, my boy, when the cacao fell like that, did it hurt you?" He said, "Yes, my king, it hurt me." King says, "OK, bring your butt over here." [laughter] He'd slice off a kilo of butt. One kilo of flesh that he just cut right off and took. When the time came, you'd just go off to your house and die.

Then the next person would come along asking for work. He'd say, "My king, I've come to ask you for a job." He'd say, "Well, no problem. In the morning, just go let those cows I've got over there, let them out of the pen and bring them outside." In the morning the man went and opened the pen right up. The cows fell down, *gúlúlúlú*, fell down, all over the ground, dead. He went back and said, "My king, I went like you said and opened the cows' pen over there. All of them fell down on the ground, dead." He said, "My boy, did it hurt you?" He answered, "Yes, my king." The king said, "Bring your butt over here." He turned his butt toward the king and went over. The king sliced off one kilo and took it. The guy went off and died.

So that's the way it went. He just kept killing people. But the name of the king—I forgot to mention that. The king was "King Nothing-hurts-him" (or "King Nothing-angers-him").

But there was a young guy who decided to go ask for work. His mother didn't want him to. She said, "Child, don't go. The place where you're going to go ask for work—Well, not a single person has gone to ask for work there and returned. If you go ask for work there, you're as good as dead and gone. Don't go!" He said he was determined to go. He arrived. He said, "My king, I've come to ask you for a job." "All right," he said. He said, "My boy, do you know who I am?" The boy said, "No. " He said, "I am King Nothing-hurts-him." He said, "OK, no problem." And he went off to the work he had. He went off to pick the cacao. As he reached up to touch it, all the beans fell down and ran *gúlúlúlú* all over the ground. He went back to the king. He said, "King, I went to touch the cacao over there to harvest it, and it fell off all over the ground, it all broke off and fell down before I even touched it." He said, "My boy, did it hurt you?" The boy said, "No. My king, it didn't hurt me." King said, "OK. No problem. That's all right." He said, "Let's go to sleep for the night."

In the morning he said, "Well, my boy? I'd like you to go harvest a field of rice I've got over there. Just go on and cut the rice." He went off, reached out to cut a stalk of rice, and they all fell and covered the whole area, *gúlúlúlú*. He went back, and he said, "My king, I went to cut the rice over there and all the stalks fell over to the ground." He said, "My boy, didn't it hurt you?" He said, "No. How could it have hurt me?" The king said, "OK." So nothing happened. The next morning, he said, "I'd like you to let out some chickens I've got over there." He went to let them out. But as he opened the door, all the chickens fell down on the ground, dead. (As things fell, he would take something and just kill them right off. It didn't bother him if things fell. This was a kid who wasn't hurt by anything. He'd just cut things down. He'd just cut it down and kill it.) The king said, "Well, my boy. In the morning you'll go and open a duck pen I've got over there." He opened it. Whoosh!! Flap! They just kept coming out and falling down. He finished every one of them off, just cut them up, dead! He went back and said, "My king, those ducks I went to let out, well, such-and-such a thing happened." He said, "Well, my boy, did it hurt you?" The boy said, "My king, it didn't hurt me." "Oh," he said. Well, this kept going on and on until there was nothing left in that place. I don't need to list all that was gone. There was absolutely nothing left. He'd killed everything. All that was left was some pigs he had.

So he said, "Well, my boy. Go open up the pig pen over there." So he went to let out the pigs. The pigs all fell down. So he jumped out and he clubbed them all to death. Cut them all up. Cut off their tails and took them. Then he buried those tails. He took the rest of the pigs' bodies and hid them off in the underbrush. He just buried those tails till all that was left above the ground was a teeny tiny bit, the tips were barely sticking up.

He just did it to make a problem with the king. He killed absolutely all of them. Then he came out and he ran to him. He went straight to his king. "My king, my king!" he said. "I went to go let out the pigs, and all of them burrowed down under the ground! So I ran back to tell you!" [laughter] The king said [very agitated], "Where?" he said, "Over there!" The king said, "Let's go!" He ran off and when he arrived he looked around. Now, the way they were buried, the pigs' tails went deep into the ground, and only a tiny little piece was sticking up. You couldn't grab it to pull it out. They grabbed them as tight as they could. The king said, "This won't work. You know what we'll do?" "What?" said the boy. "Run back to my wife, in the house over there. [laughter] Go have her give you a shovel. Quick! Bring it back." The kid ran back there. He really ran fast to get there, and he said, "Quick! Hurry up, as fast as you can. My king says to!" "All right," she said. So then he told her—"My king says to tell you—Well, what he says is that I should 'live' with you." [exclamations and laughter] "What did you say?!!" she asked. "Yes," he said. "'Quick! Quick! Quick!' That's what he said!" She said, "No way!" But the king turned and shouted back to her, "Quick! Give it to him quick! Give it to him quick! Give it to him right away!" She said, "OK, I understand." The king said "Give it to him! Give it to him! Give it to him! Fast! Fast!" [hysterical laughter] That's what he said. "Give him! Give him! Give him! Give him! Give him!" The boy took the wife and threw her right down on the bed. and then he went to work. Well, that shovel that the king sent the boy back for, in a rush, so they could dig up the pigs—Well, the boy didn't bring it back so quickly. He was gone for quite a while, and finally the king said, "Something's wrong." He ran on back to the house, looked in, and the boy was on top of his lady. [exclamations] He fell over backwards and just lay there. The boy said, "My king, did this hurt you?" He said, "Yes, this hurt me." The boy said, "Bring your butt over here!" [wild laughter] The king turned his butt toward the boy and approached him. He brought his butt on over. The boy lopped off a kilo. And then the king died. That's why things are the way they are for us. Otherwise, it would have been that whenever you asked for work from a white man, a king, he'd kill you. The boy took care of all that for us. And that's as far as my story goes.

Refusing to accept the whiteman's definition of the situation, the boy triumphed in the end. And today, however hard it is for Saramaka men to retain their inner strength and dignity while submitting to humiliating work and treatment in coastal wage labor situations (cleaning out toilets at the French missile base at Kourou, for example), tales like this—and First-Time memories of incidents like Neptune's heroic death or Étja's standing up to the colonial officer—help them keep going. Out of the ashes of destruction and death, in the crucible of conquest and colonialism, Afro-American maroons throughout the Caribbean rimland created unique cultures and societies and somehow found the strength to keep on going. Even today, when such peoples continue to be threatened by repressive national governments—as in present-day Suriname and French Guiana[43]—they fight on, refusing to forget their collective past and insisting on their own right to define themselves and their world.

PART II

Authority and Intimate Violence

Historians of the colonial Americas are by now used to analyzing power struggles and cultural contestation in borderlands at the edges of empire. In general they have understood borderlands as geographic sites, zones where competition between European and Indian groups rendered political and cultural authority fluid and negotiable. Such work has been undeniably useful in advancing understanding of the dynamics of colonial rule in the Americas—but it also begs questions about contests for power within social, as well as geographic, space. Gloria Anzuldúa has eloquently argued that the concept of borderlands encompasses psychological, sexual, and spiritual dimensions as well; a borderlands can exist anywhere that "the space between two individuals shrinks with intimacy."[1] Indeed, the colonization of the Americas involved not just extensive efforts to project authority over physical space but an intensive effort to effect rule over social space as well. And if struggles for power in geographic borderlands involved the redrawing of boundaries and the redefinition of authority at different moments, then struggles for power along the "intimate frontiers of empire" likewise involved redrawing the boundaries between church, state, and the "household" and redefining colonial authority over gender relations.[2] This struggle over intimate domains of life was crucial was crucial to the "production of colonial inequalities."[3] The chapters in Part II analyze how conflicts over authority and sanction shaped the creation of both "domestic spaces" and gendered and racial identities in colonial Quito, eighteenth-century British America, and colonial French Louisiana.

In her analysis of women's efforts to seek redress in domestic disturbances in Quito, Kimberly Gauderman argues that Spanish American women were able to take advantage of jurisdictional tensions within the colonial order to protect themselves and their interests. Aware that the colonial state took an interest in preventing domestic abuse, adultery, and the seduction of unmarried women, women found success in the legal system. The boundary between household and state authority in Quito was ultimately permeable, checking what previous scholars have seen as traditional male prerogatives in their private dealings with women. In contrast, Sharon Block and Cecile Vidal each demonstrate that state–sanctioned forms of certain types of violence shaped colonial ideologies of race and gender. In her examination of violence against slaves in Louisiana, Vidal shows that selective enforcement of the colony's Black Code led to a progressive racialization of violence and a strengthening of masters' power; while royal officials criminalized private violence between white men and intervened against whites for mistreating slaves they did not own, those sections of the Black Code that might have mitigated owners' violence against slaves were not enforced, normalizing white violence against blacks. Similarly, Block argues that rape was "situationally classified" depending on the identity of the attacker and the victim. Not only were attackers with significantly higher social status than their victims less likely to be charged with crimes, they were also, if prosecuted, charged with sexual crimes carrying a lesser penalty than violent crimes. When black men were accused of rape their actions were seen as sexually violent—and thus more serious—crimes. Thus, Vidal and Block cumulatively show the significance of legal noninterference in households and in intimate encounters between colonial men and women in gendering and racializing power relations in colonial society.

Together, these chapters reveal the contingency of colonial efforts to regulate intimate affairs. They demonstrate that while, as Ann Stoler has noted, "the making of an imperial body politic" was linked to "the making of sexualized and racialized selves," this process proceeded, at times, in fits and starts.[4] The practice of sanctioning—the selective enforcement of legal proscriptions—more than legal rules shaped the creation of these colonial subjectivities. Gauderman, Vidal, and Block thus show that the examination of the borderlands of everyday life in the colonial Americas—the internal edges of empire—can be as fruitful as analysis of the geographic borderlands scholars have traditionally explored.

Chapter 3
The Authority of Gender: Marital Discord and Social Order in Colonial Quito

Kimberly Gauderman

In 1662, Maestro Francisco de la Vega, priest in charge of the parish of San Marcos in Quito, testified that he was well aware of the illicit relationship between the married Antonio Carrillo and María de Castillo. Antonio's wife, Agustina de la Vega (not a family relative of the priest), had complained to him that her husband physically mistreated her, stole her property, and abandoned her to live with María de Castillo, a woman held in ill repute by most of the parishioners. After patiently listening to Agustina "ten or twelve times," he gave her a recommendation that might seem surprising coming from a priest. He did not encourage her to change her husband's behavior by setting a saintly example herself in the virtues of silent suffering, obedience, and patience. Instead, he advised her to sue her husband. Maestro Francisco counseled the aggrieved wife to go to the civil authorities because, he said, it was the royal justices who knew how to resolve Agustina's problems with her husband.[1]

Agustina took the priest's advice and brought criminal charges against her husband before the royal authorities for physically mistreating her and adultery. We too would be wise to heed the priest's counsel and move beyond the traditional view of the church as the main instrument of social intervention into the otherwise private realm of intimate relations between men and women. Adultery, physical aggression, and abandonment were criminal acts, and women routinely used the criminal justice system against men who abused them. I describe the limitations women faced in resolving domestic disputes through the ecclesiastical system of justice and then, through an examination of court cases, explore how and why women of different social rank and ethnicity sued men, the punishments men received, and why the local community and the royal government often supported women in domestic disputes. The results put into question the view that a sexual double standard for women and men was universally accepted by colonial Spanish American society and that men's physical aggression against female family members was considered acceptable behavior.

Women's strategies for confronting men's disloyalty and physical abuse also provoke deeper questions about the connection between gender and authority in colonial Spanish America. Researchers traditionally use a patriarchal model to show how men, on the basis of their gender, held greater economic, social, and political power than women. As commonly used, the patriarchal model assumes that Spanish society was hierarchically arranged around a central authority and that this cultural framework also explains relations between men and women in society and the family. The existing work on colonial Spanish state structure, however, shows that political and economic relations were decentralized. Interpreting women's status through the specific cultural matrix of decentralization that defined colonial Spanish society reveals greater authority for women than researchers have usually acknowledged. The successes and failures of women to compel ecclesiastical and civil authorities to intervene in women's intimate conflicts with men suggests that gender authority, like other forms of authority, was inherently decentralized.

Limitations of the Ecclesiastical Court System

The church held exclusive jurisdiction over the constitution and dissolution of marriages in colonial Spanish America. Once a marriage had taken place, the church considered the union permanent until the death of one of the spouses. Only in very rare cases did it grant divorces or annulments. Divorce was conceived of as a separation of the spouses and their property, but the marriage was still considered valid in that neither person could remarry. An annulment canceled the marriage, as if it had never happened, and both individuals were thus free to remarry. Accordingly, marital continuity rather than marital bliss was the overriding concern of the church. Because of its emphasis on the permanence of marriage, the church was largely uninterested in establishing firm criteria for the conduct of spouses. Clearer regulations would have made things easier for individuals seeking separation, allowing them to sue their partners for failure to meet authorized standards of conduct. As the research of many gender historians conclude, though the church did adopt egalitarian guidelines for the behavior of husbands and wives, these guidelines remained poorly defined, and the judgments by ecclesiastical courts were often contradictory.[2]

In a foundational statement concerning the definition of marriage by Alfonso the Wise in the thirteenth century, both men and women were exhorted to live together permanently and faithfully, neither one to engage in carnal relations with another person.[3] The expectation that women and men had an equal commitment to each other was also mirrored in the fact that the official causes recognized by the church for which a divorce or annulment could be granted, including adultery and domestic violence, pertained to both wives and husbands.[4]

Following canon law, it would seem that the church's expectations for conjugal life were egalitarian, demanding faithfulness and collaboration from both spouses, and that the ecclesiastical courts recognized a number of causes for legal separations. For women, however, there remained numerous ambiguities. In the case of adultery, for example, though both spouses were prohibited from committing adultery, a wife's adulterous relationship was considered a far more serious offense than her husband's. This difference in the perception of wives and husbands' adulterous activities was based, interestingly, on property rights. Because all children a married women gave birth to were considered legitimate and shared equal inheritance rights to her and her husband's private estates as well as to their community property, should a wife give birth to another man's child, that child would illicitly gain rights to property. If a husband engendered a child by another woman, no such confusion existed because that child would legally have no inheritance rights and would not, thus, affect the preservation of family property.[5]

Other than adultery, the most common complaint of wives was domestic violence, and here too the church's position was weak.[6] Though the church ostensibly discouraged domestic violence, in divorce cases it is clear that the church often recognized as legitimate a husband's right to punish his wife in order to change her behavior. Thus, though there was no actual legislation that allowed husbands to physically punish their wives, domestic abuse, like male adultery, was usually considered by ecclesiastical courts as an insufficient cause for obtaining a separation. In Natalia León's study of divorce in Cuenca, Ecuador, for example, of the 24 divorce cases encountered for the period 1750 to 1800, 21 of the demands for divorce were by wives, and in 20 of these cases, the women cited domestic violence as their central argument. The ecclesiastical court granted only 2 divorces during this period, and in neither of the judgments was the wife's mistreatment cited as a factor.[7]

León's study demonstrates other important factors when considering the effectiveness of the church in regulating conjugal relations: divorce cases were exceedingly rare; it was overwhelmingly wives who initiated the demands, and they usually lost. Silvia Arrom's study of divorce in Mexico City shows the same pattern. Between 1790 and 1856, Arrom encountered 70 divorce suits; of these cases, wives brought 63 of the demands. In the wives' suits, 62 accused their husbands of cruelty and 57 claimed actual physical abuse by their spouses. The success rate in the ecclesiastical courts was low; in only 12 percent of the total number of demands was a divorce obtained.[8] Throughout the colonial period, divorce was difficult to obtain, despite the church's official recognition of just causes for legally separating married couples.

The case of doña Rafaela Núñez de Valladolid, in the Audiencia of Quito, exemplifies the difficulties wives faced in the ecclesiastical courts even when they had ample evidence that officially recognized causes for divorce existed.[9] Doña Rafaela was the youngest of three sisters; their mother apparently died when she was quite young, and their father never remarried. Her sisters had already married, and she, having expressed a desire to live a life of chastity and religious devotion, had spent much of her life in the convent in Ibarra. On an outing to the family's hacienda, she was raped by her brother-in-law, an event that traumatized her and increased her determination not to marry but to live her life as a lay sister in the convent.[10]

Her desires for a quiet life in the convent, however, were thwarted when her sisters and father proposed a marriage for her, upon the urging of two of the convent's nuns who wanted to arrange a marriage for their nephew. Doña Rafaela's father later testified that he was in favor of the marriage because he lacked the financial means to keep her in the convent. Doña Rafaela, however, rejected the offer and insisted that she never wanted to marry. Several witnesses, including her father and sisters, later testified that the family began a campaign of intimidation, threats, and violence to force doña Rafaela to accept the marriage. Her father threw her down the stairs and threatened to kill her if she didn't accede, which, because of force, she finally did. However, when the intended groom heard of her original rejection of his proposal, he then withdrew the offer of marriage, claiming that he desired a religious vocation.

At this point, it looked like the situation was playing out well for doña Rafaela. Then came the first kidnapping. Her father, insulted by the withdrawn marriage proposal, rounded up the sisters, their husbands, and several domestic employees, kidnapped both doña Rafaela and the intended groom in the middle of the night, took them to a priest, and forced them to marry. The ceremony lacked the procedures prescribed by the church for legitimate marriages. No proclamations of the intended marriage had been read in the church in the preceding weeks, neither of the two potential spouses was interrogated by the priest in private to ensure that they were marrying of their free will, and no notary was present. After the ceremony, the two were locked in a room at a sister's house for the night. Both doña Rafaela and her then–unwilling husband claimed that the marriage was never consummated.

The two then went their separate ways; she returned to the convent, and again it looked like she might be able to enjoy a peaceful existence. Her husband, however, had a change of heart. His strategy for reuniting with doña Rafaela included kidnapping her a second time and holding her prisoner in a house in Quito. Doña Rafaela, however, managed to escape, after which she sued for annulment and divorce. The ecclesiastical court ordered her husband to pay for her expenses in the convent during the court proceedings, but he did not comply, instead beginning to sell the things she had left in Quito. Meanwhile, his aunts in the convent tormented doña Rafaela by verbally abusing her and depriving her of food. Doña Rafaela's situation was growing precarious: not only did she lack financial support and necessities in the convent; she was isolated and forbidden from communicating with family members. Despite testimonies by her father, sisters, neighbors, domestic employees, and even her husband himself verifying her early vow of chastity, her desire for a religious vocation, the use of threats and physical force against her, the procedural irregularities of the ceremony, and the acknowledgment by both of the partners that the marriage had never been consummated, the case was still being disputed nearly a year and a half later.

Although doña Rafaela's demand united all the major causes officially recognized by the church as invalidating a marriage, in his initial judgment, the bishop's lieutenant recommended that she be forced to live with her legal husband. Even so, the suit was allowed to continue despite the lieutenant's objections, though it is not clear that the case was ever resolved. Her husband seems never to have responded to the demand for divorce and was cited with *rebeldía*, or failure to appear in court. Doña Rafaela's side of the case was considered complete, and the last information available is her lawyer's request that the final judgment be issued on the basis of the information and testimonies compiled on her behalf.

Doña Rafaela's story demonstrates many of the limitations wives faced when using the ecclesiastical system of justice. Although her decision to seek an annulment or a divorce was an extraordinary measure for a wife to take, doña Rafaela was clearly desperate and determined to separate from her husband in whatever way possible. When her father tried to counsel her, she reportedly angrily replied "she wasn't asking for his advice but for his favor in order to leave the oppression in which she found herself; if no one in her family offered any relief and she had no other refuge she would flee to regions where no one knew her."[11]

Once a wife presented a demand for annulment or divorce in the ecclesiastical courts, she had to remain resolute in confronting the long, isolating and costly process. The law stipulated that a woman making such demands had to be "deposited" in the home of a well-reputed citizen or in a convent, with the husband obligated to pay for her expenses. Even doña Rafaela, who remained in the convent of her choice, complained of the isolation, deprivation, and harassment she had to endure. For poor working women, who would have been separated from their livelihoods, or for mothers, who might find themselves separated from their children, such a period of isolation would have been onerous if not impossible to bear. When one considers the length of the litigation (often over two years), the great expense of hiring attorneys and notaries, and the likelihood that a suit would be rejected, it is not difficult to understand why the ecclesiastical courts remained an option that only few wives took. For most women, the church was an ineffectual mediator in their conflicts with men.[12]

In his study of women in colonial Spanish America, Richard Boyer asks, "But if the church intruded little into the domestic arena, what mechanisms did regulate married life?"[13] In answering this question, he draws on research by scholars on English and French societies to conclude that, beyond ad hoc manifestations of public sentiment, always in defense of patriarchal authority and the inviolability of sex roles, the family remained an impenetrable unit controlled by its male head. And in fact, if the only recourse a wife had was the church, whose tenets encouraging gender equality were rarely enforced, one would have to accept the generalization that violence and adultery were acceptable male traits. But another formal mechanism did exist for women, the criminal justice system. In addition to being judged as immoral by the church, adultery and domestic violence were illegal acts. Women from all walks of life skipped the church courts with their difficult, expensive, and lengthy system of justice, and simply sued their husbands in the criminal justice system and had them thrown in jail. It was easy, cheap, and fast, and some wives did it over and over again in order to curb a misbehaving husband.

The Criminal Justice System

In the seventeenth century, women were legally empowered to bring criminal charges against men, including their husbands.[14] Just as it was overwhelmingly wives who brought demands for divorce to the ecclesiastical courts, it was also wives who used the criminal justice system to resolve their conflicts with their husbands. There is no record of a criminal suit being brought by a husband against his wife for any reason in the district of Quito in the seventeenth century. The definition of adultery and wife beating as crimes signifies that men who engaged in such acts risked more than the moral consternation of a few church officials. Men who were violent or dishonest in their relations with women faced possible imprisonment, fines, confiscation of their property, banishment, loss of their public offices, and forced labor in public projects, the military, or textile mills.

Women's use of the criminal justice system poses questions about the connection between gender norms and the creation and maintenance of authority and social order in Spanish American society. Traditionally, historians of Spanish American women tend to link gender norms to a particular form of political organization broadly defined as "Old Regime." In this view, society was a well-defined hierarchy with a central figure of authority, the king. The structure of the family reflected this cultural logic: the absolute power of the father/husband over his children and wife was analogous to the authority of the king. As Steve Stern noted, "the metaphor of familial patriarch readily ran up the chain of rule to higher authorities, the metaphor of kingship readily ran down the chain or rule to husband-fathers, and the patriarchal family ruled by a father-elder was the fundamental unit of social survival and collaboration."[15] In short, the capacity of men to "rule" over women within the family mirrored the centralized authority of the king over his subjects.

There is a well-established body of literature, however, that demonstrates that the Spanish political system was decentralized. Spanish administrative and judicial bureaucracies, and even the king, were not hierarchically ordered. Instead, they shared overlapping jurisdictions of authority. The conflict and competition generated through this system produced its own network of checks and balances and negated the need for a centralized position of authority to stabilize social relations. Groups and individuals, jealously guarding and trying to enhance their own spheres of status and influence, vigilantly prevented each other from overextending their authority and consolidating positions of centralized control. Government bureaucracies at all levels were encouraged to watch and report on each other in order to ensure that this network of authority remained permeable and flexible. Within this system, the exercise of authority was never absolute but required negotiation between various groups empowered to protect their particular interests. Within this cultural logic, wives were capacitated to control their own property and to litigate against male kin in order to limit the authority of individual men and, thus, to integrate the family into the broad network of relations that characterized Spanish society.[16]

Both the church and the state recognized the family as a source of social, economic, and political power. However, while both were interested in preserving families intact, their tactics for doing so were distinct. For the church, once a marriage had taken place, that family unit became essentially hermetically sealed; relations between the couple became a personal matter. The attitude of the church can be partly understood in that the only official action it could take once the marriage had taken place was to dissolve the union. Though the church might encourage moderation and collaboration between spouses, it lacked any mechanism for officially censuring or punishing individuals without putting in jeopardy the permanence of the union. The church could intervene on the part of individual interests only at great risk to the institution of marriage—and thus to its own powers—since an important aspect legitimating the church's control over the family was its definition of marriage as a permanent union sanctified by God. The church instead emphasized the importance of the couple's common interest, which it saw as the continuation of their union. Goody explains that "by insinuating itself into the very fabric of domestic life, of heirship and marriage, the Church gained great control over the grass roots of society itself . . . Religion entered into the basic units of production and reproduction."[17]

Unlike the church, the state viewed marriage as a union incorporating both individual and common interests, much like any other legal institution in Spanish American society. The government enabled family members to protect their individual interests in order to prevent families from collapsing into closed corporate entities. Husbands were not legally recognized as the sole authority over family resources; wives possessed their own estates and sued their husbands in courts but because the civil authorities could not dissolve marriages, any action they took, no matter how disruptive to the marriage, could never officially end the union. State policies were not partisan to one sex over another; rather, the state used individual suits to increase the permeability of all sectors of society to external vigilance and social intervention. The state's mechanisms for legally punishing spouses increased its legitimacy by allowing it to extend its influence over individual men and women whom the church had permanently sealed together. Society empowered women with the juridical capacity to litigate independently from and even in opposition to men, including male kin, as part of a cultural strategy to maintain social stability through decentralizing relations of authority.

Independent Actions of the State

Personal relations were of public interest, and public interest was fostered by the extension of government authority into private relations between men and women. Royal and local authorities accomplished this goal by independently monitoring and sanctioning personal conduct and by prosecuting men accused by women of duplicitous and violent behavior.

Spanish conquest in America generated many conflicts, some of them marital, because men often left their wives behind in Spain for many years, sometimes indefinitely. The Crown issued numerous directives mandating that men in the Indies either send for their abandoned wives or be shipped back to Spain. Though most of this legislation was never enforced, a few men were indeed fined large amounts of money for delay in bringing their wives to Quito. The viceroy, for example, ordered the conquistador Rodrigo Núñez de Bonilla to pay three thousand pesos in gold to the Crown in 1556 for not having brought his wife from Mexico. The money was collected but was returned to him once his wife arrived. That same year, the viceroy ordered the carpenter Andrés Suara to pay five hundred pesos for failing to bring his wife from Spain. Again, the money was returned to him once his wife arrived in Quito.[18] Ten years later, the king ordered that neither the judges nor the president of the Royal Audiencia grant licenses for men to remain in the Indies if they had left wives in Spain, and that such men should immediately be sent back to Spain.[19]

Although historians generally agree that this legislation remained a dead letter, the use of it to accuse men must have been frequent, because a special licensing process existed to grant men specified periods of time to be physically absent from their wives in other regions of the Spanish Empire. The accusations and the threat of punitive action were deemed troublesome enough that at least some men did apply for such licenses from the royal government. In 1573, for example, the Royal Audiencia of Quito granted limited licenses to Alonso de Prada and Benito González to remain in the district, ordering them to immediately bring their wives from Spain.[20] Wife abandonment and men's sexual conduct were not simply ignored but were considered state matters—so much so that men wrote directly to the king from Quito, denouncing others who had abandoned their wives and set up new households with other women.[21] Though these denunciations were doubtless motivated by rivalry, it is noteworthy that the accusers chose the particular issues of wife abandonment and adultery to target the men, showing that there was a general expectation that royal authorities would intervene in such situations when it was brought to their attention.

Wives' Criminal Charges Against Husbands

Wives in seventeenth-century Quito initiated criminal charges against their husbands for adultery, domestic violence, abandonment, and lack of financial support. In Quito, the royal courts could even take the preemptive move of ordering the arrest of husbands who physically threatened their wives. The royal court of the Audiencia took such a preventive measure to protect doña Ventura de Zárate from the physical aggression of her husband, don Juan de Encalada, in 1685.[22] After years of violent encounters with her husband, doña Ventura moved herself and her children to her mother's home. Though doña Ventura's husband traveled frequently outside of Quito on business, he continued to live in their house in Quito and constantly menaced both doña Ventura and her mother when he was in town. Both women probably felt great relief the morning that don Juan left Quito to conduct business in Lima. However, they learned the next day that he had secretly reentered Quito, dressed as a cleric to hide his identity, and that he was rounding up a group of men to attack the two women. Alarmed, the women sent word to the Royal Audiencia, asking for protection. The president of the Audiencia ordered captains don Nicolás de Arguello and don Nicolás de la Carrera to gather a group of men to arrest don Juan and his accomplices. In the ensuing armed conflict with the royal authorities, don Juan was killed, and the men who accompanied him were arrested. The death of don Juan was unintended, yet this situation demonstrates that, at least in some instances, political authorities acted to protect wives' safety by intervening in internal family matters at the women's requests.

Neighbors also responded to wives' complaints about their husbands. Many wives who accused their husbands of physically mistreating them also accused them of adultery and, indeed, tended to attribute their husbands' violent behavior to their relationships with other women. In doña Francisca de Barrionuevo's suit against her husband in 1680, officials themselves presumed the connection between domestic violence and adultery "Nicolás de Escobar, married to doña Francisca de Barrionuevo, has been publicly living in sin with Alfonsa Grado for more than six or seven years with great notoriety and scandal, for which reason he is abusing his wife, treating her badly in words and actions. And so that such excess should be rigorously punished, it is ordered that proceedings begin so that in respect to this official injunction witnesses will come forth and be examined."[23] Several Spanish and mestizo women neighbors came forth and testified that they had seen Nicolás with his lover and had also seen them both mistreat doña Francisca. All the witnesses, however, attributed Nicolás's escalating violence to doña Francisca's public complaints about his behavior. As one witness succinctly put it, "doña Francisca always publicly complained that her husband was in an illicit relationship with Alfonsa, and this was the reason he abused his wife in both words and deeds."[24]

Witnesses commonly made the connection between male violence and female public complaints, but not, as might be assumed, to imply that a wife should accept her husband's affairs and mistreatment and learn to be silent. The connection made by witnesses between escalating male violence and female persistence in publicizing their maltreatment suggests the general opinion that women's speech was powerful. Men knew that wife beating and adultery were not male prerogatives but could, in fact, be defined as illegal acts. Wives who revealed their husbands' illicit behavior exposed the men to possible public censure and punitive action at the hands of the government. A reputation as an abusive man could bring a man dishonor. Diego Nagales, for example, who was involved in a criminal suit against his brother, found his testimony discredited because he was "known by all to have beaten his wife."[25] It was generally assumed, then, that husbands had a lot at stake in keeping their unlawful behavior secret and would thus use violence to silence the victims, their wives. The chatter of women was not idle. In doña Francisca's criminal suit against her husband, he was ordered arrested and his property confiscated on the basis of the testimony of her women neighbors.[26]

Wives who did not publicly air their grievances with their husbands were at a disadvantage when they initiated criminal charges against their spouses because they could not rely on the validation of outside testimonies. Such seems to have been the situation of doña Juana Requejo, married to Captain Andrés de Sevilla, whose suit is unusual in that she relied only the testimonies of people in her own household and not outside witnesses.[27] Doña Juana claimed to have lived in physical danger for over twenty years because of her husband's violent temper. What seems to have provoked her into criminally charging her husband with multiple counts of physical violence and adultery was the forced entrance into her house by his steward, whom she had jailed and sued for assault and property damage. Even as a married woman, doña Juana was able to bring a criminal suit in her own name against the steward for physically endangering her and her household.[28]

Feeling empowered, or simply fed up, the following day she also sued her husband. Doña Juana claimed that she and her husband had never lived a conjugal life; instead, from the beginning of their marriage he had mistreated her, beating her and even repeatedly trying to stab and hang her. She also accused him of having long-term affairs, first with a married woman, then with two widows, and finally with her own married niece. In addition, he had stolen her property and had even given a dress of hers to his mistress. By doña Juana's account, her husband was a violent and dangerous man, and her charges are similar to, if more severe than, those in the other women's suits examined above, whose husbands were punished.

Doña Juana's husband, however, received only a reprimand from Audiencia authorities and was ordered to treat his wife better.[29] A main difference in her case is that, while the other wives repeatedly alerted the public about their husbands' conduct, doña Juana apparently made no mention of her husband's activities to anyone outside of her household. The only testimonies she compiled to corroborate her charges were from her own servants. Having kept silent for over twenty years, thus effectively isolating herself from her community, her case against her husband was substantially weakened. In the end, although the state condemned her husband's behavior, it did not intervene forcefully on her behalf.

Community knowledge about familial relations was an important part of the legal process, especially considering that wives presenting charges against their husbands were usually held to a lower burden of proof than claimants in other similar kinds of criminal cases. In other types of physical aggression, for example, the victim of an attack, or a representative, called for a notary to certify the location and gravity of the wounds, their number, and probable cause. With or without eyewitnesses, the notary's report was the official evidence that the person had indeed been the victim of an attack. In seventeenth-century Quito, wives did not present notarized descriptions of the injuries inflicted on them by their husbands; other evidence substantiated their accusations. A strong case would include witnesses from the wife's neighborhood, whose testimonies would appear more disinterested than those of people within her own household.

By considering the testimony of neighbors as sufficient evidence to punish husbands, the legal system encouraged wives to report their husbands' activities to the community. Community members held husbands accountable for their behavior by acting both as an informal source of pressure on the men to modify their conduct and as agents in the formal mechanisms for apprehending and prosecuting husbands who mistreated their wives through physical violence or adultery. The mestizo neighbor of doña Francisca, for example, felt justified in confronting her neighbor's husband when she testified that she had personally admonished him for mistreating his wife.[30]

Networks of acquaintances also intervened directly in apprehending wayward husbands. In 1697, for example, the indigenous Gerónima Chuquillanqui complained to her nephew that her husband had abandoned her and was living with another indigenous woman. She wanted to sue her husband and have him punished. Her nephew contacted the Indian in charge of the hacienda's indigenous workers, who in turn informed the hacienda's Spanish steward of Gerónima's complaint. The steward, together with Gerónima, went to the mistress's house, seized the couple, and turned them over to royal authorities, who ordered the lovers jailed.[31] Gerónima's initiation of the apprehension of her husband and the legal charges against him suggests that the Spanish legal system regulating gender norms incorporated indigenous peoples. Gerónima and her nephew clearly knew that her husband's adultery could be prosecuted in the Spanish criminal system, and at her request, Spanish officials jailed the offending husband and his mistress.

The government's zeal in prosecuting husbands could, however, have unintended consequences by exceeding the original intentions of the wives they had betrayed. Judgments against adulterous men could result in the destitution of their wives and the long or permanent separation of spouses. The objective of most wives was the correction and not the destruction of their husbands. For this reason, wives could find themselves in the position of pleading for leniency for the men against whom they had originally sought criminal charges. An example of such a situation is the criminal case pursued by doña Angela Hurtado de Mendoza in 1662 against her husband, Francisco Gómez de Acevedo, for adultery.[32]

Francisco was a functionary (*escribano receptor*) of the Royal Audiencia and apparently incorrigible in his affection for his mestizo mistress, Petrona de Escobar. Francisco and Petrona had already been picked up and jailed by city patrols three times for being found in bed together when, in March, they were arrested again because of a formal complaint filed by doña

Angela. At the time of the arrest, testimonies were taken from several neighbors, including Petrona's mother. All the witnesses gave details of the relationship and voiced their disapproval of it. Many said that they had tried to intervene, but that Francisco was a violent man and had threatened them and Petrona when she had tried to end the relationship.[33]

In April, Francisco was condemned to six years of exile in the army in Chile and the loss of his office. Exile to Chile was commonly understood to be a death sentence, as few men ever returned from the war the Spaniards were fighting against the Araucanian Indians. Doña Angela wrote to the court asking that the sentence be suspended because "there was no hope that he would ever return from the war," and that therefore her husband's parents, with whom she was then living, would have no reason to continue to care for her. She also argued that the removal of her husband from office would leave the family with no economic resources. She complained that, as she was the person who had denounced his adultery to authorities, it was unfair for them to issue a ruling so detrimental to her. Finally, she claimed that Francisco had mended his ways and was now living tranquilly with her. Francisco's parents wrote a letter on his behalf as well. Royal authorities did change their ruling, suspending the exile to Chile; instead, Francisco was exiled to the town of Ibarra, north of Quito, for four years, fined three hundred pesos, and still ordered to resign from his position with the Audiencia. Because Francisco was now destitute, his father paid the fine for him, and he was freed from jail.[34]

The following month, in May, Francisco was found naked in bed with Petrona by the senior judge of the Audiencia, who had accompanied the regular patrol because of information he received concerning Francisco's continuing affair. Both Francisco and Petrona were shackled during the arrest and were kept continually in chains during their imprisonment of several months. After two months of imprisonment, Francisco asked that his shackles be removed because his foot was being crippled, but this request was denied.[35] Doña Angela again pleaded for leniency for her husband but the royal court finalized the sale of his office.[36] In his fourth month in jail, Francisco claimed that he should be freed because of the general pardon given by the king in honor of the birth of his son. His request was denied because, as the royal court determined, such pardons were not for people who had repeatedly committed "scandalous crimes."[37] In the court's final judgment, Francisco was ordered to comply with the exile to Ibarra.

The experiences of doña Angela and Francisco reveal both the various mechanisms used to stop adulterous liaisons and the repercussions for the people involved. Francisco was first apprehended and jailed by authorities, after which his wife initiated criminal charges against him. The court's decision to exile him to the war in Chile and deprive him of his office, however, was life-threatening to Francisco and economically disastrous to his wife, so she was forced into the incongruous position of pleading for a suspension of the court's ruling in the criminal case that she had originally pursued against him.

The definition of adultery as not only a grave offense but also one committed against the government itself becomes even clearer during Francisco's final imprisonment of over five months. Not only did the government reaffirm its decision to exile him to Ibarra and divest him of his official government position by finalizing the sale of his office, it refused to free him through the general pardon granted by the king. General pardons applied to all those who had committed common crimes, such as debtors, thieves, and most murderers. But they excluded criminals who had committed particularly grave offenses such as treason, insurgency, counterfeiting, heresy, and premeditated murder.[38] The royal officials of Quito, then, considered Francisco's crime of adultery equivalent in gravity to those offenses that automatically merited punishment. Indeed, the magnitude of his crime warranted, for government officials, severe treatment in jail, where he was continually shackled at the risk of crippling him.

It seems clear that the government was not operating on promasculinist policies, but it is also evident that its firm stance against male adulterers was not motivated by a concern for women. Any basis for familial life that remained between doña Angela and Francisco was destroyed by government judgments eliminating Francisco's livelihood and separating the couple by exiling him first to Chile, then to Ibarra. Doña Angela was left alone, with no financial support and dependent on the charity of her in-laws. The issue for historians is not whether Spanish state and society privileged men or women, but rather to determine to what extent both women and men were used as extensions of social control through continually shifting positions of authority and subordination. Conflicts between men and women within the family, like conflicts in other institutions, were the point of entrance for social vigilance and control. In the struggle between keeping and revealing secrets, both husbands and wives could reinforce their positions of power in the family or, indeed, they could both be destroyed.

Seduction

Married women used the criminal justice system to force husbands to honor their vows to physically protect, financially support, and faithfully respect their wives. Marriage was a witnessed, legally binding act, and therefore it might be expected that either spouse could sue if the other broke the terms of their agreement. Unmarried women who voluntarily engaged in sexual relations with married men had legal recourse as well. In addition to facing charges by their wives, adulterous husbands could also face government prosecution on behalf of the unmarried women they seduced. In the two cases examined below, the authorities defended the honor of the women and severely punished the offenders, despite the fact that both women admitted that they had voluntarily engaged in sexual relations with the men because of the promise of financial compensation.

In 1692, doña Juana Martínez Cabeza de Vaca brought criminal charges against the married Matías Correa for seducing her illegitimate daughter (*hija natural*), Petrona Martínez Cabeza de Vaca.[39] Several witnesses testified that they had often seen Petrona and Matías together and had noticed that the two hid whenever any of Petrona's relatives happened by. Then Petrona disappeared. She claimed later that Matías had deflowered her and taken her to many different houses to prevent anyone from finding her. In her declaration she stated that she had engaged in sexual relations with Matías because he had promised to pay her two hundred pesos, of which he claimed he kept one hundred at the monastery of the Franciscans and the other hundred in the city of Riobamba. He also promised to buy her clothing and to support her financially. On the basis of this financial arrangement they had sexual intercourse, but then afterward, when she asked him for the money, he did not pay her.[40]

Royal authorities jailed Matías and confiscated his goods. In his declaration from jail, he claimed that Petrona had run away from home and, because he was the one who had found her and returned her to her mother's house, Petrona was fabricating lies against him out of spite. In his defense, he produced witnesses who testified that Petrona was known in the neighborhood for behaving loosely. Various people testified that Petrona frequently left her house at night by herself, wore low-cut dresses to fiestas, and accepted gifts of food and money from men. Her virginity was suspect. Now, it would seem that maligning the reputation of a woman of illegitimate birth who freely admitted to exchanging sex for money would have been an easy task, but this was not the case. And indeed, Matías's legal defense became even more difficult when two midwives examined Petrona and declared that she was four months pregnant. The government did not accept his defense and condemned him to two hundred lashes, ten years' service in a military post, and confiscation of all his property in favor of Petrona. Matías did not, however, wait around for his punishment to be carried out. He escaped the Quito jail, dressed as a woman, with the help of women accomplices who smuggled women's clothing in to him. What surprised witnesses who saw him after his escape before he fled the district was not that he had escaped the jail but that he had shaved his beard and mustache to do so. What was a Spanish man without hair on his face?

Witnesses on both sides of this suit testified that Petrona was a gregarious young woman. Indeed, though witnesses on her behalf believed she was a virgin before consenting to Matías's overtures, no one claimed that she had led a quiet and reserved life. She herself did not initially complain that she had been corrupted or left in dishonor by Matías, simply that he hadn't paid her. The one expected witness who never appears in the suit is Matías's wife, who could have provided some background on his character. She never testifies and, though some people claim to have known her, no one gives any information about her; even her name is not known. The only reason we know she existed is that Matías was described as a married man. But perhaps that is all we need to know; it seems at least that was all the state needed to know in order to prosecute and punish him with such vigor. The fact that he was married was a major element in the court's decision, one that weighed more heavily than even the fact that Petrona was left pregnant.

It might be claimed that married men were considered generally suspect and were thus easier to prosecute than single men. Indeed, at least one woman took advantage of this situation to falsely accuse a married man of seducing her and fathering her child. Francisca Ruiz de Padilla was able to concoct an elaborate story of adultery and incest against Maestro Flores, convincing the woman she lived with, neighbors, and government authorities.[41] Francisca was a young widow who, because she was orphaned, lived with her widowed sister-in-law, doña María de Salazar. Maestro Josef Flores was a former business partner of doña María's deceased husband and was a boarder in her house. Doña María stated that she had suspected something between Francisca and Maestro Josef Flores and therefore had interrogated Francisca, "who tearfully admitted that she had been guilty, because he had promised to favor her and used persuasions and she was a poor woman."[42]

The gravity of Maestro Josef Flores's offense was made to seem even greater when it was supposed that the first night he seduced Francisca was the night the volcano Pichincha erupted in Quito. One witness lamented that "while Christians were making confessions and carrying out acts of penitence because they thought it was the end of the world, Maestro Josef Flores had Francisca locked in his room and was committing adultery all night long."[43] He was also accused of committing incest for having sexual relations with Francisca's sister, Andrea, whom it was claimed he kidnapped and deflowered after she had left the convent only two days earlier. Maestro Flores was jailed, and things kept looking worse for him. Francisca gave birth to a baby she claimed was his, and his own wife showed up to denounce him publicly for hitting her three or four years earlier. Neighbors testified that they had seen him with both sisters. Nuns testified in favor of Francisca.

Maestro Josef Flores's guilt seemed certain, and after over a year in jail he was still awaiting sentencing. Then Francisca confessed. She explained that she had really been involved in a long-term relationship with a priest, and, wanting to hide the relationship after she became pregnant, she accused Maestro Flores of seduction. He had never touched her or her sister and, in fact, she had hardly even spoken with him. Citing her confession, the courts absolved Maestro Josef Flores.

The situation of Maestro Josef Flores suggests that the elements that traditionally are thought to have made men invulnerable to prosecution by women might have in some cases made them more susceptible. As a man who had graduated from his studies in arts and theology with a master's degree, Maestro Flores's social prestige should have made his declarations of innocence credible or his guilt possible to overlook. But, in fact, people were far more willing to give credence and defense to the young, penniless widow than to him. His status as a married man increased the gravity of his crimes and the likelihood of his prosecution. The eagerness of the community and government prosecutors to punish the unfortunate Maestro Flores suggests that what researchers often dismiss as "male prerogatives" were considered disruptive and abusive and were condemned by society and by law.

Conclusion

What kind of society made it possible for women to act independently, even when this caused conflict with the men around them? Because marital conflicts occurred within a cultural framework of decentralized authority, women's ability to protect their interests against men was not exceptional but was culturally necessary in a society that thrived on difference, competition, and even conflict. Like slicing through an onion, analyzing the mechanisms of power in Spanish society reveals layers of authority held together through tension instead of by a central core. There is a large body of evidence in the early Latin American field demonstrating that social stability was, in fact, guaranteed through decentralized power relations. The government itself was composed of multiple hierarchies with overlapping and competing jurisdictions. Authority was produced within a network that prevented any individual or group from consolidating a position of absolute control.

The general tendency of scholars on Spanish American women has been to embed their research within a different matrix of authority. For such researchers, patriarchal gender norms are the cultural reflection of a centralized, hierarchical political regime. Just as good political order required an absolute monarchy, social stability required that men occupy a political, social, and economic status superior to women. The tendency to multiply and diversify, rather than to unify and centralize, was a cultural characteristic of Spanish American colonial society, one that also defined the logic of family structure. Family members were joined in a union that created shared domains of interest while preserving the interests of individuals. The potential for husbands to consolidate positions of patriarchal authority was recognized by society. But rather than viewing semiautonomous, male-headed households as elements of social stability, the colonial government viewed patriarchy as disruptive to a social order that culturally and institutionally undermined all forms of centralized control. In order to check the possible formation of patriarchal authority within the family, wives were legally empowered to defend their interests against their husbands. Spanish courts upheld women's legal rights through a large body of gender legislation that applied to all racial groups.

The legal system recognized that a wife's interests could diverge substantially from her husband's, and therefore wives had legal recourse to defend themselves against their spouses. Far from being considered male prerogatives, domestic violence and adultery were defined as criminal offenses. Although the church also condemned such behavior, it lacked official mechanisms for censuring or punishing spouses for their misconduct. The only official action the church could take to resolve marital discord was to dissolve the union temporally or permanently. The church considered the separation of spouses, however, a threat to the sanctity of marriage in general and to the church's institutional legitimacy, as its control over marriage was based on a definition of marriage as a sacred and inviolable union of the souls of men and women. For women who suffered from their husbands' physical violence and adultery, the church was therefore not a practical recourse because such male conduct was rarely considered sufficient for dissolving the marriage.

Women had the option, however, to sue their husbands for domestic violence and adultery in the criminal justice system. There, women found almost immediate relief; husbands were often jailed for the course of the suit. If found guilty, men faced potentially severe punishments, including imprisonment, confiscation of their property, fines, loss of office, forced labor, and long exiles. The government took a special interest in adultery and even continued the prosecution of a man on these charges after his wife had pardoned him and desisted from pursuing the case. Severe judgments against husbands had an equally disruptive effect on the well-being of wives and children. In that light, and unlike many other types of crimes, officials considered adultery an offense against the government and they felt compelled to prosecute it.

The testimony of witnesses in suits initiated by wives against husbands demonstrates that physical abuse and adultery were not tolerated. In many cases, men and women intervened to stop a husband's violence against his wife and to publicly berate a husband for his illicit sexual relationships. The public reputations of men could, in fact, be diminished on the basis of their relationships with their wives. Neighbors and acquaintances volunteered incriminating information about husbands, denounced men to authorities, and even aided in finding and arresting offending husbands. Community censure of violent and unfaithful men was not, therefore, only an informal pressure exercised on men. Women who complained publicly about their husbands and aroused the interest of neighbors had a much better chance of winning their suits. Community involvement was thus also an element in the formal mechanisms used to prosecute men; on the basis of a wife's formal complaint and the corroborative testimony of a few neighbors, a husband could find himself in jail and his property confiscated. Not only did married men face legal charges by their wives, they could also face criminal complaints by women they seduced. In cases of seduction, single women, even those with questionable backgrounds and motivations, successfully won judgments against married men.

Government and society recognized the potential for married men to consolidate their power within their families and become patriarchs. But husbands were the object of community vigilance and the targets of criminal prosecution precisely to prevent them from forming enclaves subject to their personal authority. Women's juridical capacity in Spanish American society was not due to enlightened notions of women's rights, equality between the sexes, or even fairness. However, the shifting alliances and conflicts that quickened the Spanish concept of authority also created spaces where women, like members of other social groups, could exert their autonomy and protect their interests.

Chapter 4

Private and State Violence Against African Slaves in Lower Louisiana During the French Period, 1699–1769

Cécile Vidal

Until the middle 1980s, the subject of colonial Louisiana attracted the attention of very few American historians.[1] Since then, historians' interest in the French colony has grown. Most of this work deals with interethnic relations between European, African, and Amerindian communities, and with black slavery in particular.[2] The sheer size of the African community in the region justifies this strong interest. By 1731, when the slave trade to New Orleans had nearly ceased, black laborers made up the largest ethnic group in the French establishments and outnumbered whites four to one; by 1760, the ratio had shrunk to two to one. A large Afro-Creole community also developed. Of the approximately four thousand slaves who lived in Lower Louisiana in the 1740s, nearly two-thirds were Creole.[3] If American historians studying African slavery in the lower Mississippi valley agree about these major demographic characteristics, however, they disagree about the ethnic diversity among Africans, the importance of spreading slaves among settlers, and the relationship between the region's black and white residents.

These differing interpretations are grounded in discussions about the African community and on contradictory visions of European society. On one side, historians see that disorder and chaos in Louisiana reigned as the result of failed economic development, the long periods of war and rupture with the home country, and the presence of a sizable Amerindian community on which Europeans grew economically and strategically dependent. According to this interpretation, corrupt and tyrannical local authorities combined with numerous convicts and soldiers of low moral character to breed the deep social and cultural antagonisms among the European community. On the other side, historians have found that during the period of royal administration between 1731 and 1769 social and political order prevailed. In general, they argue that European society was relatively united thanks in large part to a broad distribution of slaves, the abundance of land, the early death of most of the convicts, a European culture dominated by Canadians, Catholic conformity, the necessity for Europeans to unite against other ethnic groups after the Natchez uprising in 1729, and the exclusive political control of royal authorities.[4]

My own work on the Illinois Country,[5] along with the judicial records of New Orleans, reveals a persistent violence among white inhabitants, who frequently insulted each other, fought, and committed more serious crimes that disrupted daily life. That violence, however, does not seem particularly unusual or exceptional when compared to customary levels of violence in the home country in the eighteenth century.[6] I trace that relationship by investigating how state sanctioned violence in the multiethnic and slave society of the colony differed from that of the home country. I do so by studying violence against black slaves in Lower Louisiana during the French period, 1699–1769.[7] I consider private violence—the violence exercised by masters against their slaves and the violence of white people toward slaves who did not belong to them—as well as institutional violence against black laborers. It goes without saying, perhaps, that slave societies were much more violent than societies made up of free people.[8] Slavery is based on violence, deprivation of freedom, constraint by force, and domination of one individual or group by another. But one can nevertheless explore the forms taken by that violence and the limits to it that the society and the state could have established.

During the French period, royal power never ceased trying to reinforce its absolutism. The preeminence of royal justice and the monopoly on violence that the state tried to impose and defend was a privileged means of firmly establishing that absolutism. In a society where order was constantly threatened by the violence occasioned by the social and economic system of slavery, the nature of state attempts to control the violence is of fundamental interest and raises several questions. What limits did the state impose on the violence masters used against their slaves and that which whites directed toward blacks? What forms did state violence and repression against slaves take? What was the relationship between private and state violence toward slaves? Did this violence between masters and slaves, whites and blacks, influence the intensity and the forms of violence between other ethnic groups, and did some "racialization" of violence between these groups occur? Finally, did either the state or private individuals modify their violent practices according to the social status and ethnic origins of their victims?

We can perhaps answer these questions by examining the various legal disputes in the region. The Superior Council of Louisiana, established temporarily in 1712 and permanently in 1716, functioned as high court of first instance and last appeal for civil and criminal cases for New Orleans and the region.[9] The composition of the council varied, but, after 1731, when the colony returned to royal supervision after having been administered by the Company of the Indies between 1718 and 1731, the council was composed of the governor, the *commissaire-ordonnateur*, the king's lieutenant, several councilors, a public prosecutor, and a clerk.[10] Both the governor and the *commissaire-ordonnateur* had the title of first councilor, but the role of the governor was mostly honorific and it was the *commissaire-ordonnateur* who served as the first judge and presided over the council. The other councilors were chosen from among the settlers. Contrary to the situation in France, these judicial offices were not venal and hereditary. Instead, the king commissioned councilors for an unspecified period of time. They received a salary and were more dependent on the central power than their colleagues in France.

Most of the 150 cases against slaves that took place between 1723 and 1769, for which records survive, were criminal procedures for *marronage* (desertion), theft, or both. Slaves were less frequently tried for assault or homicide.[11] All the civil or criminal procedures against whites for mistreatments or homicides of black slaves have been studied; so have cases concerning whites that reveal the interethnic relations in the colony. Because of a lack of diaries, correspondence, and slave accounts, these statements and interrogations are the only documents which provide the voice of the individuals, free or enslaved, of that time. Very often, the clerk transcribed the witness's or the defendant's very words, sometimes even using the incorrect vocabulary or syntax of the speaker. If the defendants were being questioned, the judges let them speak freely and at great length. As a result, these statements and interrogations often reveal a great deal about the concerns and small events of daily life at the same time they provide a way of understanding the daily realities of master/slave relations.

Extreme Violence Against Slaves

Slave narratives housed in the judicial archives clearly illustrate how masters violently imposed their will on their slaves. This violence was omnipresent. Planters or their white or black overseers punished their slaves if they came late to work, took too long for lunch, refused to work because of illness, worked badly, stayed out all night to see a mistress, went dancing, argued, or stole. Masters were also violent for no apparent reason. They beat slaves with a stick or whip, sometimes for several days, clapped them in irons, deprived them of food, and tied them outside for hours or days. The violence so terrified slaves that many tried to escape. When judges asked maroon slaves why they had run away, most of them answered that either they were mistreated or they were scared of being mistreated.[12]

Violence was also a tool of menace and terror. The threat of it allowed masters to obtain their objectives without having to inflict punishment. One example proves the point. In 1744, Jupiter (called Gamelle), a slave belonging to a former officer, Sr. Pradel, was sentenced to death for breaking and entering into numerous private houses in New Orleans. Several times, Jupiter explained to the judge, he stole because his master had sent him every day to sell milk, eggs, and vegetables in the town market; but Sr. Pradel gave him too many vegetables and forced him to sell them at too high a price for the market. As a result, Jupiter often failed to sell everything and was generally scolded and even whipped for failing at his task. To escape the beatings, he began stealing to raise the money his master expected, and he tossed the unsold vegetables into the river or gave them to the soldiers to hide the evidence. He also told the story of a young slave belonging to another planter who had brought back some unsold vegetables from the market and had been force-fed the leftover supplies. It is impossible to know if Jupiter was telling the truth, since under questioning it soon became clear that he was, in fact, able to lie to defend himself. At one point, for example, he falsely accused another slave of the robberies and only admitted having committed the crimes himself during the last interrogation. Thus it was the fear of being mistreated that led Jupiter to his death and coerced most slaves into obeying their owners.[13]

Not surprisingly, the forms of violence masters used against their slaves influenced notions of violence throughout European society in Lower Louisiana. In some whites' minds, the relationship of domination, superiority, and inferiority that existed in slavery was precisely expressed through such extreme violence and through the excessive mistreatment masters inflicted on slaves. Thus, when one white inhabitant inflicted excessive or unjustified violence on another, the victim often felt reduced to the lowest rung of society, to the status of a slave. Whites saw extreme violence as more than an attack on the physical integrity of an individual; it was also a strike against someone's honor and called into question the victim's status and ethnicity.

Such violence was unbearably humiliating. In 1726, for instance, the surgeon of the Paris-Duvernay and Associates concession lodged a complaint before the council about the mistreatment he received at the hands of Sr. Verteuil, manager of the concession. The surgeon complained that his employer "lost his temper with him threatening him and treating him more badly than a Negro, which he used to do with all the whites of the concession, because he felt he was the most absolute of all men."[14]

The same issue appears in a suit between two whites connected by friendship or family ties. Louis Faugere entered Herbert's house to do him a small service. Suddenly, Herbert forced Faugere onto the bed, took off Faugere's trousers, and spanked him. Then, Faugere was put in a barrel full of tar, in which an accomplice tried to plunge him to the shoulders, while Herbert forced him to drink alcohol. Herbert called in all his neighbors, inviting them to laugh at Faugere's expense. One of the bystanders told the judge that at one point Herbert "took the whip for Negroes to use it against Faugere, the Canadian called Abel said 'Stop this Mr. Herbert, one don't whip the French like the Negroes,' and he grabbed the whip and threw it in the attic." In fact, two men intervened at this time, although no one had moved before despite Faugere's calls for help. Herbert prevented anyone from interceding by insisting that he was the master in his house; but, at least in the eyes of two bystanders, the situation became intolerable and the violence excessive when Herbert wanted to punish Faugere by beating him with an instrument usually used against black slaves.[15]

Whites also refused to be punished by black slaves. Such an obsessive fear appears in another case that took place in Natchez. A gypsy, sentenced to hard labor in 1741 and sent to Natchez to be in the service of the commandant of the outpost, Chevalier Dorgon, had an argument with the white cook. They fought, and the cook made a complaint to the commandant. The officer was infuriated with this affair "because a slave do not have the right to hit a free man." He ordered some black slaves to tie up the gypsy, at which point the man stabbed himself with a knife. Since attempted suicide was regarded as a crime, the convict was prosecuted. To justify his actions, he said that he was completely drunk and that he grew "angry when he heard that Mr. Dorgon wanted to make him tie by a Negro, it is what despaired him, since he did not deserve to be mistreated by some Negroes."[16]

Such extreme violence humbled and segregated its victims from the rest of society thus perpetuating a virulent strain of racism in Louisiana.[17] Still, custom and public opinion put limits on what masters, and whites in general, could do to slaves. In 1730, Mr. D'Ausseville, a former councilor in the

Superior Council, sued his overseer, Charpentier, for being the worst kind of torturer. D'Ausseville reproached his employee for not giving slaves enough food, and for making them work too many hours every day, even on Saturdays and Sundays when slaves were traditionally allowed to cultivate their own gardens. The overseer was also particularly harsh with female slaves: he did not protect pregnant women, nor did he respect the custom of letting the women leave work two hours before nightfall so that they would have time to prepare food, and he sexually abused all the women. Finally, Charpentier allegedly caused a suicide, several deaths, and various injuries through neglect, beatings, and abortions.

Even if he sued his overseer in the civil courts to gain some financial compensation, and even if it was his interest to paint a darker picture of the situation to get the judges' approval, it is clear that Charpentier's behavior offended D'Ausseville. In a letter to his employee, he wrote, "I could not understand your method, in your ferocity you will only make them rebel or throw themselves in the river. How can you thus claim to make them be devoted to work and faithful?" In a later petition, he spoke of the "violent passion [of his overseer] for mistreating slaves." D'Ausseville thus condemned this violence for moral and practical reasons. Such methods only led the slaves to revolt, run away, or commit suicide, causing the master to lose his capital and work force.[18] In D'Ausseville's mind, slaves should have been handled with a combination of gentleness and force, in a paternalistic spirit, as Le Page du Pratz, a former planter, recommended in his *Histoire de la Louisiane*.[19] This method came partly from the Black Code and partly from customs collectively established and accepted by society as the proper way of dealing with slaves. It corresponded to the difficulty masters faced in obtaining slaves, their high price for those settlers of limited means in the 1720s, and the impossibility of replacing slaves after the interruption of trade in 1731.

By suing Charpentier in the civil courts, D'Ausseville followed the typical procedure used in all the affairs involving a planter and his white overseer.[20] To prosecute these torturers in the criminal courts would have constituted a dangerous precedent that might have eventually hurt other masters. Such realities should not suggest that the wider society approved of these overseers' behavior, but it is difficult to know just how this condemnation was expressed. It is possible that even when condemned by their peers, these torturers did not suffer a loss of social status, since even more significant than the social pressure to be less violent was the firm belief that one was always the master in one's own home.[21]

The Black Code and Permissible Violence

In addition to mounting social pressure to control extreme violence against slaves, the state also tried to limit the extent of this violence, relying in particular on the Black Code. The code, promulgated in Louisiana in 1724, was based on a modified version of the original text of 1685 drafted for use in the French West Indies.[22] The king ordered a new promulgation of the code in 1732.[23] Local authorities issued several edicts reminding subjects of the Black Code's provisions, and they augmented the laws to deal with new problems. But they always kept to the spirit of the original Black Code. The most complete and coherent ordinance was Governor Vaudreuil's code of 1751.[24] The Black Code and the subsequent edicts were not fully enforced, even though they were not completely ignored.[25]

First, articles 38 and 39 of the Black Code forbade masters from torturing their slaves, under fear of prosecution in the criminal courts. Rather, owners and overseers only had the right "when they think that the slaves deserve it to chain them up and to strike them with a stick or a whip." This disposition was aimed not so much at protecting slaves against their masters' abuses as it was directed at imposing the preeminence of royal justice.[26] But, since planters were the only ones who could appreciate the necessity of the punishment, these rules lent them power and authority. During the entire period, in fact, no criminal proceedings were launched against a slaveholder for such crimes following a complaint from a private person or the public prosecutor.

This is not to say that masters and overseers refrained from using violence to punish slaves or draw confessions from them; in fact, several cases record such practices.[27] The planter Dumont de Montigny, for instance, recalled in his memoirs that runaway slaves could be punished severely by their masters, even branded, with no intervention by the authorities.[28] In another exceptional case, a female slave was confiscated from her owner by the council and sold at an auction to benefit the charity hospital because her master had repeatedly mistreated her. Nevertheless, he was not prosecuted in the criminal courts.[29]

This example should not suggest that the authorities paid no attention to masters' mistreatment of their slaves. When interrogating runaways, judges usually tried to understand the slave's motivations and whether the flight had been caused by the planter's mistreatment. Because looking for runaway slaves was a financial burden for the Company of the Indies or the state, the judge had an interest in understanding and limiting the phenomenon. In March 1728, Governor Périer suggested that the company give the Amerindians a reward of 160 livres worth of goods for each captured runaway slave. In describing the financing of this measure, he wrote: "It would be unfair if all inhabitants paid what it cost to reward the savages for runaway slaves, [since] often [only] one inhabitant is responsible for a slave's flight because of the inhumane mistreatments he imposes on the slave, [rather], it is fair that he be the only one to pay what it costs to get the slave back, being so happy to have him returned. You would object that some slaves run away as the fancy takes them, it is true, but this is not a reason to make all the inhabitants bear what it will cost to get these slaves back."[30] However, during the trials for *marronage*, the judge never accepted mistreatment as a mitigating circumstance and never prosecuted the masters for it.[31] Moreover, no procedure started by a slave because he was not well fed, clothed, or supported, as Article 20 of the Black Code guaranteed him, is recorded in the archives.[32]

In fact, the only cases where royal justice was willing to sue a white person in civil courts for forcing a slave to flee was when the person in question was not the master but the plantation's director or overseer or someone who had rented the slave, since article 49 of the Black Code obliged such individuals to take care of their slaves "as a good father would do" and made them liable for the slaves if they did not die a natural death.[33] Most of all, the state tried to protect the owners' interests. This is why Sr. Péry, director of Mr. Coustillas's plantation, rushed to report the death of a runaway slave to the clerk's office. He testified that the slave had been punished by the overseer "with the number of slashes proportionate to the fault he had committed," had not been "whipped wrongly or unjustifiably," often ran away for no reason, and died of hunger and exposure during his last desertion.[34] However, another case suggests that even when the person being accused was not the owner but the overseer, royal justice did not easily condemn him for forcing slaves to run away.[35]

Royal justice also intervened in cases where whites had mistreated slaves who did not belong to them or over whom they had no legal authority. Eight cases involved whites in conflict with one another when one, often himself a slaveholder, mistreated or punished another man's slave for having done something prejudicial to him: one slave owner shot another master's slave for having stolen a pig; another mistreated a slave because he let his master's cattle graze on the other man's plantation; a third whipped a slave because she had slept with one of his own slaves.[36] These quarrels were always settled in the civil courts. While focused primarily on awarding material damages to the injured parties, these cases also involved broader questions about the limits of power and territory between white colonists. Indeed, to beat someone else's slave was to usurp the master's right to punish his own slave, to tread on his property without permission. In this process, the slave was completely dehumanized, viewed only as property.

In three other cases, conflicts among white inhabitants erupted when one insulted or physically mistreated another's slave. In one case, a slave gleaned corn which had been separated from its stalks by a storm. En route home, he passed Joseph Chaperon's plantation, which was located next to his own master's residence. Chaperon attacked the slave, saying that "in the past when you belonged to Sr. Chamilly you were an honest man because your master was honest, while now that you belong to Brosset you are as much of a rascal as he is." Then Chaperon beat the slave and broke his arm. Brosset told the judge that Chaperon had routinely taunted him and claimed some damages for his slave's broken arm. This case, like others, was settled in a civil court, and it focused as much on issues of the master's honor as on financial damages to the injured parties. The incident also reveals how mistreated slaves were thus used as instruments in rivalries between whites, making slaves catalysts for verbal and physical violence that would have been too dangerous to express directly between white people. The financial damages could thus repair the material loss (the working time of the hurt slave) but also indirectly allay the blow to a man's injured honor.[37]

Regardless of the kind of mistreatment inflicted, the circumstances of the incident, and who was responsible for the attack, almost no white person was ever prosecuted in a criminal court by royal justice for mistreating a slave, whether or not the slave belonged to him.[38] And yet one can find in the archives two exceptions to this rule, both involving criminal proceedings against soldiers accused of having killed one or several slaves. Each time, the serviceman was sentenced to be hung. These death sentences can be explained by the fact that the accused was a soldier and in one case because the man was suspected of being a violent recidivist whose victims belonged to the king or to the Ursuline nuns. In Louisiana society, troops made up the lowest social group among whites; as such, they were closer in social status to slaves. Soldiers, sailors, and slaves thus shared the same sociability in the inns and taverns of New Orleans. They also shared the sad privilege of suffering the hardships of a royal justice less merciful toward them.[39]

The Private Use of Public Justice

Willfully or unwillingly, masters turned to royal justice to punish slaves for committing particular crimes such as running away, stealing, employing physical violence, and murder. This collaboration was not systematic. For example, slave owners did not always fulfill their obligation to report their runaway slaves to royal authorities, although it is not possible to determine the frequency of their notifications. In the same way, they very rarely declared domestic thefts committed by their slaves.[40] In the cases when a white person's property was stolen, the parties sought an agreement outside the judicial system, and masters usually agreed to punish the slave and to pay back the value of the stolen goods.[41] Planters were reluctant to turn slaves over to judicial authorities because they were obliged to pay all jail as well as justice costs and the value of the stolen goods (unless they gave up the slaves in question and abandoned them to royal justice), and because their slaves lost value if mutilated. In cases where a slave was put to death, his or her value was assessed by two experts and the amount was given to the master. Often, however, this exchange could not make up for the loss, since the slave owner had generally been forced to part with an important laborer who could only be replaced with great difficulty, particularly after 1731 with the interruption of the slave trade to Louisiana.[42]

Planters sometimes took the initiative in resorting to royal justice. They appealed to the law when they were unable to punish their slaves themselves, such as when a slave ran away for an extended period, very frequently, or with other slaves.[43] Similarly, slave owners who usually took the law into their own hands at other times respected the Black Code in the most serious cases where slaves physically attacked their masters or when they murdered one another.[44] They resorted to royal justice because they needed to eliminate dangerous elements who could have threatened them or their other slaves or who might have served as a bad example to fellow slaves. They let the state punish such individuals publicly and solemnly in order to dissuade other slaves from doing the same thing. In this way, planters and authorities collaborated to prevent further disorder.

The archives reveal an exceptional case where a planter sent one of his slaves to jail in order to have him judged and punished, apparently because the master could not make the slave obey. However, he did not want to lose his property, so he succeeded in obtaining only a light punishment for his slave. In 1753, Mr. Dubreuil, one of the richest inhabitants of the colony, who concluded numerous agreements with the authorities for the construction of public buildings, sent a letter to the public prosecutor, Raguet, to inform him that he had sent his slave, Joseph, to jail.[45] Joseph was, according to the planter, a "rascal" who had repeatedly stolen chickens and other goods, had borrowed horses every night for his licentious outings, had insulted an officer's wife, and had threatened another slave with death because he refused to give him his canoe. At the end of the letter, Dubreuil wrote that "as it is not just to suffer his mischievous behavior anymore, would you please be so kind as to cut one of his hamstrings. That is the only thing that will stop him because he is so nimble that he runs like a deer and he is such a good swimmer that when he is pursued he throws himself in the water, emerging more than two miles away." In this case, then, the master himself decided on the appropriate sentence for royal justice to impose on his slave! Although legally Joseph should have faced death because of his relapse into crime, the council ordered that both hamstrings be cut and that Joseph be imprisoned for fifteen days. Furthermore, the judgment was only partially executed because the executioner was not familiar with this corporal punishment. As a result, in 1755, the prosecutor had to ask once again that Joseph's two hamstrings be cut, when Joseph was again arrested for a theft and mischievous behavior.[46]

This affair shows that in some cases planters could turn to local authorities but without resorting to legal procedure. As a matter of fact, before having been arrested and judged in 1753, Joseph had already been sent to jail by his master for a theft, had spent a few months in prison, had escaped, and had been forgiven by his owner, all without any legal proceedings.[47] Although Joseph's case may be illustrative, it was not unique. Several other slaves were whipped by the public executioner or sent to jail by their masters with the formal agreement of the authorities and without any proceedings.[48]

Regression and Torture in the 1760s

Colonial officials did more than simply act as a slaveholder's enforcers: they guaranteed order in the colony and protected people's property from thieves. Officials prosecuted thieves and runaways more than any other criminals because one of the most serious problems they confronted was endemic theft on plantations and in town.[49] Slaves, and especially runaway slaves, were invariably held responsible for these crimes wherever they were committed.[50] Indeed, state authorities systematically prosecuted and severely punished runaways because they suspected that they stole to survive while on the run. The great concern with theft can be explained by the fact that the economic development of the colony was always difficult and slow, and that most of the settlers were not very rich, did not own much, and needed their cattle and food stocks to survive. Preventing theft was thus a way of pre-serving the inhabitants' material security.[51] Interestingly, in the same period, a similar phenomenon was taking place in France, where judges prose-cuted more frequently and punished more severely crimes against property, even if the number of thefts had not risen in comparison with preceding centuries.[52]

In Lower Louisiana, the status of the victim, the number of times the slave had been accused of stealing before, whether the crime was commit-ted at night, the quality and quantity of goods taken, and the finding of a weapon on the thief all factored into the sentence imposed on the criminal. Runaways faced sterner punishment if they had tried to escape more than once, had stayed away for a long time, had convinced other slaves to desert too, or had taken up arms while running away. Only those slaves who had fled for a second time or for a particularly long duration were convicted; there was no case in the archives in which a slave was prosecuted for a first short flight. Penalties ordinarily ranged from whipping to severing one or two hamstrings or ears to jail time. Other criminals were beaten with a stick, branded with a fleur-de-lis on the right shoulder, or beaten and branded with a letter V on the shoulder or the right cheek.[53] In violation of the Black Code, no slave was ever sentenced to death simply for running away, even when it was for the third time, because the master would have lost his slave's services.[54] One slave convicted of both running away and theft was sen-tenced to death because of aggravating circumstances. Two others were sentenced to be hanged and two others to be broken alive on the wheel after having made amends (one had also his right hand cut off, while the other benefited from a *retentum* saying that he must be strangled before being struck by the executioner's axe).[55]

When they decided to prosecute certain crimes or specific slaves, judi-cial authorities in Louisiana generally respected the Black Code's provisions regarding penalties, but they also took it upon themselves to determine the application of the death penalty. When selecting penalties, judges rarely took into account the defense put forward by accused slaves. When they refused to admit their crimes, the magistrates sometimes, but very rarely, resorted to torture. Although torture was uncommon, it was not reserved for slaves. According to law, preparatory questioning, that is the torture imposed before the final sentence in order to elicit the accused person's confession, could only be used if the crime for which the accused was prosecuted was subject to the death penalty and if strong presumptions of guilt already weighed heavily on the accused. Preliminary questioning, in contrast, was applied before the execution of the sentence to obtain a confession of other crimes or the denunciation of accomplices. The torture could be ordinary, extraordinary, or both, corresponding with the level of punishment.[56]

The use of torture in the 1760s in Louisiana, however, indicates that authorities were willing to severely and violently repress potentially subversive black slaves. Still, few officials went that far. According to the judicial archives, judges resorted only five times to this practice. In two cases, preparatory questioning was applied, and each time only ordinary torture was inflicted. In three other cases, judges ordered the application of preliminary questioning, each time using both ordinary and extraordinary torture (the latter by means of ankle-boots). In one case of cattle theft, preparatory questioning was imposed on both a white butcher and his black slave.[57]

Four of these five cases took place in the same year, 1764. The settlers in Louisiana could not have been aware that 1764 was also the year of the publication of the *Traité des délits et des peines* by Cesare Bonesana, marquis de Beccaria, the Italian jurist, which was translated and published in France two years later and which elicited tremendous debate. However, Beccaria had not started the debate. The Enlightenment elite had long been interested in the issue of torture, and their focus had begun to influence judicial practices in the home country. In the seventeenth century, even when torture was ordered, it was lightly applied by magistrates, as demonstrated by the fact that most of the accused did not confess to a crime, unlike their fourteenth-century counterparts. From the mid-eighteenth century onward, torture was rarely ordered by *parlements*. When Louis XVI abolished preparatory questioning in 1780 and preliminary questioning in 1788, he only confirmed in law the end of a practice that already had fallen into disuse.[58] In fact, most of the documented sentences that imposed corporal punishment were dated in the 1760s. During this period, the public prosecutor was Nicolas Chauvin de La Frénière, a Creole and son of one of the richest planters in Louisiana. Having spent several years in France, where he studied law, he returned to Louisiana in January 1763 after the king commissioned him the public prosecutor in the Louisiana Superior Council. He became the first Creole public prosecutor in the colony. Several years later, in the fall of 1768, he led a rebellion against the new Spanish governor. While the eastern part of the colony had been ceded to Great Britain in the Treaty of Paris in 1763, the western part of Louisiana, including New Orleans, had been transferred to Spain by the Treaty of Fontainebleau in 1762, but Spanish authorities were slow to take possession of the colony.[59]

Once in office, the new public prosecutor initiated a campaign against slaves accused of running away and theft. In 1764, and again in 1765, the prosecutor instructed the clerk of the council to list all the "justiciary Negroes" from the preceding months (seventeen slaves in seventeen months, among whom three were sentenced to death).[60] Likewise, increased repression is clear from the number of slaves prosecuted and condemned in the 1760s in comparison with the number from the beginning of the French period (with a maximum in 1764). Justice was also hastier. Before the 1760s, judges often subjected suspects to two or three interrogations for the most serious crimes, as had been the custom in France. In the 1760s, however, judges usually recommended just one interrogation of the accused. Worse, the use of torture and agonizing corporal punishment increased in that decade.

Whereas French officials sentenced criminals to be mutilated less and less often during the eighteenth century, officials in Louisiana continued the practice of cutting off slaves' ears, severing their hamstrings, and—more rarely—amputating hands.[61] They hoped both to prevent repeat offenses, and to allow the immediate identification of a previous offender. They also intended these victims to serve as examples. Any slave encountering another slave whose ears had been clipped immediately saw what he risked if he committed a similar crime. In addition, the public nature of state-imposed punishments served a pedagogic purpose. In general, punishments were carried out in the area where crimes had been committed. Whippings were inflicted in every town square of the city; making amends took place before the church doors; and mutilations and death penalties were executed in the main square of New Orleans. After executions, bodies were exposed for twenty-four hours and then buried or left on the bayou road. In some cases, the wives of executed slaves, accused of complicity, were sentenced to attend the execution of their husbands. Overall, the public execution of corporal punishments and death sentences by the most horrible methods, such as breaking on the wheel, despite the addition of *rententum* twice, were intended to be dissuasive. Even if such harsh measures only lasted for a few years, one can speak of the *temps des supplices* (time of severe corporal punishments) just as during the sixteenth and seventeenth centuries in France, when royal justice was particularly severe and merciless as the king sought to assert his absolute power.[62]

In Louisiana, this period was the first time that the Superior Council tried to limit black slaves' criminal behavior by systematically applying the Black Code. Because the system had relaxed over several decades, officials passed a local ordinance in 1751 to strengthen their control over slaves. In this edict, Governor Vaudreuil warned that if the slaves were not correctly punished by their masters when necessary, royal justice would do so with exemplary severity.[63] Judges, however, did not apparently comply with the stricter law: only thirteen cases dealing with slaves exist in the archives for the 1750s, and many lack a sentence. Thus, although the king's representative wanted to impose stricter laws on slaves, it seems clear that councilors did not exercise repressive power with particular severity, perhaps because they did not have the means to do so or perhaps because that kind of repression did not suit planters' interests.

Several reasons drove authorities to pursue a wave of repression during the 1760s. In 1763, in the lower Mississippi valley, black slaves were still more numerous than white residents. Outside the colony, massive slave revolts rocked Saint Domingue in 1751 and ravaged Guyana. La Frénière had certainly heard of these revolts on his way back to New Orleans from Cap français. By 1764, rumors were also spreading that the king had abandoned Louisiana. For all these reasons, the settlers felt particularly vulnerable. Inside the colony at much the same time, many plantation owners had sold their properties, leading to the dispersal of slaves and forcing new planters to impose their authority on their recently acquired laborers. These new slave owners imposed their authority more violently than did longtime slaveholders. Finally, La Frénière tried to advance himself politically and socially with a more repressive campaign, which was especially popular among new planters.[64] But not all went as La Frénière planned. After the failure of the revolt led by the Creole public prosecutor against Spanish authorities, a new era began in Louisiana when a new judicial system replaced the Superior Court (even though there was significant continuity in the laws' spirit and practice with regard to slaves between the French and Spanish periods), the renewal of slave importation to the colony, and the development of an important community of free blacks.[65]

Conclusion

As in every slave society, master-slave relations in Louisiana were shaped by constant, omnipresent, and permanent violence. Although most whites agreed that the master exercised absolute power to constrain and punish his slave with the greatest severity, all did not agree on the way violence should be used to control slaves. Indeed, the fate of individual slaves varied tremendously according to whom they belonged. Some slave owners were pitiless torturers who displayed extreme cruelty. Most slave owners, however, condemned excessive violence for both moral and practical reasons and because it contradicted the goal of an exploitative system based on the maintenance of cheap labor. Progressively, by consensus, officials and masters established collective customs that determined how slaves should be treated. Sharing a paternalist perspective, most slaveholders concurred that they should use a combination of kindness and force toward slaves.

In their daily dealings with slaves, planters only partially took the Black Code into account. However, if most of them did not apply all the provisions of the code, they respected its paternalistic spirit. According to the king's injunctions, masters had to behave as "good fathers," which did not exclude the use of extreme violence. This model drew from the monarchist conception of authority.[66] As the king was his subjects' father and exercised (or tried to exercise) absolute power over them, masters were their slaves' fathers and maintained absolute power over them. This paternalistic power could be defined either by its moderation, its capacity for forgiveness and clemency, or, on the contrary, by its severity, its capacity for punishment and harshness. Under the Old Regime, royal justice was precisely characterized by this duality: a great leniency toward most of the accused, illustrated by royal reprieves, on the one hand, and an unmerciful severity toward individuals considered unredeemable, on the other. Whether severe or forgiving, these policies shared the same goal, the submission of the subjects to the monarch's authority.[67] A similar situation existed between masters and slaves. Allowing women to leave work two hours before nightfall so that they could pound corn for the families to eat or whipping a slave who refused to work had the same goal: to make the slaves accept their position and to take advantage of their labor as much as possible.

The king, source of all authority, delegated some of his power to planters, as is demonstrated in the Black Code. As such, local authorities usually let masters punish their own slaves. This had two apparently contradictory consequences. On the one hand, it allowed slaveholders to inflict more severe punishments. Royal authorities rarely intervened to protect slaves against their masters' abuse, meaning judges contradicted the spirit of the Black Code. Leaving humanitarian concerns aside, the code's dispositions forbidding excessive mistreatment were aimed at maintaining order in the colony by preventing revolts, theft and flight and could have been used to assuage the slaves' fears of being mistreated.[68] However, colonial officials did not possess the financial resources, the police, or the judicial means to apply the Black Code. Furthermore, they could ill afford to alienate the white inhabitants of a faraway colony that played such an important strategic role in the Anglo-French rivalry in America.

On the other hand, this delegation of authority allowed slave owners a means of escaping the most severe measures of the Black Code, which called for the death penalty for slaves who carried arms illegally or for their mutilation in the case of flight—since owners sought first and foremost to preserve their capital and work force. In fact, in the same way that they relied on the Black Code when it suited them, masters turned to authorities to punish their slaves when they needed help, thus using either a judicial or or unofficial process. When royal justice punished slaves, it also took the masters' interests into consideration. This collaboration between authorities and planters served both parties' interests since both benefited from exploiting slaves. Individually, all council members were slaveholders and hence earned profits from slave labor. Generally, both royal power and the home country elite benefited from the growing colonial economy.[69]

Officials intervened in slave owner's prerogatives only to protect the state's peculiar interests and missions. Royal justice reserved the right to punish the most important crimes, acts of violence against free persons and murders committed by slaves against white or black people, thus asserting the preeminence of royal authority over local inhabitants. Royal power also fulfilled its role of arbitrator and guarantor of order by intervening in cases involving disputes between white people about slaves, especially in cases of flight and theft, or in cases of abuse of a slave by a white who did not own him. The only time when authorities threatened not to let slave owners punish their own slaves anymore followed a scandal in 1751 about alcohol sale to inhabitants and slaves that implicated the general lieutenant of the king in Louisiana. If Governor Vaudreuil reacted so vigorously in promulgating his new ordinance he did so not as a planter but as the king's representative in the colony. Individually, he might have defended his interest as a slaveholder, but in this instance his career in the monarch's service was more important in shaping his decision. As governor, he had to privilege the state's interests, which generally but not always coincided with the planters' interests. As such, he tried to restore order in the colony by relying on the spirit of the Black Code. Nevertheless, his regulation was not followed by increased punishment of slaves' crimes by royal justice, because the authorities did not have the means to do so and because slave owners—like royal power more generally—were driven by two contradictory tendencies: on the one hand, they sought to chastise slaves severely as a means of making them obey and work and of maintaining order; on the other hand they adopted a moderate approach hoping to preserve the work force their slaves represented.

Paradoxically, it was only in the 1760s, when royal power had been weakened in Louisiana, when the king of France had lost the Seven Years' war and decided to abandon the colony to two rival monarchies in America, that royal justice was the most severe and exemplary. To explain this apparent paradox, one must remember that this repressive wave was the work of the first Creole public prosecutor. La Frénière used his role as royal attorney to defend his own political agenda and to promote the Creole elite's interests. Even if the revolt of 1768 directed against Ulloa, as representative of the Spanish monarchy, was mainly motivated by the planters' and traders' anger over measures that were intended to limit Louisiana's trade for the benefit of mercantilism in the home country, and thus did not concern the question of slavery, La Frénière's arguments against arbitrary government and for the necessary "consent of the governed" and "the right of the people to decide any act touching their welfare," as well as his presentation of the council as "depositories of the laws under whose sanction the people may live in happiness," demonstrate that the Creole elite had reached a new level of political consciousness and wished increasingly to govern the colony themselves.[70] In the years before 1768, such ideas were gaining ground, and thus the repression of the slaves in the early 1760s was more likely a result of Creole initiatives than of the state seeking to control slaves more aggressively.[71] This repressive campaign attested both to the hardening of master-slave relations and to the increasing violence towards slaves and was the first sign of the transformation of the relations between the monarchy and the planters.

While slaves experienced a particularly severe campaign of repression in the 1760s, the forms and methods of private and state violence they endured throughout the French period worked to distinguish them from the rest of society, to give them an inferior status within the social and ethnic hierarchy that was developing in the colony, and thus to progressively "racialize" Afro-European relations. The state, in particular, played a great part in propagating the notion that violence against slaves should be the norm between whites and blacks, since it hardly ever prosecuted and imposed corporal penalties on white settlers for the abuse of slaves, instead demanding only material damages from the culprit, which reduced slaves to the status of property. The state's position toward violence in Louisiana was,

thus, in opposition to the rising criminalization of violence by royal authorities in France under the Old Regime.[72] While at first glance the kinds of
penalties that royal justice imposed on slaves were not all that different
from those inflicted on white criminals (for example, torture was applied
equally to white and black individuals), the authorities were far more likely
to enforce corporal penalties against slaves. Indeed, such punishments had
been disappearing in France during the same period, and in Louisiana even
soldiers did not have their ears cut off or their bodies broken alive on the
wheel and abandoned on the road. Thus, even if Afro-European relations
were not characterized by the virulent racism that one associates with the
nineteenth century, private and state violence against slaves in the eighteenth century was instrumental in the birth of a certain form of racism in
that society as well.

Chapter 5
Violence or Sex?
Constructions of Rape and Race
in Early America

Sharon Block

Is rape an act of sex or an act of violence? In the past thirty years, we have been schooled to view rape as a violent, not a sexual, crime. A quick search of rape-related Web sites in 2001 came back with a police site that proclaims, "RAPE is an act of violence." An online teen-support center based in Florida boldly summarizes that "Although rape involves the sexual organs of two or more people, it is never about sex. Rape is an act of violence." Colleges and universities have promoted similar understandings of rape as a violent act. The University of California, Irvine's, safety tips, for example, recently included the statement: "Rape is a violent crime—a hostile attack—an attempt to hurt and humiliate. It is not the result of 'uncontrolled passions.'"[1]

Such formulations of rape have grown out of decades of feminist activism. In 1971, Susan Brownmiller's foundational book, *Against Our Will*, treated rapes as part of women's historical oppression, rather than as unconnected acts of sexual overexuberance. Catherine MacKinnon further blurred the lines between heterosexual sex and rape, seeing both as constitutive of gender inequality. Since then, other feminist scholars and activists have emphasized the ways that rape is a purposeful assault on an individual, not a sexual misunderstanding or a means of damaging another man's property.[2]

By and large, these new understandings have been part of a hard-fought movement to value and protect women's sexual choices, and to recognize the tremendous harm done by sexual assaults. Yet such reformulations have been neither comprehensively adopted nor without their own pitfalls. First, the exact classification of rape as an act of sex or violence has continued to vex scholars. Historians of crime have compiled statistics on criminal prosecutions that as often include rape under the category of "assault" as under "sex crimes" or "morals offenses."[3] A second unintended consequence arises from the feminist movement's classification of rape as a violent act: when we subsume rape under the category of violence, sexual assaults then seem to require visible marks of that violence. As Stephen Schulhofer writes, we cannot escape a "seemingly unshakeable association of rape with physically violent misconduct."[4] Indeed, we do not even have nonjudgmental language with which to address the subject: calling an incident a sexual *attack* or sexual *assault* implicitly emphasizes the violent nature of the incident, and risks implicitly negating those acts that use nonphysical means of coercion.

The ambiguity over whether rape is about sex or violence is also at the heart of how early Americans defined sexual assaults. While we might assume that rape has historically been understood as a sexual act (hence the need for twentieth-century feminist activism), early American discourses actually employed both categorizations of rape. In statutory and common law, sexual attacks might be grouped with either sexual or violent crimes. Prosecutions of lesser sexual attacks (what we might call sexual battery) could fall under charges of assault or sexual immorality. Various individuals had similarly divided viewpoints. Women's courtroom descriptions of rape suggest that they saw physical violence as a necessary part of a rape, and juries generally required evidence of physical injury for legal proof of irresistible force. Yet other commentaries on rape suggest that many early Americans believed that rape grew out of sexual, not violent impulses: religious figures tended to categorize rape as a sexual sin, and many other early Americans expressed a belief that that the cause of rape was a man's unrestrained sexual desires.

Taken together, these views amply illustrate the ways that early Americans could view rape as either sexual or violent. However, these conflicting abstract categorizations of rape shifted to a more clear division when faced with individual incidents: those who had social power and authority were most likely to be seen as sexual *or* violent offenders, while those without significant social status were seen as sexually violent attackers. In the increasingly racially polarized British American colonies, this meant that black men's sexual attacks were most easily labeled as rape, while white men's sexual attacks were more likely to be identified as sexual immorality or simple physical assault. This racialized view of rape was most extreme in cases of interracial sexual assaults: sexual assaults on black women by white men— if condemned at all—were overwhelmingly defined as unremarkable sexual mischief, while black men's sexual assaults on white women were immediately identified as violent assaults requiring criminal prosecution. Together, these situational classifications of rape underscore the racialization of authority and sanction in the definition of early American sexual violence. Rather than existing as an abstract standard, violence and the authority to address that violence were understood by early Americans in terms of their New World social and racial dynamics.

I have been able to reconstruct these multiple cultural views of rape from a wide array of sources gathered for my larger study of sexual coercion in eighteenth- and early nineteenth-century British America. My sources include manuscript court records and published criminal narratives, all known colonial publications that mention rape, as well as an array of other extralegal print and manuscript commentaries.[5] With these sources, I have reconstructed more than nine hundred incidents of sexual coercion, and hundreds of commentaries on sex and rape more generally. Despite scholars' productive efforts to define colonial America by its regional cultures, my study reveals an American view of rape that depended on largely shared beliefs about race, sexuality, and the enforcement of authority.

Categorizing Rape: Religion and Law

British and American dictionaries defined rape as a necessarily violent act. Samuel Johnson called rape the "violent defloration of chastity," and other dictionaries followed suit.[6] Legal definitions of rape similarly stressed violence. Although they did not always mention violence specifically, they generally implied the use of physical coercion by defining rape as carnal knowledge of a woman by force and against her will.[7] Even without an explicit mention of rape as violence, however, well-known transatlantic commentaries categorized rape with other physically violent acts. *Blackstone's Commentaries* listed rape as an offense against persons, alongside murder and other physical assaults.[8] In the Revolutionary era, a printed series on English law discussed rape in lecture nine, "Violence to the Person Not Destructive of life."[9]

Yet other British legal commentaries recognized that rape began as a sexual act. One 1776 commentary on criminal law suggested that rape grew out of sexual desire, "a prepensity natural to man."[10] Accordingly, some colonial legal commentaries classified rape alongside other sexual acts. In his 1723 charge to grand juries, James Logan grouped crimes into categories: against subjects, against people, against society, and "from Uncleanness." Rape was in this final category, alongside adultery, bigamy, fornication, incest, sodomy, and bestiality.[11] American statutes on the general punishment of rape also sometimes listed rape alongside other sexual crimes. In 1636, Plymouth's list of capital crimes grouped rape together with sodomy or buggery, neither of which required violence or force in their commission.[12] Likewise, New Hampshire's 1718 "Act against Murder etc." listed the punishment for rape after the punishments for buggery.[13] Nearly a century later, an 1806 review of the laws of the Commonwealth of Kentucky mentioned buggery repeatedly in the discussion of rape, and sample indictments for the sex-related crimes of "Rape, Sodomy, Forcible Abduction and Adultery" were grouped together, despite their presumably different levels of force and violence.[14] Finally, the longstanding legal holding that a husband could not rape his wife underscored the legal view of rape as an outgrowth of sex: once a woman gave her consent to conjugal relations by saying "I do" at marriage, then rape by a husband became a legal impossibility within the marital bonds.[15]

While legal documents might group rape under multiple headings, religious writers uniformly saw rape as a sexual misdeed. In 1699, Cotton Mather explained that a white man who had been executed for rape had failed to properly control his sexual desires. The man had fornicated with women throughout his life and had fathered nineteen or twenty children.[16] In Mather's reckoning, the man was a menace because he could not control his sexual urges, not because he was physically violent. With the development of the criminal narrative genre in eighteenth-century New England, ministers set rape alongside other sexual immoralities in published execution sermons for both black and white rapists. In Aaron Hutchinson's sermon on the execution of a black rapist in 1768, he repeatedly told listeners that the prisoner's lifelong "uncleanneness" had led him to this unhappy end.[17] In a 1772 sermon about a white convicted rapist, the Reverend James Diman warned listeners about an array of sins, including keeping company with "lewd" and "whorish" women, and about "intemperate drinking" that would lead to the inflammation of "men's lusts and passions."[18] Nowhere did Diman mention assaults or physical violence in his extensive list of dangerous sins. Instead, such ministers lined up rape alongside other immoralities on a continuum of sexual misbehavior. As the Reverend Timothy Langdon explicitly stated of a condemned black rapist in 1798, "His crimes are ruinous to society, whether he be an adulterer, a fornicator, or one who commits a rape."[19]

Like adultery or fornication, for New England ministers rape was another version of sexual misconduct. Their concern with rapists' sins and moral misdeeds made rape useful as an example of sexual immorality, rather than as a random act of violence. Even when the condemned rapists to which the ministers referred were of African descent, not one of these pastors referred to the violence twenty-first-century readers would consider inherent in a sexual assault. But, as we shall see, the religiously oriented New England criminal narrative genre would be the exception, not the rule, to the view of black men's rapes as sexually sinful rather than violent.

For example, most nonreligious comments—even in New England—focused on white rapists' sexual immorality but black rapists' violence. A printer who published a poem about an executed white rapist in 1772 wrote, "Your wicked Life, how lustful, how obscene! . . . To whore and drink has been your mighty Aim."[20] A witness for the defense in a 1783 Pennsylvania rape trial testified that the accused white man was of decent character and "not addicted to Women," and in another rape trial that same year, a defense witness likewise testified that the white accused "has not the Character of being a Lover of women."[21] Again, none of these statements mentioned rape as an act of violence. If the white rapists had been accused or convicted of adultery or fornication, the same comments would have been appropriate.[22]

In contrast, comments on black rapists more often focused on the violence of their behavior. In 1743, the husband of one New England rape victim spoke of the "Barbarous & Cruel Violence of an Inhuman Negro Slave."[23] The published life story of Joseph Mountain, an infamous "Negro highwayman" charged with raping a woman in Connecticut in 1790, labeled his actions as "most brutal and savage" and a "barbarity."[24] The judge in an 1817 trial of a Connecticut African American man reminded the grand jury that blacks came from a savage nation, and he ultimately condemned the rape as an act of "violence and outrage."[25] Ministers may have seen condemnation of sin as their ultimate goal, regardless of the identity of the sinner (indeed, most execution sermons spent little time discussing the individual rapist or the rape), but other early Americans saw white-on-white and black-on-white sexual assaults as profoundly different kinds of acts.

The classification of acts of possible sexual coercion for criminal prosecution also reveals the clear emphasis on racial understandings of sexual violence. This is especially obvious in instances of sexual violence that would not ultimately be categorized as rape. Rape was a capital crime in the colonial period, but such severe punishment applied only to consummated acts of intercourse. Legal manuals all agreed that, as Lord Hale wrote, "to make a rape there must be an actual penetration."[26] Because most colonies had no general statutes regarding prosecution and punishment for attempted rape, lower courts had significant leeway in deciding how to charge a man who had tried to force himself on a woman or girl. In practice, this flexibility meant that sexual assaults would often be categorized along racial lines.

White-on-white sexual assaults were repeatedly prosecuted as lesser crimes of sex or of violence, rather than as acts of sexual violence. Various courts sometimes charged white men only with assault (rather than attempted rape or assault with an intent to rape), despite the obviously sexual nature of the attack. In 1734, a Pennsylvania court brought an assault charge against a man who, as the twelve-year-old victim explained, "did with his yard Endevore to Enter her Body 2 or 3 times."[27] A New York court charged four white men with assault in 1754, yet the lawyers' opening statement clearly identified the crime as an attempted rape.[28] In 1777, a Pennsylvania court charged James McConnaughy with committing an assault, but the local newspaper identified the crime as a rape when the fair-skinned man escaped from jail.[29] And in 1793, a New Hampshire court charged Elisha Thomas with assault for grabbing a woman by the throat, throwing her on the ground, and punching her in the face while he tried to force her into sexual relations.[30]

Some courts also charged white men only with sexual misbehavior for acts that seemed to involve forced or violent sex. In 1728, a Connecticut court convicted a white man of fornication because he had forced a woman into sexual relations with "his Greater strength, and so not being by her consent."[31] Similarly, in 1738, a Pennsylvania court docket charged John West with committing fornication with Isabella Gibson, although the indictment and a witness's statement charged John with attempted rape.[32] The court may have been trying to avoid a risk of capital punishment with this odd combination of charges: it seems counterintuitive to accuse a man both of fornication (unmarried sexual intercourse) and an *attempted* rape (unconsummated sexual intercourse). Or, perhaps the court clerk saw the attack as sexual in nature and so labeled it in the court docket as fornication. Regardless, when white men were the accused, courts might interpret possible sexual force as sexual immorality or assault, rather than as the sexual violence of rape or attempted rape.

Other times, courts used adultery charges to prosecute incidents of white-on-white possible sexual force. Some courts might have found that adultery charges could be more easily proven than rape charges, which required proof of irresistible physical force. A Pennsylvania court charged David Robb, a married man, with committing adultery with his servant, Rebecca McCarter, when she became pregnant in 1787. Rebecca testified that she had often struggled with David, who repeatedly tried to have sexual relations with her when they were alone. Rebecca told the court that on multiple occasions, he "left me so that I could scarcely lift my Arm to my Head—He struggled with me . . . He threw me on the Bed."[33] Even by colonial standards, this might have been seen as forced sex—examiners repeatedly questioned whether Rebecca had consented to the sexual relations. But they did not appear to pursue a rape charge, perhaps because Rebecca's pregnancy made adultery easier to prove than the force required of rape.

Other courts mixed the theoretical consensuality of adultery into charges of forced sex against white defendants. In 1742, a Connecticut court charged Isaac Willow with endeavoring "to tempt" Margaret Pearls "to Adultery all which was done with force and violence against ye Consent" of her.[34] Individual women also adopted the language of adultery to describe incidents of forced sex. In 1737, Catherine Parry told a Pennsylvania court that Robert Mills had "Importune this deponant (attempting to force her) to Commit Adultrey with him," even though a court clerk classified the incident as "rape."[35] The use of phrases such as forced adultery or ideas such as using violence to "tempt a woman" into sexual relations suggest that early American conceptions of consent and coercion were quite different from our view of their opposition, especially when both accused and victim were white members of the community.[36]

Some of this blurring between adultery and rape developed out of Anglo-American legal traditions. Both adultery and rape had been capital crimes in the early colonial period.[37] Further, the legal language of adultery stated that a man had had sexual relations with another man's wife "with force and arms," which was also the standard phrase in any assault indictment.[38] In adultery, however, this formulaic phrase often referred not to physical force but to the removal of a wife from another man's household. This language of force in adultery prosecutions makes it nearly impossible to tell from cryptic legal records if the "force and arms" of adultery was legalistic jargon or physical coercion. But this formulation was not just abstract legal tradition. Part of the harm of both rape and adultery derived from the sexual taking of a woman without her patriarch's permission. The courts' concern was over what husbands had lost, not over a wife's consent or coercion. For instance, though increasingly unprosecuted in colonial America, the crime of marrying an heiress without her father's permission was closely allied with rape, even if the bride had consented to the marriage.[39] In this form of ravishing, the crime was committed against the patriarch, and the woman's consent was irrelevant, just as the crime of adultery "with force and arms" referred to force against the husband's marital rights, regardless of the wife's consent.[40] In either case, actual physical violence to the woman was unnecessary, and hardly the point. By mixing the language of adultery into cases of forced sexual violence, early Americans recognized the transgressive sexual nature of rape but risked minimizing the very real violence that accompanied such sexual assaults when white men were involved. Because early America's race-based slave labor system denied marital rights to slaves, most blacks had little legal protection for their marital relations.[41]

Like adultery charges, prosecutions of white men for incestuous sexual relations with their white daughters often negated the violence that may have been involved in child molestation and instead emphasized fathers' sexual crimes. In 1705, a Massachusetts court charged a father with disorderly carriage for "entertaining his daughter frequently in his bed."[42] A Connecticut court prosecuted James Benton Jr. for lascivious behavior with his daughter in 1769.[43] In 1777, a wife accused her husband of "utmost lewdness" with their four-year-old daughter during divorce proceedings.[44] This is not to say that all father-daughter sexual interactions were prosecuted as sexual crimes: occasionally, father-daughter sexual interactions were charged as rapes, such as the infamous Ephraim Wheeler rape case in 1805.[45] Yet, even in that case, Ephraim's lawyers emphasized the sexual, not the violent, nature of Ephraim's incest with his daughter. They asked the jury, "Why did she go [into the woods with him, where she was raped], without being dragged by violence? . . . Would you not strongly suspect that these transactions were not much against her will?"[46] In part, because fathers could use a variety of sanctioned means of coercion—including some degree of physical correction—toward their daughters, father-daughter rapes were more likely to be viewed as the sexual crime of incest than as the sexual violence of rape.

Such sexually based charges may have seemed particularly applicable to incestuous rapes for several reasons. First, incest itself, however heinous, was defined as a crime of relationships, not of violence. Unlike modern conceptions, the offense of incest was the violation of familial order, not child molestation as we understand it. Second, early Americans may have believed that fathers would not have to use physical violence to have sexual relations with a daughter, making assault charges less appropriate. Third, a father's physical violence was sometimes acceptable within a family unit, and thus not the court's job to adjudicate. For all of these reasons, incest provided another legal category that charged white men's sexual assaults as sexual crimes, rather than crimes of sexual violence.

Because children of slave mothers could not claim their lineage through the father, a father could not legally be prevented from having sex with his enslaved daughter on the basis of this biological relationship. As one ex-slave recounted, "My grandmother was her master's daughter; and my mother was her master's daughter; and I was my master's son."[47] An early abolitionist complained that the "innocent offspring of the master" would become "the slave of her unnatural brother" and therefore be "forced to submit to his horrid and incestuous passion."[48] Generations of incest would go unrecognized and unprohibited for enslaved women, further emphasizing the association of sexual (rather than sexually violent) crimes with white defendants and victims only.

Indeed, when we examine the legal classification of black men's sexual assaults, the picture looks startlingly different from the image of white men's sexual misdeeds. Black men (many of whom were enslaved and thus subject to slave court trials with far fewer procedural safeguards) were generally charged with far more serious crimes than whites for sexual assaults on white women.[49] While only 48 percent of white men's prosecutions for sexual assault included rape charges, rape charges accounted for 69 percent of black men's prosecutions.[50] On rare occasions, black men might be charged with a crime less than rape for a sexual attack, but this charge was almost always for an attempted rape. While white men might be charged with a variety of less serious crimes that addressed *either* sex or violence, rather than both together, courts charged black men almost exclusively with crimes of sexual violence such as attempted rape. Thirteen percent of white men's criminal prosecutions involved a charge other than rape or attempted rape, compared to only 2 percent of black men's prosecutions.[51] Indeed, I have been unable to find any black-on-white sexual assaults prosecuted under charges of fornication, lewdness, adultery or any other purely sexual crime. Neither have I located an assault charge against a black man for an incident that appears to contain possible sexual coercion. This pattern of associating sexually violent, rather than solely sexual or solely violent charges with black men's sexual misdeeds grew out of the statutory treatment of black-on-white rape.

Over the first half of the eighteenth century, colonies institutionalized a statutory emphasis on black rapists—especially black rapists of white women. In 1714, New Jersey specified punishments for enslaved men—any "negro, Indian or other Slave"—who raped any of the "Majesties Leige People, not being Slaves."[52] Maryland's 1737 act for "the more Effectual Punishment of Negroes & other Slaves" set the death penalty for a black man's "Rape upon any White Woman."[53] Although American statutes generally did not directly address attempted rape until the post-Revolutionary criminal code revisions, many colonies specified exact punishments for black-on-white attempted rape. As early as 1705, Pennsylvania specified a punishment of thirty-nine lashes, branding, and exile for a "Negro" who attempted to rape a white woman.[54] An early eighteenth-century Delaware statute specified a punishment for any slave convicted of attempting to rape a white woman of having his ears nailed to the pillory for four hours and then cut off "close to his head."[55] In 1743, Rhode Island mandated whipping, branding, and expulsion from the colony for a black man's attempted rape of a white woman.[56] In 1751, Maryland statutes condemned to death any slave who attempted to "commit a Rape upon any white Woman."[57]

The colonial statutory specifications for enslaved men's attempted rapes on white women not only set harsher punishments than those to which white men would ever be subject, they also removed local justices' flexibility to minimize the seriousness of sexual assaults by classifying a sexual assault as a lesser sexual or violent crime. Instead, statutes set black-on-white sexual assaults in a category with other rebellious and dangerous slave behavior. While general statutes on nonexpressly racial sexual assaults might appear alongside other sexual crimes such as sodomy, buggery, adultery, or fornication, black-on-white rape and attempted rape statutes were uniformly part of colonies' attempts to regulate dangerous slaves. The first mention of rape in specific relation to slavery in the British colonies may have been in a Barbados statute of 1688 that set special trial courts to deal with slaves who "many Times" committed grievous crimes, including "Murder, Burglaries, Robbing in the Highways, Rapes, burning of Houses or Canes."[58] A 1714 New Jersey law specified punishments against slaves who murdered, raped, burned, or dismembered.[59] New York's 1730 "Act for the More Effectual Preventing and Punishing the Conspiracy and Insurrection of Negro and other Slaves" included punishments for "Murders Rapes Mayhems Insurrections or Conspiracies."[60] A 1751 Maryland statute condemned slaves who had committed insurrection, murder, arson, or rape of white women to death without benefit of clergy.[61] An 1816 Georgia statute specified that slaves and free people of color would be tried for the capital offenses of insurrection, poisoning, murder, maiming, burglary, arson, and rape of whites.[62] Early American laws clearly labeled black-on-white rape as a crime of resistance to white authority, rather than a singular sexual attack. The setting of rape within statutes on slave rebellions was a crucial piece of the racialization of rape in early America. White men's sexual attacks might be understood as sexual or violent, depending on the circumstances, but black men's sexual attacks on white women were legally—and, as we will see, socially—understood as sexually violent in nature.

To summarize, in the abstract, legal treatises categorized sexual attacks as sexual offenses or violent assaults. While New England ministers focused on rape as a sexual misdeed, most other commentators tailored their classification of rape to the race of the defendant. Similarly, courts charged white and black men with different crimes for acts of possible sexual violence. Black men would not be charged with a sexual crime without the specification of violence, but white men were repeatedly charged with crimes of sex or violence, rather than the two together. All of these divisions strongly suggest that a community's perception of sexual violence depended greatly on the defendant's and victim's social position. When we examine how acts of rape were committed (rather than how they would be classified after the fact), we again see divisions across lines of race and gender.

Describing Acts of Rape Through Race

It has become a truism to describe sexual controversies as "he said, she said." But the different foci of men's and women's descriptions of the circumstances of rape may have been more than adversarial attempts to convince a courtroom of their side of the story. Descriptions of sexual assaults by the men involved suggest that they viewed their behavior as primarily sexual in nature. At the risk of sounding ridiculous, if only the women had consented, there would have been no violent rape. The few black rapists whose public words have been preserved seemed to adopt viewpoints similar to their white male counterparts, implicitly rejecting the notion that their acts were those of violence and rebellion. Yet women's descriptions of sexual assaults more often focused on the violence of the attack. Perhaps this is not particularly surprising—women needed to prove the violence of rape, and men might be able to exonerate themselves by claiming consensual sexual relations. But here, too, we see interpretations of sexual coercion that varied along racial lines. White women accusing black men of rape were more likely to see the attack as a physically violent one, while they might see a white man's attack as an incident of consensual social relations gone horribly awry.

Contrary to general images of rape, white rapists did not necessarily lay hidden, waiting to spring their violence on unsuspecting women. Instead, many early Americans saw white men's rape as an act that evolved from attempts at consensual sexual relations. Descriptions of incidents that would later be charged as rape repeatedly presented white attackers as having first *asked* to have sexual relations. Only after that offer was refused would a man proceed to successively more forceful tactics. In the first quarter of the eighteenth century, William Byrd recounted how a fellow traveler had "employ'd force, when he cou'd not succeed by fair means" in having sex with a woman.[63] In 1793, a woman recalled that a white New Yorker named Henry Bedlow "asked her consent three or four times, which she refused" so he then forced himself on her.[64] In the early nineteenth century, convicted rapist Ezra Hutchinson admitted that he would "obtain my will by compulsion, where free consent should be refused."[65] In all of these cases, white men's sexual overtures were presented as voluntary offers that preceded any attempts at forced sexual relations.

Victims also repeatedly presented rape as something white men forced on them only after they refused to comply with the men's sexual offers. In 1730s Pennsylvania, one woman testified that a neighbor had tried to convince her to have sexual relations with him for at least a year before he threw her down and raped her.[66] In mid-century New York, a young woman testified that one of the men who tried to rape her had "offered her silk for a gown, if she would comply" with his sexual overtures.[67] In Revolutionary New England, Joseph Bedford repeatedly climbed into Mary Noble's bed, leaving each time after she told him to do so. But after doing this half a dozen times, he told her "if I stirred or got up he wd beat my brains out."[68] White men had the social authority to commit sexual assaults in ways that seemed consensual and that tied rape directly to the normalcy of consensual social relations. In framing their stories in these ways, the tellers showed that they and their white attackers did not divide forced and consensual sex into clear and separate acts. The actions that might have led to a consensual sexual encounter could also be a prelude to forced sexual interactions.

Similarly, after the sexual coercion, white men might continue normal social relations with the woman or her family, as if no violent or forced sexual interaction had taken place. In 1728, in Connecticut, George Clinton walked Elizabeth Painter home after raping her.[69] In Massachusetts, in 1769, Elisha Bliss raped Mary Turner repeatedly in the woods over a two-hour period. Yet when Mary said she had some business in a nearby house, he believed her promise that she would come back out and let him walk her home.[70] After Abraham Moses raped Christiania Waggoner in 1783, he went to meet Christiania's husband, and all three spent several hours together.[71] In New Jersey, in 1788, James Rook told Polly Frees that he was "going to Shellenes Mill to fish" after raping her—hardly the actions of a man who thought he had committed a capital crime.[72] Despite threatening to slit her throat minutes before, James now put their relationship back into normal sociable terms, discussing his day's plans. Whether these white men did not believe or would not admit that their actions constituted rape, they apparently tried to keep amiable relations with these women. By placing forced sexual acts into a milieu of voluntary social relations, white men had the opportunity to make rape resemble consensual sex. But in racially divided early American society, this was not usually an option available in black-on-white sexual assaults, where friendly interracial socializing would likely be far less acceptable than that between white neighbors or community members.

Men who were defending themselves from rape convictions were not the only figures who might recast a story of rape into a consensual sexual encounter. White men's reformulation of rape into consensual sex might be repeated by the very authorities who adjudged the merits of a woman's accusation of sexual assault. An 1808 case from the Mississippi Territory exemplifies the ways in which a woman's vision of sexual violence could be rewritten by legal officials into a consensual relationship. Mary Ellis accused Francis Surgit, owner of the plantation on which she lived, of raping her. According to Mary, when the owner put his hand on her shoulder, "she told him he was a Saucy man and to begone out of her presence," but he grabbed both of her hands, forced her down on the bed, and raped her. After hearing this testimony, the judge in the case concluded that Mary "had consented to the amour" because Mary's orders for Francis to leave her alone "were Soft words, he understood them, and her pliable conduct." What Mary termed as being grabbed by the wrists and thrown on the bed, the judge saw as Francis taking "her by the hand & l[eading] her to the bed; [he] laid her on it and there Enjoyed her."[73] What Mary saw as violence or force, this legal official interpreted as consensual sexual relations, using his authority to categorize the incident as a purely sexual encounter and therefore necessarily consensual. Early Americans could imagine that women might consent to sexual overtures, but they could less easily imagine that they would willingly consent to physical violence. Thus, an Anglo-American view of white men's rapes as sexual acts gave white men a powerful defense against the charge of rape: the woman had consented.

The early American belief that white men raped out of sexual urges, not from explicitly violent attempts to dominate or control, also provided a ready means to defend accused rapists. A series of Revolutionary and early Republic-era petitions show how community members tried to defend accused or convicted white rapists. In a 1783 rape trial, a defense witness testified that since the defendant's marriage, he "has not the Character of being a Lover of women."[74] A witness for the defense in another trial that year testified that the accused was "not addicted to Women."[75] In 1816 Maryland, the petitioners asked the court to drop rape charges against John Gibson, because, the petitioner rationalized "he, being about to be married, will not, probably, Sin again."[76] This petitioner saw regular sexual access to a wife as an antidote to the sin of rape. None of these writers saw rape as violence that might make the attacker a danger to others in society. Instead, they assumed that unrestrained or unfulfilled sexual desires had led these white men to rape.

Yet when women and witnesses reacted to and recounted black-on-white rapes, they instead emphasized the physical threat of the attack, not the social relations in which the rape had occurred. When Diana Parish ran to a neighbor's house after being raped by an enslaved man in 1748, she was "crying out he has killed me."[77] A witness to one attack in Delaware in 1792 ran to tell others, "The Negro is killing my Mistress."[78] After a rape in early nineteenth-century New England, Lelea Thorp told the first woman she saw after being raped that the African American man "had almost killed me."[79] Using almost identical language, these witnesses unequivocally categorized black men's sexual assaults as obvious and extreme physical violence. Rather than conveying images of social coercion or sexual offers, they portrayed black men committing grave bodily injuries on white women.

In contrast, the few black women who formally accused black men of sexual attacks seemed to view those incidents much like witnesses viewed white-on-white sexual attacks: within the bounds of social relations gone awry. For instance, when a New Jersey slave named Jane complained that another slave named Pompey had tried to rape her in 1796, Jane recalled that Pompey had walked her part of the way home from church and had even helped her duck through a fence before he pushed her down and raped her.[80] Similarly, when free black woman Dolly Boasman complained that a slave had attacked her in early nineteenth-century Virginia, she recounted that the man had entered her house, said "he had a favor to ask, she asked him what, he told her a stroke, she told him to go away." According to Dolly, the man "then seized her, choked her and threw her down and ravished her."[81] Both of these African American women described sexual assaults by black men, not as the near-death violence portrayed in black-on-white sexual attacks, but as social relations that had turned into sexual attacks.

While these cases are suggestive, we have comparatively little overall evidence of black women's experiences with sexual assaults. Part of the reason for this is that in known court records, white women accounted for more than 95 percent of the identifiable victims of prosecuted rapes.[82] Thus, the rape of black women appears largely undocumented and unprosecuted, again making the role of authority and sanction critical to the way a sexual assault would be marked as a criminal act. White men might comment on the sexual mistreatment of black or enslaved women without feeling obligated to bring legal action on the woman's behalf. For example, in 1774, Philip Vickers Fithian noted repeated sexual attempts toward Sukey, a "likely Negro Girl of sixteen," who was a slave on the Carter family's Virginia plantation. Despite repeated rumors that a Carter son tried to force himself on Sukey, Philip dismissed the claim as "calumny" and showed little interest in finding or condemning Sukey's attacker.[83]

Thus, there is little doubt that white men raped black women with virtual impunity throughout early America. Unlike in the later antebellum period, there were no laws explicitly forbidding the prosecution of a white man for the rape of a free black or an enslaved woman. However, multiple colonies prohibited enslaved women from testifying against white in criminal cases, which would make many white-on-black rapes incredibly difficult to substantiate.[84] But while legally possible, such prosecutions were practically unheard of in colonial America: no rape conviction against a white man (let alone a slave's owner) for raping an enslaved woman is known to exist between 1700 and the Civil War.

There are, however, scattered records suggesting that enslaved black women also engaged in sexual relations—perhaps forced, perhaps nominally consensual—with their masters. In 1756, John Briggs complained to a Rhode Island court that he had been defamed by the charge that he had "offered to be naught with his Negrow woman."[85] In 1775, a Virginia Baptist church heard accusations that a Brother had offered "the Act of uncleaness to a Mulatto Girl of his own."[86] In 1783, a Delaware court brought a bastardy charge against Michael Hart for impregnating his slave.[87] The few such recorded incidents are undoubtedly the tip of a very large iceberg. Even if only a small percentage of the interracial master-slave sexual relationships that resulted in master-fathered enslaved children occurred in blatantly forced liaisons, the numbers of American mixed-race children born under slavery suggests that such relations were far more common than surviving documents might seem to suggest.[88] But without a means to legally redress the rape of most black women, there was little chance to adjudicate the violent or sexual nature of these relationships. In a perverse irony, this was something that black women had in common with white men: sexual incidents involving either regularly got read by early Americans as sexual, not sexually violent. Unfortunately, this pairing meant that white men's sexual assaults on black women were implicitly sanctioned through the legal system's studied disinterest in the prosecution of white men or the protection of black women.

While enslaved black women were the most institutionally disadvantaged, even free black women had little chance of courts seeing their complaints of sexual assaults as violent sex. In one of the few extensively documented white-on-black sexual assault cases, in 1809 a New York black woman named Sylvia Patterson accused a white man of attempted rape. Throughout the trial, Sylvia's sexual reputation came under repeated attack as witnesses were brought forward to show that because Sylvia was sexually promiscuous, the alleged attack must have been of a consensual sexual, not violent nature. Witnesses claimed that she was married to a man who had six other wives, that she was hospitalized for a venereal disease, that she associated with prostitutes, and that she improperly bared her legs in public. Those trying to convict her attacker implicitly degraded Sylvia's sexual character on account of her race, arguing that the man had tried to have sex with Sylvia because "no white woman that had the least regard for herself would have any thing to do with him."[89] For black women, especially, early Americans often saw little distinction between their consent and a white man's coercion. All women might be subject to a maligned sexual reputation, but the few nonwhite women who claimed a sexual assault could be summarily disgraced by racial associations to sexual impurity. Because black women's bodies were sexually unprotected, any assault on them was more likely to be labeled an act of sex than one of violence.

Conclusion

The ultimate effect of the racialized definitions of sexual violence is a stark and horrific one. Of the 173 men known to have been executed for criminal charges related to a rape between 1700 and 1820, 141—more than 80 percent—were of African descent. Given that whites outnumbered blacks in every region throughout this time period, this number is especially striking.[90] While some of this disparity can be attributed to a racially based slave labor system, an examination of the racialized understandings of rape itself reminds us both that we need to understand the ways that racial ideologies were reinscribed in daily life and that racial ideologies reshaped far more than the lives of black people. Abstract beliefs took shape around the very real bodies coexisting in the New World, and a racialized view of rape was no exception.

In the abstract, legal and religious publications forwarded definitions of rape that combined images of sex and violence. In theory, lawbooks saw rape as a crime against persons, but they still might group rape with other sexual crimes. New England ministers cared about the moral implications of rape as a sexual sin, rather than the identity of individual rapists. In practice, however, we see a clear racial delineation. Racially specific statutes defined black-on-white rapes as crimes related to slave rebellion. Local courts were far more likely to charge white men's acts of sexual force as either sexual misdeeds or assaults, while black men's acts would more consistently be labeled as the sexual violence of rape or attempted rape. And in actual incidents of sexual assaults, victims and witnesses saw different intent in the acts of black and white potential attackers.

Thus, race, more than any other single feature, divided acts of sex from acts of violence. Those white men with authority in early America not only had the ability to commit sexually violent acts comparatively unprosecuted or unmolested, they also had the authority to implicitly sanction those acts by redefining them into lesser sexual misdeeds. In contrast, Anglo-Americans repeatedly interpreted black-on-white sexual assaults primarily as violent attacks. For black women, perhaps some of the most vulnerable members of early American society, the emphasis on black assailants and white victims of rape meant that they had little means to define white men's unwelcome sexual acts as violent offenses. These racial dividing lines suggest that we need to better historicize concepts of violence to account more fully for the significance of race in all historical categories of violent behavior.

PART III

Colonial Space and Power

S pace, as geographers have increasingly reminded us, is a social construct. It is both the medium within which social relations occur and a crucial outcome or product of those relations.[1] Space, moreover, is also a political and cultural construct. Assertions of political authority turn space into territory; recurrent patterns of habits, values, or practices across space can help in defining a common culture.[2] Relations of power and identity exist in spatial orders, but they also produce them. Moreover, perceptions of violence—or its absence—can shape the social meaning of spaces; fear of crime and disorder, a sense of idyllic calm, and anxiety about chaos and barbarism can help install a sense of place among residents of cities, the countryside, and even the colonial marchlands, respectively.[3] As Arjun Appadurai has written, the production of space "is inherently colonizing, in the sense that it involves the assertion of socially (often ritually) organized power over places and settings that are viewed as potentially chaotic or rebellious."[4] Thus, examining violence, space, culture, and power as mutually constructed and historically interrelated can yield insights into the operation of sanction and authority within the colonial Americas. The three chapters in Part III examine jurisdictional struggles along colonial frontiers.

Cynthia Radding's comparative examination of the mission communities in Sonora and Chiquitos analyzes native cultures and ethnicities as products of conflict over resources and political authority. Over time, she argues, these mission communities served as both a site for the increase of Spanish colonial power and a space for the constitution and reconstitution of native identities and polities in response to Spanish rule and struggles between indigenous groups. Mark Meuwese and Matthew Dennis examine homicides as test cases defining the limits of colonial authority. The deaths of Jacob Rabe and Kauquatau in seventeenth-century Dutch Brazil and nineteenth-century New York each raised questions over sovereignty and sanction—over who would possess the power to define the death (as murder, the execution of a criminal, or the killing of a traitor in wartime) and punish the offenders. And in each situation these questions of whose rules were law were embedded in larger geopolitical struggles—the war among the Dutch, Portuguese, Tupi, and Tarairiu for Brazil and the struggle among the Iroquois, New York State, and the U. S. government for sovereignty during the postindependence period. In neither case was the extension of colonial sovereignty unproblematic; the resolutions of each case were grounded in pragmatism and power more than principle.

In all three cases the authors challenge us to resist easy homologies between space and sovereignty or space and identity. Did Rabe—an ethnic German working for the Dutch West India Company, specifically as a mediator between the WIC and the Tarairiu Indians, and married to a Tupi woman named Dominga—live in a "Dutch" legal or cultural space? Imperial efforts to transform Native societies into colonial spaces in Sonora, Chiquitos, and New York each accelerated the creation of new Indian identities and political movements. Writing on the impact of globalization on cultural formation, Appadurai argued that "the isomorphism of people, territory, and legitimate sovereignty that constitutes the normative charter of the modern nation-state is itself under threat from the forms of circulation of people characteristic of the contemporary world."[5] These essays on colonial space and power reveal how contested that isomorphism in the colonial Americas was; taken together, they suggest that the complexity and diversity of the contemporary world has decidedly colonial roots.

Chapter 6
The Murder of Jacob Rabe: Contesting Dutch Colonial Authority in the Borderlands of Northeastern Brazil

Mark Meuwese

On the evening of 4 April 1646, a violent incident occurred that challenged both the cultural boundaries and the social hierarchy of colonial northeastern Brazil: Jacob Rabe, a German mediator between the Dutch West India Company (WIC) and the Tarairiu Indians, was assassinated by WIC soldiers. According to eyewitnesses interviewed by colonial officials after the murder, the prominent military commander George Garstman had lured Rabe to Dirck Mulder's house in the frontier province of Rio Grande do Norte in northeastern Brazil. After drinking with colonists and military officers for some time, Garstman suddenly ordered his men to return to Fort Ceulen, a nearby Dutch fort. After Garstman's abrupt departure, Rabe decided to leave too and ordered his African slave to fetch his horse. The slave left but soon returned to tell Rabe that he could not find his horse. Irritated, Rabe went outside to look for the horse himself. But as soon as he entered the woods surrounding Mulder's residence, a pair of shots fired by two company soldiers mortally wounded Rabe. As Rabe lay dying, Jacob de Boullan, an officer under Garstman's command, slashed him several times with his sword to make sure that he was dead.[1]

The High Council, the company government in Dutch-controlled Brazil that was based in Recife, was dismayed when it heard about this gruesome murder a week later. The Recife government became even more alarmed when they found out through interrogations of Garstman's men that their superior had not only instigated the brutal assassination but had also confiscated Rabe's possessions. The council was very concerned about the effect that these two crimes could have on public order and military security in the colony. As an indication of how serious they considered these incidents, the Recife officials dispatched a special investigative team led by the *fiscaal*,

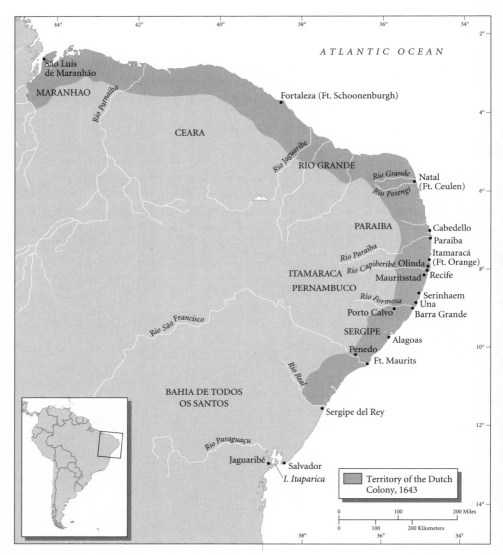

Map 6.1. Colonial Dutch Brazil, 1643. From P. J. P. Whitehead and M. Boeseman, *A Portrait of Dutch Seventeenth Century Brazil: Animals, Plants and People by the Artists of Johan Maurits of Nassau,* Koninklijke Nederlandse Akademie van Wetenschappen, Verhandelingen, Afdeling Natuurkunde, 2e reeks, deel 87 (Amsterdam: North Holland Publishing Company, 1989), 18.

the WIC's prosecuting attorney, to Rio Grande on 14 April. During a special meeting on 23 April with the Council of Justice, the highest colonial judicial authorities, the High Council identified three potential crises precipitated by Rabe's murder.

The first concerned the Tarairius, a Native people from Rio Grande who were important military allies of the Dutch in the latter's ongoing war against Portuguese guerrilla forces. Since 1642, Jacob Rabe had been the official liaison-officer and negotiator between the WIC and the Tarairius. Because the Tarairius considered the slain mediator a close friend "who they held in great esteem," the council was afraid that if they did not swiftly punish Rabe's murderers, the Tarairius would "change their old friendship in enmity, and instead of assist us, would from now on do harm and damage to us."[2]

The second potential crisis for the council was the response of Rabe's Tupi Indian wife, Dominga. Following Rabe's assassination, Garstman and local officials in Rio Grande had stolen all of Rabe's material possessions, which included "livestock, negroes, and furniture." In the Roman-Dutch legal system, which was enforced by authorities in the Dutch Republic and the overseas Dutch world, "a widow automatically received at least 50% of the marital estate upon her husband's death." Thus, according to early modern Dutch civil law, Garstman's appropriation of Rabe's belongings violated Dominga's inheritance rights. Although Dominga was seen by the council as an acculturated Indian who had adopted certain aspects of Christian European civilization, Dutch colonial officials were not sure how Dominga would react to the robbing and killing of her husband. During the special meeting in Recife the company authorities expressed the fear that Dominga might persuade her Tupi kinsmen to break off the alliance with the Dutch if her demands for justice were not met.[3]

The third crisis concerned Garstman himself. The High Council and the Council of Justice were determined to prosecute Garstman because "no self-respecting Government could let a murder go unpunished." Moreover, the killing was considered a criminal offense against the company, since Rabe had been officially appointed as liaison to the Tarairius by the Heeren XIX, the executive board of directors of the WIC in the Dutch Republic. However, at the same time, the Recife councilors realized that Garstman was a high military officer and a member of the colonial elite. Garstman had served the company as a military officer in Brazil since the early 1630s, and in September 1645 the High Council had even provisionally appointed him as a senior commander of the colonial militia. The Recife government acknowledged that "the incarceration or purge of the head of the militia was somewhat problematic" because Garstman had many influential friends among the military and civilian elite of Dutch Brazil. Moreover, the Recife authorities realized that, even if they were to convict Garstman, his status as a "high Commander" enabled him to appeal his verdict to the Heeren XIX.[4]

The multiple challenges to the authority of the government in Dutch Brazil triggered by Rabe's murder can be divided into two types of judicial conflicts. The first was the jurisdictional dispute between the High Council and the Natives over "whose rules were law" in colonial Brazil. Because the Recife authorities viewed the Rabe case as a murder committed by one colonist against another, they argued that the murder case needed to be resolved within the colonial legal system. However, since Rabe was closely associated with the Tarairius and the Tupis, the council was afraid that their valuable Indian allies would want to pursue justice against Garstman according to their own rules. Rabe's murder therefore became a case study about whether Dutch law or Indian law would prevail. The second type of judicial conflict involved intracolonial and intraimperial contestations over Garstman's punishment. In Brazil, the council could expect opposition from the colonial population, which was sympathetic to Garstman. In addition, the council knew that Garstman could take his case to the metropolitan authorities, who could overturn any sentence from the colonial periphery.[5]

Historians have usually treated these two types of jurisdictional conflicts as separate stories. While ethnohistorians have analyzed legal disputes between Indians and colonists, scholars concentrating on the social-political development of colonies have dealt with court cases that pitted colonial governments against colonists and colonial peripheries against the metropolitan center. However, the Rabe case demonstrates that Indian-European and intracolonial legal conflicts were sometimes interrelated. Analyzing the two types of judicial contestations together provides a more complete understanding of how colonial authority worked.[6]

By comparing the responses of the High Council to the challenges from the Tarairius, Dominga, and Garstman, I argue that all sides tried to compromise because they all needed each other. Recent students of Dutch colonization in the New World have argued that both metropolitan and colonial authorities often responded pragmatically to challenges to their power in order to maintain order and stability. Two factors contributed to this tolerant attitude held by Dutch colonial officials. First, the WIC was a joint stock company. If protests by colonists or a specific government measure threatened to disrupt commerce or the stability of the colony, the

Heeren XIX instructed officials in the colonial periphery to accommodate these protests or to repeal the measure. Second, like other European colonial powers in the early modern world, Dutch authorities were often forced to seek compromises with the colonial population because they lacked the resources to enforce their will.[7]

Although the pragmatic response of metropolitan authorities to political and legal crises helps explain the council's reaction to the Rabe case, it does not address the local circumstances that also shaped the outcome of the crisis. The development of Dutch Brazil as a borderland eventually led all parties involved in the Rabe murder to respond pragmatically as well. Whereas "frontiers" are usually narrowly conceived as geographic zones of interaction between Native peoples and European invaders, the concept of borderlands—defined as a geographic zone of interaction "where autonomous peoples of different cultures are bound together by a greater, multi-imperial context"—takes into account the impact of imperial conflicts upon these intercultural interactions. By connecting the localized studies of Indian-European contacts with the studies of European rivalries over control of the New World, historians can demonstrate that encounters between Natives and colonists were influenced as much by local circumstances as by imperial contexts. During the first half of the seventeenth century, northeastern Brazil was a heavily contested borderland in which Dutch attempts to conquer the Portuguese colony decisively shaped Indian-European and intracolonial relations in the region.[8]

While the Dutch heavily relied on the Tarairius and the Tupis to defeat the Portuguese, both Native peoples actively sought out an alliance with the WIC to obtain independence from Portuguese colonization. It was this context of mutual strategic dependency that conditioned the diplomatic and judicial contest between the council and the Tarairius and Dominga over Rabe's death. The borderland context was also important in determining the outcome of the struggle between the council and Garstman. Although the Recife magistrates wanted to punish Garstman appropriately for the murder of Rabe, they knew that they could ill afford to turn the colonial population, which was sympathetic to Garstman, against them at a time when Portuguese guerrillas threatened the colony. An examination both of the tensions revealed by Rabe's murder and of the extent to which colonial authorities were willing to accommodate the challenges of the Tarairius, Dominga, and Garstman reveals much about the nature of colonialism in Dutch Brazil.

The WIC's anxiety over Rabe's death was amplified by the brief history of its rule in Brazil and the longer history of Dutch expansion in the Atlantic world. After the annexation of Portugal and its overseas empire by the Spanish Hapsburg Crown in 1580, the rebellious United Provinces proceeded to extend their global war against the Habsburg double monarchy to the lucrative Portuguese colonies in Southeast Asia and Brazil. Since the late 1590s, Dutch merchants had shown increasing interest in taking control of the profitable sugar plantations of northeastern Brazil. After the founding of the WIC in 1621, this joint stock company spent most of its financial and military resources on the conquest of Brazil. By the mid-1630s, WIC troops and naval fleets had secured military control over most of the northeastern coast. But because the Dutch were unable to occupy the Portuguese colonial capital Salvador de Bahia, Portuguese guerrilla forces obtained arms and supplies to continue fighting the Dutch invaders. Since neither the Dutch nor the Portuguese could defeat the other, northeastern Brazil remained a heavily contested borderland until the Portuguese captured Recife in January 1654 and drove out the Dutch.[9]

Native peoples played an important role in the Portuguese-Dutch struggle over Brazil. During the sixteenth century, Portuguese colonists and Jesuit missionaries had attempted to forcibly incorporate the indigenous peoples of northeastern Brazil as docile Christian laborers into colonial society. However, many of the coastal Indian peoples actively resisted Portuguese colonization through warfare or through migration into the interior. Native resistance against the Portuguese was especially strong in the northeastern *capitanias*, or provinces, of Paraíba, Rio Grande do Norte, and Ceará. The Portuguese had colonized these three provinces only since the late sixteenth century and lacked the resources and manpower to defeat the local natives. Moreover, the Indians were sometimes actively supported in their armed struggle against the Portuguese by visiting French traders who supplied them with arms and often joined the Indians in attacks on the Portuguese. Only through brutal raids on Native villages in which many inhabitants were enslaved did the Portuguese succeed in establishing some control over the three provinces.[10]

It is therefore not surprising that the indigenous groups of northeastern Brazil welcomed the Dutch invaders as potential allies. During a stopover of a WIC fleet at a bay on the Paraíba coast in the spring of 1625, local Tupi-speaking Potiguar Indians took the initiative to forge an anti-Portuguese alliance with the Dutch visitors. To strengthen the diplomatic relationship, several leaders of the Potiguar people even traveled to the Dutch Republic with the returning company fleet to learn Dutch and to convert to the Dutch Reformed religion. After the Dutch conquest of Recife in the early 1630s, the WIC employed several of these Potiguar headmen as mediators to persuade other Indians to support the Dutch. Company officials also proclaimed an end to Indian slavery in all provinces under Dutch control in order to attract more Natives to their side.[11]

Like the Portuguese, the Dutch distinguished between two groups of Indians in Brazil. These distinctions were based not only on cultural differences between the two groups but also on the extent of the Indians' contacts with Europeans. The first group was made up of the Tupi-speaking coastal peoples, whom the Dutch referred to as "Brazilians." Before the arrival of the Portuguese, most Tupi peoples had formed independent semisedentary horticultural communities, which often raided each other's villages to obtain captives. By playing many of the Tupi groups against each other, the Portuguese had been able to obtain large numbers of Indian slaves that were put to work on the sugar mills and plantations in the northeast during the sixteenth century. In an attempt to curtail widespread abuse of the Tupis, Jesuit missionaries concentrated most Tupis in *aldeias* or mission villages. In these communities the Jesuits tried to transform the Tupis into sedentary Christian farmers.[12]

After the Dutch expelled the Jesuits from the northeast in the early 1630s, the WIC continued to use the *aldeias* in order to make use of their Tupi allies more efficiently. The company frequently recruited them for military campaigns against the Portuguese, and colonists hired Tupi men and women for various labor tasks in the sugar sector. Despite their use as auxiliaries and their integration into the colonial economy, the Tupis remained a segregated and subordinated segment of Dutch colonial society. In an attempt to accommodate Tupi grievances against their continued exploitation by colonists, the High Council gave Brazilians limited self-rule and their own courts in the spring of 1645. However, serious crimes such as a murder committed by one Tupi against another continued to be tried by colonial authorities.[13]

The second group of Indians in northeastern Brazil was made up of the "Tapuyas." While the Brazilians were seen as semi-civilized Indians, the Tapuyas were viewed as irredeemable savages who remained beyond the reach of colonial rule. The term "Tapuya" was originally a Tupi name with negative connotations intended for those Native peoples who were linguistically and culturally different from the coastal Tupis. Most Tapuya peoples were communities of hunters and gatherers who lived in the *sertão*, the arid backcountry of the coastal provinces. The Portuguese soon adopted the name and applied it to any Native group that lived in the *sertão* and resisted colonization. The *sertão* and the Tapuyas eventually became inseparable from each other in Portuguese eyes. The Brazilian backcountry became a region inhabited by uncivilized and barbaric peoples who were outside of the legal boundaries of the Portuguese empire.[14]

Although the Dutch also considered the Tapuyas to be uncontrollable savages, they viewed some as useful allies. In the early 1630s, WIC officials in Recife were contacted by several Tapuyas from Rio Grande do Norte to launch an assault against the Portuguese in that province. The Tapuya diplomats promised to aid the Dutch and join them in an alliance against the Portuguese. These Tapuyas called themselves the Tarairius and lived in the *sertão* of Rio Grande. After one unsuccessful Dutch attempt to capture the Portuguese coastal fort Reis Magos in Rio Grande in 1631, a WIC force occupied the strategic Portuguese stronghold in December 1633. WIC authorities appointed George Garstman as commander of Fort Ceulen. In his position as garrison commander Garstman received a large delegation of Tarairius who visited Fort Ceulen in February 1634. For several days Garstman and the Tarairius, including their leader Nhanduí, exchanged diplomatic greetings and gifts with the help of several Tupi interpreters. However, Garstman and other company officials were also skeptical about the usefulness of the Tarairius because they continued their longstanding hostilities with neighboring Indian peoples. Moreover, the Tarairiu practices of killing captives and ritual cannibalism of deceased relatives greatly disturbed European sensibilities. The seasonal Tarairiu raids against colonial ranches and farms to obtain cattle and other food resources also dismayed company authorities because they angered Portuguese colonists who had agreed to live under WIC rule. Despite their savagery and unruly behavior from the company point of view, the Tarairius remained valuable allies for the Dutch. The ferocity of Tarairiu warriors intimidated the Portuguese as well as their Indian allies and, for a relatively small quantity of Dutch trade goods, Nhanduí was willing to send Tarairiu warriors to fight alongside the Dutch.[15]

Growing Portuguese resistance to WIC rule in Brazil made the company increasingly dependent upon its Brazilian and Tarairiu allies. Roving bands of Portuguese rebels and their Indian and African allies often raided the northeastern countryside in order to keep the Dutch on the defensive. Although the Recife magistrates sometimes apprehended and executed the Luso-Brazilian rebels, the frequent references to *bosloopers*, or rural bandits, during the 1630s and 1640s strongly suggest that the High Council was ineffective in suppressing the Portuguese guerrilla activities. In the summer of 1645 the Dutch suddenly lost the military initiative after the outbreak of a Portuguese revolt against WIC rule. This carefully planned uprising was organized by officials in Salvador de Bahia and supported by most Portuguese colonists in Dutch-controlled territory. While the Portuguese rebels and their Indian and Afro-Brazilian allies quickly seized control over the northeastern countryside, the company troops and their Indian allies retained military power over most of the coastline, including the province of Rio Grande. However, in order to fight the spirited Portuguese revolt more effectively, the council grew ever more dependent upon its Indian allies. As the Tarairius and the Brazilians from Rio Grande do Norte became indispensable for the company in its struggle against the Portuguese guerillas, the council was careful not to alienate them.[16]

The Collision of Jacob Rabe and George Garstman

It is in this context of a fierce Portuguese rebellion against WIC rule that Jacob Rabe and George Garstman acted out their dramatic roles. Before discussing why Garstman had Rabe assassinated in April 1646 it is important to provide brief biographical sketches of the two individuals.[17] Rabe and Garstman had similar personal backgrounds. First of all, both men were ethnic Germans in service of the WIC in northeastern Brazil. Second, they had similar social backgrounds. While most Germans in service of the Dutch East and West India Companies were impoverished peasants or urban dwellers, some were also military officers, merchants, members of the lower nobility, or somewhat educated and skilled members of the middle classes. Garstman and Rabe belonged to this latter group. Garstman's first mention in the documents and texts about Dutch Brazil is as a captain of a company of WIC soldiers in the province of Rio Grande in December 1633. Since appointments of officers in the early modern Dutch army were often based on social and financial status, Garstman was probably a man of some standing and economic means before he enlisted in the service of the company. Likewise, when Jacob Rabe is first mentioned in the official Company papers in 1642, he is referred to as *heer,* or gentleman, a social title that set him apart considerably from the rank-and-file soldiers and lower company officials.[18]

Third, both men were closely involved in the WIC alliance with the Tarairius, a fact that would set Garstman on a collision course with Rabe. In his position as commander of Fort Ceulen, Garstman played an important role in WIC-Tarairiu relations during the early 1630s. Although the WIC occasionally deployed the Tarairius against Portuguese forces, the ongoing Tarairiu raids against European farms and ranches in Rio Grande necessitated company officials establishing more control over the troublesome but valuable Indian allies. After having relied on several other, short-lived European mediators, the council in Recife appointed Jacob Rabe as interpreter and liaison officer to the Tarairius on 25 June 1642. It is not known why the Recife officials selected the hitherto unknown Rabe for this special position. Most likely, Rabe had shown useful cross-cultural skills such as the ability to speak Indian languages and a willingness to interact with Natives on a frequent basis. Rabe's main tasks were to keep the Tarairius loyal to the company and to prevent the Tarairius from invading the coastal area of Rio Grande.[19]

Unlike Garstman and other WIC officials who dealt closely with the Tarairius, Rabe developed a hybrid identity that blended Indian and colonial European practices. Whereas other colonial mediators looked down upon the savage Tarairius, Rabe became an adopted member of this Native people. In addition to his close association with the regularly moving Tarairius, Rabe also had a small ranch or farm near Fort Ceulen. This farm was maintained by more than twenty African slaves that Rabe had obtained through the Tarairiu campaigns against Portuguese colonists. Moreover, despite the council's efforts to keep company soldiers and employees from establishing intimate relations with Indian women, Rabe was married to a Brazilian woman named Dominga who lived with him on his farm. Finally, Rabe wrote a short and sympathetic protoethnographic account of the Tarairius. In this document he depicted the Natives with whom he dealt on a daily basis as an exotic people who were radically different from Europeans. At the same time, Rabe's personal observations of the Tarairius were remarkably value-free. For instance, when describing their cannibalistic rituals, Rabe provided an explanatory and serious analysis of a cultural practice that was unanimously abhorred by other European eyewitnesses.[20]

In contrast to Rabe, Garstman refused to mix colonial and Indian identities. Although he also closely associated with the Tarairius, in his position as WIC commander of Fort Ceulen Garstman strived toward respectability and high status in colonial society. This was evidenced when, in January 1638, the company commander acquired not only African slaves but also one of the few sugar mills in Rio Grande. Moreover, while Rabe established a formal relationship with a Native American woman, Garstman revealed his preference for European ways by marrying a Portuguese woman in the 1630s. Due to a shortage of Dutch women in Brazil, marriages between company officials and Portuguese women were not infrequent. These inter-cultural unions clearly revealed that, despite the bitter Portuguese-Dutch conflict and the alliance between the WIC and various Indian peoples, prominent Protestant WIC officials such as Garstman preferred Catholic Por-tuguese women to Native women. Garstman's connection to the Portuguese community in Dutch Brazil became so close that the High Council sus-pected him of treason. In December 1636, rumors reached Recife accusing Garstman of conspiring with his wife's relatives to surrender Fort Ceulen to the Portuguese. Disturbed by these stories, the council initiated an official investigation. However, in May 1637 the council concluded that Garstman was not involved in a conspiracy with the Portuguese, and he was cleared of all accusations.[21]

A series of Tarairiu raids against Portuguese and Dutch colonists in Rio Grande in the early 1640s brought Rabe and Garstman into direct con-flict. Because Rabe had actively participated in the attacks against colonists, Garstman imprisoned the intercultural negotiator in Fort Ceulen. However, soon after his capture in February 1643, Rabe escaped and rejoined the Tarairius in their depredations in Rio Grande. The council in Recife was angry with Rabe but was also afraid to lose the alliance with the Tarairius. Despite having temporarily suspended Rabe's WIC salary, the council rein-stated him as mediator to the Tarairius soon after Portuguese rebels threat-ened to invade Rio Grande.[22]

The tension between Rabe and Garstman increased when the council considered both men for a position as provincial magistrate in Rio Grande in January 1644. It is not clear why the Recife councilors selected Rabe as one of the candidates for a task that did not involve working with Indians. However, the company government in Recife probably assessed Rabe's activ-ities in Rio Grande through a different lens than local WIC authorities of that province. And geographic distance may well have played a role in the different perceptions of Rabe. The Recife officials were only in contact with Rabe through letters, whereas Garstman and the Rio Grande magistrates dealt with Rabe on a face-to-face level. While Garstman and other company offi-cials in Rio Grande considered Rabe as a colonist who had gone native and who had placed himself outside the boundaries of colonial society, the High Council in Recife continued to view Rabe primarily as a WIC official who had successfully maintained the important alliance with the Tarairius. Garst-man was probably irritated by Rabe's candidacy, not only because he had only recently imprisoned Rabe, but also because Garstman himself had been nominated for the position of provincial magistrate.[23]

Although Garstman was suspicious of Rabe, the outbreak of the Portuguese revolt in the summer of 1645 forced both men to temporarily put aside their differences. In order to preserve the WIC presence in Rio Grande against the Portuguese rebels, the council called on the services of both Rabe and Garstman. While Rabe rallied the Tarairius to attack roving bands of Portuguese and Indian rebels, Garstman coordinated the military defenses of the WIC. From late June to early July 1645 Garstman even corresponded personally with Rabe about how to utilize the Tarairius as a defense force. Thus, given their necessary and close cooperation following the Portuguese rebellion, it is somewhat puzzling why Garstman ordered Rabe's murder in April 1646.[24]

However, by early 1646 Garstman had two motives for wanting Rabe killed. First, Garstman blamed Rabe for the violent death of Garstman's Portuguese father-in-law at the hands of the Tarairius in the summer of 1645. During the summer and fall of 1645 Tarairiu warriors led by Rabe had brutally killed several groups of Portuguese colonists in Rio Grande. In one of their raids, Rabe and the Tarairius murdered a congregation of Portuguese parishioners in a rural Catholic church. While this attack was in any case greatly upsetting for Garstman because of his close affiliation with the Portuguese community in Rio Grande, the massacre was especially disturbing for him personally because his father-in-law was one of the victims. Already angry at Rabe for his previous involvement in Tarairiu raids against colonists, Garstman now had a strong personal motive for terminating Rabe's activities once and for all.[25]

Second, Garstman had designs on Rabe's wealth. According to rumors circulating after Rabe's death, the controversial mediator had acquired a considerable amount of valuables during his campaigns with the Tarairius. Several individuals closely associated with Garstman testified to company officials that Garstman had been interested in uncovering a supposed treasure of Portuguese gold and jewelry that Rabe had buried somewhere in Rio Grande. During the days immediately following the murder, Garstman ordered his men to collect as many of Rabe's possessions as possible. Furthermore, Garstman even had one of his lower officers torture Jacob Willems, Rabe's personal servant, in order to get him to disclose the location of the supposed treasure. Local company officials initially also considered Rabe's material property as the main reason for his violent death. In order to prevent the looting of Rabe's possessions, Jan Hoeck, the *schout,* or sheriff of Rio Grande, quickly sealed and placed several chests filled with Rabe's clothing and jewelry inside Fort Ceulen. In addition, he ordered some soldiers to round up cattle and horses that belonged to Rabe's farm. Finally, Hoeck brought into Fort Ceulen twenty-two of Rabe's African slaves. Although Rabe's fabled buried treasure was never found, it is clear that the considerable material wealth he did possess might have been a strong motive for Garstman to have Rabe killed.[26]

The Tarairiu Reaction

Since Rabe had been "held in high esteem" by the Tarairius, the High Council feared that his violent death at the hands of WIC soldiers and officers would anger the Tarairius. The Recife authorities were particularly afraid that the murder would unravel the Tarairiu-Dutch alliance. It was therefore of great importance for the council to convince the Tarairius that the assassination of Rabe was an unfortunate and regrettable crime committed by a military officer who had acted without the support from the colonial authorities. To deliver this delicate message to the Tarairius, the High Council called upon the services of Roelof Baro, an experienced intercultural mediator who had been dealing with the Tarairius for several years. On 25 April 1646, the High Council ordered Baro to contact the Tarairiu leader Nhanduí and tell him that Rabe's murder was an act of a few irresponsible European soldiers who would be duly punished. The Recife magistrates also ordered Baro to bring a Tarairiu delegation to Recife in order to keep the Indians loyal to the WIC.[27]

However, when the Tarairiu delegation visited Recife, they demanded that Garstman be handed over to them. According to Pierre Moreau, a WIC secretary who provided the only account of this meeting, the Tarairiu envoys emphasized that Garstman had murdered Rabe for no legitimate reason. Fearing that the Dutch authorities would exonerate Garstman for having killed Rabe, the Indian diplomats angrily told the council that "Jakob Rabbi could not be accused of anything, and he had never been a traitor." In making their case that Rabe had not been guilty of any crimes that could have justified Garstman's actions, the Tarairius tried to appeal to a shared notion of justice among themselves and the Dutch colonial authorities. Although the legal systems of the two cultures differed substantially, the Tarairiu diplomats attempted to convince the council that Garstman's motives for killing Rabe were unacceptable to both the Tarairius and the Dutch. For example, the Tarairius rejected the explanation that Garstman had justly murdered Rabe in order to prevent the latter from organizing periodic

Tarairiu raids against Rio Grande cattle ranchers and farmers. The Tarairiu dignitaries explained that the company's failure to provide their people with enough food and trade goods had necessitated the Rabe-led raids on Rio Grande ranches and farms.[28]

Even if Rabe had been guilty of any offenses against colonists, the Tarairiu delegates argued that he should have "been sentenced according to the [legal] custom of the Hollanders; but instead they had murdered him, when he could have easily been arrested." By suggesting that Rabe could have been tried by the Dutch judicial system, the Tarairius revealed that they were willing to accept Dutch jurisdiction over Rabe, "who they loved more than one hundred other persons." Of course it was easy for the Tarairius to make this suggestion, since Rabe was now dead. It is unlikely that Rabe himself would have accepted Dutch jurisdiction. After all, he had escaped from Fort Ceulen after Garstman had arrested him for the plundering of colonial farms in Rio Grande in 1643.[29]

However, by telling the council that they would have allowed Rabe to be tried in a colonial court, the Tarairiu delegation probably hoped to establish some goodwill among the Recife magistrates so that the latter would turn over Garstman. To bolster their argument, the Tarairiu envoys even shrewdly tried to manipulate the High Council's subordinate position to the Heeren XIX in the Dutch Republic. The Tarairiu delegates referred to a special right that had supposedly been given to them by the Heeren XIX, which allowed them to bring to justice anyone who had mistreated their people. The surviving company records do not indicate that such a remarkable privilege was actually ever given to the Tarairius. Moreover, it is unlikely that the Dutch would have ever given these Indians, whom they considered uncivilized savages, the right to judge and sentence colonists.[30]

Not surprisingly, the council rejected the request of the Tarairiu delegation to let Garstman be tried by them. The council explained their decision by telling the Tarairius that "Garstman was a high commander, and that they were powerless to hand him over." In addition, the council told the Tarairius that, even if the colonial government sentenced Garstman, according to the colonial legal system he would still be able to appeal his verdict to the Heeren XIX. Extraditing Garstman to the Tarairius without allowing him to appeal his case in the Republic would have brought the council into an embarrassing conflict with their metropolitan superiors.[31]

There was also another reason why Garstman was not handed over to the Tarairius. Although the Tarairius considered Rabe as one of their own, for the council Rabe remained a company official who had been appointed as liaison officer to the Tarairius. Because Rabe was still seen as a member of colonial society by the Recife officials, Garstman had murdered a colonist and not a Tarairiu. Accommodating the Tarairiu request would have meant that the council accepted Indian jurisdiction over a murder case that involved only colonists. Like other European colonial powers, giving Native peoples the right to try colonists according to indigenous laws was out of the question for Dutch colonial authorities. Yielding to Tarairiu demands would have implied that Tarairiu laws were equal to Dutch laws, an admission that Dutch colonial officials would never have considered since they viewed the Tarairius as a culturally inferior people who did not even have written laws. At the same time, the Dutch officials wanted to keep the Tarairius as allies, so they assured native diplomats that they would mete out appropriate justice against Garstman. To emphasize that they were sincere, the council even paraded a captive and bound Garstman in front of the Tarairius. However, the Tarairiu diplomats, very disappointed that the council would not deliver Garstman to them, were not impressed. Upon leaving the special meeting in Recife, the Tarairiu delegation warned the council that the Dutch would soon regret their decision not to give up Garstman.[32]

Despite the defection of some Tarairius upset that Garstman had not been turned over to them for judgment, most Tarairius remained allied with the WIC. This was less because of Baro's intercultural diplomacy than because of the renewed outbreak of fighting between the Tarairius and neighboring Native peoples. Fortunately for the council, the Tarairius needed the Dutch more than the company needed them. Surrounded by a large number of Indian enemies who were allied with the Portuguese, Nhanduí asked Baro to provide the Tarairius with military support as soon as possible. However, the council was reluctant to provide any sustenance to Nhanduí as long as the Dutch were themselves pressured by the Portuguese rebels. The Recife officials initially supported the battered Tarairius only with cheap trade goods such as axes, knives, and mirrors. Only after Baro reported in late August 1647 that the Tarairius were driven to plundering colonists' farms and plantations on the coast did the High Council resolve to send more substantial aid in the form of soldiers. Although the anti-Portuguese alliance between the Tarairius and the company remained intact throughout the period of the Dutch presence in northeastern Brazil, the conflict over "whose rules were law" in the Rabe murder case had clearly shown that the relationship remained primarily practical. Neither the Tarairius nor the Dutch colonial officials were willing to compromise over how to punish Garstman.[33]

Dominga's Pursuit of Justice

While the Tarairius unsuccessfully attempted to punish Rabe's murderer by their own legal standards, Dominga, the Tupi wife of the slain intercultural mediator, chose to work within the Dutch judicial system to claim her rightful inheritance. Her decision to pursue justice in this way strongly suggested that Dominga felt comfortable operating in colonial society. Dominga's designation as a Brazilian by the council indicated that she belonged to those Indians who were seen by the Dutch as people who might adopt Christian European civilization. Like many other Brazilians, Dominga, whose Tupi name is unknown, probably received an Iberian name during her stay at one of the Catholic mission villages sometime before the Dutch conquest. Most likely Dominga was also baptized by Jesuit missionaries at that time. In addition, like other Tupis who were concentrated in the *aldeias*, Dominga may have learned how to read and write through Jesuit missionaries and later from Dutch Protestant schoolteachers. Finally, Dominga likely participated in colonial society because both the Portuguese and the Dutch relied heavily on Brazilian men and women as workers in the colonial economy or as military auxiliaries.[34]

In addition to being in frequent contact with colonists inside and outside her *aldeia*, Dominga gained an even closer understanding of colonial society by marrying Jacob Rabe. Although no records of a formal wedding have been found, the High Council consistently referred to Dominga as Rabe's "wife," "housewife," and "widow." Moreover, the Dutch authorities acknowledged that she had a rightful claim to Rabe's possessions, which suggested that the relationship was more than an informal liaison. Like many other Brazilian women, Dominga probably entered into a formal union with Rabe for practical reasons. Because the Tupis lived in societies that were primarily based on kinship ties rather than on centralized state rule, intermarriages solidified trade and diplomatic relations with European powers. By marrying the German-born mediator who represented the WIC, Dominga and her Tupi relatives not only strengthened the alliance with the company but also obtained direct access to valuable trade goods such as textiles and metal tools that Rabe often distributed among Indian allies of the Dutch. For Dominga the relationship with Rabe may have offered personal material benefits as well. In addition, the union enabled Dominga to move away from the *aldeias*, which were often unhealthy places where many Tupis died of epidemic diseases inadvertently imported by European colonists and African slaves. Finally, by moving in with Rabe, Dominga avoided having to do heavy labor in the colonial economy or to join Tupi men on dangerous WIC military campaigns against the Portuguese.[35]

Dutch colonial officials usually prohibited intermarriage between company employees and Indian women. Recife authorities tried to ban intercultural liaisons in the colony because they were afraid that soldiers and lower officials would exploit and abuse native women. Since the WIC was heavily dependent upon the Tupis as military auxiliaries and as laborers in the colonial economy, the council wanted to avoid any intercultural friction. In addition, the influential Dutch Reformed ministers in the colony strongly condemned marriages between Christians and non-Christians. However, the council tolerated Rabe's marriage to Dominga. The Recife councilors probably made an exception for Rabe because he was indispensable in maintaining the company's alliance with the Tarairius. Rabe's ability to speak the Tarairiu language and his willingness to associate closely with these savage Indians made him a highly useful person whom the Council could ill afford to lose. It is also possible that Rabe was allowed to marry Dominga because colonial officials and Dutch Calvinist ministers considered her a sincere Christian convert.[36]

Thus, Dominga's marriage to Rabe and her identity as a Brazilian woman familiar with colonial society help explain why she pursued justice within the Dutch legal system following her husband's death and dispossession. It is possible that Rabe and Dominga had made a will that gave Dominga the right to inherit some or all of Rabe's possessions in the case of his death. This was a common practice among married couples in the Dutch Republic and its overseas colonies. Significantly, when the *fiscaal* interviewed her at Fort Ceulen in Rio Grande on 5 May 1646, Dominga claimed ownership of Rabe's stolen goods. It is therefore possible that Dominga had some understanding of Dutch inheritance law. After describing how she had seen her husband leave their house on the day of his murder, Dominga gave a detailed account of all the material possessions that Rabe had taken along. Among the items were golden rings and jewelry and a small case in which Rabe had packed his riding cape, as well as "a silver cup and a silver spoon, and a piece of red and white silk." According to the report written up by the *fiscaal*, Dominga "therefore requested that these goods and others belonging to her" should be returned to her, "or the equivalent thereof, and that those who will be found guilty of the death of her husband, would be punished to the satisfaction of the law." Although the *fiscaal* did not imply what system of "law" Dominga meant, it is clear from the context that Rabe's widow most likely referred to the Roman-Dutch legal code rather than to Tupi Indian traditions.[37]

The council must have been relieved when they learned that Dominga would not threaten to break up the strategic Tupi-Dutch alliance over the robbery and murder of her husband. Unlike the Tarairius, who had attempted to implement justice against Rabe's murderer according to their own customs, Dominga accepted the Dutch colonial order. After being informed by the *fiscaal* of Dominga's demands, the grateful council instructed colonial officials in Rio Grande to fulfill her request for justice. By ordering the Rio Grande authorities to satisfy Dominga's wishes, the council revealed that they were still afraid that Dominga would attempt to persuade her Tupi kinsmen to abandon the Dutch if her claims were not met. On 8 August 1646, the council noted that Sheriff Hoeck "had given to the widow of Jacob Rabbi, being a Brazilian woman, on our orders, 10 negroes and some other goods belonging to the estate of the deceased." Although Hoeck did not report to his superiors whether Dominga was pleased with this transaction, he did write that "the [Brazilian] nation was satisfied." As far as the company authorities were concerned, the potential rift with the Tupis had now been repaired. Significantly, Dominga's name does not appear in any further WIC records.[38]

The Trial and Sentencing of George Garstman

The most important challenge for the council involved the prosecution and punishment of Garstman. It is a challenge for historians to reconstruct the actual events surrounding the trial, because the WIC records are incomplete and other written sources more often confuse than clarify the matter. This is partly because of lost documents but also because chaos engulfed Recife at the time of Rabe's murder. Plagued by severe food shortages and besieged by Portuguese guerrillas, the murder of Jacob Rabe was only one of the many crises facing the High Council. What follows here is therefore only an initial attempt at interpreting some of the major events involving the WIC magistrates and Garstman.[39]

When the Council instructed the *fiscaal* to travel to Fort Ceulen on 14 April in order to investigate Rabe's murder, the Recife officials were still unsure whether Garstman was behind the killing. The council did therefore not immediately arrest the prominent officer when a ship carrying Garstman and his soldiers arrived from Rio Grande in the Recife harbor on 17 April. The Recife magistrates even allowed Garstman to give a briefing about his recent improvements of the WIC defenses in Rio Grande against Portuguese

rebels. But on Saturday 21 April, the Recife councilors learned from an un-
disclosed source that several soldiers under Garstman's command had participated in the murder. Alarmed by this news, the High Council summoned
these soldiers for interrogation on the same day. Although Garstman had
clearly instructed his men to keep silent, they quickly implicated their superior in Rabe's murder, probably out of fear of being tortured. For example,
Ensign Jacob de Boullan testified on 21 April that Garstman had instructed
him to kill Rabe. Moreover, he also told the Recife magistrates that his superior had threatened to fire him unless he killed Rabe.[40]

Faced with these damaging revelations, the council interrogated Garstman himself. Expecting that his prominent position as civil militia commander would guarantee him immunity from prosecution, Garstman haughtily
asked the councilors whether it was allowed for De Boullan, a subordinate,
to accuse his superior of a crime. De Boullan, who probably feared a harsh
sentence if found guilty, turned Garstman's question around and openly
asked "whether it was acceptable that a field commander could abuse his
power and determine the life and death of his officers." For the council it
was now clear that Garstman had ordered the assassination of Rabe. In the
special meeting with members of the Council of Justice on 23 April, the
Recife government speculated that Garstman had committed the crime to
seek favors from local Portuguese colonists. The Recife government remembered that several years ago they had investigated whether Garstman had
secretly conspired with the Portuguese against the WIC. The council now
also deemed Garstman's marriage to a local Portuguese woman suspicious,
especially since she "had shown her bitterness against our nation on repeated occasions." Since Rabe had been "deadly hated" by the Portuguese
colonists of Rio Grande for having led the Tarairius in attacks against Portuguese settlers in the summer of 1645, the council concluded that Garstman
had killed Rabe to gain the sympathy and trust of the Portuguese.[41]

Although the colonial authorities considered Garstman guilty of orches-
trating Rabe's murder and endangering the company's alliances with the
Tupis and Tarairius, they were reluctant to try him quickly because of his
prominent status in the colony. At the end of the meeting, the council
resolved to arrest Garstman but decided to put him aboard the company
vessel *Hollandia* in the Recife harbor in order to avoid unrest among the
military and colonial elite in the city. Military officers and influential colonists
who were closely associated with Garstman immediately petitioned the council to obtain his release. Like the prominent classes in the United Provinces,
the influential social group to which Garstman belonged in colonial Brazil

had developed personal friendships and a code of honor to differentiate themselves from the less privileged social groups. After the council detained Garstman, his friends and colleagues consequently felt obliged to defend their
associate's honor. On 27 April, a delegation led by Majors Bajart and Piston,
the Recife civil militia commander Mathias Beck, and even the captain of
the *Hollandia* petitioned the council to release Garstman. Irritated by this
challenge to their authority, the Recife councilors rejected this demand the
following day. On 17 May, Majors Bajart and Piston again visited the council, urging them to take the Rabe murder case out of the civilian Court of
Justice and transfer it to a military court under the pretense that both Rabe
and Garstman were military men. Insulted by this renewed request, the
Recife magistrates replied that Rabe had never been a soldier and that the
council had received the exclusive prerogative from the sovereign States-
General in The Hague to deal with all criminal matters in Brazil.[42]

Even after this incident, prominent military officers appealed to the
High Council for better treatment of Garstman. Although these ongoing
petitions must have greatly upset the council, the Recife magistrates were
afraid to alienate the officer corps during the continuing war with the Portuguese guerrillas. Unwilling to make a clear decision in the contentious
Rabe murder case, the council passed this task on to their successors, who
arrived in Recife sometime in early August. Significantly, soon after the new
magistrates from the Republic had replaced their predecessors, Garstman
was put ashore. The decision by the council to accommodate protesting
colonists and officers was not unusual in the Dutch colonies of the New
World. According to a recent study of the development of government in
the Dutch Americas, colonial authorities frequently surrendered to particular demands from local settlers in order to avoid the breakdown of order.[43]

In any case, after Garstman had been put ashore, the protests from his
fellow officers ceased abruptly. Apparently his associates concluded that
their demand for fair treatment of their friend was now fulfilled and that
further complaints would only worsen their relationship with the council.
The Recife magistrates now clearly wanted to resolve the Garstman case,
and in December 1646, they ordered the Court of Justice to proceed with a
trial. Although no documents from the Court of Justice have survived, we
know from correspondence between the High Council and the Heeren XIX
that the trial was held sometime in early 1647 and that Garstman was sentenced on 20 March of that year. According to Pierre Moreau, the Court of
Justice "eventually found that Garstman and De Boullan had conspired to

kill Jacob Rabe and that they later divided the loot among themselves. For this all their possessions and wages were confiscated, they were stripped of their ranks, banished from Brazil, and they were exiled to Holland as scoundrels." This punishment was quite severe for a man of Garstman's social stature. The loss of his officer's title was especially humiliating, as was the fact that he was sent back to the United Provinces as a man without any privileges. By reducing Garstman's social status the Court of Justice clearly signified that they were upset by Rabe's murder and by his endangering the WIC's strategic alliances with the Tarairius and the Tupis.[44]

Ironically, by exiling Garstman to the Republic, the Court of Justice provided Garstman with an excellent opportunity to overturn his sentence. While metropolitan authorities often transported criminal subjects to their New World colonies to marginalize them, convicted colonists who were exiled to Europe could improve their status by appealing to these same metropolitan officials. Because the WIC had received its charter from the States-General in 1621, all company institutions in overseas territories were ultimately subordinate to the States-General. As a result, soon after his arrival in the United Provinces in the summer or early fall of 1647, Garstman presented his case to the States-General, the parliament consisting of the representatives of the seven Dutch provinces. In early October 1647, the commissioners were busily discussing his case, and on 21 December, the committee reported that it would speak favorably about Garstman in a meeting with some of the members of the Heeren XIX in Amsterdam. On 10 February 1648, the committee allowed Garstman "with official letters from the High Mightinesses to go to Brazil, to seek revision of his case." Three months later, the States-General also granted Garstman a sum of money as well as official permission to travel back to Brazil. Finally, the States-General instructed the council in Recife to have the Council of Justice revisit the court case against Garstman as soon as the latter arrived in Brazil.[45]

It is difficult to know why Garstman, an ethnic German expelled from a Dutch colony for murder, was able to receive support from the States-General. However, since the committee gave Garstman merely the right to seek a revised sentence in Brazil, it is clear that the committee itself was apparently uninterested or unwilling to get too deeply involved in the complicated affair that had taken place in the frontier province of Rio Grande. Significantly, a recent study of the relationship between metropolitan center and colonial peripheries in the Dutch overseas world demonstrated that Dutch metropolitan authorities almost always instructed colonial officials

to resolve cases that were appealed. Garstman's long résumé as military officer dating back to the early 1630s possibly impressed the committee as well.
Garstman's willingness to go back to Brazil might also have played a role in
the committee's favorable decision, especially since the WIC had great difficulty recruiting enough soldiers and officers for their increasingly costly
campaigns there.[46]

The council and the Court of Justice in Recife were obviously not amused
with the decision to send Garstman back to Brazil. In a missive addressed to
the Heeren XIX dated 19 December 1648, the High Council reported that
they had recently received the States-General's directives regarding Garstman. The council recorded that, while they would comply with the instructions from the States-General, they also "were fearful that these procedures
will cause trouble for us and bring turmoil for the Court of Justice." In addition, in a letter of 10 March 1649, the council emphasized that the Court of
Justice was upset about Garstman's right to appeal his sentence, because it
damaged the reputation and authority of the judicial branch of government
in colonial Brazil. However, there was not much the council and the Court
of Justice could do, because challenging the authority of the States-General
would have been an act of extreme subordination. Garstman was apparently
successful in his appeal for a revised sentence, as the council reinstated him
to the rank of major in a regiment of the WIC army in the spring of 1649.[7]

The council's decision was likely influenced more by military considerations than by legal ones. The company army had suffered an enormous
defeat at the hands of Portuguese rebels outside Recife in February 1649,
leaving one thousand WIC soldiers and officers killed or wounded. Seriously weakened by these losses, the WIC needed experienced commanders
like Garstman to shore up the provincial defense. In August 1649, Garstman
was dispatched as commanding officer to the company stronghold in the
province of Ceará. Interestingly, Ceará was an isolated frontier region hundreds of miles from the seat of the colonial government in Recife. By sending him to Ceará, the council wanted to make sure that Garstman would not
cause further difficulties. Soon after Garstman's arrival in Ceará, the three-
year-old conflict between the combative German officer and the council
quickly ended. Garstman remained on his post as a loyal military officer
until the council surrendered all WIC possessions in Brazil to the Portuguese in January 1654. Like many colonists and soldiers, he moved to the
Caribbean in the wake of the humiliating WIC defeat in Brazil. Garstman
died of an unnamed disease in the English colony of Barbados sometime in
July 1654.[48]

Conclusion

A comparison of the ways in which the Tarairius, Dominga, and Garstman challenged the authority of the council reveals that those who worked within the colonial legal system were more successful in obtaining their goals than those who tried to seek justice according to their own rules. At the same time, the Rabe case demonstrates that all sides sought compromises because they needed each other as allies in the heavily contested borderlands of northeastern Brazil.

Because the Tarairius did not belong to the colonial order, the conflict between them and the council centered on the issue of whether Dutch colonial rules or Tarairiu laws would prevail in the Rabe case. The Tarairiu insistence on resolving the Rabe murder according to their own laws initially made a compromise with the WIC government very difficult. Although the council wanted to preserve the strategic alliance with the Tarairius, it was unwilling to transfer Garstman to their native allies, who were viewed by the Dutch as savages beyond the bounds of colonial society. Moreover, handing over Garstman to the Tarairius would have contradicted the Dutch colonial law that gave defendants the right to appeal their verdict to metropolitan officials. The council was faced with a serious diplomatic crisis that was only partially resolved by the experienced cross-cultural mediator Roelof Baro. The deteriorating relationship with the Tarairius was eventually restored after increased intertribal warfare forced the Tarairius to compromise and renew their alliance with the company.

Unlike the Tarairius, Dominga pursued justice within the Dutch colonial legal system. Dominga's status as a semicivilized Brazilian who was married to a colonist made her feel confident enough to resolve her grievances by using Dutch legal rules rather than Native traditions. Dominga's insistence upon being rewarded materially for her lost inheritance indicated that she was familiar with Dutch civil law, which gave a widow at least a portion of her deceased husband's estate. For its part, the council was relieved upon hearing of Dominga's demands because they had feared that she would persuade her Tupi kinsmen to break off the important alliance with the company.

The council's initial apprehension that Dominga might disrupt the valuable Tupi-Dutch relationship revealed the ambivalent position of the Brazilians in Dutch Brazil. While the Recife magistrates viewed the Tarairius as not belonging to colonial society, the acculturated and Christian Brazilians were partly integrated into society as cheap laborers and military allies. At the same time, the Brazilians continued to live in their own villages and maintained some of the political and jurisdictional autonomy that set them apart from colonists. Because of this inconsistent policy, Dutch colonial officials were not sure what to make of Dominga, who lived with Rabe on a farm in Rio Grande. Although all documentary evidence suggests that Dominga acted as a member of colonial society, the council dealt with her only as a member of the "Brazilian nation."

Of the three contestants, the council suffered the greatest challenge to its authority from George Garstman. This was not only a conflict that pitted a prominent colonist against colonial officials but also a contest between the colonial periphery and the metropolitan center. The Recife magistrates had hoped to resolve the Rabe murder by demoting Garstman and exiling him to the United Provinces. However, Garstman shrewdly used the right to appeal his punishment to the Heeren XIX and the States-General. On the one hand, the instruction of the sovereign States-General to let Garstman seek a revised sentence in Recife was a blow to the prestige of the High Council as well as the Court of Justice. Because the council was subordinate to the States-General, the Recife magistrates were forced to reinstate Garstman. On the other hand, in the face of the ongoing struggle against Portuguese guerrillas for control over northeastern Brazil, the council could ill afford to neglect the services of the experienced Garstman, and they subsequently reappointed him as an officer.

While the High Council claimed to rule the Dutch colony in northeastern Brazil, the challenges from the Tarairius, Dominga, and Garstman dramatically demonstrated that people within and without the colonial order continuously contested this assertion. The Rabe case thus revealed that colonial governments in the New World needed to make compromises with both the colonists and the colonized if they wanted to maintain their prerogative of power.

Chapter 7

Forging Cultures of Resistance on Two Colonial Frontiers: Northwestern Mexico and Eastern Bolivia

Cynthia Radding

The present comparative study examines ethnicity and culture as historical processes in two colonial frontier provinces on the contested borders of the Portuguese and Spanish American empires. This view of colonial space and power questions conventional equivalences between territory and ethnic identity by arguing that commonly used ethnic labels are colonial constructs, hardened into racial categories invoked to enforce social control. Yet, these same categories are reworked into historical identities with cultural significance for the peoples living under the shadow of empire. Ethnicity establishes lines of commonality and affiliation as well as boundaries of difference and exclusion; both meanings of inclusion and exclusion are expressed through territorial claims, linguistic patterns, and societal norms.[1]

To speak of forging cultures of resistance underscores both the stratagems that indigenous peoples developed for assertive action in political settings of asymmetrical power relations and the identities they assumed through historical experience. Native communities congregated in the missions that became formative institutions in the two frontier settings of this study took on political and territorial status as ethnic polities that the Spaniards called *naciones*. Cultural practices of ethnic identity emerged as Indian peoples shaped and tested the Spanish legal formula of *república de indios* through internal governance in the missions and external representation.[2] Their cultures of resistance, forged intermittently and unevenly, limited the exercise of power by provincial authorities that were distant geographically and politically from the centers of viceregal authority in Mesoamerica and the Andean highlands.

Ethnic polities did not stand alone in juxtaposition to the colonial state. Rather, their histories were entwined with the development of colonial societies on the frontiers of empire. These frontier societies represented partial transplants of Iberian cultural and political norms placed in ecological and cultural settings that contrasted strikingly with their metropolitan points of reference. As communities-in-formation, both indigenous and European settlements generated by the colonial order were marked by repeated conflicts over material resources and cultural identity. Ethnic differences in these colonial societies were magnified in importance, as they served increasingly as the defining schema for maintaining social distance and hierarchy among "Indians," "Spaniards," and "*Negros*"—enslaved persons or freed slaves of African descent.

Native peoples, who moved in and out of these colonial spheres, understood ethnicity in a variety of ways. Ethnic labels and linguistic differences that were recognized by colonial officials often referred to band or lineage affiliation. It is probable, however, that these terms of difference signified social distinctions between chiefs and commoners and gendered dialects that distinguished forms of proper address for men and women.[3] Their diverse meanings originated in precontact times and underwent significant alterations under colonialism. The fusion of separate languages in the missions, whose speakers constituted fragmented minorities due to the impact of postconquest epidemics and migrations, produced several dominant languages with written vocabularies and doctrinal catechisms. Thus, in the Sonoran Province of northwestern Mexico, different dialects named in the early Jesuit accounts—for example, Nebome, Heve, Tegüima, Eudeve, Akimel, Hiached, and Tohono O'odham—became simplified as Opata, Pima, and Pápago under colonial rule.[4]

On the tropical frontier of eastern Bolivia, the colonial label of Chiquitos was applied to the entire province extending eastward from Santa Cruz to the Pantanal, bounded by Moxos in the north and the Chaco Boreal in the south, but numerous ethnic identities persisted in the written records of missionaries and provincial governors. The *naciones* of Chiquitanos, Ayoreos, and Guarayos—so recognized by the Spaniards as ethnic identities—further subdivided into numerous dialectical and ethnic groups; for example, Manazicas, Manapecas, Paiconecas, Paunacas, Mococas, Morotocas, Zamucos, Covarecas, Piñocas, and Guarañocas, among many others. It is probable that what the missionaries heard and transcribed as ethnic categories changed according to the status of the speaker and the circumstances of the encounter, since these names are repeated across different missions but applied inconsistently over time.[5] Native peoples attached importance to these markers of identity but may have used them differently as indicators of alliance or hostility according to their histories of interethnic warfare and colonial contacts.

Indigenous peoples developed new ethnic and social identities to deal with the colonial experience, adopting the language of Spanish colonizers to distinguish between Christians, those who were baptized and initiated into Catholic liturgical practices, and *gentiles*, those who lived beyond the pale of the organized mission or visited the pueblos from time to time. This distinction of religious identity was central to the dialogue in which Indians were obliged to engage with colonial authorities, and it was their best defense against enslavement or arbitrary service under *encomienda*. For this reason the distinction between Christians and *gentiles* was internalized in the differential treatment Indians gave one another within mission villages and among mission settlements in different districts or provinces. It was related to the degrees of difference between nomadic hunter-gatherers and sedentary agriculturalists, which further distinguished mission residents from the wandering bands who visited the missions from time to time but avoided the discipline that full participation in the religious and political life of the pueblos required.[6]

Current scholarship recognizes that missions were culturally hybrid frontier communities with complex and changing ethnic mixtures that, in turn, created new traditions and markers of identity. Mission residents included, at different times, captives, nomadic migrants, and racially mixed squatters as well as the base communities for whom the missions were nominally founded and who provided their most consistent support.[7] Following this line of research, my study focuses on the following questions: Did the missions coalesce into settled communities or did they remain temporary encampments for diverse ethnic bands? Which units of allegiance were meaningful to the indigenous peoples of both regions, and how did mission residents create their own systems of status under colonial rule? And, finally, how do we interpret the historical evidence relating to the exercise of power by ethnic polities and to the limits of their autonomy under colonialism? The following discussion brings together quotidian practices of governance, seen through the indigenous councils established in the missions, narratives of identity, and episodes of conflict, viewed comparatively in the ecological and cultural settings for both provinces under study.

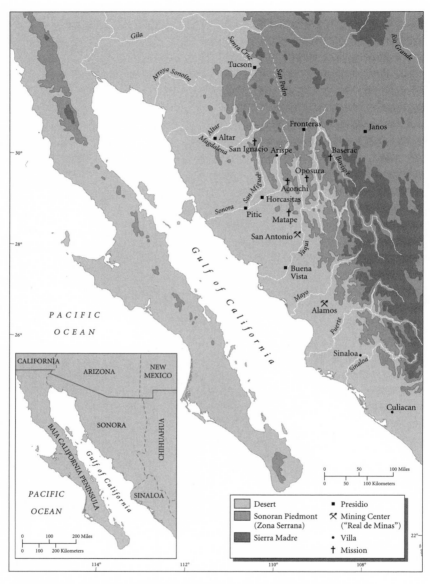

Map 7.1. Sonora: geography and major colonial settlements. Modified version of a map in Cynthia Radding, *Wandering Peoples: Colonialism, Ethnic Spaces, and Ecological Frontiers in Northwestern Mexico, 1700–1850* (Durham, N.C.: Duke University Press, 1997), 23.

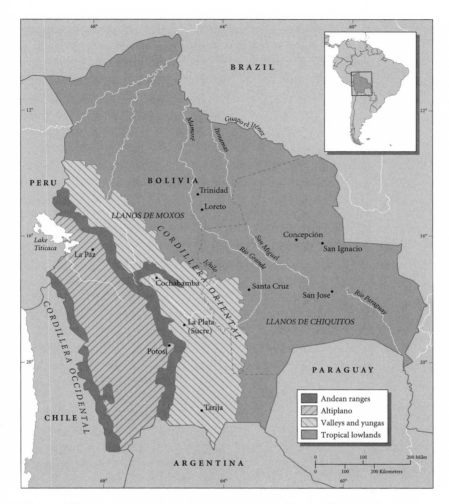

Map 7.2. Chiquitos: geography and major colonial settlements. Version of a map in Herbert S. Klein, *Bolivia: The Evolution of a Multi-Ethnic Society*, 2d ed. (New York: Oxford University Press, 1992), 5.

Cultures and Ecologies of Two Colonial Frontiers

The colonial provinces of Sonora (Mexico) and Chiquitos (Bolivia) constituted cultural and imperial borderlands in two very different ecosystems. Sonoran peoples had adapted Mesoamerican farming practices, symbolized by the trilogy of maize, beans, and squash, to the arid conditions of the Sonoran Desert and the piedmont river valleys extending westward from the Sierra Madre Occidental. Their horticulture was centered on irrigated floodplain fields supplemented with ephemeral plantings in the arroyos and swidden cultivation dependent on seasonal rainfall at higher elevations.[8] In the river valleys of central Sonora, where the mission system flourished among the Opata, Eudeve, and Lower Pima villagers, Native livelihood depended on communally maintained agricultural systems. The mission regime added a number of European cultigens—principally wheat, chickpeas, vegetables, and fruits—to indigenous horticulture and brought livestock to the Sonoran ecosystem.

Chiquitos is bounded by the western Andean foothills and the tributaries of the Amazon and Pilcomayo river basins in eastern Bolivia. It comprises a series of ecological transitions that leave their imprint on the topography and vegetation, moving eastward from the highlands through plains, shallow streams, and lagunas. Plant communities in Chiquitos range from Amazonian rain forest in the north to the scrub forest of the Gran Chaco in the south. The savannas and tropical forests with distinct wet and dry seasons favored cultivation based on root or vegetative propagation. Chiquitano subsistence depended on a variety of tubers and palm fruits that were gathered and domesticated, principally yucca (manioc) and sweet potatoes as well as maize. Planting methods did not require irrigation but centered on slash-and-burn clearings of shifting plots (*chacos*, a local variant of *chacaras*), in which two to three years of cultivation were followed by a longer period of fallow. Under colonialism Chiquitano horticulture expanded to include rice and plantains, and European livestock became an important part of the native diet. Furthermore, livestock ranches (*estancias*) were significant for the missions' communal holdings. In Chiquitos, as in Sonora, Native women grew indigenous varieties of cotton and gathered different species of palm and other plant fibers for weaving and building materials. Cotton cloth became a major staple of the Chiquitano mission economy, while surplus grains (maize and wheat) supported the commercial networks of the Sonoran missions.[9]

Agrarian technologies in both regions were inseparable from the cosmologies that gave meaning to their agrarian cycles. In the Sonoran river valleys and arid plains village farmers faced the dual risks of drought and torrential flooding that could wash away floodplain soils and destroy irrigation fences and dams. Desert o'odham as well as the piedmont nations of Pimas and Opatas punctuated their annual rhythms of cultivation, harvest, hunting, and gathering with ceremonies to bring on seasonal rains, germinate the seeds, and make the desert bloom.[10] Water held special significance in the Chiquitanía as well, where the spirits or guardians of ground-level springs, forests, and chacos, known as *jichis*, received special veneration.[11] Each of these cosmographies had territorial significance and represented sources of spiritual power that linked the Sonoran and Chiquitano communities with their environments.

Seasonal migratory patterns defined the cultural systems of Sonoras and Chiquitanos. Their physical existence depended on multiple resources of game, wild plants, and cultigens and required access to different ecological niches within a widely defined territory. Equally significant, the kinship systems that supported their rationale for conjugal coupling and social divisions implied a spatial distribution of shifting communities as well as larger nucleated villages. The spatial mobility on which the Sonoran and Chiquitano peoples relied for their economic production and their social reproduction clashed repeatedly with the Spanish colonial policy of *reducción* (congregation), the concentrated settlement of mission neophytes in fixed settlements through a combination of force and persuasion. Missionaries adapted their economy and discipline to the cultural and ecological imperatives of these environments by taking into account the fruits of gathering and alternating seasons of hunting and cultivation.[12]

Fragmented Communities in the Missions

Colonial missions were intended to amalgamate distinct segmentary groups, often dispersed spatially, into consolidated communities that were organized around Iberian institutions of local governance. Indigenous polities developed around the *cabildos*, or Native councils, established in each of the principal mission communities (*cabecera*, or "head villages"). Elected male officers, distinguished by titles and canes of office, resolved internal disputes, organized the recruitment of Indian labor, and represented the community to colonial authorities—most visibly in the defense of communal lands, cattle herds, and the fruits of the Indians' labor. Missionaries governed through the councils, in a form of indirect rule, and their presence was indispensable to implement religious observance and work discipline.

The chronology and spatial distribution of the Jesuit *reducciones* differed significantly in Sonora and Chiquitos, notwithstanding their common objectives. In northwestern New Spain, the Jesuit mission enterprise covered nearly two centuries (1591–1767), parallel to the mining frontier that moved northward from Zacatecas and Durango to Chihuahua and Sonora. While the missionaries concentrated the populations of scattered *rancherías* into fixed pueblos, missions tended to follow precontact settlement patterns by building these larger settlements in existing villages. During the first century of evangelization the Jesuits maintained the only consistent line of authority over the Indian communities. After 1732, however, the provinces west of the Sierra Madre Occidental were placed in a new governorship, creating a separate hierarchy of civilian governors that intersected with indigenous polities.

Jesuit missions developed over three-quarters of a century, from 1691 to 1767 in Chiquitos, where indigenous communities were threatened by forced servitude from Spanish *encomenderos* settled in Santa Cruz de la Sierra and from Portuguese and *mameluco* slave hunters based in Mato Grosso (Brazil). By the mid-eighteenth century, after numerous exploratory expeditions (*entradas*) to bring different bands into the missions, the Jesuits had established seven stable compounds, a number that would reach ten by 1767, comprising between one thousand and three thousand resident Indians. These concentrated settlements, laid out on a grid pattern, contrasted dramatically with the forest encampments of Chiquitano peoples. Jesuit administration was forceably terminated in both regions by the royal order of expulsion of 1767. Formal civil government began in the Chiquitanía only after the expulsion of the Jesuits, when the province was transformed into a governorship and the missions were placed under the authority of the bishop of Santa Cruz.[13] The different rhythms of the evangelizing project in Sonora and Chiquitos, and their linkages to the wider colonial order, influenced the political cultures that developed historically in each of these provinces.

Cultures of resistance took root in the interstices between colonial policy and indigenous practices. Forged in conflict, they became evident in overt episodes of defiance, as we shall see below, and in the ethnic identities that evolved under colonialism and formed part of the imperial lexicon. Indian peoples who deserted or strayed from the mission compounds were a perennial concern of colonial officials, attested to frequently in their correspondence. In Sonora, for example, the Sibubapas appear as a distinct ethnic group at the mid-eighteenth century: these were different bands of Pima speakers who had left the missions and lived largely by vagabondage, hunting, and raiding.[14] In the internal frontier areas of South America surrounding the Chiquitos mission province, the Guaycurúans were known as hunter-gatherer bands of the semiarid Chaco and the riverine plains that bordered on the Guaraní missions of Paraguay. Different chiefs and their followers, subdivided into numerous linguistic groups, negotiated their settlement in mission towns scattered among the Spanish centers of Santa Fé, Corrientes, Concepción, and Asunción. In the Chiquitanía, however, Guaycurúans were feared as raiders of the mission pueblos and they, in turn, fled before Chiquitos warriors.[15]

Chiquitos

Internal governance in the missions of Chiquitos developed in two contrasting but overlapping phases of Jesuit evangelization, during the periods of 1691–1730 and 1730–67. During the first phase, as reported by Fathers Julian Knogler and Juan Patricio Fernández, Jesuit efforts were expended in the search for new converts through repeated *entradas* that brought different bands speaking distinct languages into the villages. The mission at this time was less a settled compound than an itinerant foray into the forests, a "spiritual hunt" that resembled indigenous practices of hunting, warfare, and taking captives. Missionaries depended on groups of Christianized Indians to accompany them for up to four months at a time to locate and surround the encampments of forest peoples. Some of the expeditions were successful, bringing new groups of extended families into the missions, but often these Christians-on-trial returned to the forest.[16] The mission enterprise was contingent on their persistent migratory patterns and on the persuasive powers of the caciques, indigenous leaders of the many diverse bands that came to reside in the Chiquitos missions.

The figure of the cacique was ubiquitous among the Chiquitano and Chaco peoples, but it represented different degrees and modes of authority. Father Fernández reported that among the Manazicas, a nation of twenty-two *rancherías* whose combined territory formed a "pyramid" through the forests and savannas north of Mission San Xavier, political leadership comprised a hierarchy of "capitanes" under the command of a "principal cacique." Fernández described the relationship between the cacique and the common people as one of vassallage; the former authorized hunting and fishing expeditions and received a portion of the prey and of the cultivated harvests. Women rendered obedience to the cacique's first wife, and public ceremonies and feasts occasioned by visits among the *rancherías* marked the ascendancy of Manazica nobles.[17]

The caciques' authority among the western and southern Chiquitano peoples was less structured and more contingent on the course of events than Fernández described for the Manazica nation. Father Knogler, who served briefly in San Xavier and principally in the western mission of Santa Ana, interpreted the cacique's political role in relative terms. "The Chiquitos, more than other nations, respect persons of advanced age and position. Although there are no social classes among them, each band [*nación*] has a cacique, an accomplished person with particular prestige. Their language expresses this, since caciques are called 'fully men [men properly speaking]': *ma onycica atonie.*"[18] Caciques were equally important among the Guaycurúan bands of the Chaco, but the endurance of their authority depended on the consensus of their followers and on their skill to make war and peace and to deal with missionaries and Spanish colonists.[19]

Caciques provided the foundation for governance within the missions, from the initial phase of *entradas* to the maintenance of law and order in the settled reductions. Knogler reported, further, that missionaries enhanced the prestige of the caciques by giving them special ceremonial clothing, an elevated seat in the church, and a cane of office that they carried in all public processions. The caciques accomplished the missionaries' goals through their power to command their subjects to attend mass and religious instruction and to perform daily tasks in the mission. To the extent that caciques personified the ethnic polity of their separate bands, their elevated position in the missions defined the structure of the colonial Indian *cabildo*. Large hierarchical Native councils were a central feature of the mature phase of the ten missions of Chiquitos, although the Jesuits never ceased using the strategy of forest *entradas* to populate and maintain them. The formal structures of Native councils were not instituted at one time but developed gradually as the missions reached a stable population of different resident bands. Missionaries relied on *cabildo* officers to enforce discipline and to support the increasingly complex and voluminous production of surplus goods for trade with the Andean colonial cities and mining centers. The caciques, for their part, reasserted their authority over their separate bands through the councils and the visible signs of their investiture.

In both of these frontier provinces, the obligations incumbent on all mission Indians to attend catechism and liturgical ceremonies as well as to perform communal labor were enforced by moral suasion and the threat of physical punishment by whipping or confinement to the stocks. Punishment was carried out by indigenous officers under orders from the missionary or from the governors and magistrates. Abuses of physical punishment, often the source of bitter complaints, are recorded for both Sonora and Chiquitos, although they seem to have been more tenacious in the Chiquitanía, especially under the clerical regime following the expulsion of the Jesuits (1767). Fear and resentment of physical punishment punctuated Indians' written protests, providing a recurring theme in their acts of resistance and open rebellion.[20]

The *cabildo* institutionalized Native polities in the missions. Collaboration between missionaries and Indian officers, at times carefully orchestrated, was not merely theatrical staging. Pueblo governors and alcaldes were empowered by the missionaries' dependence on them to assign daily tasks in mission fields and workshops and to assure attendance at mass and catechism. More directly, and just as visibly, indigenous officers who held keys to the pueblos' granaries and warehouses played a central role in the distribution of food, clothing, and tools among families resident in the missions. Furthermore, the hierarchy of *cabildo* offices established a ranked order of privileges that defined concrete benefits in the form of additional rations of food and gifts, honored places to sit and stand in religious services, and access to the priests' quarters in the convents or *colegios* that comprised the architectural center of the missions.

The association between Native councils and distinct ethnic groups living in the missions is more marked for the Chiquitanía of eastern Bolivia than it is for Sonora. Periodic censuses taken of the Chiquitos pueblos under Jesuit and clerical administration identify numerous *parcialidades*, linguistic and kin affiliations that were distinguished spatially in separate residential sections. This term appears in Spanish imperial documentation throughout the Americas to refer to subunits with distinct residential and ethnic identities that either comprised larger communities or were brought together by colonial policy to form consolidated settlements. The strength and proliferation of ethnic identities through the *parcialidades* may well represent a cultural response of indigenous peoples to the fiscal and social pressures of the colonial regime.[21] It is important to distinguish between the category as used by Spanish officials to designate a tribute-paying unit or a residential area and the changing indigenous meanings of *parcialidad* to define (or contest) reciprocal relations of mutual support, alliance, or rivalry.

Tribal names recorded in Spanish documentation to distinguish among ethnic bands appeared as added surnames in mission censuses, reflecting the kin-based social and political organization of the Chiquitano peoples. Their *cabildos* were structured to accommodate representation for each of these *parcialidades* by the caciques, who acted as intermediaries between their kinfolk and the ecclesiastical and civil authorities of the missions. Jesuits and the clerical priests who followed them after 1768 recognized different *parcialidades* by name in their reports on the organizational structure of the missions. They reappear as markers of identity, but not always with the same names, in testimonial documents referring to specific grievances or uprisings that occurred in the pueblos. It is probable that some of the ethnic groups so named emerged during the colonial order and that social cleavages, both inside and outside of the missions, did not correspond neatly to band designations.[22] The dual patterns of congregation and migration that brought different linguistic and kin groups into the pueblos at different times contributed to a process of changing cultural identities and political affiliations.

In summary, the Chiquitos missions were subdivided segmentally into *parcialidades* with linguistic and ethnic connotations. These were not fixed categories but rather historical identities that emerged, split, and recombined over time. The *parcialidades* were not ranked in a consistent hierarchy, but some of them commanded greater presence demographically and politically than others; for example, the Manazica of San Xavier. The *cabildo* merged with the *parcialidades*, creating a representative structure for the caciques of different ethnic lineages, which, in turn, were distinguished spatially in each of the mission towns. Male *cabildo* members comprised a political elite that exercised disciplinary, ceremonial, and redistributive functions visible to the entire community.[23]

Sonora

Smaller and more numerous than those of Chiquitos, the missions of northwestern Mexico were not as fragmented internally as the Chiquitos pueblos nor did their administrators apply the terminology of *parcialidades* to their inhabitants. Nevertheless, Sonoran missions combined families from different *rancherías* and dialectic groups, chiefly among the distinct bands of riverine and desert-dwelling Piman speakers. Social and ethnic inequalities were expressed in the ascendancy of certain *naciones* over others and in the primacy of head villages (*cabeceras*) over smaller settlements called *visitas* in each of the mission districts. In central Sonora the Opatas and Eudeves, village agriculturalists who held the best agrarian lands in the piedmont, provided the nuclear population of the missions and exercised dominion over more nomadic groups that entered and left the pueblos, notably the Jobas of the sierra and the Tohono O'odham of the desert plains.[24] These core populations coalesced into ethnic polities through their control of mission *cabildos* and their representation of the communities to Spanish officialdom and colonial society.

Aspiring Native leaders in Sonora had two principal avenues to elite status: *cabildo* offices in the missions and military rankings in the auxiliary troops that assumed a significant role in frontier defense. The Spanish presidial system expanded during the eighteenth century to contain the northern Mexican provinces in the face of widespread raiding by Athapaskan peoples (Apaches) from the Sierra Madre and by Hokan-speaking nomads (Seris, or *Cuncáac*) from the Sonoran Desert coast. Frontier defenses depended on companies of indigenous soldiers who were salaried and organized under the command of their own captains. Furthermore, the General Commandancy of the Internal Provinces, established in 1779, created a new hierarchy to which indigenous captains appealed for prestige and gifts to redistribute to their warriors. Opata soldiers, in particular, were recruited for numerous punitive expeditions against Apache bands, traveling considerable distances from their home villages to Chihuahua and New Mexico. Three companies of Opata and Pima soldiers manned presidial garrisons at Bavispe, Bacoachi, and San Ignacio.[25] As we shall see below, these two means of social and political ascendancy generated conflicts. The presence of mission and presidio, however, was central to the history of interethnic relations in the hybrid society of colonial Sonora.

Conflict, Confrontation, and Negotiation on Two Colonial Frontiers

Indigenous *cabildo* officers and captains asserted their autonomy by leaving the confines of the mission to address their petitions and demands to provincial governors and military commanders. The following episodes illustrate concentric circles of conflict through which cultural expressions of resistance erupted into collective action involving indigenous councils and war captains in confrontation with ecclesiastical and imperial authorities in Sonora and Chiquitos. In both provinces tensions heightened due to the commercial networks that engaged the missions, escalating demands for

Indian labor, increased non-Indian settlement, and the eroding land base of the communities. Testimonials elicited by investigations into local conflicts provide evidence of different expressions of ethnic identity and modes of political action.

Sonora

Community formation was closely linked to control over arable land in the province's semiarid environment, and political tensions increased as new social and economic conditions circumscribed indigenous communities. Spanish and mixed-race colonists grew in number and, with their expanding herds of livestock, encroached on mission lands. Individual entitlements were formalized through the legal processes of *composición* and *denuncia*, leaving a documentary trail of land claims and measurements from the seventeenth century onward. In 1790, following the secularization of missions in central Sonora, colonial authorities began surveying communal lands in the heartland of Opata and Eudeve pueblos, ostensibly to assign individual plots of land to indigenous peasant families. Although aggressive privatization of village lands did not occur until the early republican era, in the 1830s, the mixture of private and communal holdings among both Indians and non-Indians in the arable valleys of the Sonoran piedmont complicated the identity of the ethnic polity—the *común*—that had been so closely tied to the land and to the mission community.[26]

Tensions erupted in a local tumult in the summer of 1790, in the Opata pueblo of Bacerác, a mission head village that shared fertile land and stream flow for irrigation with the presidio of Bavispe, established four leagues downstream only nine years earlier with a company of Opata troops.[27] On 9 July 1790, a crowd of Opatas had gathered in one of the mission fields where the wheat harvest was in progress. In the presence of the Spanish magistrate, *juez comisario* Juan Ignacio Gil Samaniego; the commanding officer of the presidio of Bavispe; the Opata village governor, Josef Antonio Mascorta; the Opata captain-general; and the Opata troop leader of Bavispe, they witnessed the attempted punishment by whipping of one their commoners accused of refusing to work and, furthermore, of offending the village governor. As the whipping began, captain-general Ignacio Noperi demanded to know, "What crime has this man committed for him to be punished so?" He then turned to the crowd, raised his cane of office, and called out: "My people, what are you waiting for? Why do you not free this man?

In the name of the king, let him go!" Two Opata soldiers rushed forward and untied the victim, Atanasio Zorrilla, as both the Spanish authorities and the Opata village governor beat a hasty retreat.

The investigation carried out a month later revealed that rivalries had been simmering for several years among the different ranks of Opata civilian and military officials, exacerbated by resentment over the intrusion of Spanish authorities into what the Indians considered to be an internal dispute. Yet, this was not a simple conflict across Spanish-Indian ethnic boundaries. Trouble began in the local community when Zorrilla threatened the governor and *alguacil* (constable) of Bacerác, refusing to follow their orders, and governor Mascorta appealed to *juez comisario* Gil Samaniego to discipline the unruly commoner through the mediation of his missionary, Fray George Loreto. When captain-general Noperi halted the punishment, he preempted the right to speak in the name of the king in full view of Opata and Spanish civil and military authorities. Prior to the events of 9 July, Noperi had humiliated Governor Mascorta and his predecesor in public meetings of the Bacerác community and taken over the office of *juez de agua*, in charge of distributing irrigation water, traditionally reserved for village councils. Following the confrontation in the wheat field, Gil Samaniego lodged an appeal with his superior *teniente de alcalde mayor* Gregorio Ortiz Cortés,[28] and Noperi rode to the provincial capital of Arizpe to lay his case directly before the intendant-governor, Enrique de Grimarest.

Indigenous officeholding was split between village councils and military captains-general even as the colonial order was visibly divided between ecclesiastical and secular arms. The fragmentary application of power compromised the Indians' defense of village autonomy and augmented political tensions at a time when private Spanish settlement was increasing and mission lands were threatened with secularization and partition. Within the indigenous world, exemplified in this case by the Opata community of Bacerác, *cabildo* offices and military rankings were increasingly concentrated in a network of extended families, not unlike the Creole propertied elite that held civil magistracies and militia titles. Captain-General Ygnacio Noperi had received the title from his elder kinsmen Gerónimo Noperi and Juan Manuel Varela; all three were natives of Bacerác.[29] Factionalism divided the Sonoran Native *común* along segmentary ethnic lines but, more visibly, along the cleavages of different colonial columns of authority. These same divisions operated in Chiquitos, but the hostilities they occasioned manifested themselves in different ways.

Chiquitos

Numerous local conflicts demanded the attention of clerics and civil authorities in eastern Bolivia, especially during the period following the expulsion
of the Jesuits. These brief but violent uprisings highlighted the separate
ethnic identities that converged in the Chiquitos pueblos during the late
colonial and early republican periods. Even at the height of the missions'
economic development, concomitant with the consolidation of their *cabildos*,
conflict simmered in this frontier province. The following case, occurring
in the same year as the tumult of Bacerác in Sonora, illustrates recurring
themes that emerge from documented uprisings, often pitting different bands
of Chiquitanos against their missionaries or the lay administrators that
oversaw the economic life of the missions. As in northwestern New Spain,
native *cabildo* officers addressed their complaints to both ecclesiastical and
civil authorities, moving from petition to open rebellion.

The council judges of San Ignacio led an armed uprising, aroused by in-
flammatory cross-accusations between the governor of the province, Antonio Carvajal, and local priests to gain control over the economic life of the
missions. The tumult began on the Eve of Corpus Christi, 5 June 1790, leaving at least five dead and a number of wounded Spanish soldiers and civilians. Indian rebels were armed with bows, arrows, and clubs (*macanas*). News
of the uprising spread to the pueblos of San Miguel, San Rafael, and Santa
Ana in the west and to San José, the principal mission of southern Chiquitos. Rebellious council judges refused to obey Governor Carvajal's order to
appear before him in Santa Ana, and they confiscated the entire store of
mission products and trade goods in the pueblo. Rumors of further uprisings circulated in the neighboring missions, where it was believed that over
two thousand Indians were armed with bows and arrows.[30]

Information about the tumult comes from Manuel Roxas, the priest of
San José mission, and the testimony given by Gregorio Barbosa, a soldier
stationed in San José. Roxas's alarmist report, despite its accusatory tone,
substantiates the Indians' fear of a more repressive work regime and their
sense of entitlement to the wealth in kind that was produced by their own
labor. Native council members (*jueces*) were alarmed when they were told
that Governor Carvajal had brought lieutenants (*tenientes*) to oversee production in the pueblos. News of the uprising in San Ignacio reached San
José at least by 19 June when Barbosa recalled that while "lying in his ham-
mock" he heard two Indians who had returned to the pueblo from working
in the cattle *estancia* say that Manuel Roxas had threatened the council

judges, saying, "Work, work harder, because the *tenientes* are coming, who will whip you to death. The *tenientes* will not hear confession nor give Mass, because only we Fathers celebrate the Mass and we are Christs on earth. What do you want governors or lieutenants for?" Then, according to Barbosa, the council judges repeated: "We do not want regulators [*reglares*], governors, soldiers, or lieutenants, for we grew up with the Fathers." Barbosa also referred to a letter the Indians had brought to Felix Ydalgo, the garrison commander stationed in San José.[31]

Father Manuel Roxas gave greater detail about the uprising in an angry letter he directed to Ydalgo, blaming the uprising on Governor Carvajal. Peppered with explicatives and swear words, Roxas's epistle provides names of the dead and wounded and references to the movement of people and rumors from one pueblo to another, revealing his intimate knowledge of the province. Roxas was born in San Miguel, the son of an artisan who had worked and lived in the Chiquitanía, producing religious imagery for the missions under the direction of the Jesuits.[32] He grew up speaking both Chiquitano and Spanish, having served as interpreter for previous governors, and was distinguished among other clerics for his ability to preach to the Indians in their language. From his letter as well as Barbosa's testimony we learn that Governor Carvajal had further angered the Indians of San José by taking away the *alférez's* (Indian constable's) cane of office, because he suspected that the *alférez* had threatened to kill him and the lieutenants. Gregorio Barbosa clarified, however, that the *alférez* had been stripped of his title because he and the Indians sent to open a road had slaughtered and eaten eight yearlings without completing the job.

The San Ignacio uprising of 1790 combined different layers of meaning with economic, political, and religious implications. It began at the beginning of the winter dry season in a year when drought was severe and it was reported that mission cattle were dying. Faced with these losses and frightened by rumors (perhaps unfounded) that lay lieutenants would be placed in the pueblos to make them work under the bite of the lash, council members of San Ignacio seized the goods from the storehouse and launched an attack on Spaniards whom they considered to be their enemies. Violence erupted on the eve of one of the most solemn feast days in the Catholic calendar; Corpus Christi. The priests' lives were spared, so it was said, because the priests "made the Mass for them, they were Christs on earth." The uprising involved all the *parcialidades* in the pueblo, and rumors of further rebellion spread to neighboring missions, even if fearful witnesses may have exaggerated the number of armed rebels. Manuel Roxas warned Ydalgo ominously that the small garrison stationed in the frontier was no match for over one thousand armed Indians (*indios de flecha*) in San Ignacio alone and perhaps an equal number of warriors in San Miguel. It occurred at a time when increasing numbers of lay civilians and soldiers lived in the pueblos or passed through on extended visits, often assuming positions of authority and, thus, posing a threat to the Native community.

Gender, ritual, and divided powers

It is evident that the formal hierarchies of ranked offices associated with the mission councils and military service in both of these frontier regions were masculine. The political functions ascribed to the caciques merged with their traditional standing as respected elders to elevate male leadership in the missions. Attendance at Christian indoctrination and liturgical ceremonies was organized by gender and age, separating men, women, and children. Behind the formal edifice of political offices, however, women contributed in fundamental ways to economic subsistence, cultural production, and public life in the missions.

Women's work in agriculture, food processing, gathering, and cloth production sustained both the households of indigenous peasants and the surpluses that, in turn, supported mission commerce. Women and children, as well as men, performed seasonal tasks in the agrarian cycle of both Sonoran irrigated *milpas* and Chiquitano *chacos*, including planting, guarding the fields from birds and insects, and harvesting the crops. Women processed grains, seeds, fruits, and stalks from planted and gathered plants, preparing food for storage and consumption. Moreover, women's central role in the production of commodities as spinners and weavers of cotton cloth, one of the principal export products of the Chiquitos missions, enhanced their importance in the pueblos even as it increased their workload.[33] Women's role in the mission economy heightened their interest in trade goods, as is seen in the kinds of merchandise routinely imported into the reductions of Chiquitos and Sonora: scissors, needles, beads, religious medallions, cloth, and ribbons produced in colonial *obrajes* of central New Spain and the Andean highlands.

Women's sexuality figured as one of the motives for conflicts that arose in the pueblos, even if women rarely comprised the leadership of rebel bands.[34] Indigenous women of Sonora and Chiquitos do not seem to have flung themselves at European men with the same alacrity that Marshall

Sahlins claims for Hawaiian women and Ramón Gutiérrez attributes to the Puebloan women of New Mexico.[35] Nevertheless, women did exercise a degree of choice in their sexual and marital partners, occasioned in part by their physical mobility between villages and *rancherías*. Late eighteenth-century census data for Sonora suggests that Opata women took Spanish or mestizo spouses. Their conjugal choices had consequences for changing ethnic identities and claims to community resources when their status changed from Indian to *vecino* ("white"): these mixed marriages either moved women out of the traditional *común* or brought new members into it, further complicating the historical production of culture.[36]

Women contributed to the ceremonial life and social bonds of their communities in important ways, as producers of fermented corn drinks: *chicha* in lowland Bolivia and *tesgüino* in northwestern Mexico. *Tesgüino* and *chicha*, in their respective domains, served as libations to enliven a good party, but they signified much more in the indigenous societies of these two frontiers. Fermented brews supplied the necessary ingredient for social conviviality even as the rituals observed for their production and consumption became conduits to spiritual power. Notwithstanding the missionaries' energetic efforts to curtail the use of *tesgüino* and *chicha* and the drunkenness that ensued in village fiestas, they remained a centerpiece of Sonoran and Chiquitano cultural practices. In Chiquitos caciques were expected to provide hospitality to visiting bands or rancherías, who would later reciprocate in kind. A good cacique served abundant food and drink and, thus, needed a wife who knew how to make good *chicha*.[37] Similarly, Sonoran fiestas accompanied with copious amounts of corn brew, often linked to the Catholic calendar, brought together extended families from different *rancherías*. The investiture of new cabildo officers or the initiation of the annual cycle of holy feast days provided the occasion for dancing and drinking ceremonies that occurred parallel to the liturgical rites intoned by the missionaries.[38]

Men and women who drank fermented brews were touched by the spiritual energies that flowed through them, thus helping to maintain the cosmic order and assuring good harvests and abundant hunting and fishing. Shamanism, only partially hidden under the mission regime, constituted an alternative source of power to Catholicism and the political culture of the missions. Female shamans were known in both regions, although men more often exercised this role. Shamanism manifested itself, above all, as esoteric knowledge derived from the environment, in association with sacred places such as caves (Sonora) and water sources guarded by *jichis* (Chiquitanía)

—knowledge that was used for healing (beneficent) or for witchcraft (evil). Preconquest Chiquitano practices, according to Jesuit Fernández, blamed the occurrence of illness on particular women, who were killed or driven from the community.[39] Jesuit missionaries and the clerics who followed them readily identified shamans as their rivals and were quick to condemn them as servants or handmaidens of the devil. Chronicles and histories from both regions reveal that however much missionaries dismissed the "barbarity" of Native sorcerers, they feared their powers and, conversely, that indigenous peoples viewed the missions, their rites, and the material innovations they brought as alternative sources of shamanic protection, especially when their traditional healers proved impotent before the onslaught of Old World diseases. Sonorans and Chiquitanos added crosses, rosaries, and religious medallions to their arsenal of talismans even as they turned to missionaries as intercessors ("Christs on earth"), but not to the exclusion of shamans whose songs and paraphernalia conserved linkages to other sources of power.[40]

Conclusion: Frontiers of Identity and Resistance

Archival testimonies about these and other conflicts provide windows onto a contextual interpretation of the political culture, ethnic identities, and ecological rhythms that framed the historical experience of indigenous peoples in the colonial missions of Ibero-American frontiers. The officers of mission councils, with their titles and canes of office, were a creation of the colonial regime; nevertheless, they assumed oppositional stances and galvanized the defense or appropriation of what they considered to be communal spaces and collective means of survival. Furthermore, they disputed colonial spheres of authority, as illustrated by Opata Captain-General Noperi's assertion of his right to speak in the name of the king or the letter directed by the Chiquitano *cabildo* of San Ignacio to the commander of the frontier garrison.

Let us return to the dual themes of ethnic identity and cultural resistance. Did the missions coalesce into settled communities or remain loose associations of ethnic bands? What were the units of allegiance and systems of ranking that were meaningful to the indigenous peoples of both regions? How do we interpret the historical evidence relating to Native communities in the missions and the colonial societies that grew up around them? The nations that peopled frontier missions created intercultural spaces that changed and developed over time, articulated with the colonial regime.[41] Their autonomy was undeniably constrained by imperial domination, but their cultural modes of material production, governance, negotiation, and defiance established markers of identity and bonds of reciprocity between indigenous elites and commoners *and* between Native communities and colonial overlords.

Native pueblos reconstituted within colonial missions over several generations coalesced into enduring ethnic polities identified as the core of mission residents who asserted their rights to the assets and their status in the political and ceremonial life of the missions. The separate ethnic identities present in the missions were a source of social divisions but also of power—albeit mediated—that placed limits on the colonial project of social control and territorial expansion. Hierarchical rankings of status and differentiation closely associated with the mission *cabildos* and, in Sonora, with service in presidial auxiliary troops created an elite corps of indigenous officers that intersected with the *parcialidades* (Chiquitos) and *rancherías* (Sonora) congregated in the pueblos. Indians living in these colonial settings faced multiple and, at times, conflicting claims on their allegiance. Chiquitanos bonded within their *parcialidades*, preserving distinctions of language and kinship among themselves, but mounted political movements that galvanized whole pueblos and spread beyond the confines of the mission in which they originated. Opata village governors and captains-general vied for ascendancy between the military and civilian spheres of authority in Sonora. Titles and canes of office that symbolized the power to command labor and to redistribute trade goods became insignia of privilege for indigenous societies among whom wealth in property was not the defining marker of social inequality.[42]

The mixed messages of resistance recorded for Sonora and Chiquitos are embedded in the cultural landscapes and political economies of both provinces and inseparable from the commercial circuits that linked mission communities to the wider colonial societies of New Spain and Alto Perú. Processes of racial *mestizaje* and social commingling had advanced more significantly in Sonora than in Chiquitos, due to the spatial proximity of missions, mines, and presidios in northwestern Mexico. In both provinces, however, mission pueblos were not closed corporate communities, but rather societies undergoing change through migration, demographic mixture, and new sources of wealth and exchange. The presence of Afro-Brazilians, Spanish/Creole priests and administrators, and mixed-race soldiers, artisans, and travelers complicated social and political relations in the Chiquitano missions, even if the majority of commoners were "Indians" of different *parcialidades*.

The particular identities designated by the rubric of *naciones* or *parcialidades* were preconquest in origin but exhibited important mutations by dual processes of merging and fragmentation under colonial rule. Some of the identities recorded as ethnic or tribal designations in colonial documentation signified differences of status or gender: captives brought into the missions constituted a kind of servant class named as such and served as both receivers and brokers of culture change.[43] In both provinces, although more notably in Chiquitos, missionaries recruited neophytes by leading forays (*entradas*) into *rancherías* or encampments to bring new contingents of non-Christian Indians into the pueblos. Thus, Piman speakers of different dialectical groups populated the northernmost missions of Sonora and, in Chiquitos, numerous bands settled in the pueblos at different times. Jesuit Julián Knogler reported that the children of new arrivals to the missions were distributed among baptized families to learn the common language, Chiquitano, and to become accustomed to the work regime in the pueblos.[44]

Sonoran and Chiquitano peoples traversed multiple frontiers, occupying within the life cycle of individuals and multigenerational families distinct ecological and cultural spaces of forest, desert, and mission towns. Shamanism intersected with Catholic ritual, even as the production and exchange of commodities served different purposes in the colonial and indigenous notions of economy. The institutionalization of the colonial mission did not separate these frontier provinces into Spanish and indigenous worlds. Rather, it created cultural nodes of confluence and dispersion through the uneven exercise of power that created unexpected cleavages and points of resistance.

Chapter 8
Sorcery and Sovereignty: Senecas, Citizens, and the Contest for Power and Authority on the Frontiers of the Early American Republic

Matthew Dennis

"In the beginning," John Locke wrote in 1690, "all the world was America." Yet even as these words were published, much of North America was no longer "America," if what Locke meant was a pure, pristine, untransformed state of nature. Permanent English settlement was nearly a century old, other Europeans had colonized the Americas even earlier, and Native people had lived on—and shaped—the continent for thousands of years. If America was a "New World" it was because colonization transformed it into something as novel to Indians and Africans as it was to Europeans. Thus, as the Americas were unsettled and settled, unmade and remade in this period, conflict over the nature and sphere of order made these continents a contested terrain of daunting complexity.

If the historical actors we study have sought to impose and maintain order in their worlds, historians too require order in their narratives about such worlds, and they employ common discourses to present comprehensible stories about their subjects. Among the conventional assumptions I challenge here is that European (and white American) discourses of law and authority uniformly operated as the dominant cultural authorities in early America, even in the postcolonial United States. Until recently, when scholars studying borderlands and transnational phenomena have attracted broader attention, the story of the nation in particular has been so mythically powerful that its status as a narrative has been largely invisible. The rise of nationalism is important, and the early national period in the United States was characterized by efforts to define and construct a nation, but national feeling and practice were complicated and diverse. The simplistic story and the aura of inevitability regarding the growth of the nation require disruption.[1]

The United States was a new political space, but it accommodated or inadvertently embraced other social, cultural, and economic arenas, which were subnational, transnational, or extranational. The country was, in some respects, a three-ring circus, except that its performative spaces were overlapping or concentric. This was surely the case in western New York State, where the Seneca-Iroquois domain was surrounded and penetrated by New York and the United States, as well as an expanding Protestant Benevolent Empire, while Iroquoia itself was fragmented and dispersed across an international borderland.

In the fifty years following the American Revolution, various Americans sought to possess or repossess this landscape in distinctive ways, in accordance with their different world views, circumstances, and interests, and grounded in the use—or potential use—of violence. The Seneca Indians occupied and maintained a tenuous sovereignty in reserved lands enveloped by the territory and polities of the State of New York and the United States. Here was an *imperium in imperio* predicament within the new federal system that posed unanticipated challenges and sometimes opportunities. In this arena, Americans worked through the implications of federalism, territorial expansion, and the economic development unleashed by the Revolution. The Senecas, a constituent member of the formerly powerful Six Nations of the Iroquois, now found themselves in an unprecedented and dangerous state of dependency, with little choice but to accommodate (while yet attempting to resist) the new forms of colonialism they faced. Their challenge was to find an effective means to conserve, or reinvent, a distinct Seneca ethnic and cultural identity, and preserve their lands, in the interstices of a dominant and expanding white, Christian American economy and society.

The conventional story of the clash between Indians and whites, who faced each other across shifting cultural and legal frontiers, must be complicated further. Senecas, like other Native peoples in the new republic, confronted not only white rivals but each other. This internal contest forces historians to move beyond a simple focus on Indian-white conflict; we must also examine the struggles *within* Native communities groping to find the best means to respond and adjust, and thus survive, in a rapidly changing world. These battles, which can only be sketched below, pitted various leaders, their villages, clans and lineages, against each other. They featured conflicting ideas, programs, and prophecies designed to embrace, reject, or refashion Seneca tradition or white innovations in varying degrees. Sometimes these struggles resembled a battle of the sexes, or a contest to transform the gender order of Seneca society. Seneca political contenders sought authority for their diagnoses and prescriptions sometimes in tradition, sometimes in a desperate pragmatism, sometimes in both. The very nature and sphere of social order was contested in this part of the early modern Americas, then, as Indians such as the Senecas sought to remake themselves to survive while they quarreled with each other over the best means to be and to remain Senecas.

The United States of America, formed in 1776, successfully maintained with military victory over Great Britain, and reorganized into a new federal system in 1787, ranks among the more significant new world orders that emerged in the Americas following Columbus's first voyage. Senecas and New York found the War for Independence and revolutionary settlement transformative. Each sought to create its own new world order in postcolonial America. In a sense, Carl Becker's old question about the Revolution remains current—was it about home rule or who should rule at home? We must answer "yes" to both parts of this query, of course: like the United States, both New York State and the Senecas sought a certain autonomy—if not complete "home rule"—in the early republic; and in every sphere the contest continued over who should rule in those expanding or shrinking homelands, and on what basis.

In the spring of 1821, as this complicated political ecosystem was still in flux, a "murder" occurred, disturbing whatever balance had emerged among these overlapping worlds. A Seneca chief commonly known as Tommy Jemmy slit the throat of a Seneca woman named Kauquatau. A Seneca tribunal had convicted Kauquatau as a witch after, it was alleged, she had killed another through her maleficium. What was the meaning of such an act? Who was allowed to decide? Was it homicide? Or was this violence authorized and thus legitimate? To what extent did authority—over this case and the world in which it occurred—depend on power and violence? A close examination of this episode illustrates the ambiguities of sovereignty, authority, law, and violence on the frontiers of the early American republic. Following discrete sketches of the new orders established by the Senecas, the United States, and New York, I will confront the curious, convoluted, but instructive case of State v. Tommy Jemmy. Its twists and turns suggest that federalism was an even more complex and ambiguous system than we might imagine, and that peoples such as the Senecas, though subordinate and dependent, sometimes found a measure of autonomy and authority by manipulating both the gaps and the overlaps in jurisdictions and authority within the nation's "more perfect union," among its states and particularly between its general and state governments.

The State of the Senecas

Although Iroquois loyalists had not been defeated on the battlefield, and though they continued to assert their independence, they were ignored and subsumed in the peace negotiated between Great Britain and the United States. The 1783 Treaty of Paris made no provision for protecting Iroquois property; indeed, it transferred all of the lands as far west as the Mississippi River to the new republic. The divided Iroquois, deserted by their ally, unless they chose resettlement in British Canada, were forced into a series of capitulations, which began with the Treaty of Fort Stanwix in 1784.[2]

The war had a horrible effect on the Six Nations of the Iroquois. Before the Revolution, life had not been without its struggles, as Iroquois communities survived only through creative diplomacy with European and provincial authorities and with other affiliated and sometimes hostile Native groups. Yet survive they did, in some thirty villages spread along an arc from the Mohawk River to Lake Erie and the Ohio country. By the spring of 1780, only two of these towns survived undamaged. The rest lay in ashes or had been abandoned, their former residents dead or dispersed into makeshift refugee camps where they struggled against the cold, hunger, scurvy, and dysentery, contemplating their future. The demographic crisis that began with the Revolution had reduced the Iroquois population by about half by 1797. The systematic destruction of their homeland—their houses burned, their orchards chopped down, their livestock or game slaughtered, their stores of corn, squash, beans, and tobacco and their standing fields of cereal and vegetable crops put to the torch—proved devastating. Pestilence soon joined death, homelessness, and famine among the Iroquois. Besides dysentery, epidemics of measles and small pox plagued them. By 1794, no more than four thousand Iroquois remained of the already diminished population of eight thousand to ten thousand People of the Longhouse alive in the 1760s.[3]

The immediate post-Revolutionary period thus found the remaining Iroquois huddled in a few small reservations, the residual properties they somehow managed to hold, in a state of disorganization and demoralization. The Senecas were arrayed in western New York primarily in villages at

Buffalo Creek, near Buffalo, at Tonawanda and Tuscarora Reservations just to the north, at Cattaraugus Reservation, to the south and touching Lake Erie, and at Allegany Reservation farther south, just to the north of the Pennsylvania line and strung along the Allegheny River. By 1838, even these homelands would be greatly reduced with the loss of Buffalo Creek and some tiny reserves along the Genesee River.[4]

In places like Cornplanter's Town, adjacent to the Allegany Reservation, Senecas resourcefully combined old ways with innovations in order to survive and forestall their complete demise. Change had always been a part of Seneca life, but now there was a particular urgency to their improvisation on tradition. In 1798, the first contingent of Quaker missionaries, or technical advisers, showed up at Allegany. The Cornplanter Senecas welcomed them and appeared open to their program of technological acculturation, which the Quakers saw simply as "civilization." Unlike other denominations to whom the United States's assimilationist program was being sublet, the Society of Friends could make a convincing case that it had no ulterior motives, would not proselytize or teach "peculiar doctrines," and did not seek economic gain, particularly through the alienation of Indian land. Their purpose, articulated generally through the newly established "Indian Committee" of the Philadelphia Yearly Meeting, was simply to introduce among the Indians "the most necessary arts of civil life" and "useful practices: to instruct the Indians in husbandry & the plain mechanical arts & manufactures directly connected with it." Among the most important, if inadvertent, gifts that Quakers bestowed upon the Senecas was the insulation they provided against other, more aggressive missionaries. While Quakers monopolized the Seneca missionary field, others were held at bay, allowing the Indians critical space to regroup and reform their society and culture.[5]

Though comparatively benign in its soft-peddling of Christian theology and religious practice, the Quaker mission did hope to transform Seneca society.[6] The Indians welcomed some technological innovations and creatively integrated new ideas and technologies into older patterns of life. Few indulged the illusion that no accommodation was necessary for their continued survival, yet bitter differences arose among the Senecas about the proper course for accommodation with the ever-encroaching white world.[7]

Permeating the history of Seneca negotiation of their colonial predicament in postcolonial America was the *Gaiwiio*, the "good word," or Code of Handsome Lake, which emerged in the apocalyptic visions of the Seneca prophet, beginning in 1799, and mediated the experience and accommodation of Seneca and other Iroquois people. Much of the success as well as the failure of Quaker "civilization," and later American Protestant Christianization and assimilation efforts, can be explained in terms of the conjunction of these Native and alien schemes. In both cooperation and conflict with outside forces, Seneca "modernization" occurred in a culturally specific way, shaped significantly by the "new religion" that became "the Old Way of Handsome Lake."

On 15 June 1799, a dissolute Seneca man, a hereditary chief, Handsome Lake took to bed in the cabin of his daughter, sick and broken. On that same day, in a state of depression, bitterness, and suspicion, he apparently passed away. But within an hour or two he revived to relate a fabulous vision, which Quaker visitors recorded and Seneca oral tradition continues to recite.[8] Another trance occurred on 8 August, and they would continue until the prophet's death in 1815. From these visions and prophecies, Handsome Lake offered his people a new social and moral code. They were instructed to avoid drunkenness, stinginess, quarreling, materialism; to honor their fathers; to remain vigilant against witches and the devil; to abandon love magic; and to "quit all kinds of frolicking and danceing except the worship dance." The prophet proposed a revised Iroquois theology and a reformed means of living in the world that blended tradition with Christian and white American ideas and practices.[9]

Handsome Lake's revelations are striking in their reworking of Iroquois gender arrangements, particularly their attempt to remake Iroquois families into patriarchal units, and in their apparent feminization of Iroquois demonology. The prophet emphasized female transgression, which the emerging code revised and elaborated. The specter of whiskey afflicted men and women alike, but witchcraft (increasingly feminized), use of charms, and abortion were *women's* offenses.[10] Such female personification in Handsome Lake's often grim visions heaped inordinate blame on women for the Senecas' fate, and the prophet's witch hunts seemed to focus special attention on an internal, often female enemy. Simultaneously, Handsome Lake's message functioned to elevate the social and political position of middle-aged men— patriarchs. Nonetheless, though Handsome Lake monopolized great amounts of power and sometimes used it to silence or defeat his political enemies locally, including high-status women who controlled kinship networks and farmland, women remained active in public affairs, even if such activity was not always obvious to outsiders. The relative failure of missionary attempts to impose exclusively male agriculture, individual (male) ownership of land, and noncommunal work patterns, the result of both male and female resistance, left women with significant reserves of power, even if somewhat diminished, and retained for them arenas outside the home. Women thus refused to shrink in the face of the "civilization" efforts either of Friends and other white missionaries or of the nativist reforms of Handsome Lake and his followers. Seneca revitalization would be negotiated, indeed even feminized.[11]

Handsome Lake's prophetic career began in an atmosphere of dread and foreboding over witchery, which gripped Cornplanter's Town in June 1799, just days before his first vision. And the prophet's ascendance was punctuated with witch hunts and executions. Treatment of these violent episodes, and their particular demonization of women, reveals these afflictions as another manifestation of the violence and disorder that troubled the post-Revolutionary Seneca world.[12] Traditionally, Iroquois men and women could, and did, embody *Agotkon, utgon,* or *otkon,* the evil power or force that witches personified, as they mobilized *orenda,* or power, for evil rather than benevolent purposes to injure others, even their own kin. As witches, they inspired near universal fear among the Senecas and other Iroquoians. Those suspected of such maleficence were hated and avoided.[13] But in a society where men and women repressed their aggression, witchcraft offered a secret, wicked means to assault antagonists, to indulge one's hatreds, rivalries, and jealousies. Such was the danger of witchcraft that the Iroquois, like the Puritans, would not "suffer a witch to live." They sanctioned the execution of witches, as quickly as the act could be carried out, and they exempted witch-killing from the rules of kin-based revenge and atonement. A witch discovered among one's own lineage or clan, after all, could be more dangerous than one operating from afar—he or she could tear the heart out of one's family.[14]

With the meteoric rise of Handsome Lake to prominence among the Allegany Senecas, witch hunting flourished. The Quaker missionary Halliday Jackson later observed that Handsome Lake "succeeded in propagating a belief among the natives, that most of their bodily afflictions and disorders arose from witchcraft, and undertook to point out the individuals who had the power of inflicting these evils."[15] The promiscuity of Handsome Lake's accusations clearly troubled some residents of the Seneca communities, both Native and white. After the execution of one "witch" at Cold Springs in about 1808, Handsome Lake's half-brother Cornplanter expressed his hope that "we shall be careful in the future how we take the lives of any for witchcraft without being sure that they are Guilty, and he thought it very difficult to prove it." Quakers residing nearby at Tunesassah later remarked with relief, "Since the subject of witchcraft was treated by the Committee who was here last fall, the Indians have concluded in council to take no more lives on that account."[16]

The Code of Handsome Lake, if not Handsome Lake himself, eventually came to reject the execution of witches, and opposition to apparent excesses—especially when prominent men were accused—forced the prophet to moderate his indictments and even to leave his residence at Cold Spring for Tonawanda. But discouraging witch hunting was hardly a rejection of the proposition that witches in fact existed, and although the purges subsided, witch hunting would not cease altogether. To their horror and embarrassment, New Yorkers would learn as much in 1821 when they confronted the sensational case of Tommy Jemmy. For Handsome Lake's followers, the prophet's witch hunts themselves, as well as continuing troubles in their world, seemed to confirm the persistence of witchcraft.

Seneca people continued to hunt witches and to follow Handsome Lake generally because they found his message compelling. It offered a means to accommodate both change and considerable stress while maintaining Seneca ethnic identity and protecting some measure of their autonomy. Handsome Lake managed to conserve Seneca tradition, for example, by advocating collective ownership of agricultural production, supporting Seneca practices of reciprocity and sharing, and rejecting production for the market (which, in any case, hardly existed for the remote Allegany Senecas). According to the Quaker Halliday Jackson, the prophet advised "that they might farm a little bit . . . but must not sell anything they raised on their land, but give it away one to another, and especially to their old people; and, in short, enjoy all things in common." Handsome Lake's reforms could be as averse to Christianity as they were to capitalism. He vociferously advocated continued observance of selectively revised ancient ceremonies, and the prophet supported older residence patterns that allowed such ritual life to continue. Such living arrangements, which drew Quaker criticism, may have been perceived by some women as supportive of their efforts to maintain female networks. Finally, tacit or explicit support of Handsome Lake might have been a means for the harassed Seneca people to construct a united front against white encroachment and dispossession. Solidarity with the prophet, an articulate opponent of Seneca land sales, may well have signified greater commitment, among both men and women, to his externally focused nativism than to his internally focused revivalism. Such was the hybrid new world order—based on tradition, custom, law, innovation, and some violence—that emerged fitfully among the Senecas of western New York.[17]

The United States

As historian John M. Murrin has brilliantly explained, the American Revolution was hardly "the logical culmination of a broadening and deepening sense of separate national identity emerging among settlers of North America." Nationalism and union itself were the belated products, not the cause, of American independence. Citizens "erected their constitutional roof before they put up the national walls." Meanwhile, the precise architecture of American government remained unclear as Americans worked out the meaning of federalism. Sovereignty might reside ultimately in "the people," but what did that mean in practice in a place such as western New York, in which jurisdictions overlapped—where lands could be, simultaneously, the domain of the United States, New York State, and the Seneca Nation? Despite the aura of inevitability in America's national myth and the sense that the nation had sprung fully born from the throes of the American Revolution, the early chapters of the country's story were complicated by the ambiguity in the relationship among national, state, and tribal governments. Vigorous policies by the central government exposed tensions in the union, not merely between general and state governments, but among diverse Americans divided regionally, ethnically, religiously, economically, and politically. Among the most vigorous and controversial federal policies were those related to Indian tribes, recognized as legal entities in the United States Constitution, to the chagrin of states such as Georgia and New York.[18]

If the 1783 Treaty of Paris settled the international conflict between Great Britain and the United States, it left much unsettled on the new nation's western frontiers. Without consulting its native allies, the Crown had ceded Indian lands south of the Canadian border to the United States. In 1784, the American states began the process of consolidating their western gains at Fort Stanwix in New York, where they initiated a treaty with the Six Nations of the Iroquois. Internal divisions in the early national period weakened the Iroquois, but as historian J. David Lehman has argued, "white factionalism" proved even more threatening to their interests. At Fort Stanwix, the Six Nations faced not merely the representatives of Congress but officials from New York and Pennsylvania as well. A series of confusing meetings discussed peace, the return of prisoners, and land. Jockeying for supremacy, the congressional delegation managed to have New York State representatives physically removed from the treaty site and to impose a major land cession on the Iroquois delegation. (New York would not stay away for long.) In the

Fort Stanwix Treaty, the Six Nations surrendered their claims to all territory outside of New York State and west of Buffalo Creek. Finally, in a separate transaction, Pennsylvania purchased lands claimed by the Iroquois within that state's boundaries.[19]

The humiliating Treaty of Fort Stanwix, while requiring substantial land cessions in the Erie triangle and the Ohio country, had at least confirmed the Iroquois's "peaceful possession" of their New York territory. But the new citizens and speculators of the American republic considered such title transitory. Immediately, agents representing Pennsylvania, New York, and Massachusetts initiated efforts to acquire Indian lands by sale or lease, through means questionable or downright fraudulent. The confusion of interstate competition for Seneca lands was compounded by the efforts of private land companies, which procured "preemptive rights" to buy land (technically, only when and if Indians chose to sell) or which sought to circumvent state or federal prohibitions on the private purchase of Indian land by fashioning clever leasing arrangements.

Meanwhile, the national government asserted its role in Indian affairs through diplomatic missions and actions of the new War Department (which assumed control of Indian affairs when it was established in 1789), as well as through trade and intercourse legislation designed to pacify the volatile frontier. Building on powers outlined in the Constitution, in 1790 Congress passed "an act to regulate trade and intercourse with the Indians tribes," which declared that "no sale of lands made by any Indian . . . shall be valid to any person or persons, or to any state, whether having the right of preemption to such lands or not, unless the same shall be made and duly executed at some public treaty, held under the authority of the United States."[20]

Seneca leaders themselves hoped to use the power of the United States to protect their interests and became frequent visitors to the seat of national government in the decade following the Treaty of Fort Stanwix, which they believed unfairly deprived them of land rightfully theirs. In a meeting at Philadelphia late in 1790, Cornplanter recounted the dizzying course of land dealings with private and state agents and declared to President Washington, "We would bear this confusion no longer . . . [We] lift up our voice that you might hear us, and to claim that security in the possession of our lands, which your commissioners so solemnly promised us." Cornplanter and other Seneca leaders sought a personal relationship with Washington, whose heroic stature and authority as chief executive of the general government made him a uniquely capable patron, one who might realistically curtail the mischief of white officials and private citizens bent on obtaining control of

Seneca land. Comparing themselves to an abandoned child, the Seneca leaders told Washington (whom they addressed as "Father"), "Our nation has looked round for a father, but they found none that would own them for children, until you now tell us that your courts are open to us as to your own people." Cornplanter challenged Washington to achieve a higher moral authority, beyond mere power. "You could crush us to nothing," he said, "and you demanded from us a great country, as the price of that peace which you offered us; as if our want of strength had destroyed our rights." Although neither had Seneca strength increased nor United States power declined since 1784, Cornplanter asked, "Were the terms dictated to us by your commissioners reasonable and just?" Washington told the Senecas that the evils connected with their loss of land "arose before the present Government of the United States was established." Now, he assured the Senecas, the case is "entirely altered. The general Government, only, has the power to treat with the Indian nations, and any treaty formed, and held without its authority, will not be binding." Washington refused to put aside the terms established at Fort Stanwix, but he promised "security for the remainder of your lands. No State, nor person, can purchase your lands, unless at some public treaty, held under the authority of the United States. The General Government will never consent to your being defrauded, but it will protect you in all your just rights."[21]

The 1794 Treaty of Canandaigua between the Six Nations and the U. S. government seemed to affirm both Washington's authority and his benevolence. The accord was a substantial success for the Iroquois, as it recognized existing reservations, ensured real peace, and in fact restored land taken from the Six Nations a decade earlier. It delineated Seneca holdings and promised that "the United States will never claim the same, nor disturb the Seneca nation, . . . in the free use and enjoyment thereof; but it shall remain theirs, until they choose to sell the same to the people of the United States, who have a right to purchase." In the Canandaigua Treaty, the Senecas seemed to have won federal affirmation of their sovereignty and federal protection against acquisitive and duplicitous land companies.[22] Nonetheless, despite the statements of President Washington, federal diplomacy, and congressional legislation, the Six Nations, and the Senecas specifically, continued to face a confusing mix of private, state, and federal jurisdictional claims and competing schemes, and they continued to endure assaults on their Native new world order and suffer erosion of their lands.

The new federal order remained ambiguous and contested, both in its delineation of authority and in its use of sanctions to enforce its mandates.

While George Washington claimed institutional authority as the nation's chief executive (as president), Senecas granted him an authority that was personal, as their champion and patron. They acknowledged his power—his ability to marshal troops and inflict violence—but they cultivated his benevolence and encouraged his sense of responsibility to them as a father. The Senecas, though weakened, retained some military resources, but they calculated that greater benefits might accrue through deference than through violence. In practice, it was unclear what sort of patron Washington, or the national government he momentarily headed, would be for the Senecas and other tribes. If the United States won the deference of Indians at least in part through threats of force, how (and how successfully) did the national government assert its supremacy over the states and their citizens? Would the United States enforce the law contained in treaties and congressional legislation when to do so entailed taking the Senecas' (or other Indians') side? To what extent did the new federal order of the United States depend on the use of violence, not merely against the Indians, but against white antagonists? The answers to these questions emerged uneasily in federal cases involving the Senecas in the 1821 and the Cherokees in the 1830s.

New York State

New York earned the nickname the Empire State for good reason.[23] Its citizens embraced an imperial objective that dramatically transformed the state in the fifty years after the American Revolution, culminating in 1825 in the opening of the Erie Canal from Buffalo to Albany, a gateway of trade connecting the Great West, New York City, and the Atlantic world. The effects of territorial expansion, white settlement, and economic development on the Six Nations little concerned white New Yorkers. Even before the end of the War for Independence, they coveted the rich lands of Iroquoia, and New York State's representatives and officials pressed their own claims of sovereignty and authority against those of the United States in an effort to acquire them.

New York rushed to assert its dominion over the landscape invaded and destroyed by General John Sullivan in 1779. New Yorker John Jay, then serving in Congress, wrote Governor George Clinton, "Would it not be proper for New York to establish Posts in that Country, and in every respect treat it as their own. In my opinion, our State has had too much Forbearance about these matters." In 1783 the state legislature sought to expropriate

Iroquois lands to compensate New York soldiers for their military service. Though the plan was challenged by Congress, New York continued to avow its sovereignty within its own borders and to frustrate the general government's conduct of Indian affairs, as it did at Fort Stanwix. Meanwhile, even those serving the state and national governments in official capacities—Philip Schuyler and his land speculator brother, Peter, for example—sought to circumvent not only federal laws but New York State stipulations as well, contained in the 1777 state constitution, that land negotiations be conducted only with the authority and consent of the legislature.[24]

Quickly following the federal Fort Stanwix Treaty, the New York State Legislature moved to promote "settlement of the waste and unappropriated lands" within the state, even arranging to advertise and distribute such lands *before* New York had gained title. And efforts by citizens and officials of New York to dispossess the Iroquois continued throughout the 1780s and 1790s, in violation of the United States Constitution and federal law. By the time the Six Nations accepted the Canandaigua Treaty in 1794, Oneida-Iroquois lands in central New York had been reduced from some five or six million acres to one-quarter of a million acres, for example, and the state illegally acquired more than one hundred thousand acres more within a few months following (and in violation of) the agreement. Ironically, the Oneidas had sided with the Americans in the Revolution and placed their trust in "friends" like Philip Schuyler. With friends like this, the Oneidas' brethren, the Senecas, were prudent to choose other patrons.[25]

The phenomenal growth of the white population in the central and then western parts of New York State increasingly enveloped the Six Nations and threatened to push them into oblivion, or at least to a trans-Mississippi reservation (in the case of the Oneidas, that meant Wisconsin). Most whites —whether nationalist or state-focused—assumed that the Iroquois would disappear as their land holdings dissolved, not only through legal, illegal, or extralegal acquisition, but also through the encroachment that undermined Native people's subsistence. New York thus planted the "roots of dependency" among the Iroquois, according to a logic well expressed by Philip Schuyler, who saw the remnants of the Six Nations in New York as "no obstacle to our future": "for as our settlements approach their country, they must from the scarcity of game, which that approach will induce to, retire further back, and dispose of their lands."[26]

This territorial aggrandizement was extralegal at best. On a national scale, President Thomas Jefferson outlined the approach in a letter to William Henry Harrison in 1803. Although Jefferson had hoped to "live in perpetual peace with the Indians," he also sought to lure them away from their traditional lives. Only after "we draw them to agriculture, to spinning and weaving," Jefferson noted, "will they give up some of their land." "We shall push," he continued "our trading houses, and be glad to see the good and influential individuals among them run in debt, because we observe that when these debts get beyond what the individual can pay, they become willing to lop them off by a cession of lands." Thus, Jefferson hoped either to incorporate the now displaced Indians as citizens or to "remove [them] beyond the Mississippi."[27]

Given this Vanishing Indian theory and program, few whites contemplated or sought to accommodate a perpetual Native presence—an undigested sovereign mass—within New York or any other American state. The later crisis in Georgia and the Removal of the Cherokees and other southeastern tribes in the 1830s were simply the culmination of these three-cornered conflicts over sovereignty. Yet New York was forced to confront the persistence of the Senecas in western New York, who maintained a land base, a tenuous sovereignty, and their own social order.

New York's presumption that its law was paramount within its borders, that it exercised sovereignty over Indian people residing within the state, met a challenge in the Stiff-Armed George case. Here we see the confrontation of state and tribal authority, in which the Senecas deployed the ambiguity of federalism to their advantage, playing the general government against the state, forcing New York to assert its dominion not merely over the Indians but also against the new seat of national government, Washington, D.C.

In 1802, a Seneca man named Stiff-Armed George was accused of assaulting and murdering a white man, John Hewitt, in an incident that occurred near Buffalo on 25 July. In two August addresses to the governor of New York in Albany, the Seneca orator and leader Red Jacket protested the arrest; he argued that Indians and whites were held to unequal standards, and, more important, Indians were not answerable to New York state law but only to that of the United States. "Did we ever make a treaty with the state of New-York, and agree to conform to its laws?" he asked. "No. We are independent of that state of New-York . . . We will never consent that the government of this state shall try our brother. We appeal to the government of the United States."[28]

Although Stiff-Armed George was convicted in state court on 23 February 1803, jurors in the case surprisingly petitioned the state for a pardon, despite their finding of guilt. They recognized the existence of extenuating circumstances—including a general pattern of "wanton and unprovoked attacks" inflicted on Senecas near Buffalo, as well as the particular assaults against Stiff-Armed George, which provoked his actions. Even earlier, Secretary of War Henry Dearborn wrote to New York governor George Clinton recommending such a pardon should the defendant be convicted. The governor indeed complied with these requests and pardoned Stiff-Armed George.[29]

Technically, Stiff-Armed George's conviction signaled a failure for Seneca assertions of independence (or, rather, their qualified dependence—on Washington, not Albany), yet clearly in winning a pardon and asserting their sovereignty Senecas prevailed. They did so by pitting federal and state governments against each other and by appealing to some New York citizens to take the Indian side against other, less savory fellow citizens. Here Senecas managed to invoke white citizens' principles and their ideal self-image and encouraged New Yorkers to act nobly and mercifully, policing their own behavior. Following a paper victory, Clinton's pardon sought to avoid a jurisdictional confrontation and trouble, both with the Senecas and with the federal government. This turn of events reflected the residual power of the Senecas—physical as well as moral—a power that was extralegal if not technically legal. The state of New York saved face, and its citizens' act of mercy allowed them to think well of themselves. Mercy presupposes the legitimacy of the sanctions imposed and the authority imposing them; suspension of sanctions is perceived by authorities as an ennobling, magnanimous act of benevolence. Did New York State hope to win the deference of Senecas and cement its dominion through this condescension? Red Jacket and the Senecas, without acknowledging New York's supremacy, managed to save the life of Stiff-Armed George and a measure of their own autonomy. The improvised solution of the Stiff-Armed George case settled little, and the contest over order, sovereignty, and legality in New York emerged more starkly in the early 1820s in *State v. Tommy Jemmy*.

Execution of a "Witch": Legal, Illegal, or Extralegal Violence? *State v. Tommy Jemmy*

In the spring of 1821, on the outskirts of Buffalo, an unfortunate Seneca Indian "fell into a state of languishment, and died." What had caused his untimely demise? To his kin it was clear—witchcraft. As William L. Stone, the nineteenth-century historian and biographer, reported melodramatically, "[The] woman who had nursed him [the victim], and anxiously watched him at his bed-side, was fixed upon as the bedlam who, by aid of an evil spirit, had compassed his death." Kauquatau, the "witch," fled to Canada but was apprehended, "artfully inveigled" back to the American side of the Niagara, tried by the local Seneca council, and sentenced to death. Without further delay, the "sorceress" was dispatched at Buffalo Creek by a chief named Sonongise, commonly known as Tommy Jemmy, who cut her throat after another executioner had botched his bloody commission. Although the "crime" involved no citizens of New York and was committed on the Buffalo Creek Reservation, the state indicted Tommy Jemmy for murder.[30]

Accounts vary regarding what happened next. According to one witness, following Tommy Jemmy's arrest, a group of angry, armed Seneca men led by Red Jacket gathered in Buffalo to protest his incarceration. Though whites feared violence, a crisis was averted after Captain Pollard, another Seneca chief and rival of Red Jacket, persuaded the Indians to disperse. But according to another witness, this confrontation never occurred. Authorities did encounter trouble finding someone willing to serve the warrant on Tommy Jemmy, but eventually one Pascal Pratt, who was friendly with the Senecas and spoke their language, agreed to take on the task. Peacefully served, Tommy Jemmy, accompanied by Red Jacket and a large contingent of Seneca men and women, turned himself in the following day. Both versions of the story suggest that, despite the commitment of the white citizens of Buffalo to extend their jurisdiction to internal Seneca matters, they nonetheless felt a sense of trepidation, intimidated by Seneca power and the potential (real or imagined) for Seneca violence. That is, they were forced to accommodate, or at least contemplate, the relationship between legal and extralegal proceedings in their world.[31]

Tommy Jemmy, his lawyer, John C. Spencer, and Red Jacket did not dispute the fact of the execution but argued that it had been performed in Seneca jurisdiction (independent of the state of New York, as defined by treaty and federal law), according to Seneca legal codes. It was thus a legal, not an illegal, act. It did not constitute murder at all but was, rather, a legitimate use of violence, sanctioned by Seneca law. "What have our [Seneca] brothers done more than the rulers of your people have done? And what crime has this man committed, by executing, in a summary way, the laws of his country, and the command of the Great Spirit?" Red Jacket asked. As the trial proceeded the puzzled white jury in Buffalo seemed convinced that the Senecas were in fact an independent people and that their own state courts lacked jurisdiction. The judge therefore referred the case to the New York Supreme Court, where it was argued in August 1821. That trial produced a wide-ranging examination of the laws, treaties, documents, and public history of the Indians from the time of discovery, and, after mature consideration, the court decided to offer no judgment. It preferred not to recognize the independent jurisdiction of Indians on reservation land within New York, yet it was unable to deny the Senecas at least a qualified sovereignty. In addition, the court seemed persuaded that the case was not one of "murder," exactly, at least as the Indians "understood it," yet it remained reluctant to sanction the act. In the end, the justices threw up their hands and, with the consent of the attorney general, released the prisoner.[32]

Governor De Witt Clinton then proposed a legislative remedy, and in April 1822 the New York Assembly passed a law specifically asserting state criminal jurisdiction over Indian tribes within state boundaries while explicitly pardoning the less-than-convicted Tommy Jemmy. This solution reflected the ironies and ambiguities embedded in the case. The state of New York seemed, implicitly, to recognize Seneca sovereignty at the same time it attempted to extinguish that sovereignty through legislation. In doing so, the state unwittingly endorsed (or at least undermined its own moral condemnation of) the Seneca act—the execution of a "witch"—which it defined as "barbaric." The series of trials and proceedings seemed to acknowledge that on Seneca reservations the rule of law—a jurisprudence more ancient than that of New York State—held sway. New York's efforts to bring "order" to this world, therefore, was hardly its own autochthonous ordering of chaos but a reordering, one based on the destruction of a pre-existing (Seneca) order with its own claims to legitimacy. While trying to ignore the fact, New York State prescribed the substitution of one jurisdiction and its laws for another, and it did so not merely at the expense of Seneca sovereignty but in competition with the national government. The state acted energetically to close a door it wanted to believe had never been open. Of course, to assert authority is not necessarily to possess it.

What was the actual meaning of the state's legislation, and did it resolve the ambiguities of jurisdiction and dissolve the region into a single social order? Did New York State law in fact apply among Indians on reservations contained within New York, diminishing Seneca and other Indian sovereignty? In retrospect, it is clear that the state had overstepped its bounds. Initially, however, a Georgia case seemed to affirm New York's stance. There in 1830 the Cherokee man George Corn Tassel was arrested and tried in a state court for a crime he allegedly committed in Cherokee Nation territory against another Indian named Sanders. Corn Tassel was found guilty and sentenced to hang. An appeal in the Georgia superior court upheld the decision, declaring that state sovereignty demanded that states have full criminal and civil jurisdiction over Indian tribes within their boundaries. The decision explicitly noted New York's 1822 legislation asserting its claims of criminal jurisdiction over Indians, which Senecas protested and rejected but which faced no federal remonstrance. William Wirt, the former United States Attorney General, quickly appealed the Georgia state decision to the United States Supreme Court, which then ordered the state to appear before it in January 1831. But Georgia convened a special session of its legislature on 22 December and acted in defiance of the Supreme Court, ordering Corn Tassel's execution to proceed. It did, on 24 December, literally killing the case and Corn Tassel himself.

Three days later, Wirt initiated another, more famous proceeding against the state, *Cherokee Nation v. Georgia*, filing it directly in the United States Supreme Court as a lawsuit involving a foreign nation and a state. The Marshall Court ultimately held that the Cherokees were not a foreign nation and therefore the Court lacked jurisdiction, an apparent victory for Georgia (and New York). But in a dictum, Marshall defined the Cherokees and other tribes as "domestic dependent nations" whose relationship with the federal government "resembles that of a ward and a guardian." This decision, along with another in *Worcester v. Georgia* in 1832 that went against the state, found the Cherokees (and by implication other Indian nations) to be distinct communities, occupying their own territory, with primary responsibility for their own affairs. If they were subordinate to the federal government, such nations were *not* subsidiary to state government; they were outside of their control altogether.[33]

Yet the dénouement of these cases is as instructive as the violent end of Corn Tassel—"legally" murdered by Georgia in defiance of the Supreme Court —with important implications for our understanding of the contested new national order in western New York State. Georgia, attempting to destroy Cherokee sovereignty and expropriate Native land, had prohibited the presence of missionaries on Cherokee territory, except when licensed by state officials. The Reverend Samuel Worcester and others refused to obtain such a permit and went to jail, offering the grounds for Wirt's test case. Yet after the missionary's (and the Cherokees') legal victory, Georgia refused to release him, and President Andrew Jackson declined to enforce the Supreme Court's order, which had reversed and annulled Worcester's conviction. Worcester remained in prison for a year and a half before accepting a deal requiring him to abandon the Cherokees and pledge allegiance to the state of Georgia in exchange for his release and pardon by the governor of Georgia.[34] Such was the victory for Cherokee sovereignty, and such was the performance of the federal government's trusteeship of an American Indian people, most of whom were subsequently removed from Georgia via the infamous Trail of Tears.[35]

Conclusion

What does this conflict tell us about the dominance and cultural authority of "the law" in the early national United States? And how does it affect our understanding of the role of legal violence (prospective, withheld, or actually executed force), as well as of extralegal means to impose particular schemes of order on the early American landscape?

On the one hand, in 1822 Tommy Jemmy and the Senecas won. The Seneca defendant escaped conviction, and his people established the sovereignty of their reservations, encircled though they were by the state of New York. Federal law and the Senecas' own residual, though greatly diminished, power proved significant, while the subsequent New York legislative act declaring state jurisdiction over civil and criminal matters on Indian reservations within the state proved legally empty, or at least unconstitutional, as the *Cherokee* and *Worcester* cases demonstrated in the following decade.

On the other hand, in 1822 the Senecas lost. Extralegal—or even illegal—forces proved more powerful than federal law in places such as New York and Georgia. In a sense, these incidents supported the adage "might makes right." States believed that civil and criminal jurisdiction followed sovereignty over land, and they imagined themselves to possess such sovereignty. It did not matter, apparently, that in New York the Six Nations had not been conquered, nor had Senecas divested themselves of their remaining territory and the authority to govern themselves within their homelands. Nonetheless, white citizens, speculators, and officials of the state acted as if Seneca sovereignty had been extinguished, and they worked to fulfill their prophecy of Seneca dispossession and disappearance. Such imperialism assumed an aura of legality, as the United States failed to challenge the Empire State and withheld the force it might have legitimately wielded against New York.

In an 1826 treaty, the Senecas lost their remaining lands in central New York and saw their reservations at Buffalo Creek, Tonawanda, and Cattaraugus substantially reduced in size; in all, the Seneca land base shrank by 86,887 acres. Twelve years later, the Senecas lost an additional 102,069 acres —all their remaining New York lands, except a one-mile-square reservation at Oil Spring—and were nearly removed to a trans–Mississippi reservation in Kansas. With Quaker assistance, however, the Senecas managed to restore their reservations at Allegany and Cattaraugus in the federal Supplemental Treaty of 1842, and in 1856 the Tonawanda Band of Senecas successfully purchased a remnant of their lost lands as a reservation and reestablished themselves in northwestern New York. In short, the Senecas did not disappear, thanks to their ability to manipulate white factionalism, exploit the ambiguities of American federalism and its divided sovereignty, and invoke the benevolence of patrons such as the Quakers. How did Senecas survive in this equivocal, complex legal and extralegal world? To what extent were they actually subjected to New York criminal justice, in violation of their own legal but unenforceable sovereignty? According to legal historian Sidney Harring, the majority of nineteenth-century Indian criminal cases were never reported; nationally, thousands of Indians were pulled into local courts, tried, sentenced, and sent to prison or executed. Was this true for Senecas, or were they able to circumvent in practice a legal system the state of New York believed it had legitimately established?

Separate worlds with separate orders continued to exist simultaneously in western New York, though white and Seneca power was hardly symmetrical. To merge these worlds definitively, to obliterate the Seneca presence, promised to be too costly, too violent. White New Yorkers, in any respect, could be satisfied that their dominion substantially prevailed, even if small reservations continued to dot the landscape. This dominion was achieved and maintained primarily through diplomacy, fraud, evasion, and wishful thinking, not through violence. Yet violence lurked under the surface and in people's memories, supporting the social order. The threat of force, or the public memory of violent coercion, was more important than actual military conquest. As Cornplanter reminded President Washington in 1790, at the Treaty of Fort Stanwix the United States delegates "told us that we were in your hand, and that, by closing it, you could crush us to nothing." Such strength gave white Americans the power, if not the moral authority, to dictate the terms of diplomacy.[36]

But the federal government and even New York State sought to cultivate the stability and legitimacy of their orders and proved reluctant to unleash violence. In the early nineteenth century, President Jefferson wrote about Indians in the Old Northwest (and, by implication, those further east) that "our strength and their weakness is now so visible that they must see we have only to shut our hand to crush them."[37] Yet he argued for a humanitarian approach, based on love. Given the course of Indian-white relations in the United States, we can conclude that this was a tough love indeed. Later executive complacency with regard to Indian rights—particularly Jackson's reluctance to use force against states such as Georgia—redirected violence toward Indians, as in the Trail of Tears. But white reticence and guilt—Americans' need to believe they were a generous and principled people—did create opportunities for the Senecas and other Indians to maneuver and preserve a measure of sovereignty. Under these circumstances, was Seneca order more "extralegal" than "legal"? If the "extra" in extralegal connotes "extraordinary"—that is, outside, exterior, or special—then it was extralegal in relation to the state of New York. Was New York's authority legal or extralegal? If the "extra" here means "superior," then it too was extralegal in terms of practical local power. If "extralegal" connotes semi-legal—outside the law but nonetheless regarded by many as legitimate—then here too New York's authority was extralegal, given the state's unchallenged violation of federal law in support of states' rights. If the postcolonial world of western New York is any guide, American new world orders remained clouded in ambiguity.

PART IV

Race, Citizenship, and Colonial Identity

C itizenship laws," Rogers Smith has written, "are among the most fundamental of political creations." Defining who is and is not a member of
a given political community, "they proclaim the existence of a political 'people' and designate who those persons are as a people, in ways that often
become integral to individuals' sense of personal identity as well."[1] Writing
about citizenship since the American and especially French Revolutions,
scholars have generally emphasized its universalist and liberal aspects in two
ways. First, looking at the logic of citizenship laws, they have seen European
and American citizenship "almost invariably universal, or at least potentially so," with an emphasis on the possibilities for an increasingly inclusive
polity.[2] Second, they have treated the Euro-American model of citizenship
as replicable and exportable, the core of modern nationalism throughout
the world.[3] But as Karen Sykes has pointed out, this emphasis has missed
the specific meanings that citizenship has carried in different times and
places. Even the seemingly "routine acts of citizens," she argues, can take on
unexpected meanings. Thus, debates over civic practice can both reveal and
reshape the meanings of citizenship in daily life. They can also illuminate
the unspoken assumptions that have shaped citizenship, unofficial attitudes
about who should be part of a community that often exert a powerful legal
influence. The chapters in Part IV examine conflicts between official practices of defining legal status and identity and unofficial means of defining
social status and communal rights and obligations.

Each of these authors finds a tension between metropolitan and colonial understandings of the relationship between social status and legal status, and all trace the increasing significance of race in shaping colonial
understandings of civic privileges and obligations. While Tamar Herzog finds
that Spanish and Spanish American authorities used increasingly divergent
means of defining membership in a community to achieve the same end—
an identification of "Spanishness" and citizenship, Ann Twinam sees colonial elites and Spanish officials disagreeing sharply over the meaning and
mutability of racial categories that defined civic status in Spanish America.
Provincials, Twinam argues, resisted the Council of the Indies' various efforts

to make the *gracias al sacar*—a royal decree allowing petitioners to change their race—easier to obtain. Both Herzog and Twinam emphasize the significance of community sanction in defining colonial identity: membership in a civic community, social status, and race were ultimately defined by local communities based on reputation, social ties, and actions, even in the face of royal attempts to impose control on the official processes through which civic identity was defined. Gene Ogle, meanwhile, uses a moment of public violence in which Raymond, an enslaved man, beat Jean-Baptist Huet, a white peddler, to explore the production of social status from the complicated relationship between race, honor, and violence in colonial Saint Domingue. Examining legal proceedings surrounding the incident, Ogle shows how the economy of violence that defined relations between social classes in France was transformed in a slave economy. Fearful of slave revolt, the white community in Saint Domingue defined itself, to a great extent, through its prerogative to inflict violence upon—and be exempt from violence by—the colony's black residents, free and enslaved. This prerogative, more than legal status, bound Saint Domingue's white civic community together.

These authors collectively reveal the necessity of juxtaposing official, imperial efforts to impose control and assign legal identities with the local and unofficial patterns of defining community status and the prerogatives associated with membership if we are to understand the meanings of race and citizenship in the colonial Americas. They show that citizenship's inclusive aspects depended fundamentally on its exclusivity: citizenship helped constitute a positive identity in part through the construction of negative identities. And finally, they show that citizenship was, in Michel Foucault's words, a "dense transfer point" of power, as debates over the limits of citizenship and over the meaning of those civic practices that were seen to define citizenship played a crucial role in producing colonial authority and identities within colonial polities.[4]

Chapter 9
Early Modern Spanish Citizenship: Inclusion and Exclusion in the Old and the New World

Tamar Herzog

The way Castilian local citizenship (*vecindad*) was modified in the New World in order to open local communities to Spanish newcomers and exclude from them all non-Spaniards, including foreigners and individuals of Indian, African, or mixed ancestry, is at the center of this chapter.[1] By closely examining hundreds of cases in which individuals requested recognition as citizens of local communities on both sides of the Atlantic, I wish to demonstrate that despite the close resemblance between Castilian and Spanish American citizenship practices, these practices enabled the colonial society to create new spaces for both inclusion and exclusion. Under colonial conditions, the local community was identified with the Spanish one. Although not initially, by the mid-1600s the typical citizen of Spanish American settlements was no longer the immigrant whose genealogy, place of origin, and culture were irrelevant, as was the case in Castile. Instead, in Spanish America, the typical citizen was a "native of the kingdoms of Spain" (*natural de los reinos de España*), that is to say, a member of the Spanish "national" community.[2]

Historians have affirmed that experiences in Spain shaped experiences in Spanish America. Most textbooks of Spanish American history begin with a short review of Iberian history, which is presented as a necessary background.[3] This review usually covers the medieval period and ignores developments in early modern Spain.[4] It is implicitly assumed that either practices in Spain remained untouched from 1500 (the discovery period) to the 1820s (the moment of rupture) or that events taking place in Spain during the early modern period were irrelevant for explaining developments in Spanish America. It is just as common to assert that Castilian and Spanish institutions were modified in Spanish America because of the encounter with new peoples and new conditions.[5] Many of these assertions are based on commonsense assumptions that, in most cases, are not accompanied by an analysis that actively compares Spain and Spanish America. When such a comparison is attempted at all, it is usually carried out by conducting primary research in Spanish America and consulting the secondary literature on Spain. The dominant assumption is that medieval Spain continued into the early modern period. Since Spain was allegedly a monolithic and unchanging reality and Latin American society experienced many changes, the conclusion these historians reach is simple: all modifications in medieval Spanish practices experienced in early modern Spanish America were due to circumstances that existed only in the New World. Hence, Old World practices were modified in the New World because of the conditions of the latter. Principal among these conditions were the encounter with the Indians and the competition with foreign powers.

Whereby some gesture toward Spanish history is included in most studies of Spanish America, historians of Spain have tended to ignore Spanish America altogether. Acknowledging the importance of the New World to the Spanish economy, many of them have failed to investigate the ongoing relationship between Spain and Spanish America.[6] They have assumed that what happened in Spanish America was irrelevant to their analysis of Spain, either because it was no different or because, on the contrary, differences were so substantial that there was no point of convergence and no possibility for comparison.

By analyzing discussions of local citizenship in communities on both sides of the Atlantic during approximately the same period and using the same type of sources and methodology, I wish to question these assumptions and demonstrate that neither was Castile dormant nor did the changes introduced in Spanish America necessarily result from New World conditions alone. I suggest that, ironically, some developments in Spanish America were more natural and more coherent with Spanish notions than those occurring in Spain. The question we need to ask ourselves, therefore, is not only why citizenship developed the way it did in Spanish America; we must also inquire why it did not follow the same route in the Old World.

In order to examine these questions, I will analyze the local citizenship regime as elaborated and practiced in Castile and then study its contemporary implementation and evolution in Spanish America. In the following narrative, "Castile," designates the Crown of Castile. I use this term in order to study citizenship in local communities under the jurisdiction of the Crown.[7] By Spanish America, I refer to the Spanish territories in the New

World. From a legal point of view, these territories were part of the crown of Castile and Castilian law; customs and practices were to be fully implemented in them. Although such continued to be the case until the early nineteenth century, from the late sixteenth century, if not earlier, Spaniards who emigrated to Spanish America could originate in any of the Spanish kingdoms, including the kingdoms of Aragón, Valencia, Catalonia, Majorca, and Navarre.[8] These people, legally titled "natives of the kingdoms of Spain," will be referred to in my narrative as "Spaniards."

My aim here is not to account for the birth of "national" or "colonial" identities. If such identities were created at all, they were the result of other processes, which I discuss elsewhere.[9] Neither will I engage here with the meaning and extension of Castilianness or Spanishness (*naturaleza*) nor with the appearance of a Creole discourse that differentiated between the Old and the New World. My intention is much more limited. I wish to demonstrate how certain Castilian practices concerned with membership in local communities (*vecindad*) fared in the New World; why this happened; and how processes in the New and the Old World can illuminate both.

The Development of Citizenship in Castile

The Castilian municipal regime originated in the Middle Ages. During this period the northern provinces gradually expanded south, conquering territories previously under Muslim domination.[10] This process, which began in the eighth century and lasted to the end of the thirteenth century, came to be known as the reconquest of Spain. However, despite efforts to stress continuity between the pre- and post-Muslim periods and to claim legitimacy —by portraying the enterprise as a return to a land that had previously belonged to the conquering powers—this was the beginning of a new era. During this period Christian control was extended throughout Spain, and new forms of government and territorial management gradually emerged. Among other things, from the eleventh century onward, this was an era characterized by massive migration from north to south. Often spontaneous in nature and dependent on individual or collective agency or on church-related institutions, this movement was also encouraged by the Castilian Crown, which called upon people to seize the moment and recast themselves anew.[11] Royal decrees promised freedom and a certain legal equality to those engaged in the resettlement of Castile; in this process, most new and transformed communities were recognized as corporate entities, and specific rights were allocated to people who were willing to come and settle in them. These rights, embodied in the status of *vecino* (citizen), included royal protection, and the privileges of being judged by the local courts, of receiving certain punishments and evading others, and of enjoying certain tax exemptions. In some cases, settlers recognized as *vecinos* also received title to land, as well as other economic incentives such as the exclusive use of communal lands or a monopoly on the introduction of certain goods to the local markets. Granted equally to all permanent settlers by virtue of their settlement, these specific rights were extended to people irrespective of their religion, their vassalage, and their status as villains or nobles, ecclesiastics or not.[12]

By the twelfth century, the Castilian-dominated territory was populated by a diversity of communities, each with its own particular legal regime and its own set of privileges, extended to all permanent settlers.[13] The disparity of standards between one community and another could be substantial, and a variety of local laws existed, each replicating the conditions under which a specific community was created. In the thirteenth and fourteenth centuries, the kingdom underwent processes of centralization and homogenization. Coinciding with the formation of a new European legal science (ius commune), local customary laws were written down, existing charters were extended to new municipalities, and new Castilian legal codes were enacted.[14] From the late fourteenth century and especially during the fifteenth and sixteenth centuries, many local communities began defining the ways by which citizenship could be achieved and the conditions for its achievement.[15] In contrast to the earlier period, when citizenship depended on residence in the community, this local legislation made citizenship dependent on the settlers' ties to each other. That bond could grow from external conditions such as residence, but citizenship no longer depended on external factors. Citizenship was now formulated as a contract in which a newcomer agreed to do certain things, such as live in the community and pay taxes, in return for receiving certain benefits, such as access to communal lands and office holding.

By the end of the fifteenth century, the division between citizens and noncitizens was generalized throughout Castile. Extended to people residing in both royal and seigniorial jurisdictions and in "urban" and "rural" communities alike, it was applied to individuals of all three estates; and, in the sixteenth century, most Castilian heads of households were either citizens (*vecinos*) or noncitizens (*residentes* or *forasteros*) in the community in which they lived.[16] Citizens enjoyed a wide array of privileges and were obliged to comply with many duties from which noncitizens were excluded. Principal among the rights of citizens was the ability to use communal property and, in most communities, to vote and to be elected to office. Principal among their duties was the obligation to reside in the community, pay taxes and other public expenses, and serve in the local militia.

During this period, a priori conditions for citizenship were anchored in questions of legal capacity such as the ability of women or minors to become citizens. It was generally agreed that under normal circumstances only male heads of households were eligible for citizenship and that the benefits of their citizenship extended to all members of their household. Although in each community some heads of households were citizens while others were not, from as early as the sixteenth century, and definitely in the following centuries, it was generally assumed that, exceptions aside, heads of households who were not citizens in one community were citizens in another.[17] The question, therefore, was not whether one was a citizen, but where. Heads of households could change their residence and citizenship, yet none was allowed to live without citizenship. The lack of "known citizenship" (*vecindad conocida*), it was argued, meant complete personal liberty, which could not be permitted.[18] People with no local ties were dangerous, because they "neither served the republic, nor married, nor paid taxes."[19] They were also the ultimate barbarians, since man could only lead a civil life when integrated into a community. Those who were not integrated were thus the ultimate outsiders.[20] In short, by the early modern period the quintessential Castilian was either a citizen or lived under the auspices of a citizen. By that time, citizenship was portrayed as a natural right, one that all people, including foreigners and nonvassals, shared. According to Francisco Vitoria, it was even a right Spaniards could impose on non-Hispanized Indians, and those Indians who refused to recognize it could be attacked for violating natural law.[21]

Since obtaining local citizenship implied the acceptance of a particular regime of rights and duties within a specific community, early modern Castilian communities elaborated formal procedures that allowed them to distinguish between citizens and noncitizens. These formal procedures were specific to each community, which set different rules about when could one apply for citizenship and which conditions and proofs were required. To give only a few examples: The ordinances of Ávila (1487) determined that citizens were individuals who lived in the community continuously or the greatest part of the year, owned a house, and paid taxes. According to the ordinances of Jaén (1573), citizens were individuals who resided in the community with their family or established a domicile in the jurisdiction. Citizens who wished to use the communal pasture had to request their formal admission to the community by petitioning the local council to recognize them as citizens. On this occasion they had to promise to reside in Jaén for the next ten years. In Archidona (1598), "no one would be considered a citizen . . . without first being received by the council, guaranteeing his compliance with citizenship's duties and buying a house and a vineyard within a year of his reception to the community." Citizens of Archidona were also obliged to settle their families within the jurisdiction and live there for at least four consecutive years.[22] In most communities, decisions concerning citizenship were made by the local council or, in very small settlements, by the community as a whole. These decisions could be appealed to a provincial judge or to one of the royal courts.

Despite the existence of these formal procedures, the status of people within Castilian communities was not necessarily tied to official declarations. Debates about citizenship could also occur when the access to certain rights reserved to citizens was questioned or when the community attempted to force one of its inhabitants to comply with a citizen's obligations. On these occasions, the issue was not the formal admission of a person into the community, but rather determining whether or not he was already a citizen. This recognition could be mechanical and could consist of verifying whether the person in question had previously been included in citizens' lists. Nevertheless, on most occasions, discussants examined the person's circumstances and behavior and measured them against a single idea: the idea that people became citizens from the moment in which they decided to become part of the community and in which they demonstrated their wish to do so by acting as citizens, mainly by complying with both privileges and duties. People who acted as citizens were thus citizens whether they did, or did not, obtain a formal declaration. Being a native of the community or the son of a citizen could be helpful in achieving recognition as a citizen, but it was insufficient on its own. Even natives and sons of citizens had to somehow demonstrate that they wanted to be citizens.[23]

This type of citizenship, defined by performance, seemed to exist equally all over Castile. It was invoked by individuals whenever their access to rights was denied or by the authorities when they wished to enforce on them certain duties. Agustín Vázquez, who resided in Pozo Antiguo (Zamora) for nine years was told one day that, because he was not a citizen, he could not use the communal pasture.[24] In order to overturn this decision, Agustín obtained from the provincial judge (*corregidor*) a ruling that, despite the fact that he had never obtained a formal recognition of this status he had always been a citizen. Similarly, the authorities of Villarramiel (Palencia) told Melchor Pardo in 1791 that he could not receive a plot of land because his citizenship status was unclear.[25] He appealed the decision to the royal court (*chancillería*) and presented proof that he was a "true and legitimate citizen." This proof included his residence, and his willingness to remain in the community and to pay taxes and make other contributions. Melchor specifically stated that in order to be recognized as a citizen, there was no need for formal approval. Indeed, the community and its authorities did not confer citizenship as much as recognize its existence. The appellate court (*chancillería*) agreed and declared Melchor a citizen from the first day on which he became worthy of this status.

These stories demonstrate that parallel to the formal procedures that declared individuals as citizens and that were indeed particular to each community, other mechanisms also existed allowing the acquisition of citizenship without the intervention of the local authorities. These mechanisms set the rule according to which citizenship depended on an individual's actions, and they allowed people to become citizens automatically by virtue of their intentions (to become citizens) and their activities (as citizens). Because of these mechanisms, which were especially powerful in the seventeenth and eighteenth centuries and were repeatedly upheld in local communities all over Castile, formal procedures for acquiring citizenship declaration were now presented as a mere formality. They allowed the community to verify the existence of an intention to become a citizen, and they publicly acknowledged people as citizens. Although this acknowledgment facilitated municipal life, because it clarified who the citizens were, it did not *make* people citizens. What made people citizens was their intention (to integrate into the community) and their subsequent activity (that proved this intention)—first and foremost, their residence in the community but also the purchase of a house, the payment of taxes, service in the local militia or in a public office, membership in a local confraternity and so forth. As the petition of Agustín Cordovilla Sánchez, who defended his right to use the communal pasture, put it: "Even without the solemnity of an expressed reception to the community, effectuated by the council, he should be considered strictly as a citizen, because of his continuous residence and the house that he owned."[26]

The principle of linking a personal decision to behavior and thus citizenship and eligibility for rights and privileges was expressed, elaborated, and reaffirmed in both judicial and administrative proceedings. It was based on the understanding that citizenship was a natural right, which people could exercise freely: "According to the freedom that according to natural law we have, each one of us can renounce the citizenship that he has and live and become a citizen in another place according to his choosing."[27] During the seventeenth and eighteenth centuries it was repeatedly asserted, at times with great lamentation, that because of the freedom of immigration, once newcomers expressed their wish to join the community, the community could not refuse to admit them: "In order to accept us as citizens, no other circumstances are needed except for an expression of will."[28] Petitioners used these arguments in order to force municipalities to accept them, and they insisted that communities were not authorized "to refuse to grant citizenship, being that the passage from one citizenship to the other was a free act."[29]

In none of the cases I reviewed were preliminary requirements addressed that would exclude a certain group of people—such as foreigners or non- vassals of the king—from ever obtaining citizenship. During the medieval period, the possibility of admitting these people to Castilian communities was openly admitted, and their presence, especially during the reconquest and resettlement period, was even encouraged.[30] The openness of Castilian communities to Catholic foreigners and nonvassals continued during the early modern period. There are multiple examples of individuals belonging to both of these categories being accepted as citizens[31] and on many occasions it was openly attested that questions of foreignness and the "right to be in Spain" were irrelevant to the admission of people as local citizens. Foreigners "could become citizens in any of the villages of these your domains without the councils being able to impede it in any way, or speak against it, as it is expressly ordered in your royal orders on the matter."[32]

While Catholic nonvassals and non-Spaniards were welcomed, by the fifteenth century it became clear that in order to be a citizen one had to be a Christian, and from the sixteenth century, a Catholic. This fact was so obvious to contemporaries and so consensual in nature that it was rarely discussed or justified. The question had both theoretical and practical implications. From a theoretical point of view, local communities were considered associations of people who wanted to live together under a single law. This law was founded in local and royal legislation, but, first and foremost, it was embodied in religious teaching.[33] For early modern Spaniards, religion was also a culture and an identity: "Religion is the tie of human society and it sanctions and sanctifies the alliances, the contracts and even the society itself."[34] Religion supplied Spaniards with a moral code, a prescription for behavior, and a key to understanding the world. These codes, behaviors, and understandings were shared with other Catholics outside Spain. Thereafter, Spaniards asserted that apparent cultural, linguistic, and behavioral differences between themselves and foreign Catholics were inconsequential: what mattered was not what separated Catholics from one another but what united them.[35] Agreement about a common law could thus easily be achieved with foreigners and nonvassals as long as they were Catholic; however, it was practically impossible to conceive of in the case of Protestants and non-Christians. From a practical point of view, it was generally assumed that, after the expulsion of Jews at the end of the fifteenth century and of the Moors in the beginning of the seventeenth century, only Christians (and eventually Catholics, that is, nonheretic Christians) could live on Spanish soil, integrate into communities, and acquire rights and privileges.[36] Although by virtue of "international" treaties certain Protestants were allowed to reside in Spain, this residence was considered by definition temporary.[37] Tolerated rather than accepted, they gained no rights from their residence, however long it lasted—unless they agreed to convert to Catholicism.

The Development of Citizenship in Spanish America

Initially, the Spanish American urban experience was a repetition of what had been the Castilian experience during the Middle Ages.[38] As was the case for participants in the reconquest and resettlement of Spain, local citizenship could be obtained by the mere fact of being part of the group that founded the community. All that was required of the conquistador—now made citizen—was to be present at the foundational act or to settle in the community shortly thereafter.[39] Once this first phase was completed, most Spanish American communities developed procedures that enabled newcomers to petition for citizenship.[40] In accordance with the Castilian precedent, candidates for citizenship could be Spaniards, Indians, or foreigners.[41]

Petitions for citizenship, which were very common during the sixteenth century in all of the cities examined,[42] gradually disappeared from municipal records by the second, third, or fourth decades of the seventeenth century. Although people continued to refer to themselves as *vecinos* in notarial acts, legal declarations, and their social interactions, the archives tell us nothing about how they achieved or maintained this status. As a result, it was customary among Spanish American historians to ignore issues of citizenship or to assume that, in the Americas, either *vecindad* was the exact replica of citizenship in medieval Spain or it was a simple honorary title that was no longer attached to notions of citizenship and belonging.[43]

Despite these assumptions, and although in Spanish America by the seventeenth century formal procedures for acquiring citizenship had indeed disappeared, nevertheless, citizenship as a tie between people forming part of the same community persisted. Also persisting was the idea that citizenship implied both privileges and duties and that people who "acted" and were "reputed" as citizens were indeed citizens. Given that by the late sixteenth and clearly in the seventeenth century citizenship could also be achieved by performance in Castile, it becomes clear that the modifications introduced in Spanish America in the seventeenth and eighteenth centuries were but a variation of those taking place at the same time also on the Iberian Peninsula. This said, seventeenth- and eighteenth-century Spanish American developments did allow the appearance of new forms of exclusion that theoretically were absent in Castile. Most important among them was the tendency to exclude Indians, Africans, and individuals of mixed ancestry from citizenship. Another was the introduction of restrictions on granting citizenship to foreigners.

The first indication of the particular path taken by Spanish American communities was already present in the foundational period, which is where my study begins. In order to account for local differences, my analysis will follow the developments in two very distinct enclaves: Caracas and Buenos Aires. These cities were marked by different types of tensions, which lead them in different directions. Nevertheless, considered together, Caracas and Buenos Aires indicate some of the potentialities involved in the implementation of Castilian citizenship in Spanish America. Although I do not mean to suggest that the exact same thing was happening elsewhere in Spanish America, such could have been the case, and indications of similar developments in other Spanish American enclaves are not wanting.

The Case of Caracas

The transformation of local citizenship into a status completely dependent on reputation and the subsequent exclusion of non-Spaniards from citizenship are best exemplified by the case of Caracas, which serves here as the first model for how Castilian citizenship could have been modified in the Americas. Caracas was founded in 1567 as a military garrison.[44] In 1578, only 14 of the 136 people who participated in its foundation were still present in the community and, until the 1580s, its permanent population remained very small. Protected by a mountain range, yet close to the sea, Caracas soon became a trading post for agricultural products coming from the hinterland and supplying the Spanish fleets in the Caribbean. During the next thirty years (1580s–1610s), coinciding with the pacification of the territory, wheat, tobacco and cattle hides provided its inhabitants with profitable exports. In the following decades, the local economy gradually shifted to the exportation of cacao to Mexico. This export trade, which sustained the growth of the city for two hundred years, transformed Caracas into a colony of New Spain and converted it into a major slave labor economy. Although it had only about 90 citizens at the end of the sixteenth century, by 1633 the city had virtually doubled in size.

Formal petitions for citizenship in Caracas were fairly frequent until the 1620s.[45] In accordance with the Castilian regime, these petitions were presented to the city council, whose members decided whether the person should, or should not, be recognized as *vecino*. During this period many petitioners were recently arrived individuals; thus, rather than being the last step toward integration in the local community, as was the case in Castile, their petition for citizenship actually initiated their contact with Caracas.[46] This was not surprising, given the fact that most of them requested admission into the community in order to be eligible, as citizens, to receive land (*solar*).[47] Also during this period, people who left Caracas continued to be considered citizens of there as long as they delegated the actual exercise of their obligations to another person. Caracas was also willing to admit absentee members: in 1597, Nofre Carrasques, representing Fernán de Zárate, requested that his client be recognized as a citizen.[48] His petition was granted, although it indicated that Fernán was absent and did not promise that he would ever come to the city. Attempts to compel obedience from those failing to comply with citizenship obligations, especially the obligation to reside in the jurisdiction, were also ignored, as affluent members continued to disobey municipal orders and replaced obedience with the casual payment of penalties.[49] This became a frequent practice from the 1610s, and, by the 1650s, certain people were automatically exempted from citizenship duties—residence included—because they were willing to pay the municipal authorities certain sums in advance.[50]

In this early stage, it was clear that Caracas gave less weight to actual residence than did its Castilian counterparts, who insisted that citizens have a prolonged and stable relationship with the community both before becoming citizens and after. Also noteworthy was the lack of a clear definition of what was municipal, what was provincial, and what was Spanish. People residing in the province could claim that they were integrated into the local community, and services to the Crown were also considered to constitute ties between the individual and the city.[51]

The demise of formal procedures of acquiring citizenship in Caracas began at the end of the sixteenth century. By that time, people requesting the allocation of certain resources described their attachment to the community in qualitative terms, rather than by simply asserting that they were citizens. For example, Tomás de Aponte, who requested a land grant in 1597, explained that he had come to the city with his wife, sons, and family and that he intended to live and remain in the jurisdiction.[52] Francisco Carbajar declared that he had been living in Caracas for over seventeen years, that he occupied a house with his wife and children, and that he had always complied with all citizenship obligations.[53] Although some people continued to request formal admission to the community by petitioning for citizenship, and others mentioned their citizenship when petitioning for specific rights, both practices were diminishing. By the 1640s, the traditional association between citizenship and land grants was also fading away. During the second half of the century, people petitioning for land no longer necessarily mentioned their citizenship,[54] and those petitioning for citizenship no longer necessarily requested land.[55] The same time period also saw the end of free land grants and the beginning of a new regime that allocated land by virtue of monetary payments. As access to land became increasingly independent of citizenship, the recording of citizenship petitions virtually ceased.

By the middle of the seventeenth century, formal citizenship declarations were thus giving way to social categorizations and the ability to acquire rights usually reserved to citizens was now based on reputation. In 1650, for example, Francisco López stated that "it was well reputed and established" (*es notorio y consta*) that he had been a citizen of Caracas for over thirty years. In 1652, Juan Rodríguez argued that his citizenship could not be doubted, since both in the city and in its province "he must be taken as such" (*debe ser habido por tal*) because of his many services to the Crown.[56]

Despite its apparent novelty, citizenship by reputation had a Castilian counterpart. As mentioned earlier, by the early modern period Castilian citizenship also could be acquired without the intervention of the authorities. Yet, while early modern Castilian communities fought against these practices and, in the name of good government, attempted to monopolize the classification of people as citizens and noncitizens, the authorities of Caracas did nothing of the sort. I could not find even one attempt to support the continuation of formal procedures for acquiring citizenship or to ensure municipal control over the classification of people as citizens and noncitizens.

Another innovation introduced in Caracas was the ineligibility of Indians, Africans and individuals of mixed ancestry for local citizenship. As seen earlier, in Castile not only were origin and genealogy irrelevant to acquiring citizenship, there was no mechanism for examining the candidate's ethnicity. In theory, therefore, Indians, mestizos and mulattoes should have been eligible for citizenship in Spanish American communities. It is true that, on occasion, Spanish American legislation separated Spaniards from Indians and stipulated that they reside in different communities. Yet this structure, which prohibited Spaniards from residing in Indian villages, never completely prohibited the emigration of Indians to Spanish settlements.[57] Such migration was not only allowed, it was also very frequent.[58] This fact was evident in early Caracas, where several Indians and mestizos were granted citizenship.[59] Nevertheless, such cases completely disappeared from municipal records after the 1620s.

The Case of Buenos Aires

The second model of the modification of Castilian practices in the New World is Buenos Aires.[60] Initially a military outpost at the mouth of the River Plate, by the early seventeenth century it had become a bustling port city, primarily exporting metals coming from Potosí in exchange other European products and slaves, most of which came to the city though contraband networks. Buenos Aires' initial years were humble. Founded in 1580 by sixty citizens, it was abandoned by many of them in subsequent years, and its population did not stabilize until the beginning of the seventeenth century.[61] During the first half of that century, it had some three hundred citizens as well as a huge military regiment. This military presence was justified by the need to protect the river but also by the proximity of Brazil. This closeness, which converted Buenos Aires into an important enclave against Portuguese expansion, also enabled it to flourish, transforming it into a point at which the Portuguese and Spanish trade networks converged. One important result of this proximity and collaboration/competition was the presence of many Portuguese merchants in the city. Their presence internally divided Buenos Aires, as most commerce was in the hands of the Portuguese and most agriculture in the hands of Spaniards. The uneasy relationship between the two communities led to several campaigns against the presence of the Portuguese. During this period, Buenos Aires also faced a growing threat to its control of the countryside as a consequence of the expansion of the Arauncanian people of southern Chile across the Andes.

According to municipal records, in the late sixteenth and early seventeenth centuries, Buenos Aires defined itself as a frontier settlement antagonistic to (yet also collaborating with) the Portuguese and the Indians.[62] Since war was a permanent preoccupation, contrary to Caracas, where this issue was hardly ever discussed, those wishing to become citizens of Buenos Aires had to express their desire to remain in the community as they would in any Castilian community.[63] Yet, first and foremost, they were required to have a horse and arms and to guarantee—when they were absent—that another person would fulfill their military obligations.[64] The proximity to Brazil and to hostile Indians and the struggle against the Portuguese both inside and outside Buenos Aires also produced an acute awareness of the Spanish character of the city, which was expressed in two different ways. On one hand, the distinction between what was local and what was Spanish was unclear. For example, it was generally argued that "services to the crown" were also services to the local community. Those engaged in expanding Spanish–controlled areas, in discovering gold mines, and in paying money to the royal treasury could claim that these activities qualified them as citizens, since they also demonstrated their attachment to the local community.[65] On the other hand, which was even more surprising, the authorities of Buenos Aires insisted that under normal circumstances only "natives of the kingdoms of Spain" could be accepted as citizens. This demand was a clear departure from the Castilian precedent, as Castilian communities easily (and frequently) admitted foreigners as citizens. In Buenos Aires, on the contrary, only exceptional foreigners who were very "useful" to the community and highly immersed in its society could be granted local citizenship.[66] Some leniency was demonstrated towards the Portuguese during the union of the Crowns of Portugal and Castile (1580–1640), yet this leniency was reversed in the following years.[67] People requesting citizenship in Buenos Aires thus had to prove that they were "natives of the kingdoms of Spain," and by 1610s the inclusion of a candidate's birthplace in citizenship petitions became the usual practice in the city.[68] When the actual place of birth was unknown, it was at least formally stated that the person's presence in the Americas was legal. Given the rules of the Spanish monopoly in the Americas, this determination necessarily meant that the person in question was a "native of the kingdoms of Spain."[69]

In contrast to the situation in Caracas, land distribution was hardly ever mentioned in Buenos Aires, and it was only in the 1610s that newcomers' duties were formally extended from having arms to also possessing a house. It was also during this period that both requirements were integrated into a formal oath that all candidates for citizenship had to take.[70] Nevertheless, even as late as 1619 and 1620, Buenos Aires still admitted absentee citizens.[71] By the late 1620s, the number of citizenship petitions was dropping; in the next few decades, citizenship petitions practically disappeared from municipal records. The abandonment of Castilian procedures was such that when in 1774 a Castilian newcomer requested a formal declaration of his citizenship, the municipal authorities were unsure about how to proceed.[72]

Local Citizenship in Spanish America: An Overview

Despite differences in their particular development and in their reading of citizenship, in Buenos Aires as in Caracas the principal traits of Castilian local citizenship were maintained. As in Castile, in the sixteenth and early seventeenth centuries, citizenship could be acquired by petitioning the town council; success depended on the establishment of ties with the community, or at least the promise to establish them. The interrelation between privileges and obligations, which was closely observed in Castile, was also maintained. In Caracas, those who wanted to receive land had to reside in the settlement or pay fees. In Buenos Aires, citizens had to comply with military duty. What was new in both cities was the complete abandonment of formal procedures for acquiring citizenship. Also new was the ill-defined frontier between the local and the Spanish communities, which were often identified as one and the same thing. This led in Caracas to the exclusion of Indians, Africans, and people of mixed ancestry and in Buenos Aires to the demand that citizens also be natives of the kingdom of Spain.

Caracas and Buenos Aires had traits that could explain these developments. Caracas gradually became a slave labor economy, leading to heightened ethnic/racial awareness. Because of the presence of many non-Spanish Europeans, especially the Portuguese, Buenos Aires experienced continuing social tension. Yet it is clear that similar processes were happening elsewhere. Although we lack precise information about these processes, we do know that historians have affirmed in the past that in sixteenth-century Spanish America Indians, mestizos and mulattoes could become citizens of

Spanish communities but that this was no longer true in the late seventeenth and eighteenth centuries.[73] Historians have also assumed that all over Spanish America, in order to be a citizen, one had to be Spanish.[74]

Similar affirmations can be made with regard to the abandonment of formal procedures for acquiring citizenship in the beginning of the seventeenth century. The disappearance of formal citizenship petitions in Caracas in the 1620s and 1630s could be explained by the gradual disassociation between land grants and citizenship and the passage from the free allocation of land to a paid one. As in Buenos Aires, it was tied to the city's coming of age. In the early 1600s both Caracas and Buenos Aires were already self-sustaining cities, with a stable population, a fairly flourishing economy and stable institutions. Under these circumstances, they no longer required an aggressive immigration policy and, as established communities, they could close ranks by linking citizenship (and rights) to reputation rather than to legal procedures. Nevertheless, there are many indications that the abandonment of formal citizenship procedures was also happening elsewhere. By the 1620s, formal citizenship petitions had also disappeared from the town records of Mexico City.[75] In seventeenth-century Popayán, citizenship was a status that did not depend on the inclusion of a resident's name in official registries. It was constituted socially and granted automatically to people who had integrated into the community.[76] In eighteenth-century Quito and Cuenca, citizenship was instituted by "public knowledge" that required no proof.[77] This coincidence indicates that the exclusion of non-Spaniards from citizenship in local communities in Spanish America as well as the continuation of formal citizenship procedures in Castile and their abandonment in the New World cannot be explained by observing local circumstances alone.[78]

The Traditional Interpretation: The Development of "National" Identities

The developments I have described so far could lead easily to the conclusion that in Spanish America Castilian local citizenship was both "essentialized" and "nationalized." Local citizenship was essentialized because instead of maintaining a regime that constituted citizenship by declaration and/or by intention, as was the case in Castile, Spanish American communities adhered completely to the idea that status was linked to reputation. This meant that in Spanish America Castilian local citizenship was stripped of its outer layers and reduced to the most essential characteristic, that is, the candidate's intent. It also meant that, contrary to Castile, where different formal procedures for acquiring citizenship existed in each community, yet citizenship by performance operated equally in all places, in Spanish America a coherent regime emerged, one that ignored the particularities typical of each Castilian community and centered on what was common to all of them. Local citizenship was nationalized because the local community now considered those who were socially external to the group, such as foreigners or Indians, as noncitizens even when they acted as citizens. The contrary was also true: all Spaniards, even those not residing in the jurisdiction or those who performed service for the Crown and not directly for the local community, could be considered citizens, because in comparison to the foreignness of other people the mere fact that they were Spanish, lived in Spanish America, and obeyed the same interests, made them part of the local community.

It would also be tempting to conclude that those developments happened because of the conditions in the New World. Such a conclusion would back what by now is a common assumption: the idea that "national identities" were forged first in the colonies and then imported back "home."[79] But are these conclusions necessary? Do we have sufficient information to back them? I would like to answer these questions by first explaining why practices in Spanish America differed from practices in Castile, then looking at the issue of the birth of identities in the colonies.

Examining the Theory: Differences Between Castile and Spanish America

There are several key factors that can explain the differences between the Castilian and the Spanish American experience. The first factor is the legal meaning of citizenship. In Castile, citizenship allowed people to enjoy many rights and forced them to comply with many duties. As a result, both the local authorities and individuals had a vested interest in clarifying who the citizens were. Citizen lists were elaborated, formal procedures for acquiring citizenship were adopted, and people often became involved in long and tedious litigation in order to ensure that they would be treated as citizens or in order to bar others from achieving such treatment. A system that by the sixteenth and seventeenth centuries theoretically allowed the autogeneration of citizenship was thus constantly pressured to create and preserve procedures for bestowing citizenship with the hope of circumscribing conflict. This resulted in the (not necessarily peaceful) coexistence between formal citizenship procedures on one hand, and citizenship by performance on the other.

Similar pressures did not exist in Spanish America. Indeed, by in the sixteenth century many New World communities no longer maintained a fully discriminatory regime that clearly distinguished between the rights of Spanish citizens and noncitizens. There are literally hundreds of examples of cases in which Spanish noncitizens enjoyed rights that in Castile would have been reserved for citizens. In many Spanish American communities communal property was open to both citizens and noncitizens, and noncitizens could also be employed in municipal offices.[80] In some jurisdictions, taxation and military duty were equally applied to both citizens and noncitizens.[81] Emptied of many (although not all) of its pragmatic implications, by the late sixteenth century Spanish American citizenship mainly embodied the social and cultural recognition that one was a permanent member of the community. It instituted people as both members of the community and "civilized." It even recognized them as Spaniards. The fact that citizens and noncitizens were treated alike on many practical issues eliminated the main motivation for establishing citizenship lists. Under these circumstances, existing only in Spanish America, the Castilian early modern idea that citizenship was an autogenerated status could be fully implemented in a way impossible to achieve in Castile. Thus, in both Castile and Spanish America there was a contemporary move from formal declarations to citizenship by reputation. However, while in Castile this move was only partially successful, in Spanish America it was complete.

The partial success of Castilian municipalities in conserving a monopoly over the classification of citizens and their distinction from noncitizens and the complete Spanish American lack of interest in doing so was probably due to the different circumstances under which local citizenship emerged. In Castile, citizenship was defined at the same time in which the kingdom itself was created. This coincidence guaranteed a regime that was initially very localized and that admitted great differences between one community and another. Processes of homogenization within the kingdom gradually closed the distance between the practices of different communities. Yet, until the end of the Old Regime, some differences, especially with regard to formal requirements and procedures, remained in place. It was also clear that in Castile municipal entities were contemporaneous with the kingdom. Their residents forged an identity of their own at the same time in which they gradually integrated, through their local membership, into the kingdom.[82] In short, while local communities were a fact, the kingdom was not yet fully consolidated. The contrary was true with regard to Spanish America. The settlement of the New World happened after the kingdom of Castile had undergone processes of homogenization and consolidation. While the kingdom was a fact, the local community was a project. In the Americas, settlers from different parts of Spain (Castile, Aragón, Catalonia, Valencia, Navarre, and Majorca) came together to form new communities. Each settler brought his own understanding of citizenship as practiced in his hometown. Many settlers moved from one community to another. Although over the years some localism emerged, given the inflow of immigrants from Spain and the constant movement between communities, this localism was constantly modified by the integration of new elements, some Castilian and some not.[83] This reality was echoed in Spanish American legislation, which, contrary to Castile, never took up questions of citizenship.[84] With the lack of clear guidance in local laws or traditions but with a cultural understanding of what citizenship "really meant," it was natural that Spanish Americans neglected the peculiarities typical to Castilian local communities and adopted instead a local citizenship regime that was common to all Castilians, and most probably to all Spaniards.

Another important distinction between Castile and Spanish America is found in the differences in immigration strategies. By the seventeenth century, permanent resident foreigners were welcomed in Castile, yet internal emigration inside the kingdom, once so desired, was no longer encouraged because it was feared that less fortunate settlements would be depopulated and subsequently abandoned.[85] In Spanish America, the contrary was true. The monopoly instituted by Spain in the New World specifically prohibited foreign immigration to the Americas.[86] Because the presence of foreigners was illegal and, furthermore, considered highly dangerous, it became reasonable to exclude all non-Spanish Europeans from citizenship in local communities. Also in Spanish America, some attempts were made to create an Indian republic that would be distinguishable from a parallel Spanish one. By the seventeenth century, this wish was reinforced by a growing awareness that the integration of Spaniards and Indians into a single community, an integration initially sought after at least by the Crown, would not be easily accomplished.[87] First defined mainly as a religious, political and cultural difference, the distinction between Spaniards and Indians was gradually being portrayed as an ethnic or even a racial distinction.[88] Under these circumstances, it is not surprising that Indians, Africans and individuals of mixed ancestry who might once have been considered potential "Spaniards" were now deemed permanently foreign to the community.

While the immigration of foreigners to Spanish American communities was discouraged, and while Indians, Africans, and individuals of mixed ancestry gradually were classified as irredeemable outsiders, the emigration of Spaniards from Spain to Spanish America and from one Spanish American enclave to another was considered highly beneficial, as it ensured Spanish control over a territory that was still largely unexplored and beyond Spanish reach. Local identities may have existed or were gradually being formed; yet, the sixteenth- and seventeenth-century Spanish American community was still viewed as a single community in which the distinctions between one settlement and the other were not (yet) clearly marked. One result of this development was that in this hectic and constantly changing world, there was an overpowering sense of intimacy: of people knowing who the others were; of individuals moving across dozens, hundreds, and even thousands of miles, yet still acting as if they were in familiar territory.[89] It was as if in their joint opposition to foreign and seemingly hostile elements, in Spanish America all Spaniards were members of a single community and all non-Spaniards were classified as aliens. From this perspective, the question of whether one was Peninsular (born on the Iberian Peninsula) or Creole made no difference.[90]

A One-Way Street?

Were the processes I describe particular to the Americas? Had I only compared medieval Spain to early modern Spanish America I would have concluded that Old World practices changed in the New World. However, having closely observed both early modern Castile and early modern Spanish America, I must conclude that practices changed on both sides of the ocean. We already know that citizenship by reputation was not an American invention. But what about the identification between citizenship and Spanishness? What I have exposed so far would lead us to believe that at least this identification was indeed invented in the New World. However, such was not the case. As I have argued elsewhere,[91] in seventeenth-century Castile the same identification was also reached, although by taking a different route. Instead of ensuring that only Spaniards could be admitted to local citizenship, as was the case in Spanish America, Castilians declared that all those who were local citizens should be considered, by extension, also natives of the kingdoms of Spain. That is to say, at stake there was not who was a citizen (as in Spanish America) but who was a Spaniard. The mechanism was different—indeed, almost the inverse—but the results were similar: a growing identification between local citizenship and Spanishness and a growing sense that either people commit themselves fully to both the local and the "national" community by being both citizens and natives or they lose the right to remain in Spain.

Rather than changing in the New World, in both Castile and Spanish America Castilian local citizenship adapted equally to local needs as its different parts were stressed in different moments and for different ends. Some things were possible in Castile, others in Spanish America, but neither place was dormant. Precisely for these reasons, I would be very cautious to conclude that a Spanish identity was first forged in the Americas and then brought back to Spain. Canonized by the writing of Benedict Anderson such interpretations of colonial history have been taken almost for granted.[92] Nevertheless, the Spanish case calls for a much more nuanced understanding. Similar yet not identical processes did happen on both sides of the Atlantic. The reasons may have been different and the results individual, yet it was clearly the case that the colonial situation was just as important as was the situation in the so-called motherland.

Chapter 10

Natural Movements and Dangerous Spectacles: Beatings, Duels, and "Play" in Saint Domingue

Gene E. Ogle

The slaves, free people of color, poor whites, and rich whites who were gathered in the marketplace of Petite Rivière Sunday morning, 1 May 1774, had the opportunity to witness an uncommon spectacle. Around nine o'clock, those paying attention saw a slave dressed in the Delaville heirs' livery whipping and chasing a white peddler across the marketplace. Several witnesses also noticed the slave's master ordering him to do so and threatening him with a cane. A smaller number had seen the reverse tableau shortly before, as the peddler had chased the slave across the marketplace, stick in hand. Soon after the second, more spectacular scene took place, a *maréchaussée* brigadier appeared and arrested the slave.[1]

Over the course of the following five years, this case passed from Saint Marc's senechal to Port-au-Prince's conseil supérieur to the colony's royal administrators to the minister of the navy in Versailles and then back to the conseil. Raymond, the slave in question, passed from the hands of the *maréchaussée* to those of Saint Marc's jailer to those of Port-au-Prince's jailer and back before apparently being released to his owners. The documentation produced by these proceedings is, if limited, extremely rich in comparison with that regarding most criminal cases involving slaves in Saint Domingue.[2]

This trial record provides an invaluable opportunity to explore the relationships between violence, status, and race beyond the plantation and patriarchal household. During the trial and its aftermath, the individuals involved alluded to a range of violent interactions whose meanings depended upon the perceived identities of the actors as much as the practices themselves. In doing so, they enunciated a series of sometimes complementary, sometimes contradictory discourses about these matters. Claims to distinctions among whites were pitted against those for upholding racial hierarchies. Arguments for masters' authority contested those for the maintenance of a visual economy in which white bodies were sacrosanct while black and colored ones were subject to exemplary beatings. The rights of white (and perhaps all) men to physically avenge wrongs done to them by their equals or lessers conflicted with the absolute monarchy's claim to a monopoly on legitimate violence.

As the multiplicity of claims made to explain, evaluate, and contest the meanings of Raymond's lashing of the peddler makes clear, French colonists, royal officials, and slaves possessed a wide-ranging cultural vocabulary for discussing public violence. The fact that the participants in the trial explicitly or implicitly referred to nearly the entire range of possible violent interaction between equals and nonequals also suggests that individual practices derived much of their meaning from their place within the totality of "thinkable" violence.[3] In other words, a beating like that of the peddler by Raymond could (and can) only be fully understood in reference to the economy of violence in which it occurred.[4]

As the case of Raymond illustrates, the particular economy of violence that governed extralegal public violence in Saint Domingue was a racialized one that derived its principal features from two sources. First, honor provided its language. The need to defend personal honor underlay both the peddler's and Raymond's master's actions before and after the whipping. Raymond knew its flip side, deference, to be the comportment demanded of him. Second, fears of slave revolt shaped colonists' justifications of their violence along with the king's agents' treatment of it. The demographic imbalance of the colony, which in 1775 was peopled by approximately 261,000 slaves, 6,000 free people of color, and 20,000 whites, was evoked repeatedly during Raymond's trial and its aftermath.[5] For the officials charged with deciding the enslaved coachman's fate, the matter ultimately became one of determining whether respect for masters' authority or deference to white skin was more essential to maintaining the slave regime.

The day after the whipping, the instance entered the court system. Jean-Baptiste Huet, the peddler, hired a lawyer to demand "just reparation" before Saint Marc's judge. With this complaint, Huet was not simply denouncing a crime. Legally, a denunciation was unnecessary, for the king's justice should have prosecuted the public beating of a white by a slave in any case. Instead, Huet was joining a civil plea to criminal proceedings already under way. Huet's plaint made clear that the need for this intervention came not from the injury but rather from the insult inflicted by the lashing. Nowhere did his deposition speak of bodily harm or the costs of medical assistance. The wrongs he had suffered were those to his honor, as he "had been abandoned to the affront and ignominy of being beaten publicly by a Negro slave on the orders of a White."[6]

Huet's request dovetailed neatly with the aims and methods of Old Regime criminal justice. Trials and executions were, among other things, shaming rituals meant to destroy whatever public honor the criminal might possess and, in doing so, to reaffirm the monarchy's might and legitimacy.[7] The reparation of an individual subject's honor could easily be joined to this process, since one of the major wrongs done to the king by the criminal was the violation of the natural order he defended. Huet's complaint made this connection explicit, as it called for the courts' vengeance because "the safety of the colonist [had been] attacked, liberty [was] groaning, the political order [had been] revolted against, all laws [had been] violated."[8] In restoring the natural order, the king's courts would also repair Huet's damaged honor.

According to Huet, what had happened resulted from a slave's petty theft and a master's overindulgence. He claimed that Raymond had tried to steal a trumpet from him. His response had been to chase the slave away with a stick in hand. Afterward, Bernard Cardeneau, the Delaville plantation's manager, had had the "weakness" to listen to the slave's complaints and the "audacity to tell this dear protégé, *give a few lashes to that rascal there.*" Raymond, "criminally docile," obeyed and struck him five to six times.

The plaint closed by once again tying the exigencies of royal justice to Huet's cause. This time, however, the matter was distinctly one of social control. Huet's lawyer highlighted how what had happened to his client threatened the entire colonial order: "a White beaten by a Negro slave on the orders of a White, in a colony where there are 100 slaves against one free person: one shivers at the thought."[9] According to his unspoken reasoning, a spectacle like that of Raymond whipping Huet was a bad example that could spread by eroding the respect due to "whiteness."

Despite its conclusion, the primary cause of Huet's legal action was his damaged honor. He had suffered what most colonists would have considered to be the most humiliating beating possible, that "by a Negro slave on the orders of a White."[10] The shame inflicted by such a beating derived from multiple sources. In France, elites humiliated enemies and disrespectful inferiors by having their male servants deliver such thrashings. Voltaire's beating by the Chevalier de Rohan's lackeys is but the most famous example of this practice.[11] Since almost all domestic tasks done by servants in France were performed by slaves in Saint Domingue, for some slaveowners it probably came naturally to use them for this one as well.

Still, colonists were well aware of the fact that slaves were not simply servants. In Saint Domingue, the shame attached to such a beating was even greater due to the meanings attached to skin color and slave status. Color difference visually underlined the differing status of whites and those beating them. The fact that the most shaming figure in colonial society, the executioner, was a provisionally pardoned slave probably strengthened associations between having one's body mistreated by a man of color and dishonor. In any case, the executioner's execration and the shame of being beaten by a slave on his master's orders had the same sources. Such beatings were not only denials of any implied equality of "whiteness," they also put the recipients in positions subordinate to those of slaves, who in the eyes of their superiors embodied honor's antithesis.[12]

These beatings were all the more powerful due to their transgressive nature. Slaves were the individuals in the French Antilles who faced the most draconian penalties for attacking whites. According to the Code Noir, the basis of slave law from 1685 until the Revolutions, any slave who struck his or her master or a member of his or her master's family "with contusion or the shedding of blood, or in the face" was to be punished by death. "Excesses and aggressions" against free people were to be "severely punished, even by death."[13] In general, colonial magistrates punished slaves for striking whites with the full rigor of the law.[14] Due to the severity of these legal sanctions, using slaves to beat another white was claiming an authority above that of the king's law, and as such even greater social distance between the slave's master and the beating's recipient.[15]

The day after Huet deposed his complaint, the judge ordered the first witnesses to appear. He added a second group four days later. These witnesses included a saddlemaker in whose shop Huet had taken refuge, a merchant, a tailor, two French peddlers, and two German peddlers. On the appointed days, the judge asked each of them to comment on Huet's complaint. Overall, their stories concurred, although each touched on different fragments of what had happened.

Several discussed the incident that gave rise to Huet's beating. These witnesses had seen Raymond take a trumpet from Huet's stand, "put it to his mouth to play it," and leave. Huet then chased after him, stick in hand. During the chase, Raymond's hat fell off and Huet took it. A few minutes later, Raymond returned, grabbed his hat and escaped.

Most of the testimony focused on the lashing itself. All had seen or heard Cardeneau order Raymond to whip Huet, and most claimed that he did so "with an angry tone of voice." While the syntax recalled by the witnesses varied, the plantation manager basically had told the slave "to fuck [*f——*] that rascal up with a bunch of lashes." The only substantive matter on which they differed regarded the slave's reaction to these orders. Some claimed Raymond hesitated before submitting to his master's orders, while others mentioned no such hesitation.[16]

The final witness, the German peddler Georges Kolp, provided the sole indication of how the crowd in the marketplace that Sunday reacted to the whipping. Immediately afterward, he said, several people asked Raymond why he had attacked Huet. The slave's answer was the same he would later give in court—he was obeying his master's orders.[17]

While, as Kolp's testimony made clear, the moment of violence in which Raymond whipped Huet was spectacular and elicited immediate responses, the other moment of violence that had led to it was passed over almost without comment by all involved in the trial. Two of the witnesses possibly did not even notice Huet's threats, although they could have been absent at that point. More tellingly, all who spoke of Huet's attempt to beat Raymond, including Huet and his lawyer, mentioned the act with no concern for the fact that it too was illegal, as only slaveowners or their delegates could legally beat their slaves. At no point in the proceedings did any of the judges, suspects, or officials involved challenge Huet's menacing behavior. Rather, this first attempted beating appears in the record as a natural response to a slave's petty theft.

This near passing over of Huet's violence appears to confirm Hilliard d'Auberteuil's claims that "[i]n Saint Domingue, whoever is White abuses the Black with impunity. Their situation is such that they are slaves of both their masters and the public."[18] The near complete absence of court records involving whites who simply beat another's slaves without further conse-quences also speaks in favor of Hilliard d'Auberteuil's assessment. As rec-ords of simple beatings of members of other groups making up colonial society do exist, it is extremely unlikely that slaves were immune to such violence.

Court records validate another of Hilliard d'Auberteuil's observations, namely that "in the wrong that has been done to the slave, the Judges have the practice of considering nothing beyond the diminution of their price."[19] For instance, in 1719, Léogane's conseil condemned a colonist to pay the price of a slave he had killed to the slave's owner.[20] Similarly, in 1765, Port-au-Prince's conseil confirmed a lower court decision ordering the Sieurs Giraude to pay Sieur Legendre twenty-five hundred livres for the cost of his slave Atis, whom they had killed, as well as one thousand livres in civil damages.[21]

Nonetheless, Saint Domingue's courts punished more severely those whites who killed another's slave with no justification whatsoever. In 1726, Petit Goave's conseil convicted a colonist of having "committed a murder in cold blood" in the person of another's slave. Not only was he ordered to pay the slave's price to his master, he was banished from the colony for ten years.[22] A case with a greater degree of atrocity led to a more rigorous punishment in 1780, when Port-au-Prince's conseil condemned a colonist "to be whipped, branded and sent to the galleys in perpetuity; for having in cold blood and without need for legitimate self-defense, cut the throats of two Negro maroons he had arrested."[23] Thus, if generally valid, Hilliard d'Auberteuil's statements regarding this matter were exaggerated.

They were also contested. The reactionary Dubuisson, in his point-by-point refutation of Hilliard d'Auberteuil's *Considérations sur l'état présent de la colonie française de Saint-Domingue*, flatly denied these claims, suggesting that slaves did not suffer such abuse quietly: "at the least blow they receive, they cry out loudly, and often bring their masters into the affair, who, out of pride or weakness, take their side immediately without knowing if they are in the wrong or in the right."[24]

Situations like that described by Dubuisson clearly occurred. Raymond complained to Cardeneau about Huet's abuse, and Cardeneau listened, even if the results were not those for which Raymond might have been hoping. Similarly, in the late 1760s in the Marmelade Parish, a slave driver's complaints to his mistress about a neighbor's violence against her slaves led to her writing the regional military commander to request protection, which was then granted.[25] Notably, in both of these cases, the slaves in question were elite slaves in the plantation hierarchy and as such had greater opportunities to request their masters' protection than most field hands had.

Taken together, Hilliard d'Auberteuil and Dubuisson have much to tell us about whites beating other people's slaves. Slaves were the members of colonial society most vulnerable to violence—not only did the courts remain uninterested unless a thrashing resulted in the loss of a slave's property value, slaves faced the most severe penalties for retaliating against a white attacker. In sum, social and legal sanctions against their use of violence and disrespect reinforced one another. Still, some slaves could succeed in soliciting their masters' protection. Others, of course, occasionally struck back regardless of the penalties they faced.

Two days after Huet's deposition, the judge interrogated Raymond. After establishing his identity (as a twenty-five-year-old Creole enslaved coach driver for the Delaville heirs' estate), the judge asked about the events in the marketplace. In his responses, Raymond minimized the extent of his offense to Huet. He claimed that he had not stolen the trumpet, and that instead of five or six lashes, he had given only three. Further, he asserted that he had not driven Huet to the porch of the saddlemaker, but rather only a "short distance."[26]

The remainder of the interrogation addressed issues of responsibility. Throughout, Raymond insisted that he had reluctantly obeyed his master's orders. He had hesitated "for the respect that he ha[d] for Whites," but ultimately gave the three lashes out of fear of punishment. Unsatisfied, the judge asked if he had not been motivated by a desire for revenge. He insisted that he had only done so for fear of punishment. When the judge asked him if he did not know that it was forbidden for slaves to do "illicit things" even on their master's orders, he responded "that he only . . . [knew] . . . the obedience due to Whites."[27]

Raymond's response to this last question seems extremely canny given the situation he found himself in. He did not answer that the only law he knew was obedience to his master, but rather obedience to "Whites." Even if the clerk was not faithful in rendering the suspect's words or if given the strains of the interrogation "Whites" came out of Raymond's mouth instead of "master," the slippage between the two terms remains telling. For Raymond, like all members of colonial society, was well aware of the importance of the colony's racial regime when it came to matters of authority and deference.

In fact, the violence discussed so far was inseparable from that involving Saint Domingue's free people of color.[28] For most white colonists, free people of color had to be kept in line to maintain slaves' respect for whites, which they considered necessary to both the maintenance of the slave regime and their own survival. Most would have agreed with the author of a 1787 *mémoire* on colonial policing, who argued that the free people of color needed "to be watched over . . . to contain them in the obedience they owe to the laws and in the respect they owe to Whites by the fear of a prompt punishment. It is mainly for this last reason that we need to watch over the free people of color; the Whites' safety depends on it, it is useless to enter into great detail on this subject; everyone knows that there are 10 blacks against one white, and what a misfortune it would be if a free black inspired feelings of revolt in the other blacks."[29]

For this author, it was "useless to enter into great detail" because he was stating a commonplace assumption. Like the conclusion of Huet's plaint, this *mémoire* expressed a common belief that the slave population was kept in line through everyday enactments of deference to those with white skin by those whose skin was black or colored. This deferential respect was the flip side of honor as hierarchy, as it was the comportment required (but rarely fully achieved) by elite whites from those deemed below them.

Contemporary witnesses suggested that one of the primary practices through which white colonists extracted this deference was simply beating "disrespectful" free people of color. This practice was all the more effective, these commentators claimed, because colonial authorities turned a blind eye to it. Julien Raimond, the most prominent spokesman for Saint Domingue's free colored planters, argued in 1786 that the fact that any white could excuse his beating of a free man of color by citing disrespect was the basis of the more general oppression he and his peers suffered. He claimed that through it colonial whites could take "the goods of a man of color, . . . his wife or his daughter."[30]

To back up these claims, Raimond referred to the writings of Hilliard d'Auberteuil. In doing so, he was not only citing a witness but also critiquing the fact that educated colonists defended such beatings. If Hilliard d'Auberteuil sometimes stood up for slaves, he was an apologist for beating free men of color. While he admitted that colonial prejudice was unjust, he insisted that it was needed to keep order in the ranks of society and maintain slaves' respect for whites. Claiming that "until the last few years, a White who believed himself offended by a mulatto would abuse him and beat him with impunity," he argued that colonial authorities should continue to allow this practice. Since "the superiority of Whites" required that free colored insolence be responded to "on the spot," he suggested, "there is a kind of humanity in allowing those who can to humiliate them with a punishment both prompt and in proportion to the insult."[31] Such beatings were to serve as lessons in deference to the recipients and, through their public humiliation, to all people of color, enslaved as well as free.

However, such encounters were ambivalent affairs in which a free man of color might strike back and reverse the lesson that the beating was meant to impart, as Dubuisson noted: "It is no longer possible to assure that a proud Mulatto . . . will suffer it very patiently if his physical forces are equal to those of the man hitting him; thus would result the politically dangerous spectacle of a White beaten by a man of color."[32]

In the final decades of the Old Regime, Dubuisson's predictions proved true more than once.[33] One such reversal occurred in 1781, when a white plantation manager, offended by the fact that a "free Negro" remained seated and did not remove his hat when speaking to him, attempted to remove the hat. The "free Negro" reacted by hitting and kicking the manager, tearing his shirt and pants.[34] Similarly, in one of the only recorded cases involving women as both the givers and the recipients of violence, in 1779 the attempts of a white soldier's wife to punish a woman of color who had insulted her resulted in a fight and the white woman being slapped by another "mulatress."[35]

Thus, as Dubuisson suggested, beatings could become free-for-alls, at least at the moment in which they occurred. Nonetheless, the equality born of physical strength or fighting skill was temporary, for the authorities dealt with cases in which a white was beaten by a free person of color very differently than those in which a white beat a free person of color. In the second case, the courts turned an almost blind eye, legitimizing it if not officially approving it. Criminal cases against whites for violence against free people of color are almost nonexistent in surviving court records.[36] Still, whites did not enjoy complete immunity. In a number of cases, when a free person of color who had been beaten sued his or her attacker, the courts awarded monetary civil damages.[37]

In contrast, instances in which a free person of color struck or threatened to strike a white were inevitably treated as criminal cases. While it does not appear to have been true, as Hilliard d'Auberteuil and Raimond asserted, that most free people of color who struck whites were given the death penalty, punishments were severe and usually involved public shaming and a loss of freedom.[38] The 1781 punishment of the "free Negro" who had fought back when a white tried to remove his hat was typical. Cap François's conseil sentenced him to be "placed in the iron collar for two hours in the marketplace . . . with this sign, 'Negro who is insolent towards Whites,' and then to be whipped, branded and attached to the public chain as a *forçat* [galley slave] for three years."[39] Such losses of freedom could also be permanent, either as intended punishment or as a result of the legal checks of a person of color's freedom that could occur when he or she became embroiled in the court system.[40]

The differential treatment of cases in which whites beat free people of color and those in which the opposite occurred likened people of color to slaves, reminding them of the "indelible stain of slavery" whites considered them to bear. If the public shaming they underwent did not make these connections clear, loss of freedom as a "galley slave" or through being sold into slavery did. More subtly, the form of justice they could obtain when beaten by whites did the same. They could claim monetary value for themselves, as masters could for their slaves, but they did not possess the social value whites had that made violence a criminal matter, namely honor. In other words, social and legal practice defined people of color's freedom as essentially different than that of whites. They were free to own themselves but not to participate in the public order constructed through the practices of honor.

On 14 May, the Senechal interrogated Cardeneau. After establishing his identity (as a fifty-three-year-old native of Aix-en-Gascogne serving as the manager of the Delaville heirs' plantation), the judge concentrated on questions regarding responsibility for what had happened. Cardeneau established his defense early on. He explained that from a distance he had seen someone beating Raymond, who was wearing the Delaville heirs' livery. Unable to discern whether the assailant was white or mulatto, he assumed the latter. Thus, when Raymond approached him, he responded, "How is it that you are letting yourself be beaten and you don't know how to defend yourself?" When asked if he had threatened his slave with a cane, he repeated his argument, claiming that he had only told his slave "to repel force by force, being persuaded that the Negro was in a dispute with another of his type [*espèce*] as for a long time he believed that it was a joke between them." Under the judge's continued prodding, he finally admitted that he did recognize Huet to be a white, but only after the whipping had taken place.[41]

The judge's final questions reminded his suspect of the illegality of all interpersonal violence outside institutions like the plantation or the household. He asked Cardeneau why he had authorized his slave to repel force with force rather than "presenting a complaint in court." The manager responded that he had done so without "evil intentions and always believing that the one mistreating his Negro was of the same status." Unsatisfied, the judge asked him if he could have authorized his slave to make his own justice even had Huet been a "man of the same status." Cardeneau responded that "he was not ignorant of the fact that it is not allowed to perform one's own justice, but that he had not remained master of his first reaction."[42]

Cardeneau's claims challenge the self-evidence of race as a visually definable category. His self-proclaimed inability to determine whether Huet was white or colored runs counter to the disciplinary logic that linked the deference of all people of color to the subordination of the enslaved population. However, no one else involved in the case acknowledged the possibility that such a misrecognition might be valid, nor was Huet called upon to justify his status as a white. How, then, did Cardeneau hope to succeed with this strategy?

First, for all that most eighteenth-century colonial whites were fairly secure in their use of somatic difference as a marker of social status, they were also aware that color was no sure sign of ancestral origin. As the Swiss visitor Girod de Chantrans pointed out, "Nature often ridicules these affairs in producing a slave much whiter than the Provençal who buys him."[43] The numerous cases of individuals ordered to justify their status as whites during the latter part of the eighteenth century attest to this fact as well.[44]

Second, elite whites routinely associated the colony's colored population with its poor whites, as did everyday life. Hilliard d'Auberteuil provided both an example of this association and an account of the social milieus in which such interactions took place: "These *mésalliés* that are seen in all the neighborhoods, these peddlers who only trade with Negroes, and only find asylum among them . . . these mixed companies of white and Negro cavaliers in the *maréchaussée*, this multitude of Whites who run cabarets, where wrongly they are allowed to assemble slaves . . . announce clearly that there are many whites who do not fear to compromise themselves to the highest degree."[45] Still, these associations of people of color and poor whites in everyday reality and in colonial elites' minds did not erase the racialized phenotypic characteristics used to distinguish among them. Elite commentators rarely noted physical similarities between the two, but rather interactions and similar forms of "dangerous" behavior.[46] Given those facts, and once again, the fact that no one else involved in the case questioned Huet's whiteness, how did Cardeneau expect the judge to believe his claims?

A strong possibility is that he never intended to convince the judge that he had, in fact, made such a mistake. Rather, his claims of misrecognition allowed him to sidestep his violation of the colony's racial order and, in doing so, to shift the focus of the case to matters of privilege among whites. However, he could not even appeal to personal prerogatives, for while he was socially above a peddler like Huet, he was not a planter or a royal officer but a paid director of a plantation. As such, he appropriated the prestige of his employers by emphasizing that what he had seen was someone beating a slave dressed in their livery. In Cardeneau's testimony, Huet's attempts to beat a slave thief became an assault on the property and prestige of the slave's owners.

For Cardeneau, and he hoped for his judges, this insult to him and his employers in the body of their slave necessitated a response as much as if it had been carried out by a free person of color or a slave. Elite whites demanded the same deference from all those they deemed to be below them, regardless of their skin color. In fact, commentators drew numerous analogies between Saint Domingue's nonwhite population and France's lower classes to explain colonial rank to a metropolitan audience. In his discussions of beating free men of color, Hilliard d'Auberteuil pointed out that in

France disrespect from "a man of the lowly people towards his superior" was punished with jail time. Similarly, the juriconsult Emilien Pétit, in a discussion of the particular respect owed by freedmen to their former owners, noted: "Let it be observed . . . that the police in France must equally maintain the respect owed by servants to . . . [their former] masters."[47]

Not surprisingly, some elite whites resorted to physical violence to impose deference upon other whites as they did with free people of color and slaves.[48] Similarly, differential treatment by the authorities validated some thrashings while penalizing others. However, claims to distinction among whites by way of interpersonal violence appear to have been more uncertain and contested than those involving a white and a nonwhite. In part, this difference resulted from the fact that *domingois* "white" society was on the whole more fluid than that of the metropole. The varying social origins of colonists, fortunes created through tropical agriculture, and the fact that in a world primarily populated by immigrants, the "true" family origins of many colonists were not matters of public record all contributed to this fluidity.[49] Perhaps more important, a certain process of social leveling among whites resulted from the placement of slaves and free people of color below all of them. This leveling was even more pronounced in the colony's economy of violence, for cases only involving whites were not overdetermined by its fundamental logic tying the deference of all people of color to the subordination of the enslaved masses.

Nonetheless, French social distinctions were not washed away by the Atlantic crossing. The same dynamic through which status took form in the interface between interpersonal negotiations involving violence and the royal authorities' differential treatment of that violence operated in regard to Saint Domingue's whites as well as its nonwhites. A near complete absence of cases in which clearly elite whites (for example, sugar planters or royal officers) beat whites clearly from the lowest ranks (for example, vagabonds or menial laborers) suggests that when such beatings occurred the former enjoyed a significant level of impunity. This possibility seems even stronger given the fact that in the 1660s and 1670s, Martiniquan authorities had gone so far as to authorize planters to beat freemasons and carpenters as they did their slaves and indentured servants due to their "costliness, their insolence and their laziness."[50]

In contrast, when lower-status whites attacked their superiors, they could find themselves facing both criminal and civil charges. For instance, when a fight between the slaves of two plantations developed into one between one's owner and the other's director in or around 1781, Cap François's conseil condemned the director to make a reparation of honor to the planter, apologizing for his "excesses, violence and batteries." He also had to pay fifteen hundred livres in damages and the costs of the publication of 100 copies of the sentence.[51] Similarly, in 1787, a mason was condemned to pay three thousand livres to a merchant whose leg he had injured.[52]

Further, the colonial context appears to have exacerbated some distinctions based upon profession. Such seems to have been the case with military officers, who appear to have been the group that most frequently resorted to exemplary beatings of other whites.[53] Their recourse to these practices reflects not only the violence of their professional culture but also, in all probability, a stronger sense of social distinction. While all military officers were not nobles, most were, and they represented a disproportionate share of Saint Domingue's nobility.[54] In addition, their disproportionate recourse to beatings resulted from their impunity. While more than one colonist beaten by military officers pressed charges, as did Louis Grandchamp in 1700 after Major de Brach struck him with "a stick on the bottom" and as Hilliard d'Auberteuil did when he was beaten "and left for dead" in 1772 by a group of officers, these investigations were usually quashed by colonial or metropolitan authorities.[55]

More generally, all royal officers enjoyed the greatest degree of the state's protection from real, threatened, or claimed beatings by other whites. In 1738, Léogane's conseil condemned a colonist to pay a one hundred livre fine, banished him from the jurisdiction of Jacmel for nine years, and brought him before both the conseil and Jacmel's court to be admonished and, bare-headed, on his knees, to admit that he had threatened to strike a judge and to ask his forgiveness.[56] Similarly, in 1785, Cap François's conseil declared a lawyer's clerk guilty of having "falsely and calumnously spread publicly the rumor that he had slapped" a military officer. The judges had him brought before the court by the executioner, and with the courtroom open to the public, made him perform a reparation of honor to the officer. He was also banned in perpetuity from the conseil's jurisdiction and ordered to pay ten thousand livres in damages.[57] The severity of these punishments resulted from the fact that the guilty parties had attacked both the personal honor of the officers in question and the royal authority manifest in the offices they held.

Nonetheless, due to the Old Regime's overlapping military, administrative, and judicial institutions and to the fact that these branches of government were often in conflict, even the outcomes of cases involving highly placed officials were by no means given. An extreme example of the vagaries of colonial justice occurred after Petit-Goave's conseil condemned a colonist to one month in jail, four thousand livres in fines, and the performance of a reparation of honor for having beaten and insulted one of its members in 1711. Two months later, the governor and intendant absolved the colonist and leveled accusations against the counselor, noting among other things that the "beating" had taken place in a cabaret. This series of events ultimately led to the counselor's removal from office "as unworthy and unqualified to hold it." Thus, due to the multiple and complex channels of colonial politics, a magistrate's attempt to uphold his public status in the wake of a beating led to his downfall.[58] This outcome highlights the fact that the arbitration of rank among whites was an ambivalent business.

The extent to which that ambivalence signaled a general, if uneven, leveling of distinctions among whites becomes clear in comparing the punishments meted out to lesser whites for attacking their superiors with those inflicted upon free people of color and slaves for similar offenses. Even if the same dynamic in which legal authorities selectively punished violence depending upon the perceived status of those involved held in all three cases, the forms punishments took reflected assumptions that less social distance separated any two whites than that separating any white and any person of color. Whites who beat their superiors were prosecuted criminally and faced serious penalties, including banishment and jail time. Nonetheless, these punishments were significantly less rigorous than those awaiting free people of color or slaves who beat whites, for example, serving as galley slaves or being hanged.

Moreover, the shaming elements of court sentences in these cases varied in ways that underscored the fact that the distinction between whites and nonwhites was more significant than any differences of status among whites. The admonishment or reparation of honor a white suffered in these cases, while public, was usually carried out in the dignity of the courtroom and not the chaos of the marketplace, as was the case for people of color. Further, while being forced to recant and ask forgiveness bare-headed and on one's knees was being put into a shaming posture, it was less humiliating than being placed in the iron collar with a sign around one's neck. Most tellingly, the fact that the most common form of shaming to which whites were sentenced was the reparation of honor, while people of color were almost never ordered to perform one, highlights a presumed level of equality among whites as well as the exclusion of those with African ancestry from it.[59] To perform such a reparation and as such actively participate in honorable society, an individual had to be deemed to possess some honor to begin with.

During the next six months, little progress took place in the proceedings—such delays were common for Old Regime justice. On 12 January 1775, the judge restarted the trial, and over the next two months he and his assistants completed the procedures required by French law to arrive at a judgment. They defined the crime as a felony and ordered both the witnesses and the suspects to revisit and confirm their testimony. During these reviews, held on 3 February, all who appeared before the judge confirmed the accounts they had given over six months earlier. Later the same day, Raymond was confronted with the witnesses and questioned regarding discrepancies between his testimony and theirs. He stuck to his story.[60]

The most notable event in the trial at this point was not this procedural matter, but rather the fact that Cardeneau failed to appear as ordered on 3 February. When the bailiff Jean-Baptiste Nau went to investigate his absence, he discovered that the manager had been missing for at least three months. To all appearances, Cardeneau had taken what was often an effective route for avoiding the law's rigor in the French Empire—he ran away.[61] While his motives for doing so remain unknown, his disappearance suggests that he feared the proceedings were not going his way. Undoubtedly, his interrogation had not reassured him, as the judge had remained skeptical regarding his misrecognition of Huet and had reminded him of the illegality of ordering Raymond to respond to violence with violence in any case. As the judge's pointed questioning had implied, Cardeneau's arguments betrayed a legally unfounded assumption that had Raymond and Huet been equals, the original beating would have called for direct retaliation.

In Saint Domingue, Cardeneau was far from alone in his belief that a man (especially if he was white and elite) had the right, if not the duty, to respond to violence from an equal in kind, particularly if insult had been part of the injury. Such beliefs possessed wide currency in France, whose rites of violence provided the models for colonial ones. The best known of these rites among equals was the duel. Originally a privilege of nobles and men of arms, by the eighteenth century its use had become common in bourgeois circles throughout the French Empire.[62] In Saint Domingue, many of the documented cases of duels and duel-like encounters involved commoners ranging from planters to legal clerks.[63] By the last half of the eighteenth century, even some free men of color had taken up the duel.[64]

The duel's continued existence represented one of the most visible failures of France's absolute monarchs to monopolize legitimate public violence. From the late sixteenth century forward, French kings prescribed draconian punishments for duelists. In 1679, Louis XIV declared it to be a crime of *lèse-majesté*, punishable by death and the refusal of church burial.[65] France's kings also created institutions to address the grievances that gave rise to single combat, establishing judges for "points of honor" between gentlemen and other "men of war."[66] This campaign against the duel was meant to be carried out throughout the French Empire, as Saint Domingue's conseils' adoption of the relevant royal legislation and ministerial letters attests.[67]

As was the case in the metropole, the monarchy's attempts to do away with the duel had little effect in Saint Domingue. Numerous single combats made their way into the archival record from the colony's early years through the end of the Old Regime.[68] The repeated nature of royal proscriptions points to their ineffectiveness, and some ministerial letters candidly acknowledged the failure of previous orders. In 1746, the minister of the navy wrote the colony's administrators, admitting, "It is effectively only too true that the pursuit and punishment of crimes of this sort is extremely neglected in this Colony."[69] As this quote suggests, the failure of the monarchy's campaign against dueling was largely attributable to the fact that its local agents did not enforce its laws.

This negligence, or perhaps resistance to the king's will, primarily resulted from the fact that its execution was entrusted to men who were not convinced of the duel's illegitimacy, and in any case did not believe that it merited the punishment the laws dictated.[70] On one hand, the duel was central to French military culture, and the military and police officers charged with the physical execution of the laws were unlikely to enforce them. On the other, men of law showed their acceptance of these rites of violence in their deeds and occasionally in their writings.[71] At the bottom of the legal hierarchy, two lawyer's clerks at Fort Dauphin (including a Jean-Baptiste Nau, possibly the same who as a bailiff had been sent to investigate the disappearance of Cardeneau) tried to provoke *combats particuliers* with three different colonists in 1786.[72] Further, while most such cases involved lawyers and their clerks, willingness to resort to duels also stretched to the men who filled the highest posts in the colonial judiciary. Even the colony's best-known magistrate, Moreau de Saint-Méry, confessed that during his Philadelphia exile in the 1790s he once went pistol in hand to demand satisfaction from a business associate.[73]

Reluctant magistrates were assisted in their quiet obstruction by the difficulty of defining a given encounter as a duel rather than self-defense or homicide. While some *combats singuliers* were tried as duels, others, like one that occurred in 1788, might have been "rather notorious among the public" as such, but due to "a lack of sufficient proofs to punish . . . [them] . . . properly," were defined as murders or homicides.[74] Similarly, even when the original call to fight was recognized to be such, a defendant could claim that he had refused it and then only defended himself after the caller attacked anyway, as was the case in 1742 when a lawyer claimed he had acted in self-defense in a sword fight in which he killed a colonist.[75]

Like the beatings of "insolent" inferiors, combats between equals (as long as they were free, and for the most part, white) derived their meaning from colonial conceptions of honor and hierarchy. Provocations to fight and the decision to accept can be viewed as complex negotiations of status among colonial whites carried out in the language and through the practices of honor. By definition, duels were fights among equals. As such, attempting to provoke one was a claim of equality. In the better-documented cases of such provocations, they inevitably came to involve assaults on the honor of the provoked. Such attacks could be the root cause of a fight, as was the case when Laurent de Graff killed another colonist sometime prior to 1685 in a sword fight that arose from the latter's attempts to ruin his reputation with "falsities and calumnies."[76] In other cases that arose from disputes over business, gambling, or women, the provoker's threats and insults made the affair into a "point of honor."[77]

On the other side of these negotiations, decisions about how to respond to provocations were assessments of relative social status. Agreeing to fight meant accepting one's opponent's claims of equality, and decisions to refuse a fight could be, among other things, refusals to accept such claims. The behaviors that could provoke a beating were the same as those that could provoke a fight—insults, threats, and aspersions on one's reputation. The difference between insolence requiring a disciplinary thrashing and insult requiring redress through single combat was thus primarily one of the perceived statuses of the two individuals involved. When provocations led to one-sided beatings instead of equal fights, refusals were clear. Other refusals, like simply saying that one would not fight or taking the matter before the courts, were more ambiguous, and in these cases the royal authorities, public opinion by way of gossip, or some combination of the two became the arbiters of both the claim and its refusal.

If white men's claims to inclusion through challenges to fight were contingent, the refusal of all whites to admit that slaves and free people of color could participate in the civic order defined in terms of honor was much clearer. Further, that refusal was not limited to forbidding nonwhites to join them on the terrain upon which they disputed their own hierarchies. It also involved denying the possibility that nonwhites might construct their own such order. Even if Cardeneau's defense relied upon appealing to the rights of all men, including slaves like Raymond, to physically stand up for themselves against their peers, the plantation manager had made this appeal in a way that limited the seriousness of any such fights between men of color. In his interrogation, he had insisted that "he believed that it was a joke between them [i.e., Raymond and Huet as a 'mulatto']."[78]

Strikingly, Raymond pursued a similar strategy. In his final interrogation prior to sentencing, he explained that the original incident giving rise to Huet's complaints had been his joking with one of his peers. More specifically, he had not taken the trumpet from Huet's stand but rather from another peddler's slave. He claimed that as he did so he had told this slave, "I will put it back after I've had a bit of fun with it." Huet had then mistaken it for his.[79]

This convergence in the testimony of master and slave points to the fact that both saw "play" as an appropriate mode of interaction between men of color. While white men could resolve honor-based conflicts by physical violence, slaves, by definition devoid of honor, had open to them the less "serious" realm of "play." In fact, play appears to have been a major trope by which whites tried to understand and contain the violence inherent in conflicts between nonwhites, and especially slaves, as something different than that between themselves. It was also a strategy many slaves used to preserve their senses of self in the face of the punishments awaiting them if they resorted to force.

For elite whites, the relegation of slave violence to the realm of "play" was, however, ambiguous, for at no point was the very real potential of such violence absent from their thoughts. The uncertainties involved in this transfer can be seen in Moreau de Saint-Méry's description of stick fighting. He began this account by identifying jealousy and *amour propre* as the primary causes of conflict among "Negroes." Notably, these were the motors of much honor-based conflict between whites, although he did not make this comparison explicit. The use of the term *amour propre* is particularly telling, as it conveyed the sense of one component of honor, self-image or self-worth, while remaining mute as to its other central component, the social validation of that self-image.[80]

Next, Moreau de Saint-Méry described the bloodier of two forms of stick fighting: "[A]s they aim at the head, the blows they deliver are always serious. The combatants are quickly bloodied and it isn't easy to separate them when anger transports them and when the combat is begun after each Negro wets his finger with saliva, passes it by the ground to bring it back to his tongue, and then striking his chest with his hand and raising his eyes towards the Heavens, he has thus performed, in his opinion, the most frightful of oaths."[81]

The ritual nature and the deadliness of such combat is clear, and the salute and oath beckon comparisons with the duel.[82] Immediately afterward, however, he passed on to a description of a more entertaining, less dangerous use of this "murderous stick" in "a type of contest": "One cannot help but admire the rapidity with which blows are delivered and evaded by two well-practiced Negroes. They threaten each other, turn one around the other in order to surprise, holding the stick and always moving both hands; then suddenly a strike is made, the other stick parries it, and the blows are thus delivered and riposted alternately until one of the combatants is touched by the other. This joust . . . has rules like fencing; a new athlete replaces the vanquished and the palm is given to the most skillful." He then concluded his discussion by grouping these tournaments together with dances.[83]

In the transition from deadly battle to skillful sport, Moreau de Saint-Méry textually contained some of the violence present in the first passage. As he was describing two different kinds of stick fights and acknowledged the violence of the first, the point is not that colonists could not admit slaves' violent potential. In fact, even in Moreau de Saint-Méry's second passage its threat and parallels to French rites return implicitly in his likening of these "jousts" to fencing—just as the primary practical use of fencing was, by the end of the eighteenth century, preparation for dueling, these jousts could be seen as practice for more serious stick fights, or even as a form of military training.[84] Instead, the point is that even the most self-aware colonists such as Moreau de Saint-Méry tended to displace the potential violence of slaves into the realm of "play" to whatever extent they could. It was not coincidental that of the two scenes, he included an image of the second in a collection of engravings he had made, and that in that collection, "Negroes playing with Sticks" was paired with "Negroes' Dance."[85]

For colonial whites, the ambiguities of "play" stretched even further, as slaves drawing on African trickster traditions and taking advantage of the relative permissibility of joking did not spare their "superiors" from their barbs.[86] The missionary Père Labat noted this fact in late seventeenth-century Martinique, claiming that "few people apply themselves more successfully than they to know the failings of people, and especially of whites, to then make fun of them and mock them continually."[87] The actions of Raymond in the market before the lashing suggest that he was playing the trickster, although he was more likely "having fun" with Huet than with another slave. The trumpet incident, the return for his hat, and perhaps even his original complaints to Cardeneau all suggest mockery.

Such joking, of course, could be interpreted by whites as precisely the sort of disrespect that was not permissible. Thus, it was not without its risks for the slaves who used it to cope with colonial society. In the case of Raymond, the potentially disastrous consequences are clear. Like provocative actions of whites before each other, "play" was subject to the give and take of the moment and the evaluation of the mocked as to what had happened. The difference between the two was that the provocative behavior of whites could be more direct and carried out in more serious tones. Slaves could only get away with it if they kept their provocations in the register of joking, and the butt of their jokes followed Dubuisson's advice on these matters: "The Negroes are more or less like the women of Les Halles who you have to let cry out without paying attention to their invective."[88]

At 4 P.M. on 2 March 1775, the court clerk and royal prosecutor entered Saint Marc's jails to read Raymond his sentence. The enslaved coachman was to perform the *amende honorable*, a ritual act combining penitence with a type of reparation of honor, before the church of Petite Rivière, "to then have his fist cut off before said church's door, and from there be brought in a trash cart to the marketplace . . . to be hanged and strangled until dead." Cardeneau, if he could be found, was to pay a ten-livre fine and be banned from ever owning slaves or being placed in command of them.[89] The royal prosecutor then announced that he would appeal the sentence before the conseil supérieur, as required in all cases involving the death penalty. It appears that the conseil decided that part of the trial had to be redone, since three months later, the proceedings in Saint Marc were begun again by a new judge.[90] Completed on 12 September 1775, this second trial produced a sentence that conformed in its entirety to that of the first.[91]

The royal prosecutor appealed the second sentence as well, and a little over a month later, Port-au-Prince's conseil reviewed the case, interrogated Raymond one last time, and made its decision. The counselors increased Cardeneau's punishment to include perpetual banishment from the colony and the confiscation of his belongings. Raymond's original sentence was "to have its full and entire execution."[92] Thus, while the upper court differed in its evaluation of Cardeneau's responsibility, both courts agreed that Raymond should lose the hand that struck Huet, along with his life.

The differences between Cardeneau's and Raymond's sentences did not only reflect the centrality of hierarchy to the workings of Old Regime justice.

They also resulted from magistrates' understandings of what were for them very different offenses. Cardeneau deserved punishment for his rash actions, but he had behaved more or less in accordance with his station. For all that his judges reminded him of the illegality of beating an inferior or fighting an equal, their sentences appear to reflect an understanding of the reasons behind his actions. In contrast, Raymond had, albeit under duress, violated one of the most serious taboos of colonial society—he, as a "Negro" slave, had publicly whipped and humiliated a white. He had not only broken the codes proscribing violence on the part of people of color against whites, he had done so in a way that appropriated a central practice by which hierarchy, understood in terms of honor, was enacted and maintained. Thus, he had inadvertently taken for himself, a slave defined by elites as devoid of honor, that very social distinction. The gravity of his crime resulted from the fact that this entry of a slave onto the field of honor threatened to demolish the colonial order built upon it.

DANSE DE NÉGRES.   NÉGRES JOUANT AU BÂTON.

Figure 10.1. "Danse de Négres" (Negroes' dance) and "Négres Jouant au Bâton" (Negroes paling with sticks). Engravings by Nicolas Ponce, from M. Moreau de Saint-Méry, *Recueil de vues des lieux principaux de la colonie françoise de Saint-Domingue, gravéespar le soins de M. Ponce . . . Accompagn'ees de cartes et plans de la même colonie, graves par les soins de M. Phelipeau . . . Le tout principalement destiné à le'ouvrage intitulé: L'oix et constitutions des colonies françoises de l'Amérique sous le Vent, avec leur description, leur histoire, &c. par M. Moreau de Saint-Méry* (Paris: M. Moreau de Saint-Méry [etc.], 1791), figure 26, detail of lower right quadrant. Beinecke Rare Book and Manuscript Library, Yale University.

Comprehending the differences between Raymond's violation and Cardeneau's offense requires an understanding of a variety of practices binding
status, violence, and honor to one another. Further, as the range of possible
interactions announced during the proceedings against the two suggests,
these practices were connected in the minds and deeds of the actors involved. Beatings of free people of color by whites drew much of their meaning from those attached to beatings of slaves by whites and of inferior whites
by other whites, as well as the social and legal sanctions against the reversals
of such scenes. Similarly, the well-noted inclusive and exclusive aspects of
fights between equals could only exist because other practices like beatings
were used to create and maintain the hierarchies in which such equality was
made possible.[93] The full significance of the privilege of some white men to
fight other white men only becomes clear when one considers that not only
were "colored" men, lesser white men, and women denied this right, they
could not even defend their bodies from beatings by elite white men. Not
only were the components of identity in the colonial hierarchy relational in
nature, so were the practices through which identities were claimed, contested, refused, and affirmed. In sum, understanding any of the honor-bound
practices relating violence and social status requires a comprehension of the
place of those practices in the economy of violence in which they operated.

The case did not end with the conseil's decision. On 10 November, the
governor and intendant suspended the sentence's execution and, with the
conseil's royal prosecutor, requested the king's grace for Raymond. They
summed up their arguments by insisting upon the need to reinforce masters' authority in the face of the colony's demographic imbalances. As they
put it, "[T]he obedience of a slave . . . must be servile and absolute," and
complete chaos would result "if it were to be put forth in principle [as Raymond's sentence implied] that the slave can disobey his master in particular cases of which he himself would be the judge!"[94] The minister agreed
and, on 1 November 1776, Louis XVI pardoned Raymond.

This twist reminds us that the logics linking violence and social hierarchy discussed in this chapter, while important, were not the only ones
operating in Saint Domingue. In this case, the colony's regime of "domestic
sovereignty" won out over its racially based economy of violence. At this
moment in time, the highest colonial and metropolitan authorities agreed
that the maintenance of a master's absolute discipline over his slaves was
the primary means by which the slave regime was to be preserved. Those
authorities had not always favored domestic sovereignty so strongly, nor
would they always do so.[95] For the moment, however, Raymond had chosen
the best possible defense, which also was the only real one open to him.

Still, neither did the case end at this point, for Raymond's pardon had to be registered by Port-au-Prince's conseil to take effect. Despite multiple attempts by the Delaville heirs to register it, Raymond was still in jail two and a half years after it was issued. At this point, on 10 April 1779, the minister of the navy wrote the intendant and governor, ordering them to attend the conseil and use their authority to make the counselors register it.[96] Whether this order was fulfilled or not remains unknown, for at this point, Raymond, Huet, and Cardeneau disappear from the documentary record. The motives behind the conseil's resistance also remain unclear. Perhaps they were opposed to freeing a slave who had publicly beaten a white. More likely, it was yet another moment in their continuing struggles with the colony's royal administrators.[97] In any case, Raymond had now spent almost five years in jail, and if he was freed, was then returned to his owners' plantation.

Chapter 11

Racial Passing: Informal and Official "Whiteness" in Colonial Spanish America

Ann Twinam

Throughout the centuries, a traditional privilege of Spanish monarchs was to override discriminatory laws and intervene to erase "defects" of heritage or birth. By the early eighteenth century, the crown had institutionalized this process—known as *gracias al sacar*—for the Americas. Petitioners might appeal to the Cámara, a subgroup of the Council of the Indies, to demonstrate their worth and pay for the dispensation of a variety of *gracias*.[1] Foreigners might eliminate their accident of birth by purchasing Spanish citizenship; plebeians might overcome parentage to acquire nobility; illegitimates might be transformed into legitimates. Then, in 1795, in a newly issued price list (*arancel*) for the Americas appeared these whitening clauses: "For the dispensation of the calidad of Pardo [dark skinned] one will make the payment of 500 reales. And for that of the calidad of *Quinterón* [one-fifth black], one will pay with 800 reales."[2] On their face the new provisions permitted pardos and *quinterones* officially to alter their status (*calidad*), no longer suffer prejudice, and enjoy the perquisites of whites.

From the beginning, the concept of whitening has engaged Latin Americanists, especially U.S. Latin Americanists, no doubt due to our own tortured heritage concerning issues of race. Even today, the idea that the benefits of whiteness could simply be purchased remains stunning. It highlights provocative differences between Hispanic and Anglo colonial worlds where, in the former, pardoness or darkness seems to have existed as a construct that could be bureaucratized, commoditized, and erased.

Unlike other *gracias al sacar* benefits, the purchase of whiteness was also distinguished by its colonial boundaries. While inhabitants of both the Spanish metropole and the American colony petitioned the Councils of Castile or the Indies for citizenship or nobility or legitimacy, only those of mixed African ancestry in the colonial Americas sought whiteness. Their quest illuminates what Ann Stoler and Frederick Cooper have identified as a "central . . . point of recent colonial scholarship," the recognition that the "otherness of the colonized person was neither inherent nor stable," given that "difference had to be defined and maintained."[3] This social/racial ambiguity becomes what Stoler locates as one of the central "dilemmas of colonial rule" given the ever-present "tension" between a "domination" that embodied both "incorporation and distancing."[4]

Gracias al sacar whitenings prove to be a particularly rich source for exploring colonial tensions of inclusion and exclusion. Embedded within the bureaucratic process is a dynamic that promotes rare conversations about norms and exceptions to norms. The petitioners in *gracias al sacar* are at a cusp—they are at the edge of a permeable social boundary—in their applications they articulate what their present condition is, explain why they want it changed, and argue why they deserve that it should be altered. Another dialogue occurs when royal officials at a number of levels consider norms and whether petitions meet the standards for status change.

While historians had long debated the significance of these whitening clauses, the discussion was hampered because the *gracias al sacar* petitions had not been located in the Archive of the Indies. Magnus Mörner had speculated that the whitening clauses might reflect a liberal, even a radical social policy. In that scenario, the activist Bourbon state intervened against the wishes of the Creole elite by venting the social pressure of oppressed castes through granting decrees promoting the upward mobility of selected mulattoes. In the process, the state not only won their loyalty but also benefited from their contributions. Yet others, such as Daisy Rípodas Ardanz and Susan Socolow, pointed to the racially contradictory aspects of other Bourbon social reforms. They focused on the Pragmatic Sanction on Marriages (1778), which restricted passing by giving fathers the power to prevent the marriage of their offspring to racial unequals. From this perspective, the Bourbon state was a conservative defender of colonial hierarchy; it buttressed the power of the white elite to maintain endogamy.

My breaking of an Archive of the Indies locational code and the systematic collection of the whitening materials provides a quick answer to this debate: although there were wobbles back and forth, royal officials usually came down on the conservative side.[5] Only a minuscule number of pardos and mulattoes applied for whitening, as there were only fifteen applications between 1795 and 1816. While officials were initially favorable, granting eight of the first eleven submitted, they tabled the remaining applications after 1803, sending the negative message that any future petitions would remain in limbo.[6] The suspension occurred because the Venezuelan elite so strongly protested the 1795 measure that local bureaucrats issued the famous *Obedesco pero no cumplo* (I obey but I do not comply). This was a rare and last-gap measure used only in dire necessity when local officials feared that an imperial law was so against their interests that they had to suspend its execution temporarily and then plead for revocation or revision. As Indies officials fought with the Venezuelan elites, and imperial officials debated, decisions on whitening remained suspended until a policy could be formulated. Further procrastination combined with the Napoleonic invasion of Spain in 1808 and the Spanish American Independence wars in 1810 to foreclose any effective decision.[7]

Although the 1795 *gracias al sacar* officially whitened only a handful of individuals, it generated a fascinating and insightful historical discussion between imperial and local royal officials, pardos and mulattoes, and colonial elites, over exceptions to rules. Most notable is that this conversation long predated the 1795 *gracias al sacar*. Royal decrees and legislation reveal that from the beginning of the colony, pardos and mulattoes had been petitioning the king for various forms of dispensations from the "defect" of their race. Their letters and depositions combine with subsequent royal responses to mark centuries of ongoing efforts to carve out racialized spaces, revealing both successes and failures. Exploration of such negotiations reveals some of the limits and the extent to which pardos and mulattoes, either as individuals or as groups, might negotiate niches, then toeholds, and then officially or unofficially pass to enjoy the status of whites.

The Background and Nature of Official Discrimination

Pardos and mulattoes must have found it particularly depressing to live in Spanish America during the sixteenth and seventeenth centuries.[8] With rare exceptions, the only imperial notice taken of their existence was negative and repressive. The tendency of imperial bureaucrats was to characterize pardos and mulattoes as ad hominen problems, rather than differentiating among individuals or between groups.

Although royal officials never made the analogy directly, some of their first comments reveal mounting concerns that the free black descendants of slaves and their mixed race offspring, were—somewhat like other European introductions such as pigs or horses—flourishing and multiplying at a too-rapid rate in the favorable environment of the Americas. Sixteenth-century legislation reveals a variety of attempts to control the novel and unexpected burgeoning of free mixed-blood populations. As early as 1553, officials in Central America were worrying about the clustering of free blacks in "towns, and mines, and mills."[9] By 1560, officials in Lima complained of the "excess" of free blacks; eight years later, Mexican authorities were similarly worried by the "great quantities of mulattoes . . . that have bad inclinations."[10] The next generation of Limeño officials (1586) found the situation getting worse —although here it is also possible to read between the lines of their critique and perceive that the censured may have been enjoying some distance and freedom from the colonial establishment. Peruvian officials complained that "in these provinces there are many blacks, mulattoes and mestizos and people of other mixtures and that each day the number of them increases and . . . many of them do not know their parents and they grow up in great vice and liberty without working, they have no occupation and eat and drink without order and mingle with the Indian men and women and join in their drunkenness and witchcraft and do not hear mass."[11]

Nor had the situation improved by the early seventeenth century. In 1607, Peruvian bureaucrats described the "great number of mulattoes" who, with no schools to attend, "wander without any guidance during the period when they ought to be developing good customs and they become vicious and slothful."[12] The situation was no better in Mexico that year as officials portrayed mulattoes as "hucksters" and their women as "dressed with great disorder."[13] In 1608, Peruvian bureaucrats again noted the "great quantity" of freed mixed-blood populations that "each day is multiplying." They worried "what remedy they could take [because of] the growth of that group and what form of government could be imposed."[14]

Not only were free black and mulatto populations rapidly increasing, they were intermingling with the white and Native populations, creating complicated mixtures of castas that negated the Spanish vision of the Americas as a society limited to *Dos Republicas* (Two Republics), one of Spaniards and the other of Indians.[15] From the sixteenth through eighteenth centuries, colonial policymakers strove to mitigate the propensity of free black and mulatto populations to mingle with Native peoples. A royal decree in 1551 considered blacks to be "very prejudicial" to Indians because they "helped them in their drunkenness and other bad habits . . . and do them much harm."[16] Royal decrees forbade blacks to live with Indians in 1580 in Peru, in 1584 in Chile, in 1586 in Lima.[17] In 1587, officials in Guatemala, complained of the "bad inclination" of the mulattoes and Negroes who aggravated and harmed the Indians "taking from them their food, women, and children."[18]

The frequency of later orders (1605, 1607, 1646, 1666, 1671, 1681, 1697) man-dating that free pardo and black populations maintain distance from Indi-ans can be directly correlated with their inefficacy.[19] By the late colonial period, the campaign had extended from the core Native populations of the center to the Spanish frontier where, in 1785, the bishop of Sonora was still vainly attempting to remove free mulattoes and blacks from Indian towns.[20]

Even though royal officials ordered free blacks and pardos to stay away from the Natives, both groups paid a special colonial tax, called tribute, dis-tinguishing them from whites. One of the earliest royal decrees (1574) on taxes recalled the "free blacks are multiplying" theme, noting that "many of the male and female black slaves and mulattoes that have passed to our Indies, and that have been born and live there, with the great riches that are in those parts, have saved and become free, and these have many profits and wealth."[21]

A series of royal laws, including in Mexico in 1577, Guatemala in 1587, Venezuela in 1592, and Chile in 1703, detailed the subsequent difficulties in collecting taxes from this mobile and color-shifting population.[22] By the mid-sixteenth century (1552, 1560 in Peru, 1612 in Mexico) discriminatory measures also forbade blacks and mulattoes to carry arms.[23] In Mexico and Peru, sumptuary regulations attempted to establish social distance by for-bidding black or mulatto women to wear any "jewel[s] of gold or silver, nor pearls, nor dresses of Castilian silk, nor robes of silk, or gold or silver lace."[24]

Yet the most draconian measures limiting the mobility of free mulatto and pardo populations did not derive from colonial legislation. Rather, they originated from the historic, prejudicial edicts encapsulated in the Spanish *limpieza de sangre*, clean or pure blood ordinances. Crystallizing in the for-mative era of the late fifteenth century, the purity of blood edicts were in-strumental in the forging of early Spanish nationhood, as they encouraged Spaniards to identify each other through shared discrimination against the despised "other." In the peninsula, the primary targeted "other" proved to be the non-Catholic, be it the "Jew," "Moor," or "*converso*" (converted Jew).[25]

In the colonies, the *limpieza de sangre* definition of the non-Catholic "other" became complicated with caste status. The historicizing of this trans-formation has yet to be detailed. One possibility is that the Moor, originally looked down upon due to Islam, became the template for the overlay image of the racially dark Moor, rationalizing the extension of *limpieza de sangre* discrimination to blacks, mulattoes, and the castas.[26] By the late eighteenth century, Spanish American Creoles typically defined those with *limpieza de sangre* as having "always been known, held, and commonly reputed to be white persons, Old Christians of the nobility, clean of all bad blood and without any mixture of commoner, Jew, Moor, mulatto, or converso in any degree, no matter how remote."[27]

Whether in Spain or America, discrimination against those lacking "clean blood" was extreme. The victims of that prejudice suffered what one seventeenth-century writer aptly characterized as a "civil death," as they were barred from access to political office, the practice of prestigious professions, and enjoyment of social status.[28] The Royal Pragmatic of 1501—promulgated by Ferdinand and Isabella just as Spanish ships were first charting the coasts of America—summarized much of this discrimination. The law listed more than forty offices barred to those who could not prove *limpieza de sangre.* The catalogue included not only high imperial positions such as royal councilors, judges in *audiencias* and governors, but also local officers such as *corregidores, regidores,* and *alcaldes.* Such requirements affected every "public office" throughout the realm. The 1501 Pragmatic also limited certain professions to those who could prove *limpieza.* Public notaries, lawyers, surgeons, pharmacists, and assayers also had to provide proof of their purity of blood.

Parallel ordinances demanding *limpieza* in military orders, the military, religious congregations, colleges, and universities complemented imperial regulations on *limpieza de sangre.*[29] When colonial American institutions such as colleges and universities wrote their own guidelines, they based them on peninsular models and included these prohibitions as well. The effect was to bar those without *limpieza* from obtaining formal education to practice law, enter the priesthood, or become medical doctors.[30] Both men and women with such "defects" lacked honor, marking them as social inferiors, unable to pass that elite prerequisite to succeeding generations.

Race, birth, *limpieza,* and illegitimacy were often linked because clean blood needed to be substantiated through genealogy, and those who were illegitimate could seldom prove parentage. Since illegitimacy rates were particularly high in the black, mulatto, and casta populations, these suffered dual defects that passed to their descendants.[31] For most purposes, including entrance to public office or a university, candidates had to provide genealogies demonstrating a minimum of three generations of ancestors who could prove their *limpieza.*

Such were the formidable obstacles that pardos and mulattoes faced as they sought to negotiate spaces for upward mobility. They were denigrated in early colonial legislation and singled out for special taxation and restrictions.

Historic Spanish prejudices against those lacking *limpieza* made them ineligible for public office, for military service, for the priesthood, for higher education, and for most professions. Even if they bypassed the "defect" of race, many were excluded due to illegitimacy. They lacked honor and were at the bottom of the social hierarchy.[32]

Passing as a Process

How did pardos and mulattoes subvert colonial systems of control? One answer is that embedded within the cultural codes of the Spanish system that repressed them were customary avenues of escape. The Hispanic world not only consciously recognized two spheres, a private and a public world, but also accepted that there could be passing, or a dichotomy between a person's private reality and an alternative, publicly constructed status. This dual vision complemented a monarchical tradition of altering public status through the dispensation of favors, or *gracias*, that officially eliminated selected "defects." The combination of dual worlds and royal *gracias* was at the core of traditional processes of Hispanic mobility.

Spaniards and Spanish Americans inhabited two worlds: one a private sphere where family, kin, and intimate friends shared confidences, trusted each other, provided mutual support and promoted each other's status in the outside world.[33] The other was a world where private reality might, or might not, be congruent with public status and reputation. Such bifurcation commonly occurred when violation of norms or certain "defects" threatened public status. Thus, unmarried women might be privately pregnant but have public reputations as virgins; fathers might recognize illegitimate children in private but not in public; men might be sodomites in private but officials of the church in public; illegitimates might construct public reputations that they were legitimates.

The process of passing was similar for pardos and mulattoes. Males might construct superior public personae and pass unofficially to hold public offices or practice professions traditionally reserved to whites; females might marry white husbands, enjoying reputations as women of honor.[34] This, of course, was very different from the United States, where, as Barbara Fields has noted, passing was considered "a particularly insidious form of deceit."[35] In Spanish America, passing was an openly acknowledged and widely accepted social phenomenon.

Not only popular acceptance of such social dualities but also monarchical traditions facilitated passing. From the beginning of the Spanish state, kings had dispensed favors (*gracias*) by officially altering public personae, no matter the private reality. As one Spanish historian noted, "The king counts more than blood [*Mas pesa el rey que la sangre*]."[36] Underlying the royal ability to transform public status was the legal vision that the monarch was superior to positive law and could alter its impact by eliminating prescribed discrimination. Throughout the centuries, Spanish kings had bypassed official discrimination, transforming *conversos* (of Jewish origin) into Old Christians and illegitimates into legitimates. From the Spanish legal viewpoint, the absence of whiteness was an equivalent characteristic, a "quality" or a "defect" similar to Jewish ancestry or illegitimacy, which the monarch could officially alter thus providing partial privileges or the total public personality of whiteness. In effect, mulattoes and pardos could tap into an already existing process of alteration of public personae and officially have their "defects" eliminated to pass as white.

Such royal favors were seldom dispensed lightly. Rather, they were rewards doled out by the monarch or his bureaucratic agents to deserving vassals who had demonstrated exceptional merit and service to the state. To be able to access traditional Hispanic mobility pathways, pardos and mulattoes, like other stigmatized groups, had to overcome the generalized negativity toward their very presence, such as their increasing numbers and their interactions with Natives; they had to bypass the legislation targeted against them, and they had to subvert the *limpieza de sangre* restrictions that barred them from public service and professions—the traditional arenas for service.

Analysis of royal decrees from the early to late colonial period reveals how pardos and mulattoes negotiated spaces where they might demonstrate their merit and services and make credible appeals for royal *gracias*. Two overarching patterns emerge. First is that dispensation from discrimination was usually first given to exceptional individuals; as time passed, the Crown might extend the benefit to designated pardo or mulatto groups. Second, pardos and mulattoes approached their ultimate goal of whiteness through an incremental subversion of colonial "categories of control."[37] Their strategy differed over time: in the early colonial period they sought to shed a specific kind of discrimination attached to their caste; by the mid-eighteenth century they tried to appropriate a limited perquisite of whiteness; by the end of the eighteenth century they requested total whiteness.

Official and Unofficial Passing: Sixteenth and Seventeenth Centuries

Exploration of royal decrees in the early colonial period, from the mid-sixteenth through the seventeenth centuries, suggests that the first imperial orders favoring pardos and mulattoes were not to make them white. Rather, the Crown issued partial dispensations to a favored individual or group providing relief from a specific discrimination attached to caste. The early strategy of pardos and mulattoes was thus to cast off negatives attached to their caste status and to better their position compared to peers, rather than seeking white privileges.[38] Almost without exception, pardos and mulattoes found military like or militia duties to be one of the first arenas where they might demonstrate royal service, making them eligible for some forms of *gracias*. As a result, official dispensations were, at least at the start, necessarily restricted to men—although wives, sisters, and daughters might receive contingent benefits from the raised status of the family's male.

One of the earliest such exemptions occurred in 1578, when Sebastian de Toral, a *moreno* (dark-skinned male) from Yucatán, Mexico asked to be excluded from the Crown's assignation of tribute payments to mulattoes. His petition noted that he was among the first settlers of the region—he had already lived in Yucatán for forty years. Furthermore, he had served as a guard and performed sentry duty without salary. The decree granting exemption to himself and his offspring agreed that the tribute imposition "had caused offense, because [Toral] was worthy of receiving much favor given he has served us greatly."[39] Considered from another perspective, the Crown had indirectly begun a process of potential whitening. With Toral removed from the mulatto tribute rolls, he—as well as his wife and his children—would be taxed as whites, a key step toward the blurring of racial identity over the generations.

Freedom from paying tribute payments, which marked the payer as racially inferior, was expanded from individuals to a selected group, the pardo/mulatto militia, in the seventeenth century. The Crown had balanced the prohibition that individual mulattoes not carry firearms with the pressing need for trained militias to repel foreign invaders. One turning point occurred in Peru, when free black and mulatto companies helped defend the port of Callao against a Dutch attack in 1627. In reward, the crown exempted them from paying tribute and extended the favor to similar companies in the port of Paita a decade later.[40] By 1670, members of free mulatto militias in Vera Cruz, Mexico, were also exempted from tribute assigned to their race.[41] Just as with the case of Toral, the result was that the next generation of men and women could proclaim that their parents were not relegated to the tax status of pardos and mulattoes, but paid the taxes of whites.

Another potential step in pardo/mulatto mobility occurred when militias were permitted to choose their own officers, rather than serve under white officers. Again, the process occurred first with individual requests for dispensations that were later extended to groups. By 1657, the existence of pardo militia units meant that someone like Peruvian Juan de Valladolid Moboron, a free *moreno*, could present evidence of substantial service. He was of legitimate birth, so only his race was a "defect." He had begun his career as a soldier, then became the head of a squadron, later an ensign and an aide-de-camp to six companies of free blacks and mulattoes. During these years he had helped repel an invasion at Valdivia, contributed to the construction of the port of Callao, and served for eleven years in the Southern Armada. He asked to be appointed head (*maestre de campo*) of the militia companies of Lima and Callao, although such a position was normally reserved for whites. Royal officials agreed that it would be "proportionate . . . to honor and favor him according to the merits."[42]

By the mid-seventeenth century, the previous, almost uniformly negative descriptions of pardos and mulattoes had altered when royal officials described the militias. In 1663, while bureaucrats still spoke disparagingly of the "great number" of mulattoes and blacks, they now also singled out the "courage" of the militia companies, their bearing of "work and discomfort," and their "vigor"—in this instance, in the defense of Santo Domingo against an English attack in 1655.[43] The reward for Mexican mulattoes and pardos was to receive permission to nominate their own members for "captains and other posts." By 1708, similar militias in Panama were also reminding the Crown of their "courage and zeal" for royal service and asking for the same favor. In 1718, they successfully pleaded that their own members first serve as "soldiers, squadron heads, sergeants and lieutenants" and then "pass to be captains of their companies, without conferring them on Spaniards," a privilege that was already customary in Mexico and Peru.[44]

The creation of mulatto and pardo military officers marked a significant step in the potential for whitening, as these formed an cohort that possessed serious credentials according to traditional Spanish standards for *gracias*.[45] The stage was set for the granting of royal favors either on their own behalf or for the mobility of their children. It is no accident that in future years a notable number of petitioners for whiteness would either have served in the free pardo/mulatto militias themselves or had fathers with military records.[46]

One of the consistencies of Spanish processes for awarding *gracias* was that exceptions might always be made to discriminatory norms. It was thus that Panamanian Vicente Mendez, a *moreno*, achieved the colonial office of governor of a town in 1687—a position reserved solely for whites.[47] Mendez was at the cutting edge of this cohort of upwardly mobile pardos, as he served in the military, first as a soldier, then as the head of a squadron, a sergeant, a lieutenant, and a captain. In the relative backwater of Panama, he had distinguished himself by routing pirates and rounding up the Indians of Darien to found the town he eventually governed. The local bishop wrote to support his assumption of that post, praising Mendez's "valor" and adding that the "pirates . . . know and fear him, and the Indians of Darien, rather than fear him, love him."

The letters of Panamanian elites did not employ a vocabulary that in-dicated—as would some counterpart endorsements in the eighteenth cen-tury—that they ever accepted Mendez as a peer.[48] Rather, his advocates more commonly argued that he did not share in the "defects" of his race. The bishop, for example, proclaimed that Mendez had "contradict[ed] with his actions the color that in others that is disrespected," while the admiral in charge of the Tierra Firme galleons concluded that "if the works of this man had been done by a Spaniard, it would be worthy for Your Majesty to honor him greatly." Royal officials agreed that "it is very just to reward him" and confirmed him in the government of the new town.

While extraordinary, such racial mobility was typically more possible in hinterlands such as Panama where there were comparatively fewer tal-ented individuals. In one respect, Mendez's mobility did not directly chal-lenge the status quo, for even though he held a position reserved for elites, he governed a town of Indians and did not have direct authority over whites. Yet his mobility proved characteristic of the process whereby Span-ish traditions of *gracias* provided interstices where the racially mixed might bypass the *limpieza de sangre* restrictions on officeholding.

While Governor Vicente Mendez had to receive official permission from royal officials to hold an office forbidden him due to his race, others passed unofficially and informally to enjoy the perquisites of whites. The link between historic agendas of discrimination and the daily prejudices faced by pardos and mulattoes was not always consistent. Written laws and traditions set overarching guidelines establishing customary agendas for discrimina-tion, which colonial officials and local elites might or might not enforce.

Such attempts to construct alternative public personae through informal passing was part of a traditional and accepted Spanish strategy that had been employed for centuries in issues of religion (*converso*) and illegitimate birth. In the instance of caste, pardos and mulattoes with whitish appearance, useful professional skills, and prominent family connections might also attempt to pass unofficially by enjoying the partial or full privileges of whites in the public sphere.

Gender, however, necessarily differentiated male and female potentials for passing.[49] While barred from most civic (militia service, public office) or occupational arenas where passing occurred, pardo and mulatto women still had impressive opportunities to pass informally in their own right. The vast majority of interracial sexual or marital relationships between whites and pardos or mulattoes was gendered, usually involving Spanish males and pardo and mulatto females. These women might experience significant informal mobility when they became the mistresses, and especially the wives and daughters, of white men. In contrast, mulatto and pardo men were more likely to pass when they held offices or occupations traditionally reserved for white males.

Whatever their gender, pardos and mulattoes found that informal mobility had limits. Someone might pass in one arena and encounter discrimination in the next; passing might be challenged at any time and mobility curtailed. When that occurred, the only remedy was to appeal for a royal *gracias* officially confirming that the individual could bypass public discrimination.

Inferential evidence of informal passing emerges, somewhat ironically, in documents that condemned such mobility after the fact. Some decrees repeated and reminded of the mandate to enforce the *limpieza de sangre* prohibitions; others referred to specific instances where pardo and mulatto men (since offices and occupations were involved) had passed. For example, as early as 1584 a royal decree prohibited the sale of public offices to mulattoes; one in 1621 forbade they be notaries; one in 1636 barred their ordination.[50] A 1623 decree in Panama conceded that pardos who were already serving as notaries might keep their posts but prohibited others from obtaining that office in the future; a 1713 document from Campeche complained that *regidores*, holders of one of the highest local offices, "were part mulatto and their quality is not equal to what is required."[51]

Other royal decrees penalized individuals who had passed. In Lima, the son of a mulatto was deprived of the position of porter of Lima in 1620; another lost the position of *caniculario* (church beadle) in 1717.[52] Such individual examples appear only where passing ultimately proved unsuccessful.

There were certainly untold numbers of instances where mulattoes and pardos enjoyed partial or total status as whites without challenge. While female mobility remains less documented, it seems likely that female pardos and mulattoes enjoyed substantial opportunities for informal passing when supported by white family members.[53]

Analysis of royal actions in the mid-eighteenth century underline's the critical role that such informal passing played in pardo and mulatto mobility. Bureaucrats were much more likely to issue an official decree validating a fait accompli erasing the "defect" of a petitioner who was already passing than to innovate and issue general or open-ended rewards to individuals who had served the state. During the closing colonial decades, pardos and mulattoes pushed the racial envelope yet further receiving exemptions from tribute and privileges for militias. They sought places in universities and in professions; finally, they directly asked to be whitened.

Bourbon Response to Passing, 1750–1780

The 1750s and 1760s marked both continuity and further progress in those two arenas—tribute and the militias—where mulatto and pardo men had already made progress. The issue of tribute is particularly revealing, for by the 1780s officials essentially conceded that so many Mexican pardos and mulattoes had informally passed that they no longer had public personae designating them as tribute payers due to caste. Officials explained that "if there are some [pardos/mulattoes] of means, they succeed due their wealth not to be listed on the census, but live jumbled with the Spanish." The result was that tribute payers were limited to "some miserables reduced to beg or live on a daily pittance."[54] By the late colonial period, masses of pardos and mulattoes had escaped paying levies that marked them as racially inferior, instead paying the taxes assigned to whites.

Members of pardo and mulatto militias took an even more substantial step toward mobility when the later Spanish Bourbons, starting with Charles III (1759–88), began a series of reforms in the Americas. An important concern was to encourage colonial self-defense, which included buttressing the militias. A 1765 decree praised the pardo and mulatto militias, noting the "great utility" that they "provide to the State and to the royal service in organizing soldiers that serve without salary, with uniforms at their own cost, that . . . is ready in all military functions."[55] The decree was among a series that extended the *fuero*—or special privileges previously reserved to the white military—to pardo and mulatto militias. The *fuero* provided special legal status to members of militia companies, exempting them in certain cases from the legal jurisdiction of local civil officials. Since these officials were white, it meant that pardo militia members would escape such civil jurisdiction, substituting that of their own officers, their racial peers.

This was one of the first royal decrees favoring pardos and mulattoes that evoked a quick negative response from colonial elites. The Caracas establishment bitterly protested the privilege, reminding Spanish bureaucrats that "the officials of the mulatto companies . . . are also mulattoes," who are "people of low sphere" compared to the white militias, staffed by "men of form and distinction."[56] The Venezuelans feared that mulattoes were "looking for ways to distinguish themselves even more, and to confuse themselves in some way with white and noble persons, even arriving [at the] wearing of wigs." Already, they noted, there had been a confrontation when a white city official had arrested a "*moreno* named Juan Bautista" who served in the pardo militia and who had exchanged "indecorous and denigrating words" with the arresting alcalde.

Such vocal protests presaged later Venezuelan outbursts protesting the whitening clauses of the 1795 *gracias al sacar*. More than any other region in the empire, Venezuela was a site both of substantial racial passing and of elite discrimination against it.[57] In this instance, the crown reviewed the situation and decided that the pardo militias would receive "the privileges of the military in future cases."[58] Such a ruling marks a turning point in royal legislation toward pardos and mulattoes—rather than eliminating an effect of caste defect, the *fuero* added a positive privilege reserved to whites.

In the 1750s and 1760s pardo men moved beyond exemption from tribute or favors limited to service in militias to receive dispensations to pass into new occupational arenas. One of the first professions where mulattoes broke the *limpieza* restrictions was to become surgeons and medical doctors. This became an entry point because, although medical skills were needed, these were not high-status occupations desired by elites. Furthermore, it was possible to obtain the necessary expertise informally, through apprenticeship, although the customary medical education for whites occurred at the university level. Both *limpieza de sangre* restrictions as well as specific ordinances gave the head of the local medical establishment, the Protomedicato, the responsibility to license medical practitioners and to forbid pardos to practice.[59] Even so, a series of cases reveals how pardos and mulattoes negotiated racial restrictions to pass informally, establish medical practices, and then be officially whitened. Yet others requested official permission to study medicine at the university, an effort that remained generally unsuccessful until after 1795.

Evidence that pardos might informally pass to practice medicine was evident in a 1760 petition from Cuban Josef Francisco Baez y Llerena, given that he had already practiced surgery for thirteen years with the informal approval, although not the official license, of the Havana Protomedicato.[60] He petitioned for a royal decree "dispensing the point of *limpieza*" so that in the future any "Protomedicato could not impede [his surgical practice] with some pretext." His petition was typical of those that were successful, for he had already unofficially passed. Yet, the question still arises how Josef Francisco had overcome racial barriers to acquire the skills of a surgeon and be permitted to practice.

While Josef Francisco provided few details, his parental background yields intriguing hints that he belonged to an emerging cohort of pardos with privileged connections and resources. His pardo father, Don Ignacio, had also informally passed, for he had held the office of notary on a frigate, served as an official in the fleet accounting offices, and enjoyed the honorific address of "Don"—all privileges typically reserved for whites. Don Ignacio's father had been a Spaniard serving on the galleons, who had an affair with an unmarried pardo woman and who had recognized and educated their illegitimate son. When this son, Don Ignacio, married, he did so to a social and racial peer, given that his wife, Maria Raphaela Guerrero, was also the illegitimate daughter of an affair between a Spanish father and a pardo mother. Their marriage produced a legitimate son and future surgeon, Josef Francisco, both of whose grandfathers were white.[61] It is notable that unlike petitioners later in the century, Josef Francisco never argued that he had a white appearance, although this must also have been likely. Yet it seems probable that his family connections facilitated his medical training and the informal passing that eventually led to the issuance of an official dispensation waiving his race for the purposes of his surgical practice.

Surgeon Josef Francisco Baez was not the only pardo passing in Havana, for his success occasioned a similar petition by Miguel Joseph Aviles three years later.[62] Precedent always influenced bureaucrats, and the royal official who reviewed the request commented that the profiles of both men were fairly similar, given they had practiced for some years with the unofficial permission of the Protomedicato. Aviles had the additional benefit of having served as a lieutenant in the militia, the typical venue where pardo males rendered royal service and earned rights to *gracias*. He had distinguished himself providing medical care for troops during the British attack on Havana in 1762. The Council of the Indies agreed to waive Aviles's racial defect and permit him to take the examinations to practice officially as a surgeon.

Aviles' petition was also notable for its introduction of a topic that would dominate pardo applications in later years. While his formal letter asked only for the narrow dispensation to practice medicine, his letter to his legal representative (*apoderado*) showed that he initially had higher hopes. He suggested that his counsel might "ask his majesty to extend . . . this *gracias* to the sons of the recipient in case they grow up with the same ability." His advice was ignored, and he received a dispensation limited to his own practice.

At the heart of Aviles' request were some complicated issues concerning official whitening that had yet to be worked out. The dispensation of royal *gracias* had a tradition developed over the centuries concerning those effects when the king eliminated other "defects," such as illegitimacy or Jewish ancestry. In those cases, the dispensation of the public "defect" was not just limited to the individual who received it, for the fault that occasioned such discrimination would no longer be handed down to the next generation to stain their *limpieza de sangre* and prejudice their opportunities. Since dispensation of racial defects was not a category that had received royal *gracias* on the Spanish peninsula, royal officials on the Council and Cámara of the Indies seemed to be working out the individual and societal consequences on a case-by-case basis. Up to this point, officials had carefully limited the effects of the *gracias* to the individual, and for narrow purposes. But the door had now been opened, as later petitions would show, for pardos and mulattoes to expand the benefits of official whitening and to attempt to extend them to succeeding generations.

One partial step to prolong whitening occurred when pardo fathers petitioned for *gracias* not for themselves, but so their sons might enter the university, particularly to study medicine. Such passing had already occurred informally. For example, even though a royal decree in 1752 from Lima forbade *zambos* (Native/black), mulattoes, and *quarterones* from matriculating in the university it conceded that some had been admitted and already graduated with medical degrees.[63] By the 1760s in Havana, not only were pardo surgeons like Baez and Aviles asking for personal dispensations to practice, but a pardo father like Antonio Flores would ask that his sons be permitted to study medicine formally, at the University of Havana.

Although his petition ultimately failed, the deposition of Antonio Flores revealed how an elite pardo cohort was developing a viable platform of public service, facilitating appeals for royal *gracias*.[64] Flores had taken a traditional pathway to mobility, given that he served in the pardo militia where he now held the rank of commander. Also typically, the family included numerous white relatives. Flores noted that his son, Joseph Ignacio, could trace six generations of white ancestors, including Flores's own father, who was white.[65] He wrote that even though his sons "were not embarrassed by reason of their birth," since they were legitimate, the university statutes against mulattoes meant they could not "study and practice medicine and surgery entering to take courses in the designated classes."

Antonio Flores's deposition included compelling vignettes certainly crafted to appeal to royal officials accustomed to rewarding excellence and making individual exceptions to rules. He recalled that even when son Joseph Ignacio was just nine and "small," the father had begun to teach him his own occupation of carpentry. However, Flores also paid for private grammar lessons, where his son proved to be "the best of all." His teacher had noted "a special talent and genius" and told Flores that "it would be a shame that such an excellent intellect should be dedicated to work with wood." Encouraged, Flores sent his son for advanced studies, where his teachers praised him as "the best student [in] grammar, philosophy, and theology within the patios of the colegio." Such arguments appealed to a classic bureaucratic discourse that those with talents to serve the king should be permitted to develop them.

Additionally, Flores's arguments provided further insight into an elite pardo cohort that had developed in Cuba. He pointed out that "in Havana, not only the nobility and the whites are professors of letters, but even the pardos, and that these . . . are cultured men." It was not only the "whites and nobles" that aspired to letters but "the pardos also look for and seek knowledge." The increase in learned pardos, he concluded, added "special timber" to the city. Yet, such appeals did not move the Council of the Indies. The reviewing official agreed that the doctors of the University of Havana had "just motive" to deny entrance to Flores's son.

During the 1760s, royal officials held the line and did not facilitate mulatto entrance into higher education. In 1764, Juan de la Cruz y Mena, himself a pardo surgeon, found that his two sons were still prohibited from entering the University of Havana to study medicine.[66] As late as 1793, royal officials would only intervene to permit mulattoes already certified as surgeons to attend special classes at the university—in this case a needed seminar on anatomy.[67]

Beyond Cuba, pardos did informally pass and graduate from colonial universities, although an advanced degree did not eliminate discrimination against them. At least, this was the experience of Don Christobal Polo, who had graduated from the University of San Bartolomé in Bogotá with a law degree. Yet when he tried to set up a legal practice in Cartagena, local elites protested. Royal officials followed their usual pattern, as they validated his informal passing after the fact, accepting his university degree and permitting him to practice. In his case, the signal services rendered by his military father during the defense of Cartagena proved an important factor. However, royal officials still refused to open university doors to others, as they then issued a 1765 decree insisting that Polo's privilege was unique and that no other mulattoes should be permitted to matriculate in Bogotá.[68] Even after 1795, whitening for university entrance would remain one of the most sought-after and one of the most controversial benefits of the dispensations of the *gracias al sacar.*

Consistent with the incrementalism of Spanish bureaucratic practice toward pardos and mulattoes, one of the most important precedents for the whitening decree of 1795 initially seemed neither striking nor controversial. Just as with surgeons, another skilled occupational arena attracting pardo attempts to pass were the offices of scribe and notary (*escribano, notario*). Juan Evaristo de Jesus Borbua, the illegitimate offspring (*hijo natural*) of a single white father and a pardo mother, had informally passed to hold several offices limited to whites, including working as a scribe in the royal offices of Portobello, for the city council, as a public notary for the church court, and as a probate official. He applied for a royal appointment as a notary in 1767, forwarding rave reviews from Panamanian royal officials who praised his "intelligence," his "application," and his "acceptance" in those offices.[69]

The reviewing official (*fiscal*) in the Cámara of the Indies noted that not only did laws prohibit mulattoes from serving as *escribanos* but later legislation ordered that they be deprived of those positions if caught holding them. Yet the *fiscal* then went on to admit that in Cartagena, Panama, and Portobello it was so difficult to find individuals qualified to be *escribanos* that the crown had made some exceptions and accepted "*quarterones* [one-fourth black] or *quinterones*" in the posts. For that reason, he recommended that the Cámara "take away from him [Borbua] the defect of *quinterón* that he suffers, so that he might be conceded the title of royal notary." The official noted that Borbua should pay twenty-two hundred reales, which was the sum regularly charged to purchase of the title of notary. He then added—in a novel departure—that Borbua should also pay forty pesos "for the dispensation of *quinterón.*"

This decision was provocative, for the language used to whiten Borbua preshadowed the words of the 1795 *gracias al sacar*, suggesting that this decision, or one like it, became the template for the official whitening clauses. This was likely the first, or at least one of the first decisions on whitening that shifted the procedure so that it followed the usual bureaucratic process for the issuance of *gracias al sacar*. Up until then, when royal officials had dispensed the defect of color for some purpose, they had done so generally, as a favor from the monarch granted for the merit or service of the petitioner, but they had not asked for monetary payment. In contrast, the Borbua decision followed the *gracias al sacar* procedure with a petition and a decision on the merit, which, if favorable resulted in the payment of a stipulated amount. This decision thus began the process of shifting the dispensation of whitening from being a general *gracias* awarded occasionally without payment to a regularized favor that might be purchased if merit could be demonstrated.

Whether royal officials were aware they had crossed a whitening Rubicon is unclear. However, the suggestive nature of the Borbua precedent was furthered in 1783 when Panamanian Don Luis Josef de Paz applied first to purchase the title of notary and then to be whitened.[70] Initially, Don Luis had purchased a royal decree in 1783 to practice as a notary. However when royal officials issued the approval, they ordered local officials to "verify with more precision his birth quality," given that he was an *expósito*, someone baptized as a child of "unknown parentage" with no specificity as to his race. Even though Luis Josef had this ambiguous public persona, the whole town knew his private reality, as the local investigating official conceded that it was "generally known" that Luis Josef "was publicly raised at the breast of Maria del Carmen Masso, his mother, a *quarterona.*" She proved to be the sister of pardo Pedro Josef Masso, a royal *escribano* of the *cabildo* of Portobello, who had "obtained a dispensation to exercise that office" and who likely had tutored his nephew in the same profession.

Barred from exercising his notary title due to his race, Luis Josef made a formal application to the Cámara of the Indies to be relieved of the defect of pardo, providing examples of three others (including Borbua) who had received similar dispensations to become *escribanos.*[71] Panamanian officials provided letters assuring his "good conduct" and "aptitude" for the post and reminding Spanish officials of the "lack of *escribanos*" in Portobello. When the *fiscal* reviewed the case, he noted that the Cámara had made other such "dispensations as seen in the collected examples." He suggested they dispense the defect of race for a payment of one hundred pesos. The Cámara agreed, but reduced the cost to forty pesos, the same sum paid by Borbua.

More important, the *fiscal's* decision had set a precedent: he directly recognized the bureaucratic shift in the categorization of whitening, noting that this dispensation was part of the *gracias al sacar*. The result was critical: the implicit linkage of *gracias* and payment in the Borbua decision was now explicitly confirmed. Purchase of whiteness—at least for the position of notary—was included in the *gracias al sacar*. Even through this decision occurred twelve years before the issuance of the official 1795 price list that first contained the whitening option, it remained in the Council of the Indies archives, establishing one of the first pieces of a paper trail that would set a precedent when royal officials would begin to revise the *gracias al sacar* legislation.

The Quest to Be White: 1780–1790

The 1780s and 1790s marked a substantive shift in pardo and mulatto aspirations concerning whitening. In the sixteenth and seventeenth centuries, the strategy of pardos and mulattoes had been to end specific discrimination attached to their caste status such as terminating individual or group tribute payments or validating their capability to serve as militia officers. By the mid-eighteenth century, pardos and mulattoes sought less to end the negatives of their "defect" than to appropriate positive attributes normally reserved to whites be it the military *fuero* or occupational choices such surgeon, lawyer, or notary. In the last two decades of the eighteenth century, pardos and mulattoes ended this incremental strategy. Petitions make clear that they wanted more than just to have the "defect" of their caste dispensed for limited purposes—they wanted to pass to be officially and fully white. One of the first cases where a pardo requested such benefits originated, perhaps not surprisingly, in Guatemala, one of those Central American regions where informal mobility was greatest.

In 1783, hydraulic engineer (*fontanero*) Bernardo Ramirez began his quest for total whitening, asking that his "sons and descendants could hold positions and honors that are appropriate for Spaniards and honored artisans."[72] Ramirez could make a substantive case that he had performed exemplary royal service: he headed the public waterworks of Guatemala City. When an earthquake destroyed the capital and it was moved a new spot, he had planned the water supply for the new capital, saving the royal treasury the very substantial sum of eighty thousand pesos. Both his father and his uncle had served the king, planning and constructing local fortifications and a gunpowder factory; Bernardo and his father served in the pardo militias. High officials, including the president of Guatemala, praised his help in the movement of the capital. The latter noted that such a *gracias* "would stimulate many of the class of pardos" to strive for similar dispensations.

Bernardo Ramirez also emphasized a theme, hinted at in previous cases but made more explicit here and after 1795. This was that there were a number of pardos on the edge of legally passing as white, who looked white. In Spanish America, once the proportion of Native or black ancestry fell below one-eighth, the person was legally white.[73] Ramirez noted that "neither his father nor grandfathers were of the color and name of Negroes or pardos." He reminded officials that "the birth of a mulata and white, as seen in his paternal grandparents, produces the category of *tercerón*, whose succession with white leads to *quarterón*, and erasing all the note [of color] the next generation and family passes in the class of Spaniards." Ramirez acknowledged that he had reversed the family racial progress somewhat with his marriage to pardo Albina de Rivera, for his offspring had temporarily lost "the direction that carries it to white." Yet, his case was typical of a number to follow where petitioners and those who supported them noted their proximity to whiteness.

As royal officials reviewed Ramirez's petition, they never questioned their legal authority to make pardos or mulattoes officially white.[74] The Council of the Indies agreed that the king "because of his sovereignty can take whatever vassal from the obscurity of his birth placing him in a distinguished sphere." The real issue, they debated, was whether Ramirez deserved such a privilege. The *fiscal* who reviewed the petition admitted that Ramirez was a "vassal" who had demonstrated "care, zeal, and love" in the service of the state and public and was "worthy of attention and some recompense." However, he considered Ramirez' request to be "repugnant or at least excessive, since Bernardo Ramirez cannot . . . take away his infected quality even though he tries to do it."

This official had anticipated what would become a critical problem in the grants of whiteness after 1795. He suggested that the ultimate effect of dispensing whiteness to Ramirez might be a weakening of royal authority, and yet he worried that if the Cámara "released him from the infection he suffers," then Ramirez would aspire to the "honors and employment" of whites. If he then encountered obstacles and local elites thwarted his mobility, he "would complain that the orders of the king are not obeyed." Royal officials would then have to intervene to enforce them. Yet, this would produce "bad consequences and worse results among the Spaniards and

Americans of distinction." This was a particularly sensitive issue for royal officials in 1783, as two major revolts in 1781 (Tupac Amaru in Peru, Communeros in Colombia) had made them unwilling to alienate local elites. The official concluded that the ultimate result "on one or the other side" would be "dissention and complaints."[75]

Even though the *fiscal* did not recommended whitening, he did feel that Ramirez deserved royal favor. He suggested, much along lines of previous dispensations to mulattoes, that Ramirez might receive "some purely personal distinction," possibly an "office in the Battalion of Pardo Militias of Guatemala, exemption from some charge or tribute, some one-time pecuniary recompense, or one of the medals handed out by the Royal Academy of the Three Nobles." Ramirez bitterly rejected the proffered post of officer in the pardo militia, complaining that "it is of no estimation in that kingdom, and positively unbecoming to the object of his pretensions . . . the quality of a Spaniard."

Much had changed in the last hundred years. Mulattoes and pardos had first petitioned to be relieved of burdens attached to their caste status; then they appropriated perquisites of whites, serving in the militia, becoming militia officers, practicing as surgeons and as notaries. By the late eighteenth century, an elite cohort of men like Bernardo Ramirez wanted much more—university for their sons and whiteness for themselves and their posterity. When the 1795 *gracias al sacar* appeared with two new royal favors, one granting "the dispensation of the quality of pardo" and the another "the dispensation of the quality of *quinterón*," it appeared that the Spanish state might have favorably responded to their interests.

Conclusion

Yet, had there really been change? One of the mysteries surrounding the purchase of whiteness is why and how it appeared in the 1795 price list in the first place. Understanding the historic paths trodden by pardos and mulattoes over the colonial centuries as they pursued upward mobility provides a striking and revisionist answer to that question.

By the 1790s, when the revised *gracias al sacar* was compiled, revenue enhancement was a royal priority, given that the French Revolutionary Wars were putting excessive demands on the Spanish treasury. The preface to the 1795 *gracias al sacar* complained that royal favors had been sold too inexpensively, thus leading to the promulgation and raised prices of the 1795 *gracias.* Rather surprisingly, documentary evidence suggests that the bureaucrats of the Council and Cámara of the Indies, those who regularly dealt with issues of royal favor, did not compile the decree.[76] Instead, their comments as they evaluated petitions from the Americas after 1795 made clear that they were surprised by some of its provisions. The introduction to the *gracias al sacar* reveals that bureaucrats in *Contaduria*, or the finance ministry, prepared the lists of purchasable favors. The result was that royal officials more interested in revenue enhancement than familiar with colonial social policy were responsible for crafting the 1795 decree. In the introduction to the *gracias al sacar*, these compilers noted that they had been guided by historical precedents. They had consulted the 1773 *gracias al sacar* that had been "formed by the Cámara of Castile," and indeed, much of the American decree was a direct copy of its Castilian counterpart. Since the dispensation of color was not an issue in Spain, the whitening clauses did not appear in the peninsular version. Additionally—and here the more speculative part begins—the compilers reported that they had also considered the "practice observed by [the Cámara] of the Indies."[77]

The traditional way that bureaucrats discovered such "practice" was to read the documents saved in the relevant archive, in this case, that of the Council and Cámara of the Indies. If they had done this, what would they have found? They would have discovered a number of cases where the "defect" of race had been partially or totally dispensed: perhaps the petitions of *morenos* Sebastian de Toral not to pay tribute in Yucatán, of Peruvian Juan de Valladolid Moborbón to be a military officer, or of Panamanian Vicente Mendez to be a governor. They almost certainly encountered the petitions from Cubans Joseph Francisco Baez y Llerena and Miguel Joseph Aviles to be able practice as surgeons, and pleas from Antonio Flores and Juan de la Cruz y Mena that their pardo sons might enter the university. Almost without question they discovered that notary Juan Evaristo de Jesus Borbua had paid forty pesos "for the dispensation of *quinterón,*" as had Don Luis Josef de Paz and—that time—officials had called his dispensation a "*gracias al sacar.*" Even Guatemalan Bernardo Ramirez' petition to be white was in the Council of the Indies archive, for it still—as do these others—remains there today. Given such a series of documents and evidence of such "practice," might treasury officials simply have added the dispensation of whiteness to provide completeness to the *gracias al sacar* list?

Location, price, and terminology support the "bureaucratic tidying" thesis. The two whitening dispensations are out of place. They are the last two items listed on the American *gracias al sacar*, essentially tacked on to everything else rather than appearing in the center of the document where other personal status-changing clauses tended to be grouped. The prices for whitening are out of proportion to the benefit—they are far too low. For example, a simple legitimation in 1795 was priced at four thousand reales. Yet the dispensation of color—a much greater *gracias*—was an eighth of this cost for pardos (five hundred reales) while *quinterones* paid but a fifth (eight hundred reales) of the sum charged to certain illegitimates (*hijos naturales*). The differential pricing between pardos and *quinterones* also presents an anomaly, given that *quinterones*, who were closer on the color scale to whites, inexplicably paid more than the darker (and presumably more "defective") pardos for whitening. The terminology for those to be whitened is also provocative. It seems illogical to signal out *quinterones*—a narrowly defined caste group—unless there were some cases, such as those from Panama, that provided specific precedents for that whitening clause. [78] Such disparities suggest that when bureaucrats added the whitening dispensations they priced them proportionately to actual prices paid in documentary cases they had consulted in the Council of the Indies archive.

This chain of reasoning suggests that pardos and mulattoes who struggled for upward mobility from the early to the late colonial period wrought much more and much less than they would ever know. Centuries of attempts to achieve racial mobility had produced an archival trail that would lead royal bureaucrats to make whitening an official *gracias* that could be purchased from the state. In the process, pardo and mulatto efforts, first to end negative discrimination attached to their caste, then to appropriate some positive perquisites of whites, had finally led to an official process where they might apply to achieve full status as whites. After 1795, the royal officials on the Council and Cámara of the Indies, an elite cohort of pardos and mulattoes in the Americas, and colonial elites would engage in further negotiations to determine what the *gracias al sacar* dispensation might mean, and what racialized spaces would, and mostly would not, be officially opened up.

Afterword

Thomas J. Humphrey

By the summer of 1765, Daniel Nimham understood too well that New York officials were unlikely to address fairly his claims to land in the southern part of the Hudson River Valley. He and the powerful landlord Frederick Philipse claimed the same land, and Philipse enjoyed far more official support than Nimham. To get some measure of redress, Nimham gathered some of his supporters, boarded a boat, and sailed to England to present his case directly to a higher authority—the king. But the king refused to meet with Nimham and ultimately referred the case back to Henry Moore, then governor of New York. Moore and his council had already heard of Nimham's complaints, and they were unlikely to side with him. Regardless, the governor and his council heard arguments from both sides and rendered a decision. Given the council's predisposition, its conclusion was hardly surprising. Nimham lost.[1]

Nimham's unsuccessful struggle to secure land title in the Hudson Valley through official channels might seem an all too common story but for one significant fact: he was a Wappinger Indian sachem. Nimham's identity alone presented a pressing reason for the governor's council to award the land to the Philipses. John Morin Scott, a New York lawyer who represented the Philipses during the proceedings, specifically argued that the governor's council could not award the land in question to Nimham and the Wappingers regardless of who held the best claim to it. He considered legitimate ownership of the land a secondary concern. Scott was more worried that the council's decision in favor of the Wapppingers could reshape the distribution of land throughout New York, igniting tensions that surrounded European attempts to expropriate land from Native inhabitants. The titles on both sides had complex pasts and almost assuredly included a moment when some Europeans had obtained land from the Wappingers illegitimately. Thus, Scott worried that any decision in favor of Nimham threatened to throw "open a Door to the greatest Mischiefs" because, as both sides knew, a "great part of the Lands in the Province are supposed to lie under much of the same Scituation."[2]

Like the stories of Richard Price's triptych, Daniel Nimham's attempt to secure his group's land represents more than what it is. The story, its characters, and its consequences contain deeper political and cultural—and perhaps even moral—meanings. They reveal how various groups validated their claims to land by justifying the retellings of events and documents that legitimated their brand of authority over others. They show how combatants invalidated alternative accounts and the credentials of their opponents and, when necessary, prosecuted their antagonists. Moreover, Nimham's story demonstrates how history shapes contemporary communities and perspectives by uncovering how historians have restated those retellings, and thereby colonized the non-European inhabitants of the early Americas again. In short, Nimham's case addresses precisely the themes raised by the authors in this volume.

Taken together, the chapters, like Nimham's struggle for land, throw into dispute some of the terms on which scholars too often depend, compelling historians to question those deeply held assumptions that they have buttressed with words such as legitimacy, legality, and authority. They offer these views from inside a fence of ideas they have built and made more secure by analyzing their subjects through it. But these chapters knock down those barriers, pushing us outside of our comfort zones to show how people justified their specific acts of horrifying violence and how they condemned the equally vicious attacks of their opponents. Also, because the chapters span the chronological and territorial scope of the early Americas they avoid propelling a protonationalist story, thus requiring readers to think more critically about power structures and colonial rule by eliminating artificially constructed restrictions of time and place. The result is not the story of Europeans imposing order in the New World, as is often depicted. Instead, the chapters offer a fresh take on the early Americas by illuminating overlapping and competing new world orders.

Christopher Tomlins begins that reevaluation by describing how competing groups in the early Americas invoked their notion of legality to justify their authority over others. They did so by categorizing some behavior as acceptable while punishing other, often similar behavior. Historians have described that process, but too frequently their analysis smacks of unavoidability and inevitability. In fact, most of the history of the early Americas is the story of competition between groups without enough power to control and rule their opponents. The chapters here outline the period when the outcome of those interactions remained in doubt. They demonstrate how competing groups asserted their definitions of legality, legitimacy, and authority in the early Americas, and they describe that period between initial contact and the settlement of the Americas by Europeans.[3]

To explore that period, the authors accept the notion that different and often contentious legalities propelled groups to endorse competing perspectives. In doing so, the chapters highlight the immediacy of interactions that shaped new world orders and minimize the inevitability that often informs historical examinations of colonialism often depicted from over the shoulders of Europeans. In the case of seventeenth-century Brazil, for instance, Jacob Rabe's murder demonstrates that the Dutch, Portuguese, Tupi, and Tarairiu all exerted enough authority that each had to cautiously navigate the ensuing political struggle that erupted after Rabe's murder, and each had to stake their claims to power without provoking hostile responses. Similarly, centuries later and a continent away, the question of whether Kauquatau, a Seneca woman accused of being a witch, was legitimately killed or instead murdered depended on which authority was describing the situation. Ensuing debates over prosecuting the witch's killer were grounded in ongoing disputes over land, power, and sovereignty between Senecas and the state of New York.

People who sought to establish their brand of authority often used violence to legitimate the legality of their rule over competitors. In fact, authorities largely defined themselves through their right to use violence against their opponents. Both Gene Ogle and Cécile Vidal describe how the use of violence increasingly fell under the purview of white men. More than that, they reveal how authorities in slave societies legitimated their power by inflicting violent punishment on nonwhites to harden race relations and a race-based hierarchy. Through the story of the punishment handed down to Raymond, a slave who beat a white man named Jean-Baptise Huet, and to his master, Ogle uncovers who held the authority to inflict violence on others. While his master was punished very little for ordering Raymond to assault Huet, Raymond was initially sentenced to death by strangulation for violating a social and cultural taboo. Vidal takes readers from the Caribbean to colonial Louisiana to illustrate that although physical punishment was on the decline in France over the course of the eighteenth century, violent punishment of nonwhites, and especially of enslaved Africans, was on the rise. Justice in the colony became racialized because officials increasingly treated African criminals far more harshly than white ones, and they treated enslaved people worst of all.

Authorities also defined gender in daily life, like race, in terms of violence. While Kimberly Gauderman demonstrates that women in Quito knew that colonial authorities sought to prevent domestic abuse, adultery, and the seduction of unmarried women, and that they worked within the legal system to protect themselves, Sharon Block explores the overlapping issues of gender and race in her study of the ambiguity of whether rape should be categorized as a sexual or a violent crime in British North America. Early American discourses discussed rape as either a sexual or a violent crime, even though women invariably saw physical violence as part of rape. Describing rape through race, however, illustrates other aspects of early American society. While white men who raped black women did so without fear of any real consequence and white men who raped white women were often charged with physical assault rather than rape, black men who raped white women were charged with a crime akin to slave rebellion.

Even though the combatants in these disputes tried to draw hard-and-fast lines between themselves and their opponents, contests justifying one brand of authority over another sometimes generated space for maneuvering for people left without authority or legitimate power. Gauderman, for instance, demonstrates how women in Quito protected themselves by exploiting the boundaries between political and household power that grew out of tensions between church, political, and household authorities. And Ann Twinam and Tamar Herzog both discuss how members of local communities in Spanish America defined colonial identities in terms of reputation, social relations, actions, and changeable notions of race, even though royal officials tried to dictate the rules through which people defined their citizenship and, thus, their local and international identities. Finally, Cynthia Radding outlines how people in the mission communities of Sonora and Chiquito reworked their ethnicity and cultural characteristics into historical identities. At the same time, however, Spanish rulers tried to harden these categories into racial identities to impose Spanish social control over competing local indigenous groups.

Some groups pushed at the boundaries of those contests to create their own space as a way to survive otherwise terrifying conditions. In his chapter, Richard Price describes how the victims of white men's violence, usually enslaved Africans, reinterpreted the vicious assaults they endured to create alternative narratives of violence that they then used to mock the very people who beat them. The descendants of those enslaved Africans used these alternative narratives to shape not only their perception of who and what their ancestors had been to influence what they are, but also what they and their descendents may become. It is a fitting reminder, too often ignored by contemporary political leaders, that our history shapes our present and future.

These chapters also describe how various groups legitimated their violence, thereby demonstrating a brick-by-brick construction of colonialism and resistance to it. In both British and French colonies in North America, officials set up their patterns of racial behavior over the course of many years, building slowly but irrevocably toward a system that privileged white Europeans and severely punished racial "others" who violated the emerging racial hierarchy. They had to keep hammering home the point in part because doing so meant reiterating their authority. But authorities also continued to enforce their power because they felt continually threatened. In Brazil in the seventeenth century and in New York in the nineteenth, indigenous groups resisted colonialism by altering some aspects of their culture to form new, potentially stronger coalitions and to preserve some measure of themselves in the face of creeping colonialism. Similarly, white slave owners throughout the early Americas punished any kind of resistance to their authority with terrifying violence, both to reassert their control over their slaves and to show potential rebels the fate that awaited them if they took up arms against their owners and rulers.

The construction of colonialism, and resistance to it, played out in unexpected ways. Daniel Nimham, for instance, sought a Crown title to the Wappingers' land not because he regarded the king as his ruler but more because he, like many Indians in British North America, figured it was the only way he could keep the land while living under an encroaching European legal system and in the face of Europeans hungry for more land. Those charters also supplied a momentary block to European expropriation of, and expansion onto, the Wappingers' land. European colonists and authorities, in contrast, thought that Indians who had obtained a royal charter for ancestral lands had given up their land to that European authority. Matthew Dennis describes Senecas following a similar process when they adopted an Anglo-European definition of witches and how to punish them in part to hold off white expansion. These activities, however, threw the Wappingers, and other groups such as the Senecas and the Oneidas, into a double bind that continues to affects their status on the land and that has contemporary ramifications for Indians who face a renewed, if different kind of, colonialism today.

To warn of the potential difficulties that may emerge through reinterpretations of the language of authority and colonialism should not thwart efforts to address the predominant issues that plague that analysis such as, most notably, historical exceptionalism. The collected chapters show the way. Rather than celebrating the advance of European colonization in the Americas or condemning that Anglo-European settlement, the chapters address power relationships in the early Americas as a problem to be examined and, perhaps, explained. By examining the struggles for power within households and communities, the regions between cultures, and the fundamental meanings of civic identity, they reveal the contested nature of power.[4] They do so to restore historical immediacy, and the agency of the people involved, with an eye toward deeper analysis of claims to power that have too often been justified with the legal rhetoric of authority.

In the process of examining local, extralocal, public, and intimate power relations, these chapters pull us out of a reverie induced by long-held historical assumptions about colonial power, colonization, and national boundaries. Indeed, they throw such fundamental terms into great debate and raise the question of their usefulness. Author after author demonstrates how officials reshaped contentious events to express, or to remold, their identities and to suggest specific meanings to the audience. In that way, the authors show how officials retold events to legitimate their kind of authority and to justify their violent oppression of their opponents. Much of the history of the early Americas relies on those retellings. Thus, it recasts uncertain events and their outcomes to create a decidedly Eurocentric master narrative of colonial America. This is especially the case for British North America. This view has inspired a brand of North American exceptionalism that implicitly justifies the vicious acts authorities used to sanction their power when they punished their opponents. But a view of the early Americas that addresses how individuals from separate, and often competing, groups occupied different positions in the vertical and horizontal realms of authority will discourage that sort of nationalist exceptionalism.[5] While Nimham's case illustrates that point to some degree, the chapters in this volume demonstrate it clearly and powerfully. They offer us a guide for more inclusive studies of the colonial Americas and compel us to think of colonialism as an ongoing process that defies periodization.[6]

The calculus that equates periodized colonialism with protonationalism may be read the other way. Periodization contributes to a protonationalism inspired by colonialism. Strict approaches show specifics, to be sure, but the chapters reveal the power of stepping outside the traditional bounds of analysis. As Christopher Tomlins demonstrates here, and others have done so elsewhere, European colonists throughout the early Americas used those written documents and specific kinds of language to legitimate taking land and conquering natives.[7] Nimham, for example, sought to gain some leverage by infusing British rhetoric with his group's ideas of space and power, but his Crown title and the court in which he fought for it privileged the British. Worse, he knew he had to satisfy a British legal system that refused to recognize any other kinds of authority but its own. Most, if not all, official courts operated, and operate, under that kind of thinly veiled bias. To facilitate the illusion of fairness, court officials heard these disputes under the false pretext of impartiality, but these courts were not designed to mete out justice. Throughout the early Americas, courts established by European powers were organized to legitimate European, in this case British, authority first and to mete out justice second.[8]

Finally, the chapters emphasize the dependent link between authority and violence, which often goes overlooked in histories of the early Americas. In condemning their opponents and by marginalizing them as illegal, people who claimed power used violence to enforce their brand of authority, defining that force as legitimate while condemning that of their opponents. That process started immediately after initial contact when European authorities in the early Americas forced a restructuring of nature and communities to compel the indigenous inhabitants of the early Americas to abide by strange and sometimes unpopular political boundaries and to conform to unfamiliar standards of behavior. On both sides, however, authorities could not impose their will as easily as they had hoped and had to carefully navigate their attempts to direct their economic, social, and cultural allies while they tried to compel the obedience of their opponents. Over time, European authorities gained power in part by describing violence as their exclusive weapon. The chapters tell that story by illuminating the conceptual and very real connections that determined how various groups claiming authority justified their control over a region and the people living in it.

Richard Price's chapter picks up on these themes and, yet, goes further by asking us to remember that a society's history, the story of competing new world orders, tells us a great deal about who the people are and what they may become. It is a fitting reminder that perhaps too many historians ignore. More than anything else, these chapters demonstrate how historians can explore the complex relationships that characterized communities in the colonial Americas as various groups collided and then set out to forge new world orders. They illuminate potent and contentious colonial worlds that became the worlds we know and the worlds we inhabit. To move beyond the prejudices that constrain us, we need to move the racial, cultural, gendered, and economic "others" out of the margins they often occupy in our histories and incorporate them into the narrative. The chapters in this collection offer a guide.

These last points show how the chapters cross fundamental boundaries and, thus, defy easy compartmentalization. By questioning basic notions of legality, authority, and colonialism, they throw our neat historical world into flux, highlighting the artificial divisions that currently shape historical study and, especially in the case of the histories of British North America, that influence a brand of colonial exceptionalism. This collection demonstrates a broader human experience. In the end, while the chapters bring readers to a disordered close, they also inspire scholars in the future to ask questions that take into account the complexity of human endeavors.

Notes

Introduction: The Ordering of Authority in the Colonial Americas

This introduction was written while I was on a Barbara Thom Postdoctoral Fellowship at the Huntington Library. I would like to thank the Huntington Library for their support and Yanna Yannakakis, David Silverman, Tom Humphrey, Chuck Walker, Andres Resendez, Greg Smithers, Richard Koufay, and Stephanie Dyer for comments and suggestions on earlier drafts.

1. Experience Mayhew, *A Discourse Shewing That God Dealeth with Men as with Reasonable Creatures: In a Sermon Preach'd at Boston, N.E. Nov. 23, 1718: With a Brief Account of the State of the Indians on Martha's Vineyard, & the Small Islands Adjacent in Dukes County, from the Year 1694 to 1720* (Boston, 1720). My discussion of the Vineyard Indians is drawn largely from David J. Silverman's work on the topic. See Silverman, "Deposing the Sachem to Defend the Sachemship: Indian Land Sales and Native Political Structure on Martha's Vineyard, 1680–1740," *Explorations in Early American Culture* 5 (2001), 9–44; Silverman, "'We Chuse to Be Bounded': Native American Animal Husbandry in Colonial New England," *William and Mary Quarterly* 3rd ser., 60 (2003), 511–48 (hereafter *WMQ*).

2. Mayhew, *Discourse*, 45–46.

3. Silverman, "Deposing the Sachem," 35.

4. Patricia Seed, *Ceremonies of Possession in Europe's Conquest of the New World, 1492–1640* (New York, 1995).

5. On the linkages between spatial assertions of cultural and legal mastery, see Seed, *Ceremonies of Possession*; and Jack P. Greene, "Mastery and the Definition of Cultural Space in Early America: A Perspective," in *Imperatives, Behaviors, and Identities: Essays in Early American Cultural History* (Charlottesville, Va., 1992), 1–12.

6. Silverman, "'We Chuse to Be Bounded,'" 539.

7. Ibid., 537. Silverman notes that although Vineyard Wampanoags did begin marking the limits of their land with fences, their enclosure practices differed sharply from English ones. While English fences marked (or were supposed to mark) the boundaries between each individual plot of land, Wampanoag fences bounded common pastureland: "'We Chuse to Be Bounded,'" 536–37.

8. Christopher L. Tomlins, "The Many Legalities of Colonization: A Manifesto of Destiny for Early American Legal History," introduction to Christopher L. Tomlins and Bruce H. Mann, eds., *The Many Legalities of Early America* (Chapel Hill, N.C., 2001), 2. I will discuss Tomlins's use of "legality" at greater length below.

9. Silverman, "'We Chuse to Be Bounded,'" 528.

10. Robert Blair St. George defines transculturation as "the action whereby a

politically dominated culture appropriates some of the symbolic forms of a dominant or imperial culture in order to articulate its own continuing vision of autonomy." Introduction to St. George, ed., *Possible Pasts: Becoming Colonial in Early America* (Ithaca, N.Y., 2000), 26. See also Jose Antonio Mazzotti, "Mestizo Dreams: Transculturation and Hetereogeneity in Inca Garcilaso De La Vega," in St. George, *Possible Pasts*, 131–47; and Walter Mignolo, *Local Histories/Global Designs: Coloniality, Subaltern Knowledges, and Border Thinking* (Princeton, N.J., 2000), 14–16, 167–70.

11. On the *vacuum domicilium* theory legitimating English dispossession of Indian lands, see Francis Jennings, *The Invasion of America: Indians, Colonialism, and the Cant of Conquest* (New York, 1976), 82, 135, 136; David Armitage, *The Ideological Origins of the British Empire* (New York, 2000), 97; and Christopher Tomlins, Chapter 1 in this volume.

12. See, for example, Foucault's discussion of the productive relationship between sanction and power in *The History of Sexuality; Vol. 1, An Introduction* (New York, 1990), 87, 144.

13. Sir William Blackstone, *Commentaries on the Laws of England. In Four Books* (Philadelphia, 1771), 1:56.

14. Tomlins, "Many Legalities," 2–3.

15. Kahn argues that within the Western conception of legal sovereignty, legitimacy is ultimately grounded in an originary moment outside of ordinary time; locating the origin of a legal order in ordinary time would, he notes, render it subject to change and leave it vulnerable to challenge. Kahn, *The Cultural Study of Law: Reconstructing Legal Scholarship* (Chicago, 1999), 48–49.

16. For examples of work from Anglo-America, see James H. Merrell, *The Indians' New World: Catawbas and Their Neighbors from European Contact through the Era of Removal* (Chapel Hill, N.C., 1989); Daniel K. Richter, *The Ordeal of the Longhouse: The Peoples of the Iroquois League in the Era of European Colonization* (Chapel Hill, N.C., 1992). For examples from Latin America, see Nancy M. Farriss, *Maya Society Under Colonial Rule: The Collective Enterprise of Survival* (Princeton, N.J., 1984); Irene M. Silverblatt, *Moon, Sun, and Witches: Gender Ideologies and Class in Inca and Colonial Peru* (Princeton, N.J., 1987); James Lockhart, *The Nahuas After the Conquest: A Social and Cultural History of the Indians of Central Mexico, Sixteenth Through Eighteenth Centuries* (Stanford, Calif., 1992); Matthew Restall, *The Maya World: Yucatec Culture and Society, 1550–1850* (Stanford, Calif., 1997).

17. On the role of discourse in legitimating the possession of the Americas, see Stephen Greenblatt, *Marvelous Possessions: The Wonder of the New World* (Chicago, 1991). Tzvetan Todorov argues that Spanish discursive techniques were crucial in Cortés' conquest of the Aztecs in *The Conquest of America: The Question of the Other* (Norman, Okla., 1999). For the application of Foucaultian techniques of discourse analysis to European law during the colonial period, see Robert A. Williams, *The American Indian in Western Legal Thought: The Discourses of Conquest* (New York, 1990). On the rise of the British imperial ideology, see Armitage, *Ideological Origins*. For a comparative discussion of the ideologies of imperialism in the Americas, see Anthony Pagden, *Lords of All the World: Ideologies of Empire in Spain, Britain, and France, C. 1500–C. 1800* (New Haven, Conn.,1995).

18. The seminal text in this trend in scholarship is Richard White, *The Middle*

Ground: Indians, Empires, and Republics in the Great Lakes Region, 1650–1815 (New York, 1991). See also Peter C. Mancall, *Valley of Opportunity: Economic Culture Along the Upper Susquehanna, 1700–1800* (Ithaca, N.Y., 1991); Daniel H. Usner, *Indians, Settlers and Slaves in a Frontier Exchange Economy: The Lower Mississippi Valley before 1783* (Chapel Hill, N.C., 1992); Matthew Dennis, *Cultivating a Landscape of Peace: Iroquois-European Encounters in Seventeenth-Century America* (Ithaca, N.Y., 1993); Jane T. Merritt, *At the Crossroads: Indians and Empires on a Mid-Atlantic Frontier, 1700–1763* (Chapel Hill, N.C., 2003). For examples of the development of hybridity in Latin America, see Louise M. Burkhart, *The Slippery Earth: Nahua-Christian Moral Dialogue in Sixteenth-Century Mexico* (Tucson, 1989); Lockhart, *Nahuas After the Conquest*; James Lockhart, "Double Mistaken Identity: Some Nahua Concepts in Postconquest Guise," in *Of Things of the Indies: Essays Old and New in Early Latin American History* (Stanford, Calif., 1999), 98–119.

19. Lauren A. Benton, *Law and Colonial Cultures: Legal Regimes in World History, 1400–1900* (New York, 2002), 12–13.

20. See, for example, James H. Merrell's summary of this debate in his "Indian History During the English Colonial Era," in Daniel Vickers, ed., *A Companion to Colonial America* (Malden, Mass., 2003), 131–32.

21. Pagden, *Lords of All the World*, 77–79; Armitage, *Ideological Origins*, 97–98.

22. I thank David Silverman for clarifying this point for me. Nancy Shoemaker has suggested that historians have exaggerated the differences between Indian and European notions of property, causing them to misunderstand conflict over this issue. See Shoemaker, *A Strange Likeness: Becoming Red and White in Eighteenth-Century North America* (New York, 2004), 16–20.

23. Tomlins has made this point about the legal history of early America in "Many Legalities," 9–11.

24. Richard J. Ross, "The Legal Past of Early New England: Notes for the Study of Law, Legal Culture, and Intellectual History," *WMQ* 50 (1993), 32–33, passim.

25. For British America, see David Thomas Konig, *Law and Society in Puritan Massachusetts: Essex County, 1629–1692* (Chapel Hill, N.C., 1979); A. G. Roeber, *Faithful Magistrates and Republican Lawyers: Creators of Virginia Legal Culture, 1680–1810* (Chapel Hill, N.C., 1981); Bruce H. Mann, *Neighbors and Strangers: Law and Community in Early Connecticut* (Chapel Hill, N.C., 1987); Cornelia Hughes Dayton, *Women Before the Bar: Gender, Law, and Society in Connecticut, 1639–1789* (Chapel Hill, N.C., 1995); William M. Offutt, *Of "Good Laws" and "Good Men": Law and Society in the Delaware Valley, 1680–1710* (Urbana, Ill., 1995). For Spanish America, see Charles R. Cutter, *The Legal Culture of Northern New Spain, 1700–1810* (Albuquerque, 1995); and Susan Kellogg, *Law and the Transformation of Aztec Culture, 1500–1700* (Norman, Okla., 1995).

26. See Dayton, *Women Before the Bar*; Kathleen M. Brown, *Good Wives, Nasty Wenches, and Anxious Patriarchs: Gender, Race, and Power in Colonial Virginia* (Chapel Hill, N.C., 1996); Robert Olwell, *Masters, Slaves & Subjects: The Culture of Power in the South Carolina Low Country, 1740–1790* (Ithaca, N.Y., 1998); Ramon A. Gutiérrez, *When Jesus Came, the Corn Mothers Went Away: Marriage, Sexuality, and Power in New Mexico, 1500–1846* (Stanford, Calif., 1991).

27. On the use of anthropology in early American history, see Richard R. Beeman,

"The New Social History and the Search for Community in Colonial America," *American Quarterly* 29 (1977), 422–33. On the role of community studies in explicating the relationship between power and culture on a local level, see Michael Zuckerman, "Regionalism," in Vickers, *Companion*, 319; Ross, "Legal Past," 35.

28. See James Clifford and George E. Marcus, eds., *Writing Culture: The Poetics and Politics of Ethnography* (Berkeley, 1986); James Clifford, *The Predicament of Culture: Twentieth-Century Ethnography, Literature, and Art* (Cambridge, Mass., 1988); Sherry B. Ortner, introduction, in Ortner, ed., *The Fate of "Culture": Geertz and Beyond* (Berkeley, Calif., 1999), 1–13.

29. Akhil Gupta and James Ferguson, "Beyond Culture—Space, Identity, and the Politics of Difference," *Cultural Anthropology* 7 (1992), 7.

30. On hybridity in the historiography of the Americas, see St. George, introduction to *Possible Pasts*. On the turn toward Atlantic history, see Bernard Bailyn, "The Idea of Atlantic History," *Itinerario* 20 (1996), 19–44; and David Armitage, "Three Concepts of Atlantic History," in David Armitage and M. J. Braddick, eds., *The British Atlantic World, 1500–1800* (New York, 2002), 11–30. On the increased study of borderlands, or "peripheries," see Jeremy Adelman and Stephen Aron, "From Borderlands to Borders: Empires, Nation-States, and the Peoples in Between in North American History," *AHR* 104 (1999), 814–41; and Amy Turner Bushnell and Jack P. Greene, "Peripheries, Centers, and the Construction of Early Modern American Empires," in Christine Daniels and Michael V. Kennedy, eds., *Negotiated Empires: Centers and Peripheries in the Americas, 1500–1820* (New York, 2002), 1–14. For these turns in anthropology see Renato Rosaldo, *Culture and Truth: The Remaking of Social Analysis* (Boston, 1993), 25–45, 196–217; and George E. Marcus, *Ethnography Through Thick and Thin* (Princeton, N.J., 1998), esp. 79–104.

31. Some historians exploring legal relations between European colonial powers and native peoples have proven exceptions to this rule. See Katherine A. Hermes, "Jurisdiction in the Colonial Northeast: Algonquian, English, and French Governance," *American Journal of Legal History* 43 (1999), 52–73; Hermes, "'Justice Will Be Done Us': Algonquian Demands for Reciprocity in the Courts of European Settlers," in Tomlins and Mann, *Many Legalities*, 123–50; Ann Marie Plane, *Colonial Intimacies: Indian Marriage in Early New England* (Ithaca, 2000). For calls for a greater investigation of legal pluralism in the fields of colonial legal history and anthropology see Ross, "Legal Past," 36–37; and Sally Engle Merry, "Anthropology, Law, and Transnational Processes," *Annual Review of Anthropology* 21 (1992), 357–79.

32. Thomas P. Slaughter, *The Whiskey Rebellion: Frontier Epilogue to the American Revolution* (New York, 1986); Alan Taylor, *Liberty Men and Great Proprietors: The Revolutionary Settlement on the Maine Frontier, 1760–1820* (Chapel Hill, 1990); Terry Bouton, "A Road Closed: Rural Insurgency in Post-Independence Pennsylvania," *Journal of American History* 87 (2000), 855–87 (hereafter *JAH*); Thomas J. Humphrey, "Extravagant Claims and Hard Labour: Perceptions of Property in the Hudson Valley, 1751–1801," *Explorations in Early American Culture* 2 (1998), 141–66; Humphrey, "Crowd and Court: Rough Music and Popular Music in Colonial New York," in William Pencak, Matthew Dennis, and Simon P. Newman, eds., *Riot and Revelry in Early America* (University Park, Pa., 2002), 104–24. Brendan McConville has paid the greatest attention to the role of competing European legal traditions—

in his case, between Dutch and English conceptions of inheritance—in shaping conflict over property rights. See McConville, "Conflict and Change on a Cultural Frontier: The Rise of Magdalena Valleau, Land Rioter," *Explorations in Early American Culture* 2 (1998), 122–40; McConville, *These Daring Disturbers of the Public Peace: The Struggle for Property and Power in Early New Jersey* (Ithaca, N.Y., 1999), 124–29.

33. Benton, *Law and Colonial Cultures*, 18–24.

34. Seed, *Ceremonies of Possession.* Seed's subsequent work continues in this same vein: see Seed, *American Pentimento: The Invention of Indians and the Pursuit of Riches* (Minneapolis, 2001).

35. Seed, *Ceremonies of Possession*, 2.

36. Ibid., 13.

37. Ibid., 13, 14–15.

38. In her efforts to distinguish between different colonial cultures, Seed implicitly disagrees with Greenblatt's method of examining how Europeans' "differing responses disclose shared assumptions and techniques" (Greenblatt, *Marvelous Possessions*, 23).

39. Seed, *Ceremonies of Possession*, 11.

40. On Williams's integration of multiple discourses into a concept of colonial authority, see Christopher D. Felker, "Roger Williams's Uses of Legal Discourse: Testing Authority in Early New England," *New England Quarterly* 63 (1990), 624–48.

41. White, *Middle Ground*; John Smolenski, "The Death of Sawantaeny and the Problem of Justice on the Frontier," in William Pencak and Daniel K. Richter, eds., *Friends and Enemies in Penn's Woods: Colonists, Indians, and the Racial Construction of Pennsylvania* (University Park, Pa., 2004), 125–56. On Bourbon recognition of frontier Indians' autonomy, see David J. Weber, "Bourbons and Barbaros: Center and Periphery in the Reshaping of Spanish Indian Policy," in Daniels and Kennedy, eds., *Negotiated Empires*, 86; on Spain's exclusive claims to imperium in America, see Pagden, *Lords of All the World*, 46–49.

42. William Sewell Jr. has argued that historians' anthropological borrowings tend far more toward synchronic than diachronic analysis in "Geertz, Cultural Systems, and History: From Synchrony to Transformation," in Ortner, *Fate of "Culture*," 35–55.

43. On the production of colonial maps, see Barbara E. Mundy, *The Mapping of New Spain: Indigenous Cartography and the Maps of the Relaciones Geográficas* (Chicago, 1996); Benjamin Schmidt, "Mapping an Empire: Cartographic and Colonial Rivalry in Seventeenth-Century Dutch and English North America," *WMQ* 54 (1997), 549–78; Ken MacMillan, "Sovereignty More Plainly Described: Early English Maps of North America, 1580–1625," *Journal of British Studies* 42 (2003), 413–47; Cynthia J. Van Zandt, "Mapping and the European Search for Intercultural Alliances in the Colonial World," *Early American Studies* 1 (2003), 72–99.

44. Margaret T. Hodgen, *Early Anthropology in the Sixteenth and Seventeenth Centuries* (Philadelphia, 1964); Anthony Pagden, *The Fall of Natural Man: The American Indian and the Origins of Comparative Ethnology* (New York, 1986); José Jorge Klor de Alva, H. B. Nicholson, and Eloise Quiñones Keber, *The Work of Bernardino De Sahagun: Pioneer Ethnographer of Sixteenth-Century Aztec Mexico* (Albany, N.Y., 1988); Sabine MacCormack, *Religion in the Andes: Vision and Imagination in Early Colonial Peru* (Princeton, N.J., 1991); Edward G. Gray, *New World Babel: Languages*

and Nations in Early America (Princeton, N.J., 1999); Karen Ordahl Kupperman, *Indians and English: Facing Off in Early America* (Ithaca, N.Y., 2000), 104–40; Joyce E. Chaplin, *Subject Matter: Technology, the Body, and Science on the Anglo-American Frontier, 1500–1676* (Cambridge, Mass., 2001).

45. Jorge Cañizares-Esguerra, *How to Write the History of the New World: Histories, Epistemologies, and Identities in the Eighteenth-Century Atlantic World* (Stanford, Calif., 2001).

46. Van Zandt, "Mapping," 88–89.

47. Schmidt, "Mapping an Empire," 549–78; MacMillan, "Sovereignty More Plainly Described."

48. Benton, *Law and Colonial Cultures*, 10, 29, 208–9; Tamar Herzog, *Defining Nations: Immigrants and Citizens in Early Modern Spain and Spanish America* (New Haven, Conn., 2003); Gene E. Ogle, "'The Eternal Power of Reason' and 'the Superiority of Whites': Hilliard D'Auberteuil's Colonial Enlightenment," *French Colonial History* 3 (2003), 35–50.

49. See Eliga H. Gould, "Zones of Law, Zones of Violence: The Legal Geography of the British Atlantic, Circa 1772," *WMQ* 60 (2003), 471–510.

50. Pierre Bourdieu, "The Social Space and the Genesis of Groups," *Theory and Society* 14 (1985), 723–24.

51. See Twinam, chapter 16 this volume.

52. Kimberly Gauderman has suggested that the essentially decentralized nature of Spanish colonial governance in colonial Quito provided women means of avoiding the most severe disabilities they might face under either religious or legal authority see Gauderman, *Women's Lives in Colonial Quito: Gender, Law, and Economy in Spanish America* (Austin, Tex., 2003); and chapter 3 in this volume.

53. Benton, *Law and Colonial Cultures*, 101.

54. Herbert S. Klein, *African Slavery in Latin America and the Caribbean* (New York, 1986), 189–215; Sidney W. Mintz and Richard Price, *The Birth of African-American Culture: An Anthropological Perspective* (Boston, 1992); Ira Berlin, *Many Thousands Gone: The First Two Centuries of Slavery in North America* (Cambridge, Mass., 1998), 111–14, 129–41, 149–54; Philip D. Morgan, *Slave Counterpoint: Black Culture in the Eighteenth-Century Chesapeake and Lowcountry* (Chapel Hill, N.C., 1998), 261–317; John Smolenski, "Hearing Voices: Microhistory, Dialogicality and the Recovery of Popular Culture on an Eighteenth-Century Virginia Plantation," *Slavery and Abolition* 24 (2003), 1–23.

55. Greg Urban, "Culture's Public Face," *Public Culture* 5 (1993), 228. See also Urban's elaboration of his theories of metaculture in Greg Urban, *Metaculture: How Culture Moves Through the World* (Minneapolis, 2001).

56. Evan Haefeli, "Kieft's War and the Cultures of Violence in Colonial Americas," in Michael A. Bellesiles, ed., *Lethal Imagination: Violence and Brutality in American History* (New York, 1999), quotation at 18; Inga Clendinnen, "'Fierce and Unnatural Cruelty': Cortés and the Conquest of Mexico," in Stephen Greenblatt, ed., *New World Encounters* (Berkeley, 1993), 12–47; Jill Lepore, *The Name of War: King Philip's War and the Origins of American Identity* (New York, 1998).

57. Michael Taussig, "Culture of Terror—Space of Death: Roger Casement's Putumayo Report and the Explanation of Torture," *Comparative Studies in Society and History* 26 (1984), 495.

58. Rhys Isaac, "Communication and Control: Authority Metaphors and Power Contests on Colonel Landon Carter's Virginia Plantation, 1752–1778," in Sean Wilentz, ed., *Rites of Power: Symbolism, Ritual, and Politics Since the Middle Ages* (Philadelphia, 1985), 275–302; Olwell, *Masters, Subjects, and Slaves.*

59. Humphrey, "Crowd and Court," 115–19. Foucault has argued that this theatrical display of the power of life and death was central to the early modern conception of sovereignty. See Foucault, *History of Sexuality: Vol. 1,* 136–37.

60. Tomlins, "Introduction," 3.

61. Benton, *Law and Colonial Cultures,* 23.

62. Urban, "Culture's Public Face," 228–29.

63. Taussig, "Culture of Terror," 468.

64. My concept of an "economy of violence" is adapted from Dell Hymes's definition of a speech economy as the set of rules governing the circulation of speech. See Hymes, "The Ethnography of Speaking," in Anthropological Society of Washington (Washington, D.C.), ed., *Anthropology and Human Behavior* (Washington, D.C., 1962), 13–53. This theme is developed more fully in Ogle, chapter 10 this volume.

65. David Armitage has argued that this kind of "cross-fertilization" is the main benefit of linking "cis-Atlantic" histories—local case studies placed in an Atlantic context—with "circum-Atlantic" histories of the Atlantic Basin as a whole. Armitage, "Three Concepts of Atlantic History," in David Armitage and Michael J. Braddick, eds., *The British Atlantic World, 1500–1800* (New York, 2002), 26.

Indroduction to Part I

1. Benedict R. O'G. Anderson, *Imagined Communities: Reflections on the Origin and Spread of Nationalism* (New York, 1991), 200.

2. Ibid., 206.

3. Michel-Rolph Trouillot, *Silencing the Past: Power and the Production of History* (Boston, 1995), 29.

Chapter 1. Law's Wilderness

1. Joyce E. Chaplin, *Subject Matter: Technology, the Body, and Science on the Anglo-American Frontier, 1500–1676* (Cambridge, Mass., 2001), 14, and see also 8–15, 20–23; Karen Ordahl Kupperman, *Indians and English: Facing Off in Early America* (Ithaca, N.Y., 2000), 1, and see also 11, 19.

2. William Shakespeare, *Titus Andronicus,* ed. Russ McDonald (New York, 2000). All line quotations are from this edition (hereafter *TA*).

3. John Nettles, "Perverse Justice in Kyd's Spanish Tragedy," http://paralel. park.uga.edu/~jnettles/kyd.html, par. 1.

4. Jacques Berthoud, "Introduction," in Sonia Massai, ed., *Titus Andronicus by William Shakeaspeare* (Harmondsworth, 2001), 7; A. C. Hamilton, *The Early Shakespeare* (San Marino, Calif., 1967). On rough theater, see Peter Brook, *The Empty Space* (New York, 1968).

5. *TA,* 32, 42, 43. Enforced silence and helplessness in the face of textual

authority is a recurrent motif of the play. Documents have been rendered supremely authoritative, "oral testimony under oath" pointless in the determination of causes, notwithstanding the "lingering distrust of written documents" as representations of fact that persisted into the seventeenth century. Jean-Christophe Agnew, *Worlds Apart: The Market and the Theater in Anglo-American Thought, 1550–1750* (New York, 1986). For the same on the Pennsylvania frontier, see James H. Merrell, *Into the American Woods: Negotiators on the Pennsylvania Frontier* (New York, 1999), 193–97, 215–21.

6. *TA*, 68.

7. *TA*, 76–81. Berthoud, "Commentary," in Massai, ed., *Titus Andronicus*, 213, notes the continuity of these scenes.

8. *TA*, 59, 97.

9. *TA*, 61–64, quotation on 100, emphasis added. Immediately thereafter, Titus consummates his revenge upon Tamora twice over, first by revealing to her that she has consumed her own sons' flesh (incest and cannibalism), then by killing her for it. As Berthoud points out, here is yet one more legal allusion turned upside down: "The proof that Tamora is guilty of eating her own sons is her execution for that crime" (Berthoud, "Commentary," 225).

10. Robert M. Cover, "Violence and the Word," *Yale Law Journal* 95 (1986), 1601, 1609, 1610.

11. Ibid., 1614–15, 1627.

12. Robert M. Cover, "The Folktales of Justice: Tales of Jurisdiction," *Capital University Law Review* 14 (1985), 181–83.

13. Ibid., 181; Cover, "Violence and the Word," 1602 n. 2. On law as meaning, see also Robert M. Cover, "The Supreme Court, 1982 Term: Foreword: Nomos and Narrative," *Harvard Law Review* 97 (1983), 4–68.

14. Cover, "Violence and the Word," 1602. Lavinia has shown us that this is not so, and Jill Lepore seconds her. War is "a violent contest for territory, resources, and political allegiances, and, no less fiercely, a contest for meaning . . . War twice cultivates language: it requires justification, it demands description" (Lepore, *The Name of War: King Philip's War and the Origins of American Identity* [New York, 1998], x). As we shall see, the law of war is of considerable importance in justifying the violence of colonization.

15. Carol J. Greenhouse, "Reading Violence," in Austin Sarat and Thomas R. Kearns, eds., *Law's Violence* (Ann Arbor, 1995), 105–6.

16. 12 Co. Rep. 63.

17. "Sir Rafe Boswell to Dr Milborne," in Catherine Drinker Bowen, *The Lion and the Throne: The Life and Times of Sir Edward Coke* (Boston, 1956), 305; Cover, "Folktales of Justice," 188.

18. Cover, "Folktales of Justice," 186, 187.

19. Ibid., 187, 181.

20. Berthoud, "Introduction," 7; Ben Jonson, *Bartholomew Fair*, Prologue, scene 2, the Bookeholder's speech.

21. McDonald, "Introduction," in *TA*, xxxiv–v, xlviii.

22. Berthoud, "Introduction," 16, 25.

23. Saturninus and Bassianus, sons of the late emperor, are on the brink of

civil war over the succession. Marcus Andronicus is conspiring to install Titus. Bassianus plots with the Andronici against his brother. *TA*, 3–5, 10–12.

24. *TA*, 7–9.

25. Titus swears loyalty to Saturninus. Saturninus takes Lavinia to be his empress, with Titus's consent, to cement the agreement. Bassianus and Lavinia's brothers abduct her, claiming Bassianus's prior right gained through "lawful promised love," which Saturninus in turn calls "lawless" and a "rape," for Lavinia is taken from him by force against her father's wishes. Saturninus denounces the Andronici and Bassianus as traitors, conspirators, and rapists. He makes Tamora his empress. In 320 lines, Shakespeare has given every principal in the play a plausible claim to have been wronged and a reason for vengeance. *TA*, 11–12, 14, 14–16.

26. *TA*, 7, 100, 101–4, 106; Berthoud, "Introduction," 29; Berthoud, "Commentary," 224–25, 226.

27. Confirmed by the fate of Tamora (her body thrown away) and Aron (buried alive).

28. Agnew, *Worlds Apart*, 8–12, 14, 60 (emphasis in original). Among its many other things, *Titus Andronicus* is a relentless assault on all affirmative rituals—births, betrothals, funerals, processions, and pageants; rituals of law, of the hunt, of the feast, of lineage, of loyalty and obligation, of hierarchy, of fidelity, of grief. Nothing is spared. Hamilton, *The Early Shakespeare*, 74–75. On modernity's subversion of ritual in the context of colonizing, see Tzvetan Todorov, *The Conquest of America: The Question of the Other* (Norman, Okla., 1999), 53–123.

29. Robert Blair St. George, *Conversing by Signs: Poetics of Implication in Colonial New England Culture* (Chapel Hill, N.C., 1998), 150, 151.

30. Ibid., 151.

31. *TA*, 9, 14–15, 43–44, 51–53, 55, 97–98, 101–2

32. See Todorov, *Conquest of America*, 34–50, 150–254; Stephen Greenblatt, *Marvelous Possessions: The Wonder of the New World* (Chicago, 1991), 68, 128–40; St. George, *Conversing by Signs*, 154–61; Chaplin, *Subject Matter*, 116–242; Lepore, *Name of War*, 3–18. See generally Richard Tuck, *The Rights of War and Peace: Political Thought and the International Order from Grotius to Kant* (Oxford, 1999).

33. Francis Barker, *The Culture of Violence: Essays on Tragedy and History* (Chicago, 1993), 204–5; Rebecca Ann Bach, *Colonial Transformations: The Cultural Production of the New Atlantic World, 1580–1640* (New York, 2000), 113.

34. On signifiers of savagery, see Todorov, *Conquest of America*, 149–60, 177.

35. Barker, *Culture of Violence*, 3–92, 142–206.

36. Agnew, *Worlds Apart*, 56. Selves that could no longer be "authorized within the traditional religious, familial, or class frame" (10) became "artificial persons" (101–48), or as Hamlet has it "piece[s] of work" (*Hamlet*, II.ii.301). For ruined monasteries, see *TA*, 85.

37. Richard Hakluyt (the elder), "Notes on Colonisation" (1578), in E. G. R. Taylor, ed., *The Original Writings and Correspondence of the Two Richard Hakluyts* (London, 1935), 116–22. On the city in colonizing, see also Anthony Pagden, *Lords of All the World: Ideologies of Empire in Spain, Britain and France, c. 1500–1800* (New Haven, Conn., 1995), 17–23.

38. Barker, *Culture of Violence*, 4–5, 147–48; Todorov, *Conquest of America*,

149–60; Tuck, *Rights of War and Peace*, 34–50; Bach, *Colonial Transformations*, 120–24, 141–44.

39. *Bradford's History "Of Plymouth Plantation,"* from the original manuscript (Boston, 1898), 94–95.

40. Alberico Gentili, *De Iure Belli* (Oxford, 1933), in Tuck, *Rights of War and Peace*, 48.

41. Grotius, writes Richard Tuck, distinguished property and jurisdiction. As to property, anyone could assert a natural right to possess waste or vacant land. As to jurisdiction, it was a right asserted by a sovereign authority over people (subjects) exercised throughout a certain area of the world's surface (territory) where the subjects in question were located. If local sovereign authorities obstructed the occupation of waste, "the local authorities will have violated a principle of the law of nature and may be punished by war waged against them." The objective of war might be no more than to insist that local authorities allow occupation, or, more ambitiously, to establish a new "stable and effective right to command anyone who entered into a certain area of land," which meant the establishment of a new "jurisdiction over territory." See Tuck, *Rights of War and Peace*, 106–7.

42. *Bradford's History*, 110.

43. Francis Newton Thorpe, *The Federal and State Constitutions, Colonial Charters, and other Organic Laws of the States, Territories and Colonies Now or Heretofore Forming The United States of America* (Washington, D. C., 1909), 1828–29. See generally Patricia Seed, *American Pentimento: The Invention of Indians and the Pursuit of Riches* (Minneapolis, 2001), 29–44.

44. On the construction of the North Atlantic seaboard's indigenous economy of mobility as "absence," see Jean M. O'Brien, *Dispossession by Degrees: Indian Land and Identity in Natick, Massachusetts, 1650–1790* (New York, 1977), 1–30.

45. Thorpe, *Federal and State Constitutions*, 3784.

46. John Donne, *A Sermon Preached to the Honourable Company of the Virginia Plantation, 13 Nov. 1622* (London, 1623), quoted in Tuck, *Rights of War and Peace*, 124, and see also 35, 49–50 (More), 124–25 (Robert Cushman and Samuel Purchas).

47. Thorpe, *Federal and State Constitutions*, 3036 (Pennsylvania), 765 (Georgia).

48. Taylor, *Original Writings and Correspondence*, 211.

49. Ibid., 218–21, 222, 223, 327, 328, 329.

50. See Eric Hinderaker, *Elusive Empires: Constructing Colonialism in the Ohio Valley, 1673–1800* (New York, 1997); Donna Merwick, *Possessing Albany, 1630–1710: The Dutch and English Experiences* (New York, 1990); Kupperman, *Indians and English*, 110–41.

51. See Christopher L. Tomlins, "The Legal Cartography of Colonization, the Legal Polyphony of Settlement: English Intrusions on the American Mainland in the Seventeenth Century," *Law and Social Inquiry*, 26, 2 (Spring 2001), 319–20.

52. Taylor, *Writings and Correspondence*, 215, 332–33.

53. Thorpe, *The Federal and State Constitutions*, 1857. The extract quoted is taken from the 1629 Massachusetts Bay Charter, but the provisions outlined are a commonplace of all the seventeenth-century charters.

54. See Richard Lyman Bushman, "Farmers in Court: Orange County, North Carolina, 1750–1776," in Christopher L. Tomlins and Bruce H. Mann, *The Many*

Legalities of Early America (Chapel Hill, 2001), 388–413; St. George, *Conversing by Signs*, 16–113; Lepore, *Name of War*, 74, 107–13.

55. O'Brien, *Dispossession by Degrees*, 22–26.

56. *Bradford's History*, 96, 97.

57. Cover, "Nomos and Narrative," 4.

58. Chaplin, *Subject Matter*, 83; St. George, *Conversing by Signs*, 154–56; Margaret T. Hodgen, *Early Anthropology in the Sixteenth and Seventeenth Centuries* (Philadelphia, 1964), 254–353.

59. Lepore, *Name of War*, 107, 112, 119

60. Chaplin, *Subject Matter*, 83.

61. The *Lawes, Divine, Moral and Martiall* first promulgated in the Jamestown colony in 1610, three years after its establishment, forbade all contact between settlers and Indians and all running away from the colony to the Indians. On the early history of crossing between the communities, see Kupperman, *Indians and English*, 192–94, 206–7.

62. Francis Barker, *The Tremulous Private Body: Essays on Subjection* (Ann Arbor, Mich., 1995), vi, and generally v–x. On *Hamlet*, see 25–33.

63. Barker, *Culture of Violence*, 17. On the covariance of Protestantism, the political economy of colonizing, and discipline, see, for example, Stephen Innes, *Creating the Commonwealth: The Economic Culture of Puritan New England* (New York, 1995), 39–159.

64. Greenhouse, "Reading Violence," 105.

65. See Max Weber's analysis of political communities in Max Rheinstein, ed., *Max Weber on Law in Economy and Society* (New York, 1954), 338–48.

66. John Gillies, *Shakespeare and the Geography of Difference* (Cambridge, 1994), 6.

67. Ibid., 62. See also Bernhard Klein, *Maps and the Writing of Space in Early Modern England and Ireland* (Basingstoke, 2001), 6, 21–41.

68. As in Christopher Marlowe's *Tamburlaine* (1587). See Stephen Greenblatt, *Renaissance Self-Fashioning: From More to Shakespeare* (Chicago, 1980), 195–96.

69. Barker, *Culture of Violence*, 3.

70. *TA*, 58.

71. J. B. Harley, "Power and Legitimation in the English Geographical Atlases of the Eighteenth Century," in John A. Wolter and Ronald E. Grim, eds., *Images of the World: The Atlas Through History* (Washington D.C., 1997), 189.

72. J.B. Harley and David Woodward, Preface, Harley and Woodward, eds., *History of Cartography, I: Cartography in Prehistoric, Ancient, and Medieval Europe and the Mediterranean* (Chicago, 1987), xvi.

73. Klein, *Maps and the Writing of Space*, 11, 92 (emphasis added).

74. Ibid., 129–30.

75. Bruno Latour, "Drawing Things Together," in Michael Lynch and Steve Woolgar, eds., *Representation in Scientific Practice* (Cambridge, Mass., 1990), 25, 26, 44–46, 60. See also Todorov, *Conquest of America*, 251–54; Greenblatt, *Marvelous Possessions*, 9–12.

76. Anthony Pagden, "The Struggle for Legitimacy and the Image of Empire in the Atlantic to c. 1700," in Nicholas Canny, ed., *The Origins of Empire: British Overseas Enterprise to the Close of the Seventeenth Century* (New York, 1998), 37.

77. John Locke, *Second Treatise of Government*, ed. and intro. C. B. McPherson (Indianapolis, 1980), 18–30. See also Pagden, "Struggle for Legitimacy," 42–44; James Tully, "Rediscovering America: The Two Treatises and Aboriginal Rights," in James Tully, *An Approach to Political Philosophy: Locke in Contexts* (Cambridge and New York, 1993), 155–66.

78. Gentili, *De Iure Belli*, quoted in Tuck, *Rights of War and Peace*, 47.

79. Klein, *Maps and the Writing of Space*, 35.

80. Richard Hakluyt, lawyer, of London, to Abraham Ortelius, cosmographer, of Flanders (n.d., circa 1567), in Taylor, *Original Writings and Correspondence*, 81.

81. Klein, *Maps and the Writing of Space*, 44, and 61–75.

82. Ibid., 67; Edmund Spenser, *Amoretti*, quoted in Bach, *Colonial Transformations*, 48, and 37–65.

83. Klein, *Maps and the Writing of Space*, 46, 43.

84. Christopher Tomlins, "Early British America, 1585–1830: Freedom Bound," in Paul Craven and Douglas Hay, eds., *Masters, Servants, and Magistrates in Britain and the Empire, 1562–1955* (Chapel Hill, N.C., 2004); Tuck, *Rights of War and Peace*, 40–47.

85. McDonald, "Introduction," in *TA*, xxxix.

86. *TA*, 24. Later, in dialogue with Tamora, Lavinia refers to Aron as "your Moor" (*TA*, 33).

87. *TA*, 106.

88. *TA*, 31–32.

89. *TA*, 33–34, 99.

90. *TA*, 69, 70, 71, 86 (emphasis added).

91. *TA*, 72, 74, 85.

92. Berthoud, "Introduction," 41; *TA*, 89.

93. Ibid., 41. In Agnew's terms, Aron is the play's starkest embodiment of the market's erosion of organic human relations. Not only does he stand for the nullification of human communities, in person he is the market's ultimate creation and contradiction of humanity—a human commodity.

94. "Set him breast-deep in earth and famish him. / There let him stand and rave and cry for food. /If anyone relieves or pities him, / For the offense he dies. This is our doom" (*TA*, 105–6). Aron is to be tortured to death, slowly, closely observed, and enforced by a decree criminalizing the elementary human virtue of empathy. Here is one final undermining of the opposition between civitas and barbarity.

95. Cover, "Nomos and Narrative," 4–5.

96. Greenblatt, *Marvelous Possessions*, 9–11.

97. Tuck, *Rights of War and Peace*, 34, 35, 47–50, 102–3, 105.

98. Hence Rogers Smith's massive attempt to explain all forms of ascriptive inegalitarianism as always inimical to liberalism rather than as, historically, quite compatible with it. Smith, *Civic Ideals: Conflicting Visions of Citizenship in U.S. History* (New Haven, Conn., 1997).

99. See Bernard Bailyn, *The Peopling of British North America: An Introduction* (New York, 1986); and *Voyagers to the West: A Passage in the Peopling of America on the Eve of the Revolution* (New York, 1986).

100. See, e.g., Jack P. Greene, *The Intellectual Construction of America: Exceptionalism and Identity from 1492 to 1800* (Chapel Hill, N.C., 1993), 58, 66.

101. Hinderaker, *Elusive Empires*, 227. In 1867, Francis Parkman wrote, "The Indians melted away, not because civilization destroyed them, but because their own ferocity and intractable indolence made it impossible that they should exist in its presence." Francis Parkman, *The Jesuits in North America in the Seventeenth Century* (Boston, 1909), 418. "Unopened" is taken from James Willard Hurst, *Law and the Conditions of Freedom in the Nineteenth-Century United States* (Madison, Wis., 1956), 8.

102. Nowhere better epitomized than in the *Wall Street Journal*'s annual editorial invocation of William Bradford's narrative of the Pilgrim landing in the new world. See, for example, "The Desolate Wilderness," *Wall Street Journal*, 26 November 2003, A16.

103. Locke, *Second Treatise*, 21–22.

104. See Carole Pateman, *The Sexual Contract* (Stanford, Calif., 1988).

105. For a recent example, see Gordon S. Wood, *The Radicalism of the American Revolution* (New York, 1992). But for a more recent departure, see Robert V. Hine and John Mack Faragher, *The American West: A New Interpretive History* (New Haven, Conn., 2000).

106. Cover, "Nomos and Narrative," 5.

107. See Stanley N. Katz, "The Problem of a Colonial Legal History," in Jack P. Greene and J. R. Pole, eds., *Colonial British America: Essays in the New History of the Early Modern Era* (Baltimore, 1984), 465–66.

108. "Occasionally," writes Patricia Nelson Limerick, "continuities in American history almost bowl one over" (Limerick, *The Legacy of Conquest: The Unbroken Past of the American West* [New York, 1987], 48, and see generally 41–48, 55–96).

109. Hurst, *Law and the Conditions of Freedom*, 3–32.

110. Reverend Jason Lothrop, "A Sketch of the Early History of Kenosha County, Wisconsin, and of the Western Emigration Company," *Wisconsin Assembly Journal*, II (1856), Appendix 14, 450–79, esp. 461–64, 472–79.

111. For the breadth of Hurst's reading and mind, see Carl Landauer, "Social Science on a Lawyer's Bookshelf: Willard Hurst's *Law and the Conditions of Freedom in the Nineteenth-Century United States*," *Law and History Review* 18 (2000), 59–96.

112. Cover, "Nomos and Narrative," 5.

113. Hurst, *Law and the Conditions of Freedom*, 12.

114. See Hine and Faragher, *The American West*, 115; Lea VanderVelde, "Slaves in Free Territory" (Iowa College of Law, 2001).

115. Hurst, *Law and the Conditions of Freedom*, 67–8.

116. VanderVelde, "Slaves in Free Territory."

117. Barker, *Culture of Violence*, 3–4.

118. Stephen Greenblatt, *Shakespearean Negotiations: The Circulation of Social Energy in Renaissance England* (Berkeley, 1988), 5–6.

119. Ibid., 7.

120. Hurst, *Law and the Conditions of Freedom*, 3–6. On the construction of "we" as an icon of American culture and history, see also Bach, *Colonial Transformations*, 230–31

121. Pateman, *Sexual Contract*, 87; Greenblatt, *Shakespearean Negotiations*, 7.

122. On energetic colonizers and enervated Indians, see Chaplin, *Subject Matter*, 34–35, 116–279.

123. See, for example, Hinderaker, *Elusive Empires*, 244–67.

124. Locke, *Second Treatise*, 11.

125. As Jeannine Purdy writes of Frantz Fanon, "Fanon was concerned to show that the function of, and the attitudes toward, law and its violence varied according to which side of the . . . divide one stood on" (Purdy, "Postcolonialism: The Emperor's New Clothes?" in Eve Darian-Smith and Peter Fitzpatrick, eds., *Laws of the Postcolonial* (Ann Arbor, Mich., 1999), 203.

126. John L. Comaroff, "Colonialism, Culture and the Law: A Foreword," *Law & Social Inquiry* 26 (2001), 306. See also Merrell, *Into the American Woods*, 281.

127. *Poem by One Named Xu from Xiangshan Encouraging the Traveler* (written on a wall of the federal quarantine station, Angel Island, Port of San Francisco), in Him Mark Lai et al., eds., *Island: Poetry and History of Chinese Immigrants on Angel Island, 1910–1940* (Seattle, 1980), 42.

Chapter 2. Dialogical Encounters in a Space of Death

An earlier version of this chapter was published as "Encuentros dialógicos en un espacio de muerte," in Manuel Gutiérrez Estévez, et al., eds., *De Palabra y Obra en el Nuevo Mundo. Encuentros interétnicos* 2 (Madrid, 1992), 33–62. Its methodological underpinnings are spelled out in Richard Price, *First-Time: The Historical Vision of an Afro-American People* (Baltimore, 1983; 2nd ed., Chicago, 2002) and Richard Price, *Alabi's World* (Baltimore, 1990).

1. Michael Taussig, *Shamanism, Colonialism, and the Wild Man: A Study in Terror and Healing* (Chicago, 1987), 132.

2. David Scott, "That Event, This Memory: Notes on the Anthropology of African Diasporas in the New World," *Diaspora* 1 (1991), 261–84 and David Scott, *Refashioning Futures: Criticism After Postcoloniality* (Princeton, N.J., 1999).

3. Scott, "That Event," 263.

4. I engage Scott's interesting criticisms more directly elsewhere; see Price, "The Miracle of Creolization: A Retrospective," *New West Indian Guide* 75 (2001), 37–67.

5. Marcus Wood, *Blind Memory: Visual Representations of Slavery in England and America, 1780–1865* (New York, 2000).

6. "The space of death is one of the crucial spaces where Indian, African, and white gave birth to the New World" (Michael Taussig, "Culture of Terror—Space of Death: Roger Casement's Putumayo Report and the Explanation of Torture," *Comparative Studies in Society and History* 26 [1984], 468; see also Taussig, *Shamanism*).

7. Greg Dening, *Performances* (Chicago, 1996), 45.

8. Sidney W. Mintz and Richard Price, *The Birth of African-American Culture: An Anthropological Perspective* (Boston, 1992), 25.

9. Jan Jacob Hartsinck, *Beschrijving van Guiana of de Wilde Kust in Zuid-Amerika* (Amsterdam, 1770), 763.

10. As Dening has written, "Obeisance to sovereignty is the acknowledgement of both the limit on self and the openness of self to the invasion of power. This thing outside of self [in the present case, the slaveocracy] needs many plays to make

it present and real. Not least among the plays is the victim's demeanour and accep-tance and resignation. There is horror at execution when the victims see the shams and will not be killed quietly" (Dening, *The Bounty: An Ethnographic History* [Mel-bourne, 1988], 15).

11. The previous day, Stedman had witnessed various "Shocking Barbarities," his "Ears deaf'd With the Clang of the Whip, & Shreeks of the Negroes" being "pun-ished." He had also seen three American sailors, from a brig lying in the roads of Paramaribo, being brought ashore in custody "for having been Drunk on Duty," and receiving "a *Fire Cant* Each at the Captains Request, that is Bastonaded or beat on the Shoulders by two Corporals with bamboo Sticks, till theyr backs were Swell'd like a Cushion" (John Gabriel Stedman, *Narrative of a Five Years Expedition Against the Revolted Negroes of Surinam*, transcribed from the original 1790 manuscript, edited, and with an introduction and notes, by Richard and Sally Price [Baltimore, 1988], 544).

12. Stedman quotes here from (Anonymous), "Jamaica, a Poem in Three Parts. Written in that Island, in the year MDCCLXXVI" (1777, 1, vv. 186–90).

13. Stedman, *Narrative*, 546–47, 550. Accounts of slave stoicism under torture are sufficiently common in the region that some European literary scholars, unschooled in the historical realities of the colonial New World, have wondered whether such narratives simply represent a trope originating—most likely—with Aphra Behn's fictional account of the death of the slave-prince Oroonoko, set in Suriname a hundred years before Neptune's execution.

He [Oroonoko-Caesar] had learned to take Tobacco; and when he was assur'd he should die, he desir'd they would give him a Pipe in his Mouth, ready lighted; which they did: And the Executioner came, and first cut off his Members, and threw them into the Fire; after that, with an ill-favour'd Knife, they cut off his Ears and his Nose, and burned them; he still smoak'd on, as if nothing had touched him; then they hack'd off one of his Arms, and still he bore up, and held his Pipe; but at the cutting off the other Arm, his head sunk, and hie Pipe dropt, and he gave up the Ghost, without a Groan, or a Reproach . . . They cut Caesar [Oroonoko] into Quarters, and sent them to several of the chief Plantations. (Aphra Behn, "The History of Oroonoko; or, the Royal Slave" [1688], in *All the Histories and Novels Written by the Late Inge-nious Mrs. Behn, Intire in Two Volumes* [London, 1722], 199–200)

But historians familiar with this American space of death and who have carefully documented the sentences meted out and the slave-victims' demeanor, from archival journal sources, make quite clear that such events were institutionalized occur-rences, central rituals of the totalizing world of the plantation society. See, for exam-ple, R. A. J. van Lier, *Frontier Society: A Social Analysis of the History of Surinam* (The Hague, 1971), 136; Price *First-Time*, 9–10. In the early eighteenth century, Herlein had reported that a recaptured town slave, "whose punishment shall serve as an exam-ple to others," was sentenced

to be quartered alive, and the pieces thrown in the River. He was lain on the ground, his head on a long beam. The first blow he was given, on the abdomen, burst his bladder open, yet he uttered not the least sound; the second blow with the axe he tried to deflect with his hand, but it gashed the hand and upper belly, again without his uttering a sound. The slave men and women laughed at this, saying to one another, "That is a man!" Finally, the third blow, on the chest, killed him. His head was cut off and the body cut in four pieces and dumped in the river. (J. D. Herlein, *Beschryvinge van de Volk-plantinge Zuriname* [Leeuwarden, 1718], 117)

And Stedman himself described how "even So late as 1789 On October 30 & 31 /at Demerary/ Thirty two Wretches were Executed, Sixteen of Whom in the Above Shocking Manner, Without So much as a Single Complaint was Heard Amongst them, & Which days of Martyr are Absolutely a Feast to many Planters" (Stedman, *Narrative*, 1988, 47–549). Should any doubts remain, I cite just one more example, from a little-known book by a German Moravian missionary who was visiting the capital of Suriname in 1779; this sample, again, stresses the everydayness of such executions as well as the absolute insistence of the Afro-American victims (whom the missionary sees merely as "frivolous") on making a final statement of individuality and resistance.

When I returned I found out that there would be an execution in which seven slaves would lose their lives. Such executions take place once a month and are normally scheduled for a half hour past sunrise. I felt it my duty to attend and was there at quarter to six . . . Soon, six negroes were brought, bound with ropes to one another. The seventh, who was old and sick, was brought in a handcart. Of the six, only one looked melancholy. The others seemed cheerful and kept trying to humour the other who finally became a bit happier. The judicial officials were on a special structure for their use, in front of which the delinquents were made to stand in a row. Each was made to say what he had done wrong, and their death sentences were read out to them in their own language. But while their crimes or sentences were being pronounced, they just kept talking and laughing together. To their comrade who was so sad, they said "Fie! Shame on you. You're not a brave negro." After all the formalities, the delinquents were unbound from one another by the executioner, who is also a negro. Then the sick man was pulled with great difficulty from the cart and had to be bound with ropes. Then came the four others, including the melancholy one, who shared the same fate. This last was temporarily released from the bonds tying his hands behind his back and said [to the one who untied him], "You are a good negro. You've given me back my freedom," and he clapped his hands. But this freedom of course was short-lived since the executioner and his assistant soon bound his hands with thin cord and ordered him to lie on his back on the ground. Under his head they placed a piece of wood. The executioner wanted to bind the negro's eyes but he did not want this. He said he was a negro and brave, so then the executioner cut off his right hand, after which the negro raised his bloody arm and said, "Well, at least I am free again, even though my arm is too short." The other negro who was to suffer the exact same fate, commented with humor, "Well, your head will soon become too short as well." Quickly, they turned to him, so that the piece of wood was placed under his chin, and they cut off his head with an axe. When it was time for the last one to be executed, he turned out to be the most frivolous *[Leichtsinnig]* of them all. He was at most seventeen years old and had poisoned his mistress called Missi, and he looked as if he were facing death with complete defiance. After he had lost his hand he screamed out at the executioner, "Your axe works wonders! I hardly feel anything!" (Johann Andreus Riemer, *Missions-Reise nach Suriname und Barbice* [Zittau and Leipzig, 1801], 103–6)

It may be worth noting that Stedman's description of Neptune's suffering and death was quoted in full in Knapp and Baldwin's *Newgate Calendar*, where it formed the centerpiece of their discussion of torture; see Andrew Knapp and William Baldwin, *The Newgate Calendar* (London, 1824), 1: 136–43. "No longer deemed compatible with freedom...[execution by torture] was therefore abrogated in the year 1772. Yet . . . the inhuman practice still prevails in some of the English settlements abroad" (ibid.).

14. Stedman, *Narrative*, 547.

15. Ursy M. Lichtveld and Jan Voorhoeve, ed., *Suriname: Spiegel der Vaderlandese Kooplieden*, (The Hague, 2nd ed., 1980), 288.

16. Aleks de Drie, *Sye! Arki Tori!* (Samengesteld door Trudi Guda) (Paramaribo, 1985), 48–51, 342–43; Lichtveld and Voorhoeve, *Suriname*, 80–102.

17. See Stedman *Narrative*, passim.

18. Marcus Wood gives a very different reading of Stedman's descriptions of Surinamers (including Neptune) under torture, claiming that they portray "a fantasy of complete insensitivity [on the part of the victims], . . . an inability to suffer which is inhuman . . . Stedman's set piece descriptions of the torture of black men present the victims as dropping into a nihilistic buffoonery" (Wood, *Blind Memory*, 231–34). And he goes so far as to write of "the disempowering aspects of Stedman's accounts." Leaving aside what I see as a serious misreading of Stedman's work, I would note that with all his concern about discourse (and Foucault), Wood never tries to imagine what the victims (except, perhaps, as generalized, unhistoricized human beings) might have been thinking and feeling and acting in terms of. When he writes, "The black male victim in Stedman's writing is an involved parody of the controlled violence of European torture," he is denying the possibility that parodic agency (and the ability to enact an ultimate act of resistance) could be the prerogative of the victim and not just a device of the clever writer's imagination. My own claim, once again, is that more than a trope is involved in such narratives and that we can read—peering through the multiple sources in several languages—something about the actors', and not just the observers', mind-set. (Michel-Rolph Trouillot's recent warning about African American historiography may be worth repeating: "As social theory becomes more discourse-oriented, the distance between data and claims in debates about creolization . . . increases. Historical circumstances fall further into a hazy background of ideological preferences" [Trouillot, "Creolization on the Edges: Creolization in the Plantation Context," *Plantation Society in the Americas* 5 (1998), 15].)

19. Detailed citations for this paragraph are found in Richard Price, ed., *Maroon Societies: Rebel Slave Communities in the Americas*, 3rd ed. rev. (Baltimore, 1996), 16–19.

20. The protagonist of this wartime story was a most unusual African-born slave (the man whom John Gabriel Stedman later referred to as "The Celebrated Graman Quacy . . . one of the most Extraordinary Black men in Surinam, or Perhaps in the World," and whose portrait was engraved by William Blake). In 1755, Kwasímukámba, the double agent supreme, played the Dutch colonists' hand against the Saramakas' aged but still redoubtable tribal chief Ayakô, himself supported in these events by Wámba, a forest-spirit god. The psychologically complex drama

(which is recorded in both Dutch documents and Saramaka memory) witnessed the slave Kwasí arriving in Saramaka pretending to be a new recruit from the plantations, using his powerful ritual knowledge to befriend Chief Ayakô, and almost becoming privy to the ultimate secrets of Saramaka invulnerability, with Wámba—speaking through the mouth of Ayakô's sister's daughter—warning Ayakô that Kwasí was in fact a secret agent; Ayakô setting a trap and allowing Kwasí to escape back to the whites; Kwasí returning the next year at the head of a colonial army of hundreds of men; and then, during the final battles deep in the interior of Suriname, the Saramakas finally claiming their sweet revenge. No set of wartime incidents so well expresses the fierce and defiant ideology that Saramaka Maroons call "First-Time." Indeed, it was just after telling me some details of this highly secret and dangerous story that Peléki, a Saramaka descendent of Ayakô, remarked,

And that's why, Friend, Maroons do not trust Creoles [non-Maroon Afro-Surinamers] . . . Because of what happened to our ancestors. If you take one of them as a *máti* [formal friend] that's what they'll do with you. You must not trust them with a single thing about the forest. City people! They fought against us along with the whites. Like you. I must not [am not supposed to] tell you anything! It isn't good. Because whites used to come fight them. Well, Kwasímukámba was a Creole and he joined up with the whites to bring them here . . . But if you teach an outsider something, well, little by little he'll use it to come kill you . . . Well, they didn't trust him [Kwasí] fully. They didn't teach him all of their knowledge. And that's why he didn't triumph in the end. That's why we say, if you teach a Creole or a white person, that's what they'll do with you. This is the one thing Maroons really believe. It's stronger than anything else . . . This is the greatest fear of all Maroons: that those times [the days of war and slavery] shall come again. (Price *First-Time*, 153–59)

21. For the Moravians, *wísi* meant "poison," not "witchcraft" or "sorcery"—as it did for the Saramakas.

22. F. Staehelin, *Die Mission der Brüdergemeine in Suriname und Berbice im achtzehnten Jahrhundert* (Herrnhut, Vereins für Brüdergeschichte in Kommission der Unitätsbuchhandlung in Gnadau, 1913–19), 3: pt. 2, 51–52.

23. Ibid.

24. Divination with a coffin was one of the most widespread "Africanisms" in the colonial Americas (Mintz and Price, *Birth of African-American Culture*, 55–56). For illustrations of the practice in eighteenth-century Suriname and elsewhere, see Price, *Alabi's World*, 87–89, 312–13.

25. The kerosene, an anachronism in the narrative, contributes to the story's verisimilitude for modern Saramaka listeners.

26. Price, *Alabi's World*, 223–24. Four years before, the missionaries had already witnessed two spectacular public executions of Saramakas who had been convicted of witchcraft. Brother Riemer, who arrived in Saramaka two years after these events, left a detailed description of one of them, based on the graphic account given to him by Captain Alábi, a Moravian convert who often mediated between the whites and his own people.

This is the frightening story of a young negro who believed that he had so angered his god, a big Boma [anaconda] snake, that the snake could only be reconciled to him if he killed three innocent children . . . This negro knew a family with three small boys, the oldest being five and the youngest a year-and-a-half old. These he chose as the sacrificial victims of his idolatrous craze. Since this negro was well-known in the house, he entered on some pretence and took the occasion to offer the oldest child a fruit which contained a strong poison [Alábi would probably have said "prepared with witchcraft-medicine"], from which the boy died the following day. Afterwards, he watched with care to see where the father had buried his dead son, and the next day, unnoticed, he took the body from the grave to bring to his idol as a sacrifice. He then let some time pass, after which he gave the second child a piece of very tasty fruit which also contained strong poison, and from which his death quickly followed. The death of one healthy child so soon after another aroused suspicions among both the parents and relatives. But they knew no one who might be suspect. The sad father went with bleeding heart to bury this child beside the first. But he noticed that the body of the first child was missing, and his suspicions grew. After a few days, the murderer came to take the body of the second child and sacrifice it to his idols. Next came the turn of the third little innocent. The monster, after several vain attempts, finally found a means to get this year-and-a-half-old child in his clutches, and once they were alone he gave him a piece of poisoned fruit. As he must not have eaten that much fruit, he did not die as quickly as his two brothers, and had to suffer for many days before he succumbed. During his long battle against death, this extraordinary adventure was much discussed in the neighboring villages. People came from far and wide to comfort the despairing parents. Among these was the murderer, who came to show the father his grief. But he was to pay a price for his duplicity. The sight of the tiny, innocent child suffering so severely moved the rest of those human feelings he still possessed, so that he was unable to leave the baby's side. And, finally, when he managed to force himself to leave, he found himself returning soon after. His exterior, and facial expression, betrayed so much fear and anxiety that people, with sound suspicions, finally placed him in chains and forced him to stay by the child's bedside for an uninterrupted period of time, so that he would witness the child's sufferings. During this time, the prisoner's agitation grew to such an extent that the relatives called the captain and some elders to arrest this man. Some queried him about his anxiety and agitation, to which he replied that he did not wish to submit to the Kangra [*kangáa*] ordeal of the Obia men but would instead make a free and open confession. But the murderer trembled and quaked; his tongue seemed paralyzed and he was silent. Meanwhile, the captain urged him to confess. Finally, he pulled himself together and confessed his horrible deed. Soon thereafter, the long-suffering child passed away.

After the burial, during which time the murderer remained in chains, a Grang-Kruttu [*gaán kuútu*—tribal council meeting] was called. The tribal chief [Riemer refers here to Alábi] opened the council meeting by relating the gruesome series of events, after which the murderer was led in and confessed his crimes without hesitation, in the presence of all the relatives of the poisoned children. Thus, no extensive Kangra ordeals were necessary. The tribal council condemned the criminal to death and presented him to the parents for their decision as to how the execution should be carried out, for they should not lack their well-deserved revenge.

The execution of this negro is supposed to have been one of the most frightening and monstrous ever carried out by this nation. They tortured the offender for each murder, one day at a time, and gradually mutilated him completely with the choicest tortures. They cut the limbs off his body and, finally, on the third day of torture they allowed him slowly to fry to death at the stake. (Staehelin, *Die Mission,* 3: pt. 2, 270–72)

Another missionary, who was present at these events, added that

> We had hope that this poor soul could be spared and asked Brother Johannes [Alábi], who served as captain at this trial, whether he would not be able to speak to this poor slave of Satan about the love and the compassionate heart of God, and to proclaim Salvation to the whole world through the Savior's Passion and Death, and to assure him that his own redemption was still just as possible as that of the Savior. Johannes did this on the night before the execution. However, the criminal gave him no response and the conversation did not hinder him from screaming out to his god as he was dying. (Staehelin, *Die Mission*, 3: pt. 1, 337–38)

27. Like Dening, I some time ago learned "to distinguish between the set descriptions of the Other and the descriptions of being with the Other." And, like him, I believe "that we have a better chance of writing history out of the latter than the former" (Dening, *The Bounty*, 95). Nevertheless, in the case of some travel writers (including the author of this passage about Saramaka executions)—and, one fears, even some anthropologists—the difference becomes a particularly fine one, in that they sometimes take a single specific case of observation and cast it in a general, normative mode to lend a greater authority to their account.

28. Staehelin, *Die Mission*, 3: pt. 2, 268–69.

29. See Price, *First-Time*, 12–14.

30. It seems worth emphasizing that the Dutch documents, by insistently characterizing newcomers as *slaves*, foster the illusion that this status is somehow inherent to these people's character, that they are a radically different kind of person (if it is admitted that they are "persons" at all). That Saramakas may have considered newcomers simply as people newly arrived from plantations is not allowed for in colonists' discourse, making it very difficult to sort out what the relationships between newcomers and Saramakas must really have been like. It does, however, seem clear that the status of individual newcomers varied considerably in post-treaty Saramaka. As a rule, women were taken as wives and directly assimilated, and likewise with any man who already had ties of kinship or friendship, no matter how distant, with a Saramaka and could easily be included in his village. It was among all the others that precise status was open to negotiation: powerful Saramaka men often hosted a newcomer or two in a decidedly patron-client relationship, with the latter knowing that his continued welcome, indeed his very life, depended on his carrying out his end of the relationship satisfactorily. One frightened newcomer generally tried to stay with at least some others, as a kind of security; there was some safety (e.g., against hasty witchcraft accusations) in numbers. (When a whole group of newcomers was taken in by a Saramaka village or clan and given its own land, their generalized patron-client relationship has often continued, via their descendants, into the present.) But for individual newcomers, their negotiated status in regard to a particular patron could vary from that of a quasi-domestic servant or retainer to that of a close friend, from that of a prospective brother-in-law to that of a potential witch.

31. Elsewhere, I described this material dependence, this inability of maroon societies to disengage themselves fully from their enemy, as "the Achilles' heel of maroon societies throughout the Americas; [they remained] ... unavoidably dependent on the very plantation societies from which they were trying so desperately to isolate themselves" (Price, *Maroon Societies*, 12).

32. De Salontha, *Précis de deux lettres* (Nimmegue, 1778), 5–6.

33. Archives of the Societeit van Suriname 155, 15/xi/1763 (The Hague: Algemeen Rijksarchief). There is evidence that during the 1770s, even the governor of the colony admitted *in private* that the whites were cheating on the Saramaka Maroons every chance they got. In 1776 Stedman (who received his information on such matters from his good friend Governor Nepveu) allowed as he "must Acknowledge that they [the Maroons] are unfairly Dealt with, the Society of Surinam not Sending the Yearly Presents . . . without Which Perhaps they would be more true and faithful Allies than they have been" (Stedman, *Narrative*, 510). And Stedman's diary entry for 26 July 1776 is still more explicit.

The white peaple are the occation of it [the Maroons or Free Negroes being "exceedingly dangerous"]—for making an inglorious peace with them and now wanting to break their word in not Standing to their promises and feading them with trifling preasents, and [demanding] a most unmanly Submission for those black gentlemen, where ever they appear[.] The [Free] negros are no fools and in return presume impertenence trying daily to keep the whites more and more in awe of their long beards and Silver headed [captains'] Staves, whom they wil (at least at this rate) I am afraid try in futurity to extirpate all together . . . Nb. their number is incredible and all are armd. (Manuscript papers including Suriname diaries, Minneapolis, James Ford Bell Library, University of Minnesota)

In their own language, Saramakas called these goods *fri*, their word also for "peace," "freedom," and "peace treaty." Saramakas clearly saw them as a right, an earnest of the new relationship that the whites desired with them; for them the goods were tribute. Yet, for the Saramakas, these goods were also far from being mere symbols, and, *pace* Stedman, they were certainly not "trifling preasents"; indeed, they were sorely needed supplies for a people whose access to Western manufactured goods was otherwise limited.

34. Tzvetan Todorov, *La conquête de l'Amérique* (Paris, 1982).

35. Richard Price, *To Slay the Hydra: Dutch Colonial Perspectives on the Saramaka Wars* (Ann Arbor, Mich., 1983), 1–2.

36. Taussig, *Shamanism*, 109.

37. Archives of the Hof van Politie en Crimineele Justitie 90, 5/viii/1774 [30/v/1774] (The Hague: Algemeen Rijksarchief).

38. Étja's brother, Captain Kwakú Kwádjaní, compelled Daunitz to include a P.S. in one of his 1774 letters to the Court of Paramaribo: "Captain Kwaku [Kwádjaní] wishes to inform Your Excellencies that one of Etja's two slaves is married to Etja's sister, and that this slave cannot, therefore, be turned in to the whites." Daunitz, however, added a word of his own: "Might I suggest that as a reply Your Excellencies remind him that Your Excellencies did not order Etja to give his sister to a slave?" (Archives of the Hof van Politie en Crimineele Justitie 90, n.d. [May? 1774], The Hague: Algemeen Rijksarchief).

39. Documentation and citations for this period may be found in Price, *Alabi's World*, 1990, 145–66.

40. J. W. S. van Eyck, "Algemeen verslag van den tegenwoordige staat en huisselijke inrigtingen, benevens de levenswijsen der bevredigde boschnegers binnen deze kolonie" (manuscript, Amsterdam: Koninklijk Insituut voor de Tropen, 1828),

28. The Moravians—for once—understood what was happening rather more clearly, commenting that the Saramakas "only return those [slaves] who are useless to them, and they keep the best ones for themselves" (Staehelin, *Die Mission*, 3: pt. 1: 117, 99).

41. Saramaka folk tales are told as a part of funeral rites. Dynamic and filled with performative nuance, they are—in their natural settings—supremely interactive, with the teller engaging the listeners in an ongoing give-and-take as the tale unfolds. *Two Evenings in Saramaka* by Richard Price and Sally Price (Chicago, 1991), presents English translations of two full evenings of Saramaka taletelling, recorded during wakes in 1968. The tale presented here was told by a man in his late twenties to an enthusiastic group of relatives, friends, and neighbors of the deceased. As presented here, it is a truncated one-person narrative, abstracted from the fuller communal version presented in *Two Evenings*, 126–38.

42. John Wideman makes much the same point with regard to language.

In simple terms, the "inside" of black speech is just as important as its outside . . . At one end of the continuum measuring this distance between black speech and standard English is bilingual fluency; at the other, silence. Play is the esthetic, functional manipulation of standard English to mock, to create irony or satire or double-entendre, to signify meanings accessible only to a special segment of the audience. Play creates a distinctly Afro-American version of English; the speaker acknowledges to himself and announces to his audience that he's not taking the language of the slavemaster altogether seriously. But the play is serious business. (John Wideman, "The Black Writer and the Magic of the Word," *New York Times Book Review,* 24 January 1988, 28)

We are dealing, then, with a widespread Afro-American phenomenon.

43. See Richard Price and Sally Price, *Les Marrons* (Châteauneuf-le-Rouge, 2003).

Introduction to Part II

1. Gloria Anzuldúa, *Borderlands/La Frontera: The New Mestiza* (San Francisco, 1987), Preface.

2. Albert L. Hurtado, *Intimate Frontiers: Sex, Gender, and Culture in Old California* (Albuquerque, 1999).

3. Ann Laura Stoler, "Tense and Tender Ties: The Politics of Comparison in North American History and (Post)Colonial Studies," *JAH* 88 (2001), 831.

4. Ibid., 832.

Chapter 3. The Authority of Gender

1. Maestro Francisco de la Vega's testimony reads: "esta dicha mujer legitima llego mas de dies o doce veces a este testigo siendo cura a quejarse como el dicho su marido unas veces entraba tan colerico contra ella que le puso muchas veces las manos por haber dado quejas a los vecinos que le quitaba todo lo que tenia para dar

lo a la dicha María de Castillo y entendiendo la dicha mujer del dicho Antonio Carrillo hallaba alguna ampara en el dicho cura theniente le respondio este testigo que
en todas occasiones que no era justicia para remediarlo y que asi le dijo este testigo
acudiese a las reales justicias que ellas eran quienes remediaban esas cosas" (Criminales, 4 November 1662, Archivo Nacional del Ecuador [hereafter ANE/Q], fol. 52).

2. Important studies of the gendered impact of the church's control over
marriage in colonial Spanish America include Silvia Arrom, *The Women of Mexico
City, 1790–1857* (Stanford, Calif., 1985); Richard Boyer, *Lives of the Bigamists: Mar-
riage, Family, and Community in Colonial Mexico* (Albuquerque, 1995); Asunción
Lavrin, ed., *Sexuality and Marriage in Colonial Latin America* (Lincoln, Nebr., 1989);
Natalia León Galarza, *La primera alianza. El matrimonio criollo: honor y violencia
conyugal. Cuenca 1750–1800* (Quito, 1997); Patricia Seed, *To Love, Honor, and Obey in
Colonial Mexico: Conflicts over Marriage Choice, 1574–1821* (Stanford, Calif., 1988).

3. Partidas, P.4.2:1. The Siete Partidas, as seen in Francisco López Estrada and
María Teresa López García-Berdoy, eds., *Las siete partidas: Antología* (Madrid, 1992).
"P" after "Partidas" refers to the specific partida, not to a page number.

4. Divorce could be granted if one of the spouses committed adultery, was
cruel, or physically mistreated or threatened to kill the other; if one of the spouses
attempted to convince the other to commit crimes; if one committed "spiritual fornication" by engaging in heretical or pagan acts; if one contracted an incurable and
contagious disease or suffered from insanity; or if one of the parties was infertile.
Another reason was the entrance into a religious order of one of the spouses after
having obtained the license of the other spouse. An annulment was granted only on
the basis of an impediment that was unknown at the time of marriage, such as a
prior marriage of one of the parties or if the two individuals were prohibited from
marrying because of a spiritual or blood relationship. Annulment could also be
granted if one of the parties had taken a vow of chastity before the marriage, if the
marriage had never been consummated, or if the proper procedures for the marriage had not been followed, for instance if one of the partners had entered the marriage under force. See Partidas, P.4.10; Arrom, *Women of Mexico City*, 208–9; Boyer,
Lives of the Bigamists, 63–65; León, *La primera alianza*, 59–60; Asunción Lavrin, "Sexuality in Colonial Mexico: A Church Dilemma," in Lavrin, *Sexuality and Marriage in
Colonial Latin America*, 55–56; Seed, *To Love, Honor, and Obey*, 32–40.

5. Partidas, P.7.17:1. The legislation reads: "porque del adulterio que hiciese ella
puede venir al marido muy gran daño, pues si se empreñase de aquel con quien hizo
el adulterio, vendría el hijo extraño heredero en uno con sus hijos, lo que no occu-
ria a la mujer del adulterio que el marido hiciese con otra." Arrom also notes the
importance of inheritance in the determination that a wife's adultery was more detrimental than her husband's (*Women of Mexico City*, 71). On the general perception
that male adultery was a lesser crime, see Arrom, *Women of Mexico City*, 240–47;
Lavrin, "Sexuality in Colonial Mexico," 68; Boyer, *Lives of the Bigamists*, 140–45.

6. On sanctions against a husband's use of violence against his wife, see
Arrom, *Women of Mexico City*, 72. On the impact of domestic abuse on wives, see
Lavrin, "Sexuality in Colonial Mexico," 78; Boyer, *Lives of the Bigamists*, esp. 128–40.

7. León, *La primera alianza*, 96–97.

8. Arrom, *Women of Mexico City*, 228–29.

9. Matrimoniales, 11 September 1724, ANE/Q.

10. For an explanation of the difficulties of prosecuting rape in this period, see Lavrin, "Sexuality in Colonial Mexico," 71–72.

11. Matrimoniales, 11 September 1724, ANE/Q, fol. 10.

12. Arrom notes that nonelite women were more likely to forgo official procedures for an ecclesiastical separation and opt to informally separate themselves from their spouses; See *Women of Mexico City*, 245. Certainly, Boyer's work on bigamy shows that de facto separations were quite common in colonial Mexico; See esp. 109–64. Nancy van Deusan's study of divorce cases in Lima between 1650 and 1700 indicates that the number of marital litigation suits increased during this period. Although women made up 95 percent of the litigants, the majority dropped their suits, perhaps because of the difficulties mentioned. See van Deusan, "Determining the Boundaries of Virtue: The Discourse of Recogimiento Among Women in Seventeenth-Century Lima," *Journal of Family History* 22 (1997), 373–89.

13. Boyer, *Lives of the Bigamists*, 109.

14. To underscore the historical novelty of women's juridical capacity in colonial Spanish America, women living in modern Ecuador only regained the right to sue their husbands for any reason, including domestic violence, on 12 November 1995. Unidad de Modernización Judicial de la Comisión Andina de Juristas; http://www.cajpe.org.pe/RIJ/BASES/mujer/1htm (6/13/01).

15. Steve Stern, *The Secret History of Gender: Women, Men, and Power in Late Colonial Mexico* (Chapel Hill, N. C., 1995), 311. For other examples of this methodological tendency see Arrom, *Women of Mexico City*, 76–77; Boyer, *Lives of the Bigamists*, 230. Many influential scholars of women in colonial Spanish America frame women's lives within a patriarchal paradigm. Within this model, women in colonial Spanish America are depicted as perpetual minors under the tutelage of fathers and then husbands. For scholars who ascribe to the patriarchal paradigm, men represented women in the public sphere and, within the family, controlled women's sexuality, reproductive roles, and labor power. My study, however, asserts that Spanish culture traditionally undermined the establishment of centralized positions of authority through which a patriarchal system might operate. By contesting the relevance of the patriarchal paradigm for understanding colonial Spanish America, I am not arguing that women were more liberated than they are today. Rather, evidence supports the conclusion that to the extent that women as individuals faced subordination in colonial society, it cannot be attributed to the Spanish legal system or to essentialized notions of gender within Spanish society. Both Boyer and Stern rely on a patriarchal model in their analyses. Boyer concludes that women were subjugated absolutely to fathers and husbands; Stern, while showing a more nuanced vision of women's status, still includes women's use of the criminal justice system as part of a strategy he identifies as "the multiplication of patriarchs." Representative research on the Andean region includes Irene Silverblatt, *Moon, Sun, and Witches: Gender Ideologies and Class in Inca and Colonial Peru* (Princeton, N.J., 1987) and Luis Martin, *Daughters of the Conquistadores* (Albuquerque, 1983). General social historians of early Spanish America have long seen women's relative independence and assertiveness; for them patriarchy is hardly a factor. See, for example, James Lockhart, *Spanish Peru, 1532–1560: A Social History*, 2nd ed. (Madison, Wis., 1994), 169–92.

16. See Clarence Haring, *The Spanish Empire in America* (New York, 1975 [1947]). See also John Phelan, "Authority and Flexibility in the Spanish Imperial Bureaucracy," *Administrative Science Quarterly* 5 (1960); and *The Kingdom of Quito in the Seventeenth Century: Bureaucratic Politics in the Spanish Empire* (Madison, Wis., 1967). For a fuller discussion reinterpreting colonial Spanish gender norms through a framework of decentralization see Kimberly Gauderman, *Women's Lives in Colonial Quito: Gender, Law, and Economy in Spanish America* (Austin, Tex., 2003), esp. 12–29.

17. Jack Goody, *The Development of the Family and Marriage in Europe* (Cambridge, Eng., 1983), 45. According to Goody, although marriage had been considered a sacrament since the beginning of the thirteenth century, it was not so declared until the sixteenth century in the Council of Trent, when the church claimed exclusive rights to determine marriage validity (Trent, Canon 1). The thirteenth-century Partidas recognized what was essentially self-marriage; relationships in which individuals exchanged marriage vows and physically consummated their union were considered valid marriages (Partidas, P.4.1:204).

18. Ricardo Descalzi del Castillo, *La Real Audiencia de Quito Claustro en los Andes, Siglo XVI* (Barcelona, 1978), 176–77.

19. Ibid., 204.

20. Ibid., 222.

21. Fundo Especial, vol. 1, 1625, ANE/Q, fol. 63; vol. 6, 1646, ANE/Q, fol. 10; vol. 8, 1672, ANE/Q, fol. 131.

22. Criminales, 18 September 1685, ANE/Q.

23. Criminales, 2 January 1680, fol. 1.

24. Criminales, 2 January 1680, fol. 2.

25. Criminales, 5 March 1695, fol. 96.

26. Criminales, 2 January 1680, fol. 3.

27. Criminales, 28 June 1636.

28. Criminales, 30 June 1636. The file is misdated; the actual date of the suit is 27 June 1636. For another example of a married woman bringing criminal charges in her own name against a third party see Criminales, 22 March 1691. Doña Francisca Arias de la Vega, legitimate wife of Diego Rodríguez Zambrana, sued Francisco de Paredes and his mulatto servant, Pedro, for assault and robbery. Both men were jailed and their property seized.

29. Criminales, 28 June 1636, fols. 1–2, 11.

30. Criminales, 2 January 1680, fol. 2.

31. Criminales, 14 January 1697.

32. Criminales, 30 March 1662.

33. Criminales, 30 March 1662, fols. 1–7.

34. Criminales, 30 March 1662, fols. 9–14.

35. Criminales, 30 March 1662, fols. 17–24.

36. Criminales, 30 March 1662, fol. 31.

37. Criminales, 30 March 1662, fol. 43.

38. Francisco Tomás y Valiente, *El derecho penal de la monarquia absoluta (siglos XVI–XVII–XVIII)* (Madrid, 1969), 397–405.

39. Criminales, 21 August 1692.

40. Criminales, 21 August 1692, fols. 21–22.
41. Criminales, 27 September 1661.
42. Criminales, 27 September 1661, fol. 2.
43. Criminales, 27 September 1661, fol. 1.

Chapter 4. Private and State Violence Against Slaves in Lower Louisiana

1. French Louisiana was a huge territory that extended from the Great Lakes to the Gulf of Mexico and from the Appalachians to the Rocky Mountains. In Illinois Country, the French established six villages on the Mississippi between the Missouri and Ohio Rivers. However, here I examine only the Lower Louisiana region, which extended between the Arkansas River and the Gulf of Mexico, and focus on the area that included New Orleans.

2. M. Allain, "Slave Policies in French Louisiana," *Louisiana History* 21 (1980), 127–38; G. Aubert, "'*Français, Nègres et Sauvages*': Constructing Race in Colonial Louisiana" (Ph.D. diss., Tulane University, 2002); C. A. Brasseaux, "The Administration of Slave Regulations in French Louisiana, 1724–1766," *Louisiana History* 21 (1980), 139–58; G. M. Hall, *Africans in Colonial Louisiana: The Development of Afro-Creole Culture in the Eighteenth Century* (Baton Rouge, La., 1992); T. N. Ingersoll, *Mammon and Manon in Early New Orleans: The First Slave Society in the Deep South, 1718–1819* (Knoxville, 1999); J. T. MacGowan, "Creation of a Slave Society: Louisiana Plantations in the Eighteenth Century" (Ph.D. diss., University of Rochester, 1976); J. M. Spear, "Whiteness and the Purity of Blood: Race, Sexuality, and Social Order in Colonial Louisiana" (Ph.D. diss., University of Minnesota, 1999); and D. H. Usner, *Indians, Settlers, and Slaves in a Frontier Exchange Economy: The Lower Mississippi Valley Before 1783* (Chapel Hill, N.C., 1992).

3. Hall, *Africans in Colonial Louisiana*, 2–10, 29–95, 156–61, 175–77, 182; T. N. Ingersoll, "The Slave Trade and the Ethnic Diversity of Louisiana's Slave Community," *Louisiana History* 37 (1996), 133–61; Ingersoll, *Mammon and Manon*, 17–18, 67–74, 124; D. H. Usner, "From African Captivity to American Slavery: The Introduction of Black Laborers to Colonial Louisiana," *Louisiana History* 20 (1979), 25–48.

4. Hall, *Africans in Colonial Louisiana*, 2–27; Ingersoll, *Mammon and Manon*, 35–65; J. Zitomersky, "Race, esclavage et émancipation: La Louisiane créole à l'intersection des mondes français, antillais et américain," in M. C. Rochman, dir., *Esclavage et abolitions: Mémoires et systèmes de représentation* (Paris, 2000), 283–308.

5. C. Vidal, "Les implantations françaises au pays des Illinois au XVIIIe siècle (1699–1765)" (Thèse de doctorat, Paris, Ecole des Hautes Etudes en Sciences Sociales, 1995).

6. B. Garnot, "La violence et ses limites dans la France du XVIIe siècle: L'exemple bourguignon," in *Crime et justice aux XVIIe et XVIIIe siècles* (Paris, 2000), 93–110; B. Garnot, *Justice et société en France aux XVIe, XVIIe, et XVIIIe siècles* (Paris, 2000), 250; R. Muchembled, *La violence au village: Sociabilité et comportements populaires en Artois du XVe au XVIIe siècle* (Turnhout, 1989), 419; J. Quéniart, *Le grand Chapelle-tout: Violence, normes, et comportements en Bretagne rurale au 18e siècle* (Rennes, 1993), 181.

7. Criminality and the repression of crimes have already been studied in Louisiana for the Spanish period, but the analysis is mainly quantitative. See D. N. Kerr, *Petty Felony, Slave Defiance, and Frontier Villainy: Crime and Criminal Justice in Spanish Louisiana, 1770–1803* (New York, 1993).

8. I. Berlin, *Many Thousands Gone: The First Two Centuries of Slavery in North America* (London, 1998), 98.

9. H. P. Dart, "Courts and Law in Colonial Louisiana," *Louisiana History Quarterly* 4 (1921), 255–89; M. Giraud, *Histoire de la Louisiane française* (Paris, 1953–74), 1: 279–80; 2: 85–87 and 94–96; 3: 291–93; 4: 342–48; J. D. Hardy, Jr., "The Superior Council in Colonial Louisiana," in J. F. McDermott, ed., *Frenchmen and French Ways in the Mississippi Valley* (Urbana, Ill., 1969), 87–100; J. A. Micell, "From Law Court to Local Government: Metamorphosis of the Superior Council of French Louisiana," *Louisiana History* 9 (1968), 85–107.

10. The governor and the *commissaire-ordonnateur* were the two most important officials in the colony. The governor was a military officer, the representative of the king in the province, and in charge of defense and Amerindian policy. The *commissaire-ordonnateur* was responsible for finances and trade. Both were responsible for the *police*, or the general administration of the colony. Their respective attributions were not clearly defined, hence some ongoing conflicts.

11. The Records of the Superior Council of Louisiana (hereafter RCSL), kept in the Louisiana State Museum in New Orleans, are referenced as they are in the last microfilmed version. The figures correspond to the date (year/month/day) and the number of the document. The numbers, however, are not always accurate; hence, they do not always correspond to the order of the procedure. The spelling and punctuation have been modernized. For the 1720s, there are 14 cases; 40 for the 1730s; 44 for the 1740s; 13 for the 1750s; and 44 for the 1760s. There were no cases at all between 1754 and 1762, years that correspond to Kerlérec's government and the Seven Years War.

12. RCSL, 1728/07/10/01, 1729/09/05/03, 1729/09/05/05, 1729/11/16/01, 1736/09/18/01, 1737/01/10/01, 1738/04/11/02, 1741/01/16/01, 1741/01/16/02, 1741/01/16/03, 1742/01/09/04, 1743/09/10/02, 1745/05/30/01, 1748/05/18/03, 1751/06/21/01, 1752/02/17/02, 1764/01/01/01, 1764/01/25/01, 1764/04/12/01, 1764/05/18/01, 1764/07/06/01, 1764/07/06/02, 1764/07/08/01, 1764/07/31/02, 1764/08/02/01, 1764/08/10/01, 1764/09/04/02, 1765/02/16/01, 1765/10/29/02, 1767/02/21/01, 1767/06/10/02, 1767/07/04/01; Brasseaux, "Slave Regulations in Louisiana," 154; Hall, *Africans in Colonial Louisiana*, 142; Ingersoll, *Mammon and Manon*, 74. Because most runaways were men, judicial archives did not usually document violence against female slaves. However, one exceptional proceeding deals with a slave called Marguerite who ran away because her masters incessantly beat her. Her mistress also forced her to go back to work while she was still ill. See RCSL, 1764/10/23/01.

13. RCSL, 1744/03/03/01, 1744/03/05/01, 1744/03/12/01, 1744/03/14/01, 1744/03/14/02, 1744/03/21/01, 1744/03/21/03, 1744/03/21/05.

14. RCSL, 1726/10/14/02.

15. RCSL, 1741/01/23/01.

16. RCSL, 1743/06/18/01, 1743/07/06/01, 1743/07/06/02.

17. G. M. Hall argues that there was no racism in Louisiana by pointing to the

fact that the public executioner was a black man. According to her, the authorities would have never chosen a black executioner if whites would have felt humiliated by being executed by a black man. More likely, however, is that the officials had trouble finding a white executioner. See Hall, *Africans in Colonial Louisiana*, 131–32.

18. RCSL, 1730/04/06/01, 1730/04/29/01, 1730/09/05/02, 1730/09/05/05, 1730/09/07/01, 1730/09/18/01; Brasseaux, "Slave Regulations in Louisiana," 150–51; Hall, *Africans in Colonial Louisiana*, 150–52; Ingersoll, *Mammon and Manon*, 82; Usner, "The Introduction of Black Laborers," 38.

19. A. S. Le Page du Pratz, *Histoire de la Louisiane* (Paris, 1758); Brasseaux, "Slave Regulations in Louisiana", 140–41; Ingersoll, *Mammon and Manon*, 81–82.

20. RCSL, 1730/04/29/01, 1741/02/04/02, 1741/10/06/01; Ingersoll, *Mammon and Manon*, 98–99.

21. For another interpretation of society's standpoint on the extreme violence torturers imposed on slaves, one that has the masters accepting abuses as a way of dissuading their slaves from disobeying, see Hall, *Africans in Colonial Louisiana*, 154–55.

22. Archives des Colonies (hereafter AC), B, 43, fols. 388–407, March 1724, Versailles.

23. AC, B, 57, fols. 854–55, 14 October 1732, Fontainebleau, to Salmon.

24. AC, C13a, 33, fols. 150–62, 1749; C13a, 35, fols. 40–51, 1751; F3, 243, fols. 253–55, 3 March 1764.

25. Allain, "Slaves Policies in French Louisiana"; Brasseaux, "Slave Regulations in French Louisiana"; M. Giraud, *A History of French Louisiana* (Baton Rouge, La., 1991), 5: 322–26; T. N. Ingersoll, "Slave Codes and Judicial Practice in New Orleans, 1718–1807," *Law and History Review* 13 (1995), 23–62; Ingersoll, *Mammon and Manon*, 104–7, 134–42; G. Martin, *Histoire de l'esclavage dans les colonies françaises* (Paris, 1948), 27–28; K. Saadani, "Une colonie dans l'impasse: La Louisiane française, 1731–1743" (Thèse de Doctorat, Paris, Ecoles des Hautes Etudes en Sciences Sociales, 1993), 149–50 ; Usner, "The Introduction of Black Laborers," 25–48.

26. Allain, "Slave Policies in French Louisiana," 134.

27. RCSL, 1723/05/25/01, 1753/01/13/02.

28. Brasseaux, "Slave Regulations in Louisiana," 142; Usner, "The Introduction of Black Laborers," 42.

29. RCSL, 1737/11/06/05, 1737/11/20/02.

30. AC, C13a, 11, fols. 66–103, 30 March 1728, New Orleans, Périer and La Chaise to the Compagnie of the Indies; Giraud, *History of French Louisiana*, 5: 322–29; Hall, *Africans in Colonial Louisiana*, 98–99; Usner, "The Introduction of Black Laborers," 44–46.

31. RCSL, 1737/01/04/02, 1737/01/10/01, 1764/04/12/01, 1764/07/06/01, 1767/02/21/01, 1767/03/11/01, 1767/03/12/01, 1767/03/12/02, 1767/03/14/02, 1767/03/14/07; Ingersoll, "Slave Codes and Judicial Practice," 32.

32. Brasseaux, "Slave Regulations in Louisiana," 149; Ingersoll, "Slave Codes and Judicial Practice," 30–32; Ingersoll, *Mammon and Manon*, 136.

33. Brasseaux, "Slave Regulations in Louisiana," 149.

34. RCSL, 1738/12/12/01.

35. RCSL, 1736/08/04/01, 1736/09/18/01.

36. RCSL, 1731/10/13/01, 1735/10/31/01, 1737/02/12/01, 1739/04/10/01, 1742/03/13/01, 1745/03/15/02, 1745/06/11/01, 1764/06/11/04; Ingersoll, *Mammon and Manon*, 100.

37. RCSL, 1737/06/03/03, 1743/11/04/02, 1746/08/23/02; Ingersoll, *Mammon and Manon*, 99–100.

38. Ingersoll, *Mammon and Manon*, 142.

39. RCSL, 1752/06/28/01, 1764/02/21/01; Hall, *Africans in Colonial Louisiana*, 152–54.

40. RCSL, 1739/11/07/02, 1765/10/09/01.

41. Ingersoll, *Mammon and Manon*, 100–101.

42. Brasseaux, "Slave Regulations in Louisiana," 142; Hall, *Africans in Colonial Louisiana*, 144–45; Ingersoll, *Mammon and Manon*, 84–85.

43. RCSL, 1737/01/04/02, 1752/02/17/01, 1764/10/23/01.

44. RCSL, 1723/10/01/01, 1728/07/08/03, 1729/09/27/01, 1729/10/21/03, 1736/07/06/05, 1742/01/09/03, 1743/06/26/01, 1745/02/09/01, 1745/04/01/01, 1748/02/09/02, 1751/04/14/01, 1756/07/29/01, 1764/06/10/02.

45. Hall, *Africans in Colonial Louisiana*, 137–42.

46. RCSL, 1753/04/23/01, 1753/04/03/02, 1753/05/04/01, 1753/05/05/04, 1753/05/05/05.

47. RCSL, 1753/04/23/01, 1753/04/03/02, 1753/05/02/01.

48. RCSL, 1736/06/29/01, 1743/09/10/02, 1744/02/22/02, 1764/07/19/01, 1764/07/20/01, 1764/07/28/02.

49. RCSL, 1728/07/10/02, 1765/09/16/02.

50. RCSL, 1737/03/19/02, 1738/02/24/02, 1745/05/15/01, 1746/11/27/01, 1747/12/31/01.

51. Garnot, *Justice et société en France*, 15–16.

52. A. Farge, *Le vol d'aliments à Paris au XVIIIe siècle* (Paris, 1974); Garnot, *Justice et société en France*, 12–13, 15–16, 19, 44–45, 208, 212–13; A. Lebigre, *La justice du Roi, La vie judiciaire dans l'ancienne France* (Paris, 1988), 123–27; A. Zysberg, *Les galériens. Vies et destins de 60,000 forçats sur les galères de France, 1680–1748* (Paris, 1987).

53. RCSL, 1737/01/10/01, 1753/05/05/04, 1755/04/27/01, 1764/01/04/02, 1764/02/05/01, 1764/02/14/03, 1764/03/03/03, 1764/04/23/02, 1764/05/19/02, 1764/07/07/05, 1764/07/21/07, 1764/07/28/02, 1764/08/31/02, 1764/09/01/01, 1764/09/10/02, 1764/11/03/03, 1765/03/02/01, 1765/09/21/06, 1765/11/16/04, 1766/08/02/04, 1766/11/22/04, 1767/08/13/04.

54. Hall, *Africans in Colonial Louisiana*, 149–50; Ingersoll, *Mammon and Manon*, 138.

55. RCSL, 1764/07/21/08, 1764/09/10/02, 1765/09/21/06, 1767/03/14/07; Ingersoll, *Mammon and Manon*, 90–91.

56. Garnot, *Justice et société en France*, 101, 109; A. Langui and A. Lebigre, *Histoire du droit pénal: La procédure criminelle* (Paris, 1980), 116–21; Lebigre, *La justice du Roi*, 204–10.

57. RCSL, 1744/03/21/05, 1764/02/04/01, 1764/04/07/03, 1764/04/07/04, 1764/07/24/03, 1764/09/10/01.

58. Garnot, *Justice et société en France*, 192–195; Langui and Lebigre, *Histoire du droit pénal*, 127–30; Lebigre, *La justice du Roi*, 230–42.

59. Brasseaux, "Slave Regulations in Louisiana," 147, 156–58.

60. RCSL, 1764/07/24/01, 1765/10/10/02.

61. P. Kolchin, *American Slavery 1619–1877* (New York, 1999), 58.

62. M. Foucault, *Surveiller et punir: Naissance de la prison* (Paris, 1975); Lebigre, *La justice du Roi*, 133–37; R. Muchembled, *Le temps des supplices. De l'obéissance sous les rois absolus, XVe–XVIIIe siècle* (Paris, 1992).

63. Allain, "Slave Policies in French Louisiana," 133; Brasseaux, "Slave Regulation in Louisiana," 155–56; Ingersoll, "Slave Codes and Judicial Practice," 40–41; Ingersoll, *Mammon and Manon*, 104–7.

64. Brasseaux, "Slave Regulations in Louisiana," 156–58; Ingersoll, *Mammon and Manon*, 89–91.

65. Ingersoll, "Slave Codes and Judicial Practice," 41–62; Ingersoll, *Mammon and Manon*, 145–239.

66. Berlin, *Many Thousands Gone*, 98–99.

67. Garnot, *Justice et société en France*, 179–217.

68. Allain, "Slave Policies in French Louisiana," 127–28.

69. The council was presided over by the *commissaire-ordonnateur*, who was a slaveholder and an official in the king's service. The *commissaire-ordonnateur* planned to pursue his career outside the colony after fulfilling his duties, but he could profit only by defending the monarch's interests. It was the same for the governor. The competition between both men for royal favor also profited the state interests. Furthermore, both men maintained relations with the colony's elite, to whom belonged the other councilors who were interested in getting their favor.

70. J. A. Carrigan, "Old and New Interpretations of the Rebellion of 1768," *Proceedings of the Ninth Annual Genealogical Institute* (Baton Rouge, La., 1966), 40–50.

71. Brasseaux, "The Administration of Slave Regulations," 157–58.

72. Garnot, *Justice et société en France*, 11–12.

Chapter 5. Violence or Sex?

1. http://www.ci.mesa.az.us/police/rape.htm (accessed 10 August 2001); http://www.promotetruth.org/faq/default.htm (accessed 7 January 2004); http://www.abs.uci.edu/depts/police/safetytips/sexualassault.html (accessed 10 August 2001). See also http://www.crimeawareness.com/sexual.htm (accessed 7 January 2004); http://www.gnesa.org/sexual_assault/facts.html (accessed 7 January 2004); http://people.bu.edu/buwc/rcc.html (accessed 7 January 2004).

2. Susan Brownmiller, *Against Our Will: Men, Women, and Rape* (New York, 1975); Catherine A. McKinnon, *Toward a Feminist Theory of the State* (Cambridge, Mass., 1989), esp. ch. 7. On the twentieth-century legal shift toward rape as violence, see Leigh Bienen, "Rape III: National Developments in Rape Reform Legislation," *Women's Rights Law Reporter* 6 (1980), 171–213; Leigh Bienen, "Rape IV," *Women's Rights Law Reporter*, Supp. 6 (1980), 1–61. For just some of the voluminous feminist work on rape, see Patricia Searles and Ronald J. Berger, eds., *Rape and Society: Readings on the Problem of Sexual Assault* (Boulder, Colo., 1995); Emilie Buchwald, Pamela R. Fletcher, and Martha Roth, eds., *Transforming a Rape Culture* (Minneapolis, 1993).

Despite a quarter century of feminist activism, the image of rape as a purely sexual crime still remains. In January 2004, a Florida Circuit Court Judge Gene Stephenson commented in open court about a rape victim, "Why would he want to rape her? She doesn't look like a day at the beach" (http://www.local6.com/news/2802787/detail.html [accessed 30 January 2004]). After a public outcry, Stephenson apologized to the victim, who reportedly intended to ask for his immediate dismissal from his judicial post.

3. For examples of variant classifications, see Douglas Greenberg, *Crime and Law Enforcement in the Colony of New York 1691–1776* (Ithaca, N.Y., 1976), 110–11 (discussion of rape with other violent crimes), 50, 54, 58, 74 (charts listing violent crimes that presumably include rape); Michael Hindus, *Prison and Plantation: Crime, Justice, and Authority in Massachusetts and South Carolina, 1767–1878* (Chapel Hill, N.C., 1980), 152–53 (rape as sexual crime); J. M. Beattie, *Crime and the Courts in England, 1660–1800* (Princeton, N.J., 1986), 127–29, 654 (rape as offense against person), 655 (sexual offenses against children). For similar confusion in an analysis outside of court records, see Kenneth D. Nordin, "The Entertaining Press: Sensationalism in Eighteenth-Century Boston Newspapers," *Communication Research* 6 (1979), 295–320 (unclear if discussion of "violent crimes" includes rape).

4. Stephen J. Schulhofer, "Taking Sexual Autonomy Seriously: Rape Law and Beyond," *Law and Philosophy: Philosophical Issues in Rape Law* 11 (1992), 35.

5. I have examined all rape-related statutes, and all available superior court records (where rape was usually prosecuted) from all the colonies and many of the states, as well as multiple collections of lower court records, records of slave trials, and judges' and lawyers' papers. Nonlegal documents include newspapers, almanacs, journals, letters, travel narratives, and novels gathered from more than twenty-five archives and historical societies and from Evans Early American Imprints. A full discussion of the sources from which this study was drawn will appear in my forthcoming book, tentatively titled *Rape and Sexual Power in Early America* (Chapel Hill, N.C., 2006).

6. Samuel Johnson, *A Dictionary of the English Language* (London, 1755; reprint, New York, 1967); Thomas Sheridan, *Dictionary of the English Language* 5th ed. (Philadelphia, 1789).

7. For examples of this common formulation, see William Hawkins, *A Treatise of the Pleas of the Crown* (London, 1724–26, reprint, 1972), 108; James Parker, *Conductor Generalis; or, The Office, Duty, and Authority of Justices of the Peace . . .* (Woodbridge, N.J., 1764), 360; William Simpson, *The Practical Justice of the Peace . . . of South Carolina.* (Charlestown, S.C., 1761; reprint, 1972), 207.

8. William Blackstone, *Commentaries on the Laws of England* (Philadelphia, 1803), 4: ch 14, 15.

9. Sir Robert Chambers, *A Course of Lectures on the English Law Delivered at the University of Oxford 1767–777*, ed. Thomas M. Curley (Madison, Wis., 1986), 1: 404.

10. [Henry Dagge], *Considerations on Criminal Law* (London, 1772), 377.

11. James Logan, *The Charge Delivered from the Bench to the Grand-Jury at the Court of Quarter Sessions Held for the County of Philadelphia, the 2d Day of September, 1723* (Philadelphia, 1723), 13–15.

12. William Brigham, comp., *Compact with the Charter and Laws of New Plymouth* (Boston, 1836), 43.

13. John D. Cushing, ed., *Acts and Laws of New Hampshire 1680–1726* (Wilmington, Del., 1978), 121.

14. Harry Toulimin and James Blair, *A Review of the Criminal Law of the Commonwealth of Kentucky* (Frankfort, Ky., 1806) 1: 136; also 3: 137. See also Lewis Kerr, *Exposition of the Criminal Laws of the Territory of Orleans* (New Orleans, 1806), 42.

15. Sir Matthew Hale, *The History of the Pleas of the Crown* (London, 1736), 1: 629.

16. Cotton Mather, *Pillars of Salt* (Boston, 1699), 69–71.

17. Aaron Hutchinson, *Iniquity purged by mercy and truth; A sermon preached at Grafton, October 23d, 1768* (Boston, 1769), 19, 26.

18. James Diman, *A Sermon, Preached at Salem, January 16, 1777* (Salem, Mass., 1772), 21.

19. Timothy Langdon, *A sermon, preached at Danbury, November 8th, A.D. 1798* (Danbury, Conn., 1798), 11.

20. *On Brian Sheehen, a criminal this day executed in Salem . . .* ([Salem?], 1772). American Antiquarian Society (hereafter AAS), Worcester, Mass.

21. "Notes of Evidence for Respublica v. James Paxton, for rape of Jane Mathers, May 27, 1783," Yeates Legal Papers, April–May 1783, Folder 7, Historical Society of Pennsylvania (hereafter HSP), Philadelphia; "Notes of Evidence in Respublica v. Abraham Moses for a rape on Christiania Waggoner, 21 May 1783," Yeates Legal Papers April–May 1783, Folder 7, HSP.

22. For a somewhat similar-sounding public condemnation of a man for adultery, see John Tabor Kempe Papers, Lawsuits, g–l, —ALS to either William or to John Tabor Kempe, March 10, 1758. New-York Historical Society (hereafter NYHS), New York, N. Y. Thanks to Tom Humphrey for this cite.

23. Memorial of Ephraim Andrews, 1743, *Connecticut Archives: Crimes and Misdemeanors*, 1st ser., 4: 71–73. See also "King v. Jannean for rape," Manuscript Minutes, NYCQS, 1738, 348–50, New York Hall of Records (hereafter NYHR), New York, N.Y.

24. *The life and adventures of Joseph Mountain, a Negro highwayman* (Bennington, Vt., 1791), 13.

25. *Trial of Amos Adams, for a Rape, committed on the Body of Lelea Thorp . . .* (New Haven, Conn., 1817), 8, 22, 23, AAS. For a sermon on the same rapist that emphasized sinfulness, see William Andrews, *A sermon delivered at Danbury, Nov 13, 1817, being the day appointed for the execution of Amos Adams for the crime of rape* (New Haven, Conn., 1817), 16, NYHS. See also Charges to Grand Juries, Robert Treat Paine Papers. reel 17 (near the end), Massachusetts Historical Society (hereafter MHS), Boston, Mass. For rape by Native Americans being described in similar terms, see "Letter of Alexander Steele, Sept. 12, 1792," East Florida Papers, bundle 122E10, no. 323, reel 47, pt. 2, Manuscript Division, Library of Congress, Washington, D.C.

26. Hale, *Historia Pacitorum Coronae* (London, 1736; reprint, 1971) 1: 628. For the holding that emissions and penetration were both necessary, see Hawkins, *Pleas of the Crown*, 108. For American justice of the peace manuals that specify penetration and emission, see Richard Starke, *The Office and Authority of a Justice of Peace* (Williamsburg, Va., 1774), 292; *A New Conductor Generalis* (Albany, N.Y., 1819), 394. For explicit rejections of the necessity of emission, see C. J. Tilghman, "Definition of Crimes in 1806 or After," Pennsylvania Court Papers, Tyson-Yard and Miscellaneous Papers, box 6, p. 8, HSP; *Laws of the Indiana Territory* (Vincennes, Indiana, 1807), 35.

27. D. v. Daniel Patterson, Chester County, PA Quarter Sessions File Papers, Mar 1734. Chester County Archives (hereafter CCA), West Chester, Pa.

28. The King v. Lawrence et al., Aug 1, 1754, Superior Court Pleadings, K-501, reel 48; K–650, reel 49, NYHR.

29. *Pennsylvania Gazette*, 3 Sept 1777; Chester County, PA Quarter Sessions Docket, Aug. 1777, CCA; Chester County, PA Quarter Sessions File Papers, Aug 1777, CCA.

30. Rockingham, NH Superior Court Cases no. 13253, New Hampshire Archives, Concord.

31. D. v. George Clinton, Sept 1728, New Haven County Court Files: 1720–1729 R–Y, 6; New Haven County Court, bk. 3: 270. Nina Dayton suggests a similar outcome in Rex v. Deborah Corbey, Nov 1727, New Haven County Court Files, November 1727. Dr. 6. Connecticut State Library (hereafter CSL), Hartford.

32. D. v. John West, Chester County Quarter Sessions Docket, Aug 1738, 161, 157, 153, 142, 147; and Aug 1738, separate page of QSD; Chester County Quarter Sessions File Papers, Aug 1738, CCA. See also D. v. James Benton Jr., New Haven County Court Book, Jan 1769, 7, 164; NHCC Files, drawer 45, CSL.

33. Respublica v. David Robb, 20 April 1787, Yeates Legal Papers, Mar–Apr 1789, fol. 2, HSP.

34. Rex v. Isaac Willow, 26 Feb 1742/3, Windham County, CT Court Files, Feb 1743–Feb 1744, box H-383, CSL.

35. Chester County, PA Quarter Sessions File Papers, 25 July 1737, CCA.

36. On courts' increased prosecution of outsiders as rapists, see Cornelia Hughes Dayton, *Women Before the Bar: Gender, Law, and Society in Connecticut, 1639–1789* (Chapel Hill, N.C., 1995), 249.

37. John D'Emilio and Estelle B. Freedman, *Intimate Matters: A History of Sexuality in America* (New York, 1988), 28.

38. See, for example, State of Ct v. David Gardner, 1 Jan 1793. Superior Court Files, New Haven County, 1793–1795, box 340, CSL.

39. For examples of continued discussion of forcible taking and marrying in American legal manuals, see John A. Dunlap, *The New-York Justice* (New York, 1815), 364; John Haywood, *The Duty and Office of Justices of Peace . . . of North Carolina* (Halifax, N.C., 1800), 268; "Act agst forcible and stolen Marriages, 1789," in William Waller Hening, *The Statutes at Large, Being a Collection of All the Laws of Virginia* (Richmond, Va., 1823), 13: 7. On the legal treatment of heiress stealing in early modern England, see John G. Bellamy, *Criminal Law and Society in Late Medieval and Tudor England* (New York, 1984), 159.

40. On the temerity of the ideology of husbands' sexual rights, see Hendrik Hartog, *Man and Wife in America* (Cambridge, Mass., 2000), esp. 306–8.

41. As jurist Daniel Dulaney summarized in a 1767 opinion, because slaves are "incapable of marriage," "a slave has never maintained an action against the violator of his bed" (*1 Harris and McHenry [MD]*, 563.

42. Middlesex General Sessions, 13 Mar 1705, vol. 2: p. 162, reel 0892252, Massachusetts Archives (hereafter MA), Boston.

43. D. v. James Benton Jr., Jan 1769, New Haven County Court Book 7, 164; New Haven County Court Files, drawer 45, CSL. Lascivious behavior charges may have been more common in early New England. For an early eighteenth-century case (1710) that did not involve incestuous relations, see *Province and Court Records of Maine*, ed. Neal W. Allen (Portland, Maine1958), 378–81.

44. Mary Gates Petition, Salisbury, 3 March1777, Windham County, CT Superior Court Records, Subject: Divorce 1752–1922, microfilm no. 418, CSL.

45. *Report of the Trial of Ephraim Wheeler for a Rape committed on the Body of Betsy Wheeler* (Stockbridge, Mass., 1805). For a full discussion of this case and of

Ephraim Wheeler's racial marginality, see Richard D. Brown and Irene Q. Brown, *The Hanging of Ephraim Wheeler: A Story of Rape, Incest, and Justice in Early America* (Cambridge, Mass., 2003).

46. *Liberty Hall and Cincinnati Mercury*, 29 October 1805.

47. Lewis Clarke, "Leaves from a Slave's Journal of Life" in John W. Blassingame, ed., *Slave Testimony: Two Centuries of Letters, Speeches, Interviews, and Autobiographies* (Baton Rouge, 1977), 156.

48. Theodore Dwight, "An Oration, Spoken Before the Connecticut Society, for the Promotion of Freedom and the Relief of Persons Unlawfully Holden in Bondage [1794]," in Charles S. Hyneman, and Donald S. Lutz, eds., *American Political Writing During the Founding Era, 1760–1805* (Indianapolis, 1983), 892.

49. On slave courts, see Peter C. Hoffer, *Criminal Proceedings in Colonial Virginia* (Athens, Ga., 1984), x, xlv–lii; Thomas D. Morris, *Southern Slavery and the Law, 1619–1860* (Chapel Hill, N. C., 1996), 228; Daniel J. Flanigan, "Criminal Procedure in Slave Trials in the Antebellum South," *Journal of Southern History* 40 (1974), 537–64.

50. Sexual assaults involving white defendants accounted for 442 charges; black defendants appeared in 273 cases.

51. This statistic is based on 442 criminally charged white defendants and 273 criminally charged black defendants.

52. "An Act for Regulating of Slaves, 1713/14," in John D. Cushing, ed., *The Earliest Printed Laws of New Jersey 1703–1722* (Wilmington, Del., 1978), 20–22.

53. "Supplementary Act to the Act Entitled an Act for the more Effectual Punishment of Negroes & other Slaves . . . 1737," Assembly Proceedings, 26 April–28 May 1737, *Maryland Archives*, 60: 92–93.

54. *The Earliest Printed Laws of Pennsylvania 1681–1713*, 69; *A Collection of All the Laws of the Province of Pennsylvania Now in Force* (Philadelphia, 1742), 83–84. See also "An Act for Regulating of Slaves, March 1713/1714," in Cushing, ed., *The Earliest Printed Laws of New Jersey 1703–1722*, 22; "An Act for Preventing, Suppressing and punishing the Conspiracy and Insurrection of Negroes and other Slaves [1712]," in *Acts of Assembly passed in the province of New-York from 1691–1725* (New York, 1726), 84.

55. *Laws of the government of New-Castle, Kent and Sussex upon Delaware. Published by order of the Assembly* (Philadelphia, 1742), 70 (statute is undated).

56. "An Act for the more effectual Punishment of *Negroes,* who shall attempt to commit a Rape on any white woman, 1743," in *Acts and Laws of the English Colony of Rhode-Island and Providence Plantations* (Newport, R.I., 1767), 195–96. Rhode Island was the only New England colony to pass such a law. Other New England colonies, with their minimal African American populations, may not have felt the need for such statutes.

57. "Act for the more effectual Punishment of Negroes and other Slaves [May 1751]," in Thomas Bacon, *Laws of Maryland at Large, with Proper Indexes* (Annapolis, [1765]), n.p., ch. 14; "An Act for amending the act entitled An Act directing the trial of slaves committing capital crimes [Oct. 1765]." See also William Waller Hening, *The Statutes at Large, Being a Collection of All the Laws of Virginia* (Richmond, Va., 1809), 7: 137–39.

58. "Slaves; for their Regulation, &c., Aug. 8, 1688," in Shelia Lambert, ed., *House of Commons Sessional Papers of the Eighteenth Century* (Wilmington, Del., 1975), 59, no. 329.

59. Cushing, *The Earliest Printed Laws of New Jersey*, 20.

60. *The Colonial Laws of New York from the year 1664 to the Revolution* (Albany, N.Y., n.d.), 2: 679–85.

61. Bacon, *Laws of Maryland at Large*, n.p.

62. Lucius Lamar, *A Compilation of the Laws of the State of Georgia, 1810–1819* (Augusta, Ga., 1821), 804. For a similar listing in an earlier Georgia law, see the 10 May 1770 act in Horatio Marbury and William H. Crawford, eds., *A Compilation of the Laws of the State of Georgia, 1755–1800* (Savannah, 1802), 429–31.

63. Louis B. Wright and Marion Tinling, eds., *The Secret Diary of William Byrd of Westover 1709–1712* (Richmond, Va., 1941), 91.

64. *Report of the Trial of Henry Bedlow for Committing a Rape on Lanah Sawyer* (New York, 1793).

65. *The Solemn address and dying advice of Ezra Hutchinson* (Stockbridge, Mass., [1813]), 9.

66. Examination of Catherine Parry, 25 July 1737, Chester County, PA Quarter Sessions File Papers, CCA.

67. The King v. Lawrence et al., Aug 1, 1754, Superior Court Pleadings, K–501, (reel 48); K–650, reel 49, NYHR.

68. "Indictment of Joseph Bedford, Sept 1784, in Notes of Evidence taken by Increase Sumner, 1782–1786, 2: 329–30, MHS.

69. D. v. George Clinton, Sept 1728, New Haven, CT County Court Files: 1720–1729 R–Y, no. 6, CSL.

70. *Virginia Gazette*, 13 July 1769.

71. "Notes of Evidence in Respublica v. Abraham Moses for a rape on Christiania Waggoner, 21 May 1783," Yeates Legal Papers, April–May 1783, folio 7, HSP.

72. "State v. James Rook, 1788," New Jersey Supreme Court Actions at Law, no. 37902, New Jersey State Library, Trenton.

73. Territory of Mississippi v. Francis Surget, Oct 1808, in William Baskerville Hamilton, ed., *Anglo-American Law on the Frontier: Thomas Rodney and His Territorial Cases* (Durham, N.C., 1953), 419–22.

74. "Notes of Evidence in Respublica v. Abraham Moses for a rape on Chritiania Waggoner, 21 May 1783."

75. "Notes of Evidence for Respublica v. James Paxton for rape of Jane Mathers, 27 May 1783."

76. Petitions for John Gibson, 1816, Governor and Council Pardon Papers, box 17, folder 87, 91, Maryland State Archives, Annapolis.

77. Cuff indicted for rape on Diana Parish, 1748, New Haven, CT Superior Court Files, Dr. 327, September 1748, CSL.

78. Trial of John Morris, Dec 1792, Kent County, DE Oyer and Terminer Papers, Delaware State Archives, Dover.

79. *Trial of Amos Adams, for a Rape, committed on the Body of Lelea Thorp . . .* (New Haven, 1817), 14, AAS. See also Virginia Executive Papers, box 254, June 1819, Folder June 24–30, Library of Virginia (hereafter LOV), Richmond.

80. Documents related to attempted rape of Jane by Pompey, Nov 1796, Indictments, no. 3376 & unnumbered doc., Hunterdon Hall of Records, Flemington, N.J.

81. Virginia Executive Papers, 22 January 1810. Box 164, Folder Jan 11–20, LOV.

82. Of 557 prosecuted cases involving victims whose racial identity can be

identified, 22 were of African descent and 4 of Native American. For a summary of historians' attempts to quantify the sexual exploitation of enslaved women, see Joshua D. Rothman, *Notorious in the Neighborhood: Sex and Families Across the Color Line in Virginia, 1787–1861* (Chapel Hill, N.C., 2003), 249 n. 14.

83. Hunter Dickinson Farish, ed., *Journal and Letters of Philip Vickers Fithian 1773–1774: A Plantation Tutor of the Old Dominion* (Williamsburg, Va., 1957), 86, 184–85.

84. For examples of statutes that denied slaves the ability to testify against whites in criminal cases, see Hening, *The Statutes at Large*, 4:327 [1732]; Marbury and Crawford, *Laws of the State of Georgia, 1755–1800*, 429 [1770]. See also Thomas D. Morris, "Slaves and the Rules of Evidence in Criminal Trials," *Chicago-Kent Law Review* 68 (1993), 1209–39. On nineteenth-century prohibitions of rape prosecutions with enslaved victims, see Morris, *Southern Slavery and the Law*, 305–7; Peter Bardalgio, "Rape and the Law in the Old South: 'Calculated to excite indignation in every heart,'" *Journal of Southern History* 60 (1994), 756–58.

85. "John Briggs v. Elizabeth Palmer, Record of Settlement in Indictment of Job Almy for Arson, Nov. 1758," Newport, RI General Sessions File Papers, Rhode Island Supreme Court Judicial Records Center, Pawtucket, R.I.

86. Meharrin Baptist Church Record, September 1775, 35–36, LOV.

87. "Examination of Phyllis, Nov. 6, 1783," Northampton County Miscellaneous MSS., 1778–1797, 53, HSP.

88. On America's mixed-race history, see Gary Nash, "The Hidden History of Mestizo America," *Journal of American History* 82 (1995), 941–64.

89. *The Trial of Captain James Dunn, for an assault, with intent to seduce Sylvia Patterson, a Black woman* (New York, 1809), 16, 5, NYHS.

90. For colonial population statistics, see U.S. Bureau of the Census, *Historical Statistics of the United States, Colonial Times to 1957* (Washington, D.C., 1960), 756. For census data from 1790 to 1820, see http://fisher.lib.virginia.edu/census/ (accessed 1 July 2003).

Introduction to Part III

1. Edward W. Soja, *Postmodern Geographies: The Reassertion of Space in Critical Social Theory* (New York, 1989), 129.

2. On authority and territory, see Benedict R. O'G. Anderson, *Imagined Communities: Reflections on the Origin and Spread of Nationalism* (New York, 1991), 7; Paul W. Kahn, *The Cultural Study of Law: Reconstructing Legal Scholarship* (Chicago, 1999), 55–65. On the classic definition of culture as located in a particular space, see Greg Urban, *Metaculture: How Culture Moves through the World* (Minneapolis, 2001), 69, 274–76 n. 10; Renato Rosaldo, *Culture & Truth: The Remaking of Social Analysis* (Boston, 1993), 26–28.

3. Yi-fu Tuan, *Landscapes of Fear* (Minneapolis, 1979), 130–44; Bernard Bailyn, *The Peopling of British North America: An Introduction* (New York, 1988), 112–31.

4. Arjun Appadurai, *Modernity at Large: Cultural Dimensions of Globalization* (Minneapolis, 1996), 183–84.

5. Ulf Hannerz, *Cultural Complexity: Studies in the Social Organization of Meaning* (New York, 1992), 261; Appadurai, *Modernity at Large*, 191.

Chapter 6. The Murder of Jacob Rabe

1. This reconstruction of the Rabe murder is based on the testimonies of Roelof Baro, Dominga, Dirck Mulder, Jan Hoeck, Abraham Rouff, and Willem Beck, in "Informatien noopende de manslach geperpreteert aen den persoon van Jacop Rabij" (Information regarding the murder committed against the person of Jacob Rabe), The Hague, sec. 1, Acquisitions, Inv. no. XL 01 (1906), Dutch National Archives (hereafter NA). This manuscript was translated into Portuguese by A. de Carvalho as "Um intérprete dos Tapuios," in his *Avonturas e avontureiros no Brasil* (Rio de Janeiro, 1930), 165–204. All translations from the Dutch are mine unless otherwise noted. I would like to thank the National Archives (formerly the General State Archives), and the Royal Library, both in The Hague, as well as the Rare Books Collection, Memorial Library, University of Wisconsin-Madison, and the John Carter Brown Library, Providence, Rhode Island, for accessing materials used. For helpful comments on an earlier version, I would like to thank Ernst van den Boogaart, Gregory Dowd, Kathleen DuVal, Kristin Lovrien, John Smolenski, Scott Stevens, and the participants of the New World Order conference.

2. The High Council first learned of the murder around 14 April. See NA, Secret Minutes of the High Council, 14 April 1646, Inv. no. 76, Archive of the First West India Company (1621–1674) (hereafter AFWIC). On 21 April, the High Council interrogated several soldiers under Garstman's command who admitted to having participated in the killing of Rabe; see Secret Minutes of 21 April 1646, Inv. no. 76: ("who they held in great esteem"). For the special meeting of 23 April and the last quote, see Secret Minutes of 23 April 1646, Inv. no. 76.

3. For the council's fear that Rabe's Tupi wife and her kinsmen would turn against the Dutch, see Secret Minutes, 21 April ("livestock, negroes, and furniture") and 23 April, Inv. no. 76, AFWIC. For Dominga's demand for the return of the goods stolen from her, see her testimony in the file "Information Regarding the Murder of Jacob Rabe." For Dutch inheritance customs and the rights of widows, see Susan Elizabeth Shaw, "Building New Netherland: Gender and Family Ties in a Frontier Society" (Ph.D. diss., Cornell University, 2000), 41, especially note 46 (quotation); Deborah A. Rosen, "Women and PropertyAcross Colonial America: A Comparison of Legal Systems in New Mexico and New York," *William and Mary Quarterly*, 3rd ser., 60 (2003), 367; A. Schmidt, *Overleven na de dood: Weduwen in Leiden in de Gouden Eeuw* (Amsterdam, 2001).

4. Secret Minutes, 23 April 1646, Inv. no. 76, AFWIC. For Garstman's provisional appointment as militia commander see the Daily Minutes of the High Council (hereafter DM), 13 September 1645, Inv. no. 71, AFWIC. The appointment was provisional because the High Council needed official permission from the Heeren XIX. For the High Council's realization that Garstman could appeal his verdict to the Heeren XIX, see Pierre Moreau, *Klare en Waarachtige Beschrijving van de Leste Beroerten en Afval der Portuguezen in Brasil*, trans. J. H. Glazemaker (Amsterdam, 1652), 58–59.

5. I have borrowed the concept of "whose rules were law" from James H. Merrell, "'The Customes of Our Countrey': Indians and Colonists in Early America," in Bernard Bailyn and Philip D. Morgan, eds., *Strangers Within the Realm: Cultural Margins of the First British Empire* (Chapel Hill, N.C., 1991), 145. For the relationship between metropolitan center and colonial periphery in the Dutch Atlantic, see Wim Klooster, "Other Netherlands Beyond the Sea: Dutch America Between Metropolitan Control and Divergence, 1600–1795," in Christine Daniels and Michael V. Kennedy, eds., *Negotiated Empires: Centers and Peripheries in the Americas, 1500–1820* (New York, 2002), 171–91.

6. For studies of jurisdictional disputes between Indians and colonists in the New World, see Merrell, "'Customes of Our Countrey,'" 142–46; Jean M. O'Brien, *Dispossession by Degrees: Indian Land and Identity in Natick, Massachusetts, 1650–1790* (New York, 1997); Ana María Presta, "Doña Isabel Sisa: A Sixteenth-Century Indian Woman Resisting Gender Inequalities," in Kenneth J. Andrien, ed., *The Human Tradition in Colonial Latin America* (Wilmington, Del., 2002), 35–50; Yasuhide Kawashima, *Puritan Justice and the Indian: White Man's Law in Massachusetts, 1630–1763* (Middletown, Conn., 1986). For the tendency to leave out native peoples from the relationship between colony and metropolitan center, see the essays in Daniels and Kennedy, *Negotiated Empires*. Lauren Benton's, *Law and Colonial Cultures: Legal Regimes in World History, 1400–1900* (New York, 2002) is an important recent study that incorporates both types of jurisdictional conflicts into one comprehensive analysis.

7. For studies analyzing the pragmatic attitude of Dutch colonial officials, see Klooster, "Other Netherlands Beyond the Sea"; Jaap Jacobs, "Between Repression and Approval: Connivance and Tolerance in the Dutch Republic and in New Netherland," *De Halve Maen* 71 (1998), 51–58; Cynthia Jean Van Zandt, "Negotiating Settlement: Colonialism, Cultural Exchange, and Conflict in Early Colonial Atlantic North America, 1580–1660" (Ph.D. diss., University of Connecticut, 1998), ch. 4; Dennis Sullivan, *The Punishment of Crime in Colonial New York: The Dutch Experience in Albany During the Seventeenth Century*, American University Studies, ser. 9, History, (New York, 1997).

8. For the renewed interest in "borderlands," see Jeremy Alderman and Stephen Aron, "From Borderlands to Borders: Empires, Nation-States, and the Peoples in Between in North American History," *American Historical Review* 104 (1999), 814–41 (hereafter *AHR*); and the "Forum Essay Responses" in *AHR* 104 (1999), 1221–39. For the quoted definition of borderlands, see Evan Haefeli, "A Note on the Use of North American Borderlands," *AHR* 104 (1999), 1224.

9. The best overview of the Dutch in Brazil from a diplomatic viewpoint is Charles R. Boxer, *The Dutch in Brazil, 1624–1654* (London, 1957). A social history of the colony is provided by José Antonio Gonsalves de Mello, *Nederlanders in Brazilië, 1624–1654: De invloed van de Hollandse bezetting op het leven en de cultuur in Noord-Brazilië* trans. (from the Portuguese) G. N. Visser, and ed. B. N. Teensma (Zutphen, 2001). For a Luso-Brazilian perspective, see Eval Cabral de Mello, *Olinda Restaurada: Guerra e Açucar no Nordeste, 1630–1654* (Rio de Janeiro, 1975).

10. For Portuguese-Indian relations before the Dutch invasion, see M. Monteiro, "The Crises and Transformations of Invaded Societies: Coastal Brazil in the Sixteenth Century," in Frank Salomon and Stuart B. Schwartz, eds., *The Cambridge*

History of the Native Peoples of the Americas: South America, vol. 3, pt. 1 (New York, 1999), 973–1023. See also John Hemming, *Red Gold: The Conquest of the Brazilian Indians, 1500–1760* (Cambridge, Mass., 1978); Beatriz G. Dantas, José Augusto L. Sampaio, and Maria Rosário G. de Carvalho, "Os povos indígenas no Nordeste brasileiro: Um esboço histórico," in Manuela Carneiro da Cunha, ed., *História dos índios no Brasil* (São Paulo, 1992), 431–56.

11. For Tupi attempts to establish an alliance with the Dutch, see Frans Leonard Schalkwijk, *The Reformed Church in Dutch Brazil (1630–1654)* (Zoetermeer, 1998), 37, 168–73. See also Mark Meuwese, "'For the Peace and Well-Being of the Country': Intercultural Mediators and Dutch-Indian Relations in New Netherland and Dutch Brazil, 1600–1664" (Ph.D. diss., University of Notre Dame, 2003), ch. 2.

12. Monteiro, "The Crises and Transformations of Invaded Societies," 981–89, contains an excellent succinct overview of Tupi society before and after European contact. For the Tupis and the *aldeias*, see ibid., 998–99; Dauril Alden, *The Making of an Enterprise: The Society of Jesus in Portugal, Its Empire, and Beyond, 1540–1750* (Stanford, Calif., 1996), 71–75; Stuart B. Schwartz, *Sugar Plantations in the Formation of Brazilian Society: Bahia, 1550–1835* (New York, 1985), ch. 2.

13. Schalkwijk, *Reformed Church in Dutch Brazil*, chs. 8–11; Meuwese, "'For the Peace and Well-Being of the Country,'" ch. 4.

14. Robert H. Lowie, "Tapuyas," in J. H. Steward, ed., *Handbook of South American Indians*, vol. 1, *The Marginal Tribes*, Smithsonian Institution Bureau of American Ethnology Bulletin 143 (Washington, D.C., 1946), 553–56. For the relationship between *sertão* and the "Tapuyas," see A. J. R. Russell-Wood, "Centers and Peripheries in the Luso-Brazilian World, 1500–1808," in Daniels and Kennedy, *Negotiated Empires*, 123.

15. Robert H. Lowie, "Tarairiu," in Steward, *The Marginal Tribes*, 563–66. For WIC-Tarairiu diplomacy in Rio Grande, see Ernst van den Boogaart, "Infernal Allies: The WIC and the Tarairius, 1630–1654," in E. van den Boogaart, ed., in collaboration with H. R. Hoetink and P. J. P. Whitehead, *Johan Maurits van Nassau-Siegen, 1604–1679: A Humanist Prince in Europe and Brazil* (The Hague, 1979), 519–38. The Dutch mostly used the term "Tapuyas" when they dealt with the Tarairius. However, occasionally the Dutch did use the term "Tarairiu": see, for example, Johan Nieuhof, *Gedenkweerdige Brasiliaaense Zee-en Lant-Reize: Behelzende Al het geen op dezelve is voorgevallen. Beneffens Een Bondige Beschrijving van gantsch Neerlants Brasil* (Amsterdam, 1682), 222. For Garstman's appointment as commander of the newly captured fort, see S. P. L'Honoré Naber, ed., *Het Iaerlyck Verhael van Joannes de Laet, 1624–1636: Derde Deel, Boek VIII–X (1631–1633)*, Werken Uitgegeven door de Linschoten-Vereeniging 37 (The Hague, 1934), 208–16. For the diplomatic encounter between the Tarairius and Garstman, see Letter from Commander Garstman at Fort Ceulen to the High Council in Recife, March 1634, Inv. no. 50, Letters and Papers from Dutch Brazil (hereafter LPB), AFWIC. On Garstman's observations of the Tarairius, see Boogaart, "Infernal Allies," 523, 527.

16. For these *boslopers* see DM, 13 April 1639, Inv. no. 68; 25 February 1641, 12 January 1643, Inv. no. 69; 29 April, 8 June 1644, Inv. no. 70, AFWIC. For the Portuguese rebellion, see Boxer, *Dutch in Brazil*, chs. 5 and 6.

17. It is difficult to know the exact spelling of both Rabe's and Garstman's

names as their spelling occurs in various ways throughout archival records and contemporary writings. This variety is not unusual, since Europeans almost never spelled personal names consistently throughout the early modern period.

18. For Rabe's German region of origin, see Caspar Barlaeus, "De Tapoeiers, beschreven door Johan Rab van Waldeck," in S. P. L'Honoré Naber, ed., *Nederlandsch Brazilië onder het Bewind van Johan Maurits, Grave van Nassau, 1637–1644* (The Hague, 1923), 323–32. For Garstman's ethnicity, see Archive of the States-General, Secret Resolutions, Register of Resolutions Relating to West Indian Affairs, 2 October 1647, Inv. no. 4845, NA; and Secret Minutes, Inv. no. 76, 23 April 1646, AFWIC. For a study of ethnic Germans in service to the Dutch East India Company, see Roelof van Gelder, *Het Oost-Indisch Avontuur: Duitsers in Dienst van de VOC (1600–1800)* (Nijmegen, 1997). For Garstman's first mention in the sources of Dutch Brazil, see Naber, *Iaerlyck Verhael*, 208–16. For the first archival record dealing with Rabe as a *heer*, see DM, 25 June 1642, Inv. no. 69, AFWIC.

19. For interpreters among the Tarairius before 1642, see DM, 9 May 1637, 22 November 1638, Inv. no. 68, AFWIC. For the appointment of Rabe, see 25 June 1642, DM, Inv. no. 69, AFWIC. Boogaart, "Infernal Allies," p. 528, argues that Rabe was already in contact with the Tarairius in 1639.

20. For the interpretation of Rabe as a person with a hybrid identity blending Indian and European worlds, I am indebted to James H. Merrell, "'The Cast of His Countenance': Reading Andrew Montour," in Ronald Hoffman, Mechal Sobel, and Fredrika J. Teute, eds., *Through a Glass Darkly: Reflections on Personal Identity in Early America* (Chapel Hill, N.C., 1997): 13–39. For Rabe's marriage to a Tupi woman, see her testimony in "Informatien noopende de manslach geperpreteert aen den persoon van Jacop Rabij," sec. 1, Acquisitions, Inv. no. XL 01 (1906), 42–43, NA. For Rabe's material possessions, see the testimonies of Marcos Henninck (African slaves), Schout Jan Hoeck (African slaves, cattle, farm), and Willem ten Berge (farm, slave) in "Informatie noopende de manslach." Caspar Barlaeus, a noted Dutch literary figure and scholar, incorporated Rabe's notes about the Tarairius as a separate chapter in his well-known account of colonial Brazil under the rule of Governor-General Johan Maurits from 1637 to 1644. See Barlaeus, "De Tapoeiers beschreven door Johan Rab van Waldeck," in *Nederlandsch Brazilie*, 323–32.

21. For Garstman's rise to social prominence, see 9 January (African slaves), 12 January 1638 (sugar mill), DM, Inv. no. 68, AFWIC. For his marriage to a Portuguese woman and other examples of marriages between Portuguese women and WIC officers and officials, see Mello, *Nederlanders in Brazilië*, 144–45. For the rumors that Garstman conspired with Portuguese colonists against the Dutch and the subsequent investigation, see: Letter from the High Council to the Heeren XIX, 20 December 1636, Inv. no. 51, LPB; and undated later, probably May 1637, Inv. no. 52, AFWIC.

22. DM, 12 and 19 February 1643, Inv. no. 69, AFWIC.

23. For the provincial magistrate election, see DM, 8 January 1644, Inv. no. 70, AFWIC. Rabe is referred to here as "Jacob Rabboa," which I think is identical as Jacob Rabe. Eventually, the council selected Jan Soler, the son of a prominent Calvinist minister in Dutch Brazil, for the position. Rabe's Tarairiu warriors later killed Soler under mysterious circumstances. For Jan Soler, see B. N. Teensma, "The Brazilian

Letters of Vincent Joachim Soler," in Cristina Ferrão and José Paulo Monteiro Soares, eds., *Dutch Brazil*, vol. 1, *Documents in the Leiden University Library* (Ledien, 1997), 51–70.

24. For Rabe's correspondence with Garstman, see Letters from Jacob Rabe to Garstman, 28 June and 4 July 1645, Inv. no. 60, LPB, AFWIC. See also Boogaart, "Infernal Allies," p. 529.

25. For the massacre in July 1645, see the "Report on Brazil drawn up by Hendrik Hamel, Adriaen van Bullestraten, and Pieter Bas, councillors of Brazil" (undated, but probably written in late summer of 1645), Manuscript Collection, 76 A-16, fol. 18–19, Royal Library, The Hague.

26. For this motive, see the testimonies of Roelof Baro (Rabe's possessions), Willem ten Berge (treasure and torture), Jan Hoeck in "Informatie noopende de manslach,".

27. For the quotation about Rabe, see Secret Minutes, 14 April 1646, Inv. no. 76, AFWIC. See also the testimonies of Baro and Willem Beck in "Testimonie noopende de manslach." For Baro, see Teensma, "Roelof Baro's Tarairiú-monument." For Baro's mission and the letter to Nhanduí, see DM, 25 April 1646, Inv. no. 71.

28. Pierre Moreau, *Klare en Waarachtige Beschrijving van de Leste Beroerten en Afval der Portuguezen in Brasil*, translated from the French by J. H. Glazemaker (Amsterdam, 1651), 58–59. Moreau was a French-speaking personal secretary for Michiel van Goch, a member of the High Council. About Moreau, see Schalkwijk, *The Reformed Church in Dutch Brazil*, 146. For van Goch, see Boxer, *Dutch in Brazil*, 266–67. For the meeting in Recife, see Moreau, *Klare en Waerachtige Beschrijvinge*, 58–59. For the concept of a shared notion of justice, I am indebted to Benton, *Law and Political Cultures*, esp. ch. 2.

29. Moreau, *Klare en Waerachtige Beschrijving*, 58–59.

30. Ibid.

31. Ibid. For a discussion of the relationship between the metropolitan center and the colonial periphery in the Dutch Americas, see Klooster, "Other Netherlands Beyond the Sea."

32. For the passage about the bound Garstman at this meeting, see Arnoldus Montanus, *De Nieuwe en Onbekende Weereld: Of Beschryving van America en 't Zuid-Land* (Amsterdam, 1671), 515. In colonial North America, colonists also refused to allow Indians to judge colonists according to Native laws. See Merrell, "The Customes of Our Countrey," 142–46.

33. For Nhanduí's pleas for military support and Baro's diplomacy, see Moreau, *Klare en Waerachtige Beschrijvinge*, 61–62; Montanus, *Nieuwe en Onbekende Wereld*, 516. For Baro's diplomacy, see Roelof Baro, "Relação da viagem de Roulox Baro" (originally published in French in 1647) in José Honório Rodrigues, ed. and intro., and Lêda Boechat Rodrigues, trans., *História das últimas lutas no Brasil entre holandeses e portugueses e relação da viagem ao país dos tapuias*, Reconquista do Brasil 54 (Belo Horizonte, 1979), 93–107. For the initial refusal of Dutch authorities to provide military assistance, see DM, 29 August 1647, Inv. no. 72, AFWIC. For the eventual decision to send soldiers to the Tarairius, see DM, 5 September 1647, Inv. no. 72, AFWCI. For the alliance after 1648, see Boogaart, "Infernal Allies," 530–31; Merrell, "'The Customes of Our Countrey,'" 145 ("whose rules were law").

34. I have used the Iberian spelling "Dominga" rather than "Domynga" as Rabe's wife is spelled in the Dutch sources. For the Tupis in the *aldeias*, see Monteiro, "Crises and Transformations of Invaded Societies," 998–99; Alden, *Making of an Enterprise*, 71–75; Schwartz, *Sugar Plantations*, ch. 2.

35. "Testimony of Domyngas," in "Information Regarding the Manslaughter Committed Against Jacob Rabij" ("widow"); Secret Minutes, 14 April 1646 ("wife" and "housewife"), Inv. no. 76, AFWIC. For other marriages between Tupi women and WIC colonists, see Mello, *Nederlanders in Brazilië*, 216. Schwartz, *Sugar Plantations*, 43–50, discusses Indian attempts to run away from the *aldeias* to escape the harsh working conditions.

36. Mello, *Nederlanders in Brazilië*, 216, discusses WIC policy toward intermarriages.

37. Shaw, "Building New Netherland," ch. 1, discusses wills drawn up by couples when the husband went to New Netherland. For Dominga's account, see her "Testimony of Domyngas," in "Information Regarding the Manslaughter."

38. DM, 8 August 1646, Inv. no. 71, AFWIC.

39. Significantly, most scholars of Dutch Brazil mention only the murder and do not discuss Garstman's fate. See for example Schalkwijk, *Reformed Church in Brazil*, 61; Boogaart, "Infernal Allies," 530. The chaos in Recife in the spring of 1646 is vividly described in Nieuhof, *Gedenkweerdige Brasiliaaense Zee-en Lant-Reize*, 175–76.

40. For the Garstman's arrival in Recife, see DM, 19 April 1646, Inv. no. 71, AFWIC. For the interrogation and testimonies by De Boullan, see Secret Minutes, 21 April 1646, Inv. No. 76, AFWIC.

41. Moreau, *Klare en Waerachtige Beschrijving*, 58–59 (confrontation between De Boullan and Garstman); Secret Minutes, 24 April 1646 (quotations), Inv. no 76, AFWIC.

42. For the decision to put Garstman on the *Hollandia*, see Secret Minutes, 24 April 1646, Inv. no. 71, AFWIC. For the petitions, see DM, 26, 27, 28 April, 17 May, all in 1646, Inv. no. 71, AFWIC. By transferring Garstman's case from a civilian court to a military court the petitioners presumably intended to give Garstman an easy trial that would quickly find him not guilty.

43. See DM, 3, 18 July, 12, 27 August, all in1646, Inv. no. 71, AWFIC. For the new members of the High Council, see S. P. L'Honoré Naber, ed., "Het Dagboek van Hendrick Haecxs, Lid van den Hoogen Raad van Brazilië (1645–1654)" (The diary of Hendrick Haexcs, member of the High Council of Brazil [1645–1654]), *Bijdragen en Mededeelingen van het Historisch Genootschap (Gevestigd te Utrecht)* 46 (1925), 126–311, esp. 187–88. For the recent study surveying the political development of the Dutch Americas, see Klooster, "Other Netherlands Beyond the Sea."

44. For the date of the sentence, see General Missive, 10 March 1649, LPB, Inv. no. 65, AFWIC. For the quotation, see Moreau, *Klare en Waerachtige Beschrijving*, 59. For a different interpretation by a European eyewitness, see Frank Ibold, Jens Jäger, and Detlev Kraack, eds., *Das "Memorial und Jurenal" des Peter Hansen Hajstrup (1624–1672)*, Quellen und Forschungen zur Geschichte Schleswig-Holsteins 103 (Neumünster, 1995), 75–76.

45. For Garstman and the States-General committee, see Archive of the States-General, Secret Resolutions, Register of Resolutions Relating to West Indian Affairs, 2 October, 27 November, 21 December, 1647; 5, 10 February (quotation), 20 May (travel pass and annual salary), 1648, Inv. no. 4845, NA.

46. Klooster, "Other Netherlands Beyond the Sea."

47. For the complaints of the High Council, see General Missive from the High Council to the Heeren XIX, 19 December 1648 (quotation), LPB, Inv. no. 64, AFWIC; and LPB, Inv. no. 65; General Missive from the High Council to the Heeren XIX, 10 March 1649, AFWIC. For Garstman's reappointment, see DM, 23 April 1649, Inv. no. 73, AFWIC.

48. For the disastrous WIC defeat outside Recife in February 1649, see Boxer, *Dutch in Brazil,* 213–16. For Garstman's arrival in Ceará, see letter from the High Council to the Heeren XIX, 7 August 1649, LPB, Inv. no. 65, AFWIC. For the WIC outpost in Ceará from 1649 to 1654, see Rita Krommen, *Mathias Beck und die Westindische Kompagnie: Zur Herrschaft der Niederländer im kolonialen Ceará,* Arbeitspapiere zur Lateinamerika Forschung II-01 (Cologne, 2001). This study can be viewed in its entirety on the following Web site: http://www.uni-koeln.de/phil-fak/aspla/pdf/krommen.pdf (accessed on 14 May 2002). For Garstman's career in Ceará, see various journals of Mathias Beck from Ceará, 1649, LPB, Inv. no. 65, AFWIC. For the death of Garstman, see Letter from Mathias Beck on Barbados, 8 October 1654, LPB, Inv. No. 67, AFWIC. For Garstman's death and testament, see Amsterdam City Archive, Notarial Records, 28 May 1660, Inv. no. 1133, fol. 223.

Chapter 7. Forging Cultures of Resistance on Two Colonial Frontiers

1. Neil L. Whitehead, "Ethnic Transformation and Historical Discontinuity in Native Amazonia and Guayana, 1500–1900," *L'Homme* 33 (1993) 285–304; James Schofield Saeger, *The Chaco Mission Frontier: The Guaycuruan Experience* (Tucson, 2000); David J. Weber, *The Spanish Frontier in North America* (New Haven, Conn., 1992).

2. Charles Gibson, *Tlaxcala in the Sixteenth Century* (Stanford, Calif., 1952), published in Spanish as *Tlaxcala en el siglo XVI* (Mexico City, 1991), 70–123; Gibson, *Aztecs Under Spanish Rule* (Stanford, Calif., 1964), 166–93; James Lockhart, *The Nahuas After the Conquest. A Social and Cultural History of the Indians of Central Mexico, Sixteenth Through Eighteenth Centuries* (Stanford, Calif., 1992), 14–58; Robert Haskett, *Indigenous Rulers: An Ethnohistory of Town Government in Colonial Cuernavaca* (Albuquerque, 1991).

3. The Chiquitano language and a number of languages spoken by indigenous peoples of the Chaco are gendered. See P. Julián Knogler, "Relato sobre el país y la nación de los chiquitos," in W. Hoffmann, ed., *Las misiones jesuíticas entre los chiquitanos* (Buenos Aires, 1979), 143; Saeger, *The Chaco Mission Frontier,* 77–79; Sieglinde Falkinger, "'. . . cuesta entender a las mugeres . . . ' la diferencia en el lenguaje femenino y masculino en Chiquitano (besiro)," *Actas* del 1 Congreso Sudamericano de Historia, Santa Cruz de la Sierra, Bolivia, 2003 (Santa Cruz, CD, 2004).

4. Cynthia Radding, *Wandering Peoples: Colonialism, Ethnic Spaces, and Ecological Frontiers in Northwestern Mexico, 1700–1850* (Durham, N.C., 1997), 22–33; Edward H. Spicer, *Cycles of Conquest: The Impact of Spain, Mexico, and the United States on the Indians of the Southwest, 1533–1960* (Tucson, 1962), 8–15.

5. Daniel Santamaría, "Fronteras indígenas del oriente boliviano: La dominación coloniao en Moxos y chiquitos, 1675–1810," *Boletín Americanista* 36 (1986)

197–228; David Block, *Mission Culture on the Upper Amazon: Native Tradition, Jesuit Enterprise & Secular Policy in Moxos, 1660–1880* (Lincoln, 1994); Saeger, *The Chaco Mission Frontier*; Juan Patricio Fernández, *Relación historial de las misiones de indios Chiquitos*, ed. Daniel Santamaría (Jujuy, 1994), 45, 125–28. See discussion of *parcialidades* below.

6. William Merrill, "Conversion and Colonialism in Northern Mexico: The Tarahumara Response to the Jesuit Mission Program, 1601–1767," in R. W. Hefner, ed., *Conversion to Christianity: Historical and Anthropological Perspectives on a Great Transformation* (Berkeley, 1989), 129–63; Radding, *Wandering Peoples*, 1997; Radding, "Voces chiquitanas: Entre la encomienda y la misión en el oriente de Bolivia (siglo XVIII)," *Anuario del ABNB* (1997), 123–38.

7. Demographic projections of indigenous population decline and recovery have been debated for different regions and time periods, from the sixteenth to the eighteenth centuries. See Robert Jackson, *Indian Population Decline. The Missions of Northwestern New Spain, 1687–1840* (Albuquerque, 1994); Ernesto J. A. Maeder and Alfredo Bolsi, "La población de las misiones guaraníes entre 1702–1767," *Estudios Paraguayos* 2 (1974), 111–37; Block, *Mission Culture*; Santamaría, "Fronteras indígenas," 206–7; Saeger, *The Chaco Mission Frontier*, 84–97; Radding, *Wandering Peoples*, 103–70.

8. William E. Doolittle, "Aboriginal Agricultural development in the Valley of Sonora, Mexico," *Geographical Review* 70 (1980), 328–42; Gary Nabhan, *The Desert Smells Like Rain: A Naturalist in Papago Indian Country* (San Francisco, 1982); Gary Nabhan and Thomas E. Sheridan, "Living Fencerows of the Río San Miguel, Sonora, Mexico: Traditional Technology for Floodplain Managment," *Human Ecology* 5 (1977), 97–111.

9. Bernd Fischermann, "Context social y cultural," in Teresa R. de Centurión and I. J. Kraljevic, eds., *Plantas útiles de Lomerío* (Santa Cruz, 1996); Radding, "From the Counting House to the Field and Loom: Ecologies, Cultures, and Economies in the Missions of Sonora (Mexico) and Chiquitanía (Bolivia)," *Hispanic American Historical Review* 81 (2001), 45–88.

10. Campbell Pennington, *The Pima Bajo of Central Sonora*, 1: *The Material Culture* (Salt Lake City, 1969), 149–50, 252–57; Nabhan, *Desert Smells Like Rain*, 91–93; R. Jones, "The Wi'igita of Achi and Quitobac," *The Kiva* 36 (1971), 1–29.

11. Fischermann, "Contexto social y cultural," 33–36; Jürgen Riester, "Curanderos y brujos de los indios chiquitanos," *Revista de la Universidad Boliviana Gabriel René Moreno* 16, nos. 31–32 (1972); Fernández, *Relación historial*, 131–32.

12. Gathered and hunted products that became commodities in regional colonial circuits included beeswax and honey, tanned hides, and lumber.

13. Alcides Parejas, "El fin del régimen jesuítico," in Pedro Querejazu, ed., *Las misiones jesuíticas de Chiquitos* (La Paz, 1995), 296–98.

14. Radding, *Wandering Peoples*, 268–71, 361; Lorenzo Cancio to Marqués de Croix, 1766, Archivo General de la Nación (Mexico) *Provincias Internas* 48, 1, fojas 27–36.

15. Saeger, *The Chaco Mission Frontier*, 27–50; Guillermo Furlong, S.J., ed., *José Sánchez Labrador, S.J. y su "yerba mate"* (1774), Editores Coloniales Rioplatenses, vol. 10 (Buenos Aires, 1952), 37–52.

16. Knogler, "Relato sobre el país y la nación de los chiquitos," 161–65; Fernández, *Relación historial*, 135–57.

17. Fernández, *Relación historial*, 125–26. Alfred Métraux, "The Social Organization and Religion of the Mojo and Manasí," *Primitive Man*. *Quarterly Bulletin of the Catholic Anthropological Conference* 16 (1943), 20–21, relies on the same Jesuit chronicles for his description of Manasi social organization.

18. Knogler, "Relato sobre el país y la nación de los chiquitos," 178.

19. Saeger, *The Chaco Mission Frontier*, 113–18. See comparative descriptions of the limited powers of "alliance chiefs" among the Algonquian peoples of the Great Lakes region in Richard White, *The Middle Ground: Indians, Empires, and Republics in the Great Lakes Region, 1650–1815* (Cambridge, Mass., 1991).

20. Bernd Hausberger, "La violencia en la conquista espiritual: Las misiones jesuitas de Sonora," *Jahrbuch für Geschichte von Staat, Wirtschaft und Gesellschaft Lateinomerikas* 30 (1991), 27–54; Radding, "From the Counting House to the Field and Loom," 80–82.

21. W. G. Lovell and C. H. Lutz, *Demography and Empire: A Guide to the Population History of Spanish Central America, 1500–1821*, Dellplain Latin American Studies, 33 (Boulder, 1995), 77, 97, 130, 173, 175; Haskett, *Indigenous Rulers*, 9–10; M. Restall, *The Maya World: Yucatec Culture and Society, 1550–1850* (Stanford, 1997), 30.

22. Saeger, *The Chaco Mission Frontier*, 131–33, makes this point cogently in reference to the Mocobí-Abipon wars of the 1770s and 1780s.

23. Thomas Whigham, "Paraguay's *Pueblos de Indios*: Echoes of a Missionary Past," in *The New Latin American History*, edited by Erick Langer and Robert H. Jackson (Lincoln, 1995), 157–88, comments on the native elite of the Guaraní missions constituted in the *cabildo*.

24. Radding, *Wandering Peoples*, 146–50.

25. Ibid., 256–63, 276–79; John Kessell, *Friars, Soldiers, and Reformers: Hispanic Arizona and the Sonora Mission Frontier, 1767–1856* (Tucson, 1976), 137–38.

26. On division of communal lands, see Biblioteca Nacional Fondo Franciscano (Mexico) 35/722; Radding, *Wandering Peoples*, 188–93.

27. Radding, *Wandering Peoples*, 288–91; BNFF 35/767, fols. 3–11; "Conflicto entre autoridades indígenas ópatas y militares (1798–1790)," in Cynthia Radding, *Entre el desierto y la sierra: Las naciones o'odham y tegüima de Sonora, 1530–1840* (Mexico City, 1995), 179–83. The following episode is based on these documents. A league is approximately 4 kilometers (2.4 miles).

28. Gil Samaniego and Gregorio Ortiz Cortés were landowners in the fertile valley between Bacerác and Bavispe. The two families were related by marriage.

29. Fray Angel Antonio Núñez Fundidor, *Carta Edificante, Bacerác en 1777*, ed. Julio César Montané Martí (Hermosillo, 1999), 67; Archivo General de la Nación, *Archivo Histórico de Hacienda* leg. 278, exp. 20.

30. Archivo de la Catedral de Santa Cruz (Bolivia), 6–1, A-3 1790.

31. Ibid. ". . . entonces los jueces decían que no querían reglares gobernadores, soldados, ni tenientes, que ellos con los padres se habían criado . . ." *Reglares* literally translates as members of a religious order, but there are no other references to clerical orders in the document.

32. Bernd Fischermann, "Los Rojas, artesanos, y sacerdotes cruceños en la

Chiquitanía (recordando a Hans Roth)," *Festival Internacional de Música "Misiones de Chiquitos,"* 3, *Reunión Científica* (Santa Cruz, Calif., 2000), 141–50. It is not the third volume, but the third event from which the proceedings were published.

33. Cynthia Radding, "Historical Perspectives on Gender, Security, and Technology: Gathering, Weaving, and Subsistence in Colonial Mission Communities of Bolivia," *International Journal of Politics, Culture, and Society* 15 (2001), 107–23. Inga Clendinnen has made a similar observation concerning the role of Maya women in the production of cotton cloth for tribute in Yucatán (Mexico). Clendinnen, "Yucatec Maya Women and the Spanish Conquest: Role and Ritual in Historical Reconstruction," *Journal of Social History* (1983), 427–42.

34. See, for example, the uprising of Concepción in the Chiquitanía of 1779, reported in Archivo de Catedral, Santa Cruz de la Sierra (Bolivia), 6–2C, 1779. In this instance, Indian warriors of the Manapeca band rose up against their priest who, they alleged, kept one of their women as his concubine.

35. Marshall Sahlins, *Islands of History* (Chicago, 1985), 5–26; Ramón A. Gutiérrez, *When Jesus Came the Corn Mothers Went Away: Marriage, Sexuality, and Power in New Mexico, 1500–1846* (Stanford, 1991) 19, 50–51.

36. Radding, *Wandering Peoples*, 126–41, 161–65.

37. Fernández, *Relación historial,* 38–40; Knogler, "Relato sobre el país y la nación de los chiquitos," 149; interview with Justa Morón, San Ignacio de Velasco, 8/12/01.

38. Edward H. Spicer, *The Yaquis: A Cultural History* (Tucson, 1980), 59–113; Cynthia Radding, "Crosses, Caves, and *Matachinis*: Divergent Appropriations of Catholic Discourse in Northwestern New Spain," *The Americas* 55 (1998), 177–201; Pennington, *The Pima Bajo of Central Sonora*, 1:149–50; Radding, *Wandering Peoples,* 54.

39. Fernández, *Relación historial,* 35–36; Jürgen Riester, "Curanderos y brujos de los indios Chiquitanos," *Revista de la Universidad Boliviana Gabriel René Moreno* 16 (1972), 5–17.

40. Andrés Pérez de Rivas, *Historia de los Triunfos de Nuestra Santa Fé*, vols. 1–2 (Hermosillo, 1986 [1645]); Susan Deeds, "Double Jeopardy: Indian Women in Jesuit Missions of Nueva Vizcaya," in S. Schroeder, S. Wood, and R. Haskett, eds., *Indian Women of Early Mexico* (Norman, Okla., 1997); Fernández, *Relación historial,* 128–40.

41. Carolyn Martin Shaw, *Colonial Inscriptions: Race, Sex and Class in Kenya* (Minneapolis, 1995), 22–23; Sahlins, *Culture in Practice: Selected Essays* (New York, 2000) 10–21 and passim.

42. Jane Fishburne Collier, *Marriage and Inequality in Classless Societies* (Stanford, Calif., 1988), 196–221. Landed property was the chief distinction between "white" non-Indian settlers (*vecinos*) and Indians in late colonial Sonora and in nineteenth-century Chiquitos. See Radding, *Wandering Peoples*, 171–245.

43. *Nijoras,* in Sonora, were identified as a "tribe" in early colonial maps and documents, but the term referred to captives separated from their communities of origin. See H. Dobyns, P. Ezell, A. Jones, and G. Ezell, "What Were Nixoras?" *Southwestern Journal of Anthropology* 16 (1960), 230–68; Julio Montané, "De *nijoras* y 'españoles a medias,'" *Simposio de Historia de Sonora* 15 (Hermosillo, 1990) 105–23.

44. Knogler, "Relato sobre el país y la nación de los chiquitos," 182.

Chapter 8. Sorcery and Sovereignty

The author wishes to acknowledge the editors, Tom Humphrey and John Smolenski, as well as panelists and participants at the New World Orders conference, particularly Daniel Richter and Kathleen DuVal, for their comments. Thanks also to Wayne Carp, Seth Cotlar, Richard Johnson, Jacquelyn Miller, Eric Nellis, Paul Otto, William Rorabaugh, Rachel Wheeler, William Youngs, and the Northwest Early American History group for their perceptive reading and critique. Special thanks to Elizabeth Reis.

1. The point seems obvious enough today that citation of the postcolonial critic Homi K. Bhabha's influential explorations of this theme, esp. *Nation and Narration* (London, 1990) and "DissemiNation: Time, Narrative, and the Margins of the Modern Nation," in *The Location of Culture* (London, 1994), 139–70, seems hardly necessary.

2. Barbara Graymont, *The Iroquois in the American Revolution* (Syracuse, N.Y., 1972). More generally, see Colin G. Calloway, *The American Revolution in Indian Country: Crisis and Diversity in Native American Communities* (Cambridge, England, 1995), esp. chs. 4 and 5; Calloway concludes that "the Six Nations' experience in the Revolution was one of almost total disaster" (108). On the earlier history of the Iroquois, see Matthew Dennis, *Cultivating a Landscape of Peace: Iroquois-European Encounters in Seventeenth-Century America* (Ithaca, N.Y., 1993) and Daniel K. Richter, *The Ordeal of the Longhouse: The Peoples of the Iroquois League in the Era of European Colonization* (Chapel Hill, N.C., 1992).

3. See Anthony F. C. Wallace, *Death and Rebirth of the Seneca* (New York, 1970), 144, 168, 194–96. Some of these villages, especially in the Ohio Country, would have identified themselves as Iroquois more reluctantly than Six Nations leaders or imperial officials would have liked. On the contention between the Six Nations and their "client" communities and the declining influence of the former over the latter, see esp. Michael N. McConnell, *A Country Between: The Upper Ohio Valley and Its Peoples, 1724–1774* (Lincoln, Nebr., 1992). See also Dean R. Snow and Kim M. Lanphear, "European Contact and Indian Depopulation in the Northeast: The Timing of the First Epidemics," *Ethnohistory* 35 (1988), 15–33; Richter, *Ordeal of the Longhouse*, 58–59, 65–66, 114, 173, 188, 256, 331 n. 19, 355–56 n. 60. Elisabeth Tooker, "The League of the Iroquois," in William C. Sturtevant, gen. ed., *Handbook of North American Indians*, 20 vols. projected (Washington, D.C., 1978–) (hereafter HBNAI), vol. 15: *Northeast* (1978), ed. Bruce G. Trigger, 421, contains a table, "Iroquois Population Estimates by Fighting Men, 1660–1779." For the Iroquois Nation and the Revolution, see Karim Tiro, "A Civil War? Rethinking Iroquois Participation in the American Revolution," *Explorations in Early American Culture* 4 (2000), 148–65; and Tiro, "The People of the Standing Stone: The Oneida Indian Nation from Revolution through Removal, 1768–1850" (Ph.D. diss., University of Pennsylvania, 1999).

4. For a summary analysis of Seneca history and geography, see Thomas S. Abler and Elisabeth Tooker, "Seneca," in HBNAI, 15: 505–17; see 507–13 for assessment of the post-Revolutionary period through the mid-nineteenth century and for maps of the Seneca reservations. See also Tooker, "Iroquois Since 1820," in ibid., 449–65. For a contemporary description of the Allegany and other Seneca communities, see Carl F. Klinck and James J. Talman, eds., *The Journal of Major John Norton, 1816* (Toronto, 1970), 7–11.

5. The Quaker program of "civilization" among the Senecas can be reconstructed from records and minutes of the Committee Appointed by the Yearly Meeting of Friends Pennsylvania, New York, &c for Promoting the Improvement and Gradual Civilization of the Indian Natives, or "Indian Committee," of the Philadelphia Yearly Meeting, housed in the Quaker Collection, Special Collections, Haverford College, Haverford, Penn. The ten boxes of diaries, reports, and correspondence (hereafter IC Records), as well as the ten volumes of minutes (hereafter IC Minutes) and other manuscripts, are also available on microfilm at the American Philosophical Society (film 824, reels 1–12), where I examined them. See also Halliday Jackson, *Civilization of the Indian Nations; or, a brief view of the Friendly Conduct of William Penn toward them . . . and a concise narrative of the proceedings of the Yearly Meeting of Friends . . . since the year 1795, in promoting their improvement and gradual civilization* (Philadelphia, 1830); Merle H. Deardorff and George S. Snyderman, eds., "A Nineteenth-Century Journal of a Visit to the Indians of New York," *Proceedings of the American Philosophical Society* 100 (1956), 582–612; Snyderman, ed., "Halliday Jackson's Journal of a Visit Paid to the Indians of New York (1806)," ibid., 101 (1957), 565–88; Anthony F. C. Wallace, ed., "Halliday Jackson's Journal to the Seneca Indians, 1798–1800 (Part I)," *Pennsylvania History* 19 (1952), 117–47 and (Part II), ibid., 19 (1952), 325–49. More generally, see Frank H. Severence, ed., "Narratives of Early Mission Work on the Niagara Frontier and Buffalo Creek," *Publications of the Buffalo Historical Society* 6 (1903), 165–380. Quotation from IC Minutes, vol. 1 (3/8/1796). The Cherokee-Scot (and adopted Mohawk) John Norton reported similarly in 1816 at Cattaraugus (an expansion of the Allegheny mission "to promote the same end"), "The Friends (or People called Quakers) are about commencing a Settlement in the Neighborhood, with an intention of instructing these People in Agriculture, and the necessary Arts" (*Journal of John Norton*, 8).

6. On assimilationism in general, see Robert F. Berkhofer Jr., *The White Man's Indian: Images of the American Indian from Columbus to the Present* (New York, 1978); see also Berkhofer Jr., *Salvation and the Savage: An Analysis of Protestant Missions and the American Indian Response, 1787–1862* (Lexington, Ky., 1965). On the gendered nature of such assimilation campaigns, see Theda Perdue, "Southern Indians and the Cult of True Womanhood," in Walter J. Fraser Jr., et al., eds., *The Web of Southern Social Relations: Women, Family, and Education* (Athens, Ga., 1985), 35–51; and Perdue, *Cherokee Women: Gender and Culture Change, 1700–1835* (Lincoln, Nebr., 1998); Mary E. Young, "Women, Civilization, and the Indian Question," in Mabel E. Deutrich and Virginia C. Purdy, eds., *Clio Was a Woman: Studies in the History of American Women* (Washington, D.C., 1980), 98–110. Diane Rothenberg, "The Mothers of the Nation: Seneca Resistance to Quaker Intervention," in Mona Etienne and Eleanor Leacock, eds., *Women and Colonization: Anthropological Perspectives* (New York, 1980), 63–87, deals directly and provocatively with the gendered Seneca-Quaker encounter. See also Nancy Shoemaker, ed., *Negotiators of Change: Historical Perspectives on Native American Women* (New York, 1994).

7. On openness to technological innovations, "improvement" (e.g., sawmills, gristmills, roads), Western education, and moral reform, see, for example, "Extract of a letter from the Friends at Genesinguhta" (1/16/1800), IC Records, box 1; "Extract of a letter from Genesinguhta" (9/3/1800), IC Records, box 1; "Extract of a letter from

one of the Friends settled on the Alleghenny River" (2/28/1801), IC Records, box 1; "Copy of a letter from five of the Cattaraugus Indians to the Friends settled at Genesinguhta" (nm/nd/1799), IC Records, box 1; "Speech of Conidiu [Handsome Lake] on behalf of the Seneca Nation of Indians residing on the Alleghanny River . . ." (8/30/1803), IC Records, box 2. On different Allegany Seneca attitudes toward accommodation and acculturation, see, for example, Jonathan Thomas to Thomas Wistar (4/21/1804), IC Records, box 2; Friends at Tunessassah to Thomas Wistar (2/14/1807), IC Records, box 2; Friends at Tunessassah to the Indian Committee (2/3/1807), IC Records, box 2.

8. For Quaker relations of the event, see Wallace, "Halliday Jackson's Journal," I, 146–47; [Halliday Jackson,] "The Visions of Connudiu [Handsome Lake] or Cornplanter's Brother," ibid., II, 341–44; "Henry Simmons' Version of the Visions," ibid., 345–49. A Seneca testimony—a first hand account by the prophet's nephew—is in Thomas A. Abler, ed., *Chainbreaker: The Revolutionary War Memoirs of Governor Blacksnake, as told to Benjamin Williams* (Lincoln, Nebr., 1989), 210–15. The emergence of the prophet, Handsome Lake, is also noted in P. C. T. White, ed., *Lord Selkirk's Diary, 1803–1804* (Toronto, 1958), 245–46. The codified Seneca version appears in Arthur C. Parker, "The Code of Handsome Lake, the Seneca Prophet," in *Parker on the Iroquois,* ed. William N. Fenton (Syracuse, N.Y., 1968 [1913]), esp. 21–26. These events are narrated more fully in Wallace, *Death and Rebirth of the Seneca,* chs. 8 and 9.

9. "Visions of Connudiu," in Wallace, "Halliday Jackson's Journal," II, 342–43; "Henry Simmons' Version," ibid., 346–48. Wallace, *Death and Rebirth of the Seneca,* 242–48, provides a summary analysis of the second vision of Handsome Lake. The prophet's influence waxed and waned: I do not mean to suggest its universal appeal or dominance among Senecas. For an analysis of parallel developments, with peculiarities of their own, see Jay Miller, "The 1806 Purge among the Indiana Delaware: Sorcery, Gender, Boundaries, and Legitimacy," *Ethnohistory* 41 (1994), 245–66. The victims of this "witch" purge were mostly men—those, Miller writes, "at the extremes of traditional society, tainted by their involvement with conversion schemes, land sales, and prominent whites." (263). Among the Senecas, I emphasize that the nature and form of the accommodation, not whether to accommodate at all, was at issue; and defining what was or would be "traditional" was contested and negotiated.

10. According to Mary Jemison, at least among the Senecas living along the Genesee River, "women never participated" in drunken "frolics" until after the Revolutionary War; thereafter, "spirits became common in our tribe, and has been used indiscriminately by both sexes," though intoxication remained more common among men than women (James E. Seaver, *A Narrative of the Life of Mrs. Mary Jemison* [Syracuse, N.Y., 1990 (1824)], 127). According to Wallace, *Death and Rebirth of the Seneca,* 200, women in particular, as petty traders, obtained whiskey from whites and retailed it in their villages; women could thus be implicated in the alcohol crisis even if men predominated among village drunkards.

11. Jackson, *Civilization of the Indian Natives,* 76, expressed the rhetoric of domesticity and separate spheres in the following quotation of a Quaker delegation speaking to a *mixed* audience of Senecas.

12. Matthew Dennis, "Seneca Possessed: Colonialism, Witchcraft, and Gender in the Time of Handsome Lake," in Elizabeth Reis, ed., *Spellbound: Women and*

Witchcraft in America (Wilmington, Del., 1999), 121–43. This research is part of book-length study in progress, *Seneca Possessed: Witchcraft, Gender, and Colonialism on the Frontiers of the Early Republic.*

13. The term "witchcraft" is used here to refer to all forms of malevolence (and "witch" refers to those who directed it) among the Iroquois. While the diverse practices and practitioners designated generally by such terms certainly varied, especially over time and across cultural boundaries, apparently the Iroquois themselves did not divide malevolent acts or distinguish terminologically between, say, those of "witches" and those of "sorcerers." See Annemarie Shimony, "Iroquois Witchcraft at Six Nations," in Deward E. Walker Jr., ed., *Systems of Witchcraft and Sorcery* (Moscow, Idaho, 1970), 239–65, esp. 242–43. On Iroquois notions of *otkon* and *orenda* and witchcraft beliefs and practices, see William N. Fenton and Elizabeth Moore, eds. and trans., *Father Joseph-François de Lafitau, Customs of the American Indians Compared with the Customs of Primitive Times, Publications of the Champlain Society,* 48, 2 vols. (Toronto, 1974 [1724]), I, 240–41; Wallace, *Death and Rebirth of the Seneca,* 84; Åke Hultkrantz, *The Religions of the American Indians,* trans. by Monica Setterwall (Berkeley, 1979), 12; Richter, *Ordeal of the Longhouse,* 24–25; Dean R. Snow, *The Iroquois* (Oxford, 1994), 54, 96, 98; Dennis, *Cultivating a Landscape of Peace,* 90–94. See also the following: George S. Snyderman, "Witches, Witchcraft, and Allegany Seneca Medicine," *Proceedings of the American Philosophical Society* 127 (1983), 263–77; David Blanchard, "Who or What's a Witch? Iroquois Persons of Power," *American Indian Quarterly* 6 (1982), 218–37; DeCost Smith, "Witchcraft and Demonism of the Modern Iroquois," *Journal of American Folklore* 1 (1888), 184–93; Smith, "Onondaga Customs," ibid., 195–98; Smith, "Additional Notes on Onondaga Witchcraft and Hon-do-i," ibid., 2 (1889), 277–81; Lewis Henry Morgan, *The League of the Ho-de-no-sau-nee, Iroquois,* ed. William N. Fenton (Secaucus, N.J., 1962 [1851]), 164–65; Annemarie Anrod Shimony, *Conservatism Among the Iroquois at the Six Nations Reserve,* Yale University Publications in Anthropology, no. 65 (New Haven, Conn., 1961), esp. 261–88; Bruce G. Trigger, *The Children of Aataentsic: A History of the Huron People to 1660,* 2 vols. (Montreal, 1976), 1: 66–67, 81, 424–25, 500, 534–44, 589–601, 646, 657, 696, 708, 715–19; Elisabeth Tooker, *An Ethnography of the Huron Indians, 1615–1649, Bureau of American Ethnology Bulletin* 190 (Washington, D.C., 1964), 117–20. The latter two works focus on the culturally similar Iroquoians, the Hurons; most scholars of the seventeenth-century Iroquois, facing gaps in the documentary record, accept generalizations about Iroquois culture that draw on evidence from other related Iroquoians, especially the Hurons. The secondary works listed above base their discussion of Iroquoian witchcraft belief and practice in the seventeenth and eighteenth centuries on extensive contemporary references to such Native belief and practice. See esp. Reuben Gold Thwaites, trans. and ed., *The Jesuit Relations and Allied Documents,* 73 vols. (Cleveland, 1896–1901).

14. See esp. Wallace, *Death and Rebirth of the Seneca,* 76–77, 84; Shimony, *Conservatism Among the Iroquois,* 261–62. Shimony observed first hand, during her fieldwork in the late 1950s, "an almost paranoid undercurrent of suspicion, in which each person sees his health and good fortune and even his life threatened by someone or something."

15. According to Halliday Jackson, *Civilization of the American Natives,* 42, by

1801 Handsome Lake had "acquired considerable influence in the nation, so as to be appointed high priest and chief Sachem in things civil and religious"; see also ibid., 47, 50. In a 23 January 1803 letter written by Quaker missionary Jacob Taylor for Handsome Lake to the Indian Committee, the prophet asserted that the "principal part of the Sineca Nation have agreed to be under his [the prophet's] Government— and nothing in the future of any Consequences that relates to the Sineca is to be transacted without the Knowledge and approbation of Conudiu [Handsome Lake]" (IC Records, box 2). Jonathan Thomas to Thomas Wistar, representing the Indian Committee (4/21/1804), IC Records, box 2, noted that the prophet "does not pretend to have many visions of late, but his influence is great over most of the Indians of the Seneca nation and even to others of the six nations."

16. The 1808 execution is mentioned in a footnote to Deardorff and Snyderman, "Nineteenth-Century Journal [1806]," 598 n. 18; Cornplanter's speech appears in report to the Indian Committee (10/19/1809), IC Records, box 2; Joel Swain et al. to the Committee (8/16/10), IC Records, box 2, provides a follow-up.

17. See Jackson, *Civilization of the Indian Natives*, 43; Jonathan Thomas to Thomas Wistar [4/21/1804], IC Records, box 2); Elisabeth Tooker, "On the Development of the Handsome Lake Religion," *Proceedings of the American Philosophical Society* 133: 1 (1989), 45. On the dangers early nineteenth-century Senecas faced— especially to their lands and sovereignty—see, for example, State of New York, "In Assembly, March 4, 1818. Report Relative to Indian Affairs," copy in IC Records, box 3.

18. John M. Murrin, "A Roof Without Walls: The Dilemma of American National Identity," in Richard Beeman, Stephen Botein, and Edward C. Carter II, eds., *Beyond Confederation: Origins of the Constitution and American National Identity* (Chapel Hill, N.C., 1987), 333–48, quotations at 334, 347.

19. Abler, *Chainbreaker*, 153–56; Laurence M. Hauptman, *Conspiracy of Interests: Iroquois Dispossession and the Rise of New York State* (Syracuse, N.Y., 1999), 63–66; the treaty is printed in *American State Papers: Documents, Legislative and Executive of the Congress of the United States*, 38 vols. (Washington, D.C., 1832–61), Class 2: *Indian Affairs*, 2 vols. (1832–34), 1: 10. J. David Lehman, "The End of the Iroquois Mystique: The Oneida Land Cession Treaties of the 1780s," *William and Mary Quarterly* 3d ser., 47 (1990), 523–47. See also Christopher Densmore, *Red Jacket: Iroquois Diplomant and Orator* (Syracuse, 1999), 23–24; Graymont, *The Iroquois in the American Revolution*, 282–83.

20. Densmore, *Red Jacket*, 23–24. "Trade and Intercourse Act" (22 July 1790) [U.S. Statutes at Large, 1: 137–38], reprinted in Francis Paul Prucha, ed., *Documents of United States Indian Policy*, 2d ed. (Lincoln, Nebr., 1990), 14–15.

21. These speeches, delivered in Philadelphia between December 1790 and February 1791, are conveniently reproduced from the *American State Papers, Indian Affairs*, 1: 140–45, as app. 3 in Abler, *Chainbreaker*, 238–59. See Abler's useful introduction and Governor Blacksnake's recollection of the events, ibid., 160–62, 174–80, quotations at 242, 253, 239–40, 247. Ultimately Chief Justice John Marshall's 1823 opinion in *Johnson v. McIntosh* firmly established the principle that tribes held an ownership interest in their aboriginal lands superior to all but that of the United States itself, and as a result tribes could sell their lands, not to individuals or even to states, but exclusively to the federal government, see Charles F. Wilkinson, "Indian

Tribes and the American Constitution," in Frederick E. Hoxie, ed., *Indians in American History* (Arlington Heights, Ill., 1988), 120–21.

22. Densmore, *Red Jacket*, 41–45, discusses and assesses the treaty, which is conveniently reprinted as app. B, 131–34, quotation at 132. See also Jack Campisi and William A. Starna, "On the Road to Canandaigua: The Treaty of 1794," *American Indian Quarterly* 19 (1995), 467–90.

23. The origins of the nickname are "shrouded in mystery," according to Milton M. Klein, who noted some references dating as early as the 1780s (Washington apparently called New York the "Seat of the Empire" in 1785 and, later in the 1790s, the "Pathway to Empire"). By the completion of the Erie Canal in 1825 (and perhaps as early as 1819), the name Empire State was universally acknowledged. See Milton M. Klein, ed., *The Empire State* (Ithaca, N.Y., 2001), xix.

24. Hauptman, *Conspiracy of Interests*, 60–63, quotation at 62; Barbara Graymont, "New York State Indian Policy after the Revolution," *New York History* 58 (October 1976), 438–74.

25. Hauptman, *Conspiracy of Interests*, 62–81.

26. Quoted in ibid., 65.

27. Jefferson to William Henry Harrison, 27 Feb. 1803, in Prucha, *Documents of U.S. Indian Policy*, 22–23. See generally Richard White, *The Roots of Dependency: Subsistence, Environment, and Social Change Among the Choctaws, Pawnees, and Navajos* (Lincoln, Nebr., 1983).

28. *Albany Centinel*, 20 August 1802; ibid., August 24 24 1802; ibid., 3 September 1802 (quotation). At the end of the 3 September 1802 story, reprinted from the *Ontario Gazette* of 12 August, the reporter added, "At these and subsequent meetings, they [Seneca and other Iroquois leaders] still continue to insist, in long speeches, upon their entire independence of the state of New-York."

29. Quoted in Densmore, *Red Jacket*, 61–63.

30. William L. Stone, *The Life and Times of Red-Jacket, or Sa-Go-Ye-Wat-Ha; being the Sequel to the History of the Six Nations* (New York, 1841), 316; the incident is treated on 316–22. See also Robert W. Bingham, *The Cradle of the Queen City: A History of Buffalo to the Incorporation of the City*, Publications of the Buffalo Historical Society, vol. 31 (1931), 386–88. We know little about the victim beyond her sex and her alleged witchcraft. The murder was reported in the *Spirit of the Times* (Batavia, N.Y.), 11 May 1821, and the *Ontario Repository* (Canandaigua, N.Y.), 15 May 1821. Tommy Jemmy was well known locally for his travel to England with the Storrs & Co. Indian Show in 1818. Thanks to Paul Johnson for generously sharing newspaper clippings detailing these events.

31. Densmore, *Red Jacket*, 95–96.

32. Stone, *Life and Times of Red-Jacket*, 321–22; and see Stone's 1866 edition of the same work, 386–88; Bingham, *The Cradle of the Queen City*, 388; Densmore, *Red Jacket*, 96–97; *Albany Argus*, 17 August 1821. On the ramifications of the case for Indian law, see Sidney L. Harring, *Crow Dog's Case: American Indian Sovereignty, Tribal Law, and United States Law in the Nineteenth Century* (Cambridge, 1994), esp. 37–38.

33. Harring, *Crow Dog's Case*, 26–34. This principle would be more definitively established in *ex parte Crow Dog* (1883). Tribes' independence from state authority

and jurisdiction would erode over time, culminating in 1952 in Public Law 280, which extended state criminal jurisdiction over reservations in certain states.

34. Harring, *Crow Dog's Case*, 32–33.

35. See Francis Paul Prucha, "Andrew Jackson's Indian Policy: A Reassessment," *Journal of American History* 56 (1969), 527–39, though his interpretation of Jackson generally is unconvincingly apologetic. Jackson's friendly treatment of Georgia, despite Georgia's assertion of state sovereignty and its rejection of U. S. law, contrasted sharply with his conduct toward South Carolina in the nearly simultaneous Nullification Crisis. Focusing here on Cherokee challenges to Georgia rather than on Georgia's challenge to U.S. authority, Jackson wrote, "I have been unable to perceive any sufficient reason why the Red man more than the white, may claim exception from the municipal laws of the state within which they reside." The best recent treatment of Jackson is Andrew Burstein, *The Passions of Andrew Jackson* (New York, 2003).

36. Seneca Speeches, in Abler, *Chainbreaker*, 239.

37. Jefferson to Governor William Henry Harrison, 27 February 1803, in Jefferson, *Writings*, ed. Merrill D. Peterson (New York, 1984), 1118.

Introduction to Part IV

1. Rogers M. Smith, *Civic Ideals: Conflicting Visions of Citizenship in U.S. History* (New Haven, Conn., 1997), 30–31.

2. Peter N. Riesenberg, *Citizenship in the Western Tradition: Plato to Rousseau* (Chapel Hill, N.C., 1992), xix. Scholars' emphasis on the logically inclusive tendencies in American citizenship is discussed in Smith, *Civic Ideals*, 15–16. For a critique of this liberal narrative, see Kunal M. Parker, "State, Citizenship, and Territory: The Legal Construction of Immigrants in Antebellum Massachusetts," *Law and History Review* 19 (2001), 584–85.

3. Benedict R. O'G Anderson, *Imagined Communities: Reflections on the Origin and Spread of Nationalism* (New York, 1991), 156. Karen Sykes, "Paying a School Fee Is a Father's Duty: Critical Citizenship in Central New Ireland," *American Ethnologist* 28 (2001), 6.

4. Michel Foucault, *The History of Sexuality: Vol. 1, An Introduction* (New York, 1990), 103.

Chapter 9. Early Modern Spanish Citizenship

This chapter is a short, summarized version of some of the findings I describe in *Defining Nations: Immigrants and Citizens in Early Modern Spain and Spanish America* (New Haven, Conn., 2003). Copyright 2003 by Yale University. I would like to thank Yale University Press for its permission to use parts of this book.

1. Please note that this chapter describes practices of local citizenship (*vecindad*) in Castilian and Spanish American local communities. Although it mentions Spanishness (the condition of being a Spaniard, that is, a *natural de los reinos*), it

334 Notes to Pages 205–207

does not deal with this category. The classification of individuals as Spanish or non-Spanish was a complicated affair that did not necessarily depend on their birthplace or genealogy. Spanishness as a status, as well as the relationship between citizenship and Spanishness (*vecindad* and *naturaleza*), is explored in Herzog, *Defining Nations*, 64–118.

2. This category and many others are studied in Herzog, *Defining Nations*.

3. Lyle N. McAlister, *Spain and Portugal in the New World, 1492–1700* (Minneapolis, 1984), 3–40; Mark A. Burkholder and Lyman L. Johnson *Colonial Latin America* (New York, 2001), 23–32.

4. James Lockhart and Stuart Schwartz, for example, state that "the Caribbean phase [of the conquest] becomes even more complex because the Spaniards were not a previously immobile people occupying their first new area. Rather, they were inclined to view the Caribbean in the light of their own already established tradition of expansion, mainly 'reconquest'" Lockhart and Schwartz, *Early Latin America: A History of Colonial Spanish America and Brazil* (Cambridge, 1983), 62.

5. Charles Gibson, for example, states that "in Spain, Christian knights had acquired jurisdiction over lands and people captured from the Moors in a form sometimes known as encomienda. In America, occupation took place under conditions similar to those of the Spanish *reconquista* and it yielded a comparable solution . . . But . . . colonial solutions came to be more significant and more controversial than the prototype of the parent countries. With respect to encomienda, the differences are to be explained by the tradition of African enslavement, by the availability of large numbers of American natives, by their extreme vulnerability to Spanish demands, and by the need for creating, provisioning and housing a society in a new environment" (Gibson, *Spain in America* [New York, 1966], 50).

6. John Lynch, for example, refers mainly to the economic importance of the Americas in *Spain Under the Habsburgs: Spain and America, 1598–1700* (Oxford, 1981 [1969]). A somewhat similar approach is adopted by J. H. Elliot in *Imperial Spain, 1495–1716* (London, 2002 [1963]).

7. Despite many similarities, local citizenship practices differed in each of the Spanish kingdoms and Crowns. The practices I describe here were particular to Castile.

8. *Recopilación de Indias*, law 28, title 27, book 9 of 1596, refers to "natives of our kingdoms of Castile, León, Aragón, Valencia, Catalonia, Navarra, Mallorca and Menorca." Administrative and judicial records identify this group as including all individuals "natives of the kingdoms of Spain." Scholars disagree whether before this declaration natives of the Crown of Aragón were permitted to emigrate and to trade in the New World. On this point, see Demetrio Ramos Pérez, "La aparente exclusión de los aragoneses de las Indias: Una medida de alta política de don Fernando el Católico," *Estudios* (1976), 7–40; Juan M. Morález Álvarez, *Los extranjeros con carta de naturaleza de las Indias durante la segunda mitad del siglo XVIII* (Caracas, 1980), 22–24; Joseph de Veitia Linaje, *Norte de la contratación de las Indias occidentales* (Buenos Aires, 1945 [1672]), 328–29. Natives of Spanish America were considered natives of Castile.

9. The category of natives of the kingdoms of Spain was studied in Herzog, *Defining Nations*, 64–118. The relationship between this category and Creolism is described on 145–52.

10. Angus MacKay, *Spain in the Middle Ages: From Frontier to Empire, 1000–1500* (London, 1977); Jocelyn N. Hillgarth, *The Spanish Kingdoms, 1250–1516* (Oxford,

1976–78); and José Ángel García Cortázar, ed., *Organización social del espacio en la España medieval: La corona de Castilla en los siglos VIII a XV* (Barcelona, 1985).

11. Julio González, *Repoblación de Castilla la Nueva* (Madrid, 1976); Eduardo Hinojosa, *El orígen del régimen municipal en León y Castilla* (Madrid, 1896); José María Lacarra de Miguel, "Acerca de la atracción de pobladores a las ciudades fronterizas de la España Cristiana (siglos XI–XII)," in *La España medieval: Estudios en memoria del profesor don Salvador de Moxó* (Madrid, 1982), 2: 485–98.

12. Moisés García Rives, "La condición jurídica de los extranjeros en Castilla y León desde el fuero de León (1920) al código de las Partidas," *Revista de Ciencias Jurídicas y Sociales* 3 (1920), 245–83, 320–55; Manuel Álvarez y Valdés, *La extranjería en la historia del derecho español* (Oviedo, 1992), 153, 189–212, 319–70. In 1476, for example, Abenjamin Abenyahion, a Jew, become *vecino* of Murcia, where another Jew was also accepted in 1479. Luis Rubio García, *Los judíos de Murcia en la baja edad media (1350–1500)* (Murcia, 1992), 94,143, docs. 908,1009. I would like to thank David Nirenberg for sending me these references.

13. Rafael Gibert y Sánchez de la Vega, "Libertades urbanas y rurales en León y Castilla durante la edad media," in *Les libertés urbaines et rurales du XIe au XIVe siècle. Colloque international Spa 5–8.IX.1966, Actes,* 187–218 (Brussels, 1968); Alberto García Ulecia, *Los factores de diferenciación entre las personas en los fueros de la Extramadura castellano-aragonesa* (Seville, 1975); María Trinidad Gacto Fernández, *Estructura de la población de la Extramadura leonesa en los siglos XII y XIII* (Salamanca, 1977); Antonio Sacristán y Martínez, *Municipalidades de Castilla y León: Estudio histórico-crítico* (Madrid, 1981), 258–63; María del Cármen Carte, *Del consejo medieval castellano-leonés* (Buenos Aires, 1968), 81–87.

14. The evolution of Castilian local law is described in José Manuel Pérez-Prendes y Muñoz-Arraco, *Historia del derecho español* (Madrid, 1999), 2: 670–878. The reception of ius commune in Castile is studied in José María Font Rius, "La recepción del derecho romano en la peninsula ibérica durante la edad media," in *Recueil des mémoires et travaux publiés par la Société d'Histoire du Droit et des Institutions des Anciens Pays de Droit Écrit* 6 (1967), 85–104; Bartolomé Clavero, "Notas sobre el derecho territorial castellano, 1367–1445," *Historia, instituciones, documentos* 3 (1976), 3–25; Carlos Petit, "Derecho común y derecho castellano. Notas de literatura jurídica para su estudio (siglo XV–XVIII)," *Tijdschrift Voor Rechtsgeschiedenis* 50 (1982), 157–95.

15. The codification of citizenship practices is described in Miguel Ángel Ladero Quesada, *Historia de Sevilla: La ciudad medieval (1248–1492)* (Seville, 1989), 128–29, 133, 137–40; Cármen Losa Contreras, *El consejo de Madrid en el tránsito de la edad media a la edad moderna* (Madrid, 1999), 479–84; Ricardo Izquierdo Benito, *Un espacio desordenado: Toledo a fines de la edad media* (Toledo, 1996), 39–47; María Jesús Fuente Pérez, *Palencia: Cien años de vida y gobierno de la ciudad (1421–1521) através de las actas municipales* (Palencia, 1987), 29–33; Juan A. Bonachia Hernando, *El consejo de Burgos en la baja edad media (1345–1426)* (Valladolid, 1978); and Luisa Navarro de la Torre, "Avecindamientos en Huete al comenzar el siglo XV," in José Hinojosa Montalvo and Jesús Pradells Nadal, eds., *1490, en el umbral de la modernidad. El mediterráneo europeo y las ciudades en el tránsito de los siglos XV–XVI* (Valencia, 1994), 2: 693–711.

16. David E. Vassberg, *The Village and the Outside World in Golden Age Castile:*

Mobility and Migration in Everyday Rural Life (New York, 1996), 14–23; Helen Nader, *Liberty in Absolutist Spain: The Habsburg Sale of Towns, 1516–1700* (Baltimore, 1993), 27–29.

17. Exceptions include day laborers, shepherds and salaried professionals such as surgeons who emigrated from one community to another according to the demands of their profession. According to some (although not all) people, given the interested nature of their association with the community and its circumscription by time, even if heads of households they could not, by definition, become citizens. Herzog, *Defining Nations*, 38–40; Herzog, "Vecindad y oficio en Castilla: La libertad económica y la exclusión política en el siglo XVIII," in José Ignacio Fortea et al., eds., *Furor et rabies: Violencia, conflicto y marginación en la época moderna* (Cantabria, 2002), 239–52.

18. Archivo de la Villa de Madrid (hereafter AVM), secretaría 2–348–23.

19. Pedro Fernández Navarrete, *Conservación de monarquías y discursos políticos*, ed. Michael D. Gordon (Madrid, 1982 [1792]), 87.

20. This was, indeed, the main argument employed to justify the rejection of Gypsies. See Herzog, *Defining Nations*, 128–33; Alfonso García Gallo, *Los orígenes españoles de las instituciones americanas. Estudios de derecho indiano* (Madrid, 1987), 1006.

21. Francisco Vitoria, "On the American Indians," in Anthony Pagden and Jeremy Lawrance, eds., *Francisco de Vitoria: Political Writings* (Cambridge, 1991 [1539]), 239–92.

22. José María Monsalvo Antón, *Ordenanzas medievales de Ávila y su tierra* (Avila, 1990), 85, Ordinance 17; Pedro A. Porras Arboleda, ed., *Ordenanzas de la muy noble, famosa, y muy leal ciudad de Jaén guarda y defendimiento de los reinos de Castilla* (Granada, 1993 [1573]), 94–95, Ordinance 55; Juan Luis Espejo Lara and Eva Morales Gordillo, eds., *Ordenanzas de Archidona (1598)* (Málaga, 1998), 86.

23. See, for example, petitions of Juan Joseph Martín, 9 December 1767 and Felix Durán, discussed 27 May 1768, both in Archivo Municipal de Sevilla (hereafter AM/S), sec. 5 (Escribanía de Cabildo XVIII [hereafter Ecab. XVIII]), t. 298; AVM, Secretaría 2–348–36; Archivo de la Chancillería de Valladolid (hereafter ACV), Pleitos Civiles–Fernández Alonso (Fenecidos) (hereafter PC-FA[F]) 3059–3, 7; ACV, Pleitos Civiles–Pérez Alonso (Olvidados) (hereafter PC–PA[O]) 260—1.

24. ACV, Pleitos Civiles–Pérez Alonso (fenecidos) (hereafter PC–PA[F]) 3401–3.

25. ACV, PC–PA(F) 3508–1.

26. ACV, PC–PA(F) 3401–1, 15–16.

27. Opinion of Luis Verdugo, 10 February 1702 in AVM, Secretaría 2–348–23.

28. Ibid.

29. Petition of Germán Salcedo, 20 July 1788 in ACV, PC–PA(F) 3522–1. Lorenzo Santayana Bustillo, *Gobierno político de los pueblos de España y el corregidor alcalde y juez en ellos*, (Madrid, 1979 [1742]), 7, citing the works of Acevedo, Avedaño and Paz arrives at a similar conclusion according to which individuals "must be received as citizens."

30. Álvarez y Valdés, *La extranjería*, 153, 183–262.

31. Bartolomé French, native of Ireland, was accepted as a citizen of Seville in 1743 and Diego Roberto Tolosa, native of France, became a citizen of Malagá in 1748: city council meetings of 22 May 1743, AM/S, sec. 5 (Ecab. XVIII), t. 296; 22 January

1785, Archivo General de Simancas, Gracia y Justicia 873, respectively. See also ACV, PC–PA(O) 579–10.

32. Allegations of Joseph Corvillos on 22 January 1783, ACV, PC–PA(O), 579–10.

33. Helmut Koenigsberger, "Spain," in Orest Ranum, ed., *National Consciousness, History and Political Culture in Early Modern Europe* (Baltimore, 1975), 144–72; Koenigsberger, "National Consciousness in Early Modern Spain" in Koenigsberger, *Politicians and Virtuosi: Essays in Early Modern History* (London, 1986), 121–47; Stanley G. Payne, *Spanish Catholicism: An Historical Overview* (Madison, Wis., 1984), 3–70; Chiara Continisio and Cesare Mozzarelli, eds., *Repubblica e virtú: Pensiero politico e Monarchia Cattolica fra XVI e XVII secolo* (Rome, 1995); José María Portillo Valdés, "Los límites de la monarquía: Catecismo de estado y constitución política en España a finales del siglo XVIII," *Quaderni Fiorentini* 25 (1996), 183–263.

34. Juan de Mariana, *Del rey y de la instutición real* (Madrid, 1950 [1598]), 570–71.

35. Fernando Armas (Asin), "Herejes, marginales, e infectos: Extranjeros y mentalidad excluyente en la sociedad colonial (siglos XVI y XVII)," *Revista Andina* 15 (1997), 355–86.

36. The citizenship of *conversos* was studied in Herzog, *Defining Nations*, 124–28. On the role of *limpieza de sangre* categories in discussions regarding citizenship, see 27–28.

37. "Índice de los dos tomos de comercio de extranjeros en España," in Archivo Histórico Nacional, estado 647/16, ch. 33, and Archivo General de la Nación/ Buenos Aires (hereafter AGN/BA) 9–35–3–6. See also Charlotte de Castelnau, "Les étrangers protestants dans l'Espagne moderne (16e–17e siècles)," in Jean Frédéric Schaub, ed., *Recherche sur l'histoire de l'état dans le monde ibérique (15e–20e siècle)* (Paris, 1993), 143–62 ; and Leonora de Alberti and A. B. Wallis Chapman, "English Traders and the Spanish Canary Inquisition in the Canaries During the Reign of Queen Elizabeth," *Transactions of the Royal Historical Society*, 3rd ser., 3 (1909), 237–53.

38. Jorge E. Hardoy, *El proceso de urbanización en América Latina* (Havana, 1974); José Luis Romero, *Latinoamérica: Las ciudades y las ideas* (Mexico, 1976); Francisco Domínguez Company, *Política del poblamiento de España en América* (Madrid, 1984); Javier Aguilera Rojas, *Fundación de ciudades hispanoamericanas* (Madrid, 1994).

39. José Rumazo González, *Libro primero de cabildos de Quito* (Quito, 1934), 49–50; Carmelo Sáenz de Santa María, *Libro viejo de la fundación de Guatemala* (Guatemala, 1991), 19–20.

40. On 17 June 1536, Hernando Sarmiento presented himself to the authorities of Quito and asked to be accepted as a citizen. He attested that, it was well known that he would like to remain in the city: Rumazo González, *Libro primero*, 173–74. From 1541 onward, the authorities also demanded that newcomers supply a monetary guarantee that they would keep their promise to remain in the city. Town council meeting, 27 May 1541 in José Rumazo González, *Libro segundo de cabildos de Quito* (Quito, 1934), 2: 255.

41. Francisco Domínguez Company, "La condición de vecino: Su significación e importancia en la vida colonial hispanoamericana," in *Crónica del VI congreso histórico municipal interamericano (Madrid-Barcelona 1957)* (Madrid, 1959), 703–20;

Domínguez Company, *La vida en las pequeñas ciudades hispanoamericanas de la conquista 1494–1549* (Madrid, 1978), 51; Ángel Rosenblat, *La población indígena y el mestizaje en América* (Buenos Aires, 1954), 135; Oreste Carlos Cansanello, "De súbditos a ciudadanos. Los pobladores rurales bonarenses entre el antiguo régimen y la modernidad," *Boletín del Instituto de historia argentina y americana dr. Emilio Ravignani* 11 (1995), 113–39, 117.

42. Mexico City, Caracas, Quito, Lima, Buenos Aires, Santiago del Estero, and Guatemala.

43. The only study dedicated to Latin American citizenship is Domínguez Company, "La condición." Spanish American citizenship as a replica of Castilian medieval practices is described in John Preston Moore, *The Cabildo in Peru Under the Habsburgs: A Study in the Origins and Powers of the Town Council in the Viceroyalty of Peru, 1530–1700* (Durham, N. C., 1954), 15–16, 141–42. Its transformation into a purely honorary title was mentioned in Fred Bronner, "Peruvian Encomenderos in 1630: Elite Circulation and Consolidation," *Hispanic American Historical* Review 57 (1977), 633–59, 640 (herafter *HAHR*).

44. Robert J. Ferry, *The Colonial Elites of Early Caracas: Formation and Crisis, 1567–1767* (Berkeley, 1989), 1–68; John V. Lombardi, *Venezuela: The Search for Order, the Dream of Progress* (New York and Oxford, 1982), 70–94; *Hacienda y comercio de Venezuela en el siglo XVII, 1601–1650* (Caracas, 1986), 5: 47–56.

45. The following is based on a study of municipal records, mainly the multivolumed *Actas del cabildo de Caracas* (hereafter *ACC*) (Caracas, 1943, 1950–69).

46. Petitions of Fernando Sanz, dated June 22, 1592 and Bartolomé Masbel, dated 7 December 1592 in *ACC* (Caracas, 1943), 1: 192–93, 210–11, respectively.

47. Petitions of Iñigo de Sosa, 8 May 1593, and Baltazar García, 24 May 1593 in *ACC*, 1: 258–59.

48. Petition of Fernán de Zárate (represented by Nofre Carrasques), 22 May 1597 *ACC*, 1: 456–57 and 459–60.

49. Petition of Lope Díaz de León 20 October 1608, *ACC*, 3: 141–42.

50. The case of Manuel de Lemos, 28 September 1651, *ACC*, 8: 97–98.

51. Petitions of Benito Hernández, 12 January 1609, and Bernave de Oñate Mendisabal, 6 December 1611, *ACC*, 3: 165–66 and 332, respectively; petition of Jorge Amaro, 16 January 1655, *ACC*, 9: 13–14.

52. Petition of Tomás de Aponte, 22 May 1597, *ACC*, 1: 457.

53. Petition of Francisco Carbajar, 30 January 1606, *ACC*, 3: 8–9.

54. Petition of Cristóbal Martínez, 16 January 1649, *ACC*, 7: 281–82.

55. Petition of Captain Luis Fernández Ángel of March 26, 1648 in *ACC*, VII, 193–94.

56. Petition of Francisco López, 27 January 1652, *ACC*, 7: 147; and the discussion in the council meeting 11 March 1652 concerning Juan Rodríguez in *ACC*, 8: 154–211, esp. 163–64, 175–76, and 192.

57. Magnus Mörner, *La Corona española y los foráneos en los pueblos de indios de América* (Madrid, 1999 [1970]); Mörner, "La difusión del castellano y el aislamiento de los indios. Dos aspiraciones contradictorias de la corona española," in *Homenaje a Jaime Vicens Vives*, (Barcelona, 1967), 435–46; and Tamar Herzog, "On Indians and Cowboys: El papel del indígena en el derecho e imaginario hispano-colonial," in *Oltremare: Cultura e istituzioni dal colonialismo all'età postcoloniale* (Naples, forthcoming).

58. Christopher H. Lutz, *Santiago de Guatemala, 1541–1773: City, Caste, and the Colonial Experience* (Norman, Okla., 1994); Magnus Mörner, "Ethnicity, Social Mobility, and Mestizaje in Spanish Colonial History," in Felix Becker, Holger M. Meding, Barbara Potthast-Jutkeit, and Karin Schüller, eds., *Iberische Welten: Festschrift zum 65. Geburtstag von Günter Kahle* (Cologne, 1994), 301–14; and Jacques Poloni-Simard, "Formación, desarrollo y configuración socio-étnica de una ciudad colonial. Cuenca, siglos XVI–XVIII," *Anuario de estudios americanos* 54 (1997), 413–45; Poloni-Simard, *La mosaïque indienne: Mobilité, stratification sociale, et métissage dans le corregimiento de Cuenca (Équateur) du XVIe au XVIIIe siècle* (Paris, 2000).

59. For example, the case of Juan Alonso 7 April 1616 in *ACC*, 4: 101–3.

60. Jorge Gelman, "Cabildo y élite local. El caso de Buenos Aires en el siglo XVII," *Revista latinoamericana de historia económica y social* 6 (1985), 3–20; R. de Lafuente Marchain, *Los portugueses en Buenos Aires (siglo XVII)* (Madrid, 1931); C. S Assadourian, G. Beato, and J. C. Chiaramonte, *Historia de Argentina de la conquista a la independencia* (Buenos Aires, 1996); David Rock, *Argentina 1516–1987: From Spanish Colonization to Alfonsín* (Berlekey, 1987 [1985]), 1–74; Guillermo Céspedes del Castillo, *Lima y Buenos Aires: Repercuciones económicas y políticas de la creación del virreinato de la Plata* (Seville, 1947).

61. This was the second foundation of the city. The first one (1535–41) failed, as settlers abandoned the jurisdiction because of the twin threats of starvation and hostile Indians.

62. The following is primarily based on the study of municipal records, available in the AGN/BA, Archivo del Cabildo (thereafter AC) and published in the multivolumed *Acuerdos del extinguido cabildo de Buenos Aires* (Buenos Aires, 1907–34).

63. Petitions of Amador Baes (1603) and Gil Gonzáls (1603) in AGN/BA, AC 19–1–4, 168, 171.

64. Town council meetings, 8 May 1589, and petition of Bartolomé Ramírez 14 May 1590 in *Acuerdos del extinguido cabildo de Buenos Aires*. Buenos Aires: Archivo General de la Nación, 1907, ser. 1, bk. 1, 20–21. Although these requirements were also practiced in other cities as shown in Francisco Domínguez Company, "Obligaciones militares de los vecinos hispanoamericanos en el siglo XV (según se desprende de las actas capitulares)," *Revista de historia de América* (México) 79 (1975), 37–61, they were especially important in Buenos Aires: Adolfo Garretón, *La municipalidad colonial: Buenos Aires desde su fundación hasta el gobierno de Lariz* (Buenos Aires, 1933), 64.

65. Petition of Domingo Santos 12 June 12 1607, *Acuerdos del extinguido cabildo de Buenos Aires*, ser. 1, bk.1, 383; and Lucas Pacheco 12 December 1618, *Acuerdos del extinguido cabildo de Buenos Aires*, ser. 4, bk. 3, 129.

66. The case of "Jacques cirujano," discussed in the meeting of 10 June1619, *Acuerdos del extinguido cabildo de Buenos Aires*, ser. 4, bk. 3, 231.

67. The Portuguese Gil González y Amador Váez was received in 1611 as a citizen: meeting of 9 May 1611, *Acuerdos del extinguido cabildo de Buenos Aires*, ser. 2, bks. 1–2, 348.

68. Petition of Pedro Fernández de Ocampo, 1 July 1611, *Acuerdos del extinguido cabildo de Buenos Aires*, ser. 2, bks. 1–2, 379.

69. The Spanish monopoly in the Americas will be discussed in the following pages.

70. Petitions of Julián Mixel, 11 January 1610, Rodrigo Alonso del Granado 21

June 1610, *Acuerdos del cabildo de Buenos Aires*, ser. 2, bks. 1–2, 230 and 266; Petition of Rodrigo Nuñez de León 10 February 1614, *Acuerdos del extinguido cabildo de Buenos Aires*, ser. 3, bks. 2–3, 62.

71. Petition of Antonio Heris Gabiria 19 August 1619 and 6 April 1620, *Acuerdos del extinguido cabildo de Buenos Aires*, ser. 4, bk. 3, 280–81, 373–74. See also the petition of Rafael Maldonado, 19 July 1617, AGN/BA, AC 19–1–4, 69.

72. The local authorities transferred the request to the representative of local interests (*procurador*), who answered it some 3 months later, affirming that people indeed could request a formal recognition of their citizenship. Meeting 12 March 1774, *Acuerdos del cabildo de Buenos Aires*, ser. 3, 5, bks. 36–40, 52 and 86.

73. See n. 42.

74. Moore, *The Cabildo in Peru*, 141; Clara López Beltrán, "Intereses y pasiones de los vecinos de La Paz durante el siglo XVII: La élite provinciana en Charcas, virreinato del Perú," *Anuario de estudios americanos* 52 (1995), 37–56, n. 37.

75. This is clear from Mexico's *Actas de Cabildo*. See also Robert Himmerich y Valencia, *The Encomenderos of New Spain* (Austin, Tex., 1991), 8–9, 102.

76. Peter Marzhal, *Town in the Empire: Government, Politics and Society in Seventeenth Century Popayan* (Austin, Texs., 1978), 37, 70–71, and 162–64.

77. Federica Morelli, *Territorio o nazione.: Riforma e dissoluzione dello spazio imperiale in Ecuador, 1765–1830* (Soveria Mannelli, 2001), 125; Jacques Poloni-Simard, "Problèmes et tentatives d'identification des métis à travers la documentation coloniale L'exemple de Cuenca," Bernard Lavallé, ed., *Transgressions et stratégies du métissage en Amérique coloniale* (Paris, 1999), 13.

78. The existence, despite local variations, of an "American pattern of development" was also noted in García Bernal, "Las elites capitulares indianas y sus mecanismos de poder en el siglo XVII," *Anuario de estudios americanos* 57 (2000), 89–110. Also see *Cédula* of 13 September 1621, reproduced in Richard Konetzke, *Colección de documentos para la historia de la formación social de hispanoamérica, 1493–1810* (Madrid, 1953), 2 (1): 265.

79. Benedict Anderson, *Imagined Communities* (London, 1991 [1983]), esp. "Creole Pioneers."

80. Town council meeting of 1 February 1549, in *Libros de cabildo de Lima* (Lima, 1935), ser. 4, 61–63; town meeting of 17 June 1536 in J. Rumazo, ed., *Libro primero de cabildos de Quito* (Quito, 1934), 173–74 and town meeting of 16 June 1617 in *Acuerdos del extinguido cabildo de Buenos Aires*, ser. 3, bks. 2–3, 441.

81. Town council meeting of 5 February 1599, in Jorge A. Garcés, ed., *Libro del ilustre cabildo, justicia y regimiento de este muy noble y muy leal ciudad de San Francisco de Quito* (Quito, 1937), 241–42, and David Noble Cook, ed., *Numeración general de todas las personas de ambos sexos, edades, y calidades que se ha hecho en esta ciudad de Lima, año de 1700* (Lima, 1985), which included both citizens and noncitizen residents.

82. Herzog, *Defining Nations*, 91–93, 206–7.

83. Ana María Barrero García, "De los fueros municipales a las ordenanzas de los cabildos indianos: Notas para su estudio," *Revista Chilena de Historia del Derecho* 11 (1985), 29–41; Francisco Domínguez Company, "Ordenanzas municipales

hispanoamericanas," *Revista de historia de América* 86 (1978), 9–60; Fernando Alejandro Vázquez Pando, "Derecho español en América, derecho castellano vulgar, y derecho indiano (una posible interpretación histórica)," *Revista de la facultad de derecho de México* 26 (1976), 785–94; and Víctor Tau Anzoátegui, "El derecho municipal del Perú: Apuntes sobre su configuración," in *IX congreso del Instituto Internacional de Historia del Derecho Indiano, Madrid, 5 a 10 de febrero de 1990* (Madrid, 1991), 1: 111–36.

84. Spanish American legislation, whether local or common to the entire continent, lacked instructions concerning citizenship. References to citizenship were lacking, for example, in the municipal ordinances of Quito (1568), Guayaquil (1590), and many Peruvian and Mexican communities. See Archivo Municipal de Quito, Miscelánea 00012, 63–72; the *residencia* of Joseph Clemente y Mora, Archivo General de Indias, Escribanía de Cámara 911B, 15–23; Roberto Levillier, *Ordenanzas de Don Francisco de Toledo, Virrey del Perú 1569–1581* (Madrid, 1929); *Libros de Cabildo de Lima*, bk. 11, 781–813 and bk. 12, 647–88; *Ordenanzas de buen gobierno dadas por Hernando Cortés para los vecinos y moradores de la Nueva España 1524* (Madrid, 1960). When citizenship was mentioned in Spanish American law, it was usually in order to explain its administrative and political implications, such as deciding how to count the inhabitants of a new settlement in order to know which status it should receive. See *Recopilación de Indias* law 6, title 10, bk. 4 and the *Nuavas ordenanzas de descubrimiento, población y pacificacón* of 13 July 1573, reproduced in Francisco de Solano, ed., *Normas y leyes de la ciudad hispanoamericana (1492–1600)* (Madrid, 1996), 208. Ordinance 93 reads: "Declaramos que se entienda por vecino el hijo o hija o hijos del nuevo poblador o sus parientes, dentro y fuera del cuarto grado teniendo sus casas y familias distintas y apartadas y siendo casados y teniendo cada uno casa por sí."

85. These issues are treated at greater length in Herzog, *Defining Nations*, 64–93.

86. The so-called Spanish monopoly in the Americas was instituted in a series of royal decrees that were later reproduced in the main Spanish colonial legal code, the *Recopilación de Indias*, title 27, bk. 9. See also Richard Konetzke, "Legislación sobre inmigración de extranjeros en América durante la época colonial," *Revista internacional de sociología*, 11–12 (1945), 269–99.

87. Herzog, "On Indians."

88. McAlister, *Spain and Portugal*, 153–54, 179, 395; Sabine MacCormack, *Religion in the Andes: Vision and Imagination in Early Colonial Peru* (Princeton, N.J., 1991), 8.

89. Such a feeling is portrayed, for example, in Catalina de Erauso, *Memoir of a Basque Lieutenant Nun. Transvestite in the New World*, trans. Michele Stepto and Gabriel Stepto (Boston, 1996).

90. Creole claims were mainly centered on issues of *naturaleza*, not *vecindad*. Herzog, *Defining Nations*, 145–52.

91. Herzog, *Defining Nations*, 64–93.

92. Anderson, *Imagined Communities*. With reference to Spain, a similar idea appeared, for example, in Thomas James Dandelet, *Spanish Rome, 1500–1700* (New Haven, Conn., 2001), 118–19.

Chapter 10. Natural Movements and Dangerous Spectacles

1. Dossier Cardeneau, E/62, Centre des Archives d'Outre-Mer, Aix-en-Provence, France (hereafter CAOM). The *maréchaussée* was a rural constabulary.

2. Such documentation was destroyed on royal order at several points during the Old Regime. M. L. E. Moreau de Saint-Méry, *Loix et constitutions des colonies françoises de l'Amérique sous le vent*, 6 vols. (Paris, 1784–90), 2:541, 3:103.

3. On the "thinkable" and "unthinkable," see Pierre Bourdieu, *Outline of a Theory of Practice*, trans. Richard Nice (Cambridge, 1977), 21–22, 77–78, 168–70.

4. I am using the phrase "economy of violence" to refer to the range of "thinkable" exchanges involving physical violence in a society, along with the totality of those exchanges and the place of each type of exchange within that totality. In formulating this concept, I have drawn upon Deborah A. Poole's analogies between violence and economic exchange, as well as the arguments of linguistic anthropologists such as Dell Hymes regarding "speech economies:" Poole, "Landscapes of Power in a Cattle-Rustling Culture of Southern Andean Peru," *Dialectical Anthropology* 12 (1988), 374; Hymes, "Directions in (Ethno-) Linguistic Theory," *American Anthropologist*, 66 (1964), 42–43.

5. For population figures, see John Garrigus, "Blue and Brown: Contraband Indigo and the Rise of a Free Colored Planter Class in French Saint-Domingue," *Americas* 50 (1993), 235.

6. *Acte de procuration*, 2 May 1774, E/62, CAOM; *Requête en plaint de Sr Huet*, 5 May 1774, E/62, CAOM. All translations are mine unless otherwise noted.

7. Michel Foucault, *Discipline and Punish: The Birth of the Prison*, trans. Alan Sheridan (New York, 1977), 3–69; Gene E. Ogle, "Slaves of Justice: Saint Domingue's Executioners and the Production of Shame," *Historical Reflections/Réflexions historiques* 29 (2003), 275–93.

8. *Requête en plaint de Sr Huet*, 5 May 1774, E/62, CAOM.

9. Ibid.

10. He was not the only *domingois* white to suffer this ignominy. At least one other such case occurred, and given the colony's poorest whites' limited access to royal justice, it is possible that such beatings occurred more frequently than the record allows. *Arrêt du Conseil Supérieur du Port-au-Prince*, 29 september 1761, F/3/272, CAOM.

11. Julian Pitt-Rivers, "Honour and Social Status," in J. G. Peristiany, ed., *Honour and Shame: The Values of Mediterranean Society* (Chicago, 1966), 31.

12. Orlando Patterson, *Slavery and Social Death: A Comparative Study* (Cambridge, Mass., 1982); Ogle, "Slaves of Justice."

13. Robert Chesnais, ed., *Le Code Noir* (Paris, 1998), 29.

14. For instance, in 1720, the conseil of Cap François condemned a slave to be hung for having struck a white, and in 1785, Port-au-Prince's conseil condemned a slave to have his fists cut off and to be broken alive for having killed a white. That said, much of the severity of punishments depended on the identities of the person assaulted and the slave's owner as a 1778 case in which a mulatto slave was condemned only to three days in the iron collar for having tried to drown another plantation's *économe* makes clear. Moreau de Saint-Méry, *Loix et constitutions*, 2:668; 6:706; *Arrêt du Conseil Supérieur du Port-au-Prince*, 26 March 1778, F/3/274, CAOM.

15. For a similar theoretical position, see Pitt-Rivers, "Honour and Social Status," 30–31.

16. *Informations,* 4 May 1774; *Addition d'informations,* 10 May 1774, E/62, CAOM.

17. Ibid.

18. Michel-René Hilliard d'Auberteuil, *Considérations sur l'état présent de la colonie française de Saint-Domingue, Ouvrage politique et législatif,* 2 vols. (Paris, 1776), 1:144–45.

19. Ibid., 145.

20. Moreau de Saint-Méry, *Loix et constitutions,* 2:648. This reference is to a manuscript note in Moreau de Saint-Méry's handwriting in a copy of his *Loix et constitutions* at the Centre des Archives d'Outre-Mer in Aix-en-Provence. Hereafter all such references will be designated by "MS note."

21. *Arrêt du Conseil Supérieur du Port-au-Prince,* 27 May 1765, F/3/272, CAOM. The colonial livre was worth 2/3 of a livre tournois. James E. McClellan III, *Colonialism and Science: Saint Domingue in the Old Regime* (Baltimore, 1992), vii–viii.

22. *Arrêt du Conseil Supérieur du Petit-Goave,* 12 March 1726, F/3/270, CAOM.

23. *Arrêt du Conseil Supérieur du Port-au-Prince,* 11 March 1780, F/3/275, CAOM.

24. Paul-Ulrich Dubuisson, *Nouvelles considérations sur Saint-Domingue, en réponse à celles de M. H. Dl.,* 2 vols. (Paris, 1780), 1:84–85.

25. *Précis de la conduite tenue et des excès commis par M. Cappé envers l'habitation Trémais,* 25 June 1780, E/62, CAOM.

26. The transcript does not preserve the words of inquisitor or interrogated. Questions and answers were translated into single sentences, reading: "Asked if . . . he replied . . ." It is possible that the clerk translated from Creole to French, although Raymond, a servant, might have spoken French. *Interrogatoire de Raymond par le Juge de Saint Marc,* 4 mai 1774, E/62, CAOM.

27. Ibid.

28. The category "free people of color" included all free people recognized as having some African ancestry. Including African-born freedmen and women as well as the legitimate children of white planters, they were not a homogeneous social group but were tied together by discriminatory legislation and social prejudice. John Garrigus, "A Struggle for Respect: The Free Coloreds of Pre-Revolutionary Saint Domingue, 1760–1769" (Ph.D. diss., Johns Hopkins University, 1988); Yvan Debbasch, *Couleur et liberté: Le jeu du critère ethnique dans un ordre juridique esclavagiste* (Paris, 1967).

29. *Mémoire sur la Police du Cap,* March 1787, A/1/3764, Service historique de l'Armée de terre, Château de Vincennes, France.

30. Julien Raimond, *Premier Mémoire au Ministre,* Semptember 1786, F/3/91, CAOM.

31. Hilliard d'Auberteuil, *Considérations,* 2:74.

32. Dubuisson, *Nouvelles considérations,* 2:52–53.

33. Moreau de Saint-Méry, *Loix et constitutions,* 5:84; 6:225, 373, 713.

34. MS note, Moreau de Saint-Méry, *Loix et constitutions,* 6:225.

35. Moreau de Saint-Méry, *Loix et constitutions,* 6:30–31.

36. I have found only one reference to a case in which a lower court convicted a white of killing a free black. This reference comes from a ministerial letter criticizing

the court's death sentence. While it is unclear what happened when this case reached the conseil supérieur, it is likely that the minister's advice to retry it was followed. In any case, the accused had run away. *Lettre du Ministre au Comte d'Argout et de Vaivre,* 11 May 1777, F/3/274, CAOM.

37. *Arrêt du Conseil Supérieur de Petit-Goave,* 8 November 1731, F/3/270, CAOM; *Arrêt du Conseil Supérieur de Saint-Domingue,* 2 January 1788, F/3/280, CAOM; Moreau de Saint-Méry, *Loix et constitutions,* 6:295, 370.

38. Hilliard d'Auberteuil, *Considérations,* 1:145; Raimond, *Premier mémoire,* September 1786, F/3/91, CAOM; *Arrêt du Conseil Supérieur du Cap François,* 23 February 1787, F/3/278, CAOM; Moreau de Saint-Méry, *Loix et constitutions,* 5:84; 6:30–31, 373, 713.

39. Moreau de Saint-Méry, *Loix et constitutions,* 6:225. The public chain was a colonial replacement for the metropolitan punishment of galley servitude.

40. An example of the first possibility is that of the free mulatto whipped, branded, and sold into slavery for having beaten a white. Ibid., 5:84. An example of the second was a case in which a mulatto policeman was convicted of striking his (presumably white) sergeant. After his status was investigated, he was declared to be a slave and sold. *Arrêt du Conseil Supérieur du Port-au-Prince,* 5 September 1786, F/3/277, CAOM.

41. *Interrogatoire de Cardeneau,* 14 May 1774, E/62, CAOM.

42. Ibid.

43. Justin Girod de Chantrans, *Voyage d'un Suisse dans les colonies d'Amérique,* ed. Pierre Pluchon (Paris, 1980 [1785]), 166.

44. *Arrêt du Conseil Supérieur du Port-au-Prince,* 10 September 1761, F/3/91, CAOM; *Arrêt du Conseil Supérieur du Port-au-Prince,* 9 March 1768, F/3/273, CAOM; *Arrêt du Conseil Supérieur du Port-au-Prince,* 4 December 1776, F/3/274, CAOM.

45. The term *mésallié* was applied to white men who married women of color. Hilliard d'Auberteuil, *Considérations,* 2:273–74.

46. See also *Mémoire sur la Police du Cap,* March 1787, A/1/3764, Service Historique de l'Armée de terre.

47. Hilliard d'Auberteuil, *Considérations,* 2:75n; Emilien Pétit, *Traité sur le gouvernement des esclaves,* 2 vols. (Paris, 1777), 2:282.

48. For a case from the colony's early history in which a royal officer's widow attempted to beat a nobleman with a broom, see Pierre de Vaissière, *Saint-Domingue: La société et la vie créoles sous l'ancien régime (1629–1789)* (Paris, 1909), 70–71. The nobleman fought back, standing up for his own social status.

49. See Gene E. Ogle, "Policing Saint Domingue: Race, Violence, and Honor in an Old Regime Colony" (Ph.D. diss., University of Pennsylvania, 2003), 349–403.

50. Moreau de Saint-Méry, *Loix et constitutions,* 1:150.

51. Ibid., 6:116.

52. *Arrêt du Conseil Supérieur de Saint Domingue,* 23 November 1787, F/3/279, CAOM.

53. Hilliard d'Auberteuil, *Considérations,* 2:144–45; *Lettre du Ministre aux Administrateurs,* 12 February 1789, F/3/281, CAOM; Saintard, *Essai sur les colonies françoises; ou discours politiques sur la nature du Gouvernement, de la Population, et du commerce de la Colonie de S. D.* (1754), 56.

54. Vaissière, *Saint-Domingue*, 93–152.

55. Their *de facto* immunity to court proceedings derived from the military nature of colonial government and the fact that they represented the king's authority and could not be subjected to the shaming procedures of criminal justice. They were occasionally subjected to a less public, more arbitrary discipline. Moreau de Saint-Méry, *Loix et constitutions*, 1:642–644, 656–657, 663, 666; *Extrait de la lettre de Hilliard d'Auberteuil au Ministre*, January 1778; *Mémoire*, 29 March 1778; *Lettre du Ministre aux Administrateurs*, 5 August 1778, E/222, CAOM.

56. *Arrêt du Conseil Supérieur de Léogane*, 17 November 1738, F/3/270, CAOM.

57. *Arrêt du Conseil Supérieur du Cap François*, 25 October 1785, F/3/276, CAOM.

58. Moreau de Saint-Méry, *Loix et constitutions*, 2:251, 267, 276.

59. I have found only one case in which a man of color was to do a reparation of honor to a white. It occurred in the 1750s, prior to the systematic hardening of racial categories that began a decade later. MS note, Moreau de Saint-Méry, *Loix et constitutions*, 4:163.

60. Dossier Cardeneau, E/62, CAOM.

61. *Exploit de l'absence de Cardeneau, 10 February 1775*, E/62, CAOM; Arlette Lebigre, *La justice du roi: La vie judiciaire dans l'ancienne France* (Paris, 1995), 158–76.

62. François Billacois, *The Duel: Its Rise and Fall in Early Modern France*, ed. and trans. Trista Selous (New Haven, Conn., 1990), 15–20, 72–75.

63. *Mémoire*, 1742, E/9, CAOM; *Lettre de Larnage et Maillart au Ministre*, 26 janvier 1742, E/115, CAOM; *Arrêt du Conseil Supérieur du Cap François*, 26 January 1787, F/3/278, CAOM; *Mémoire des habitants demandant brevets de rémission et graces des homicides*, 1685, C/9a/1, CAOM; *Lettre du Ministre à Monsieur de Vincent*, 21 October 1787, F/3/279, CAOM.

64. Moreau de Saint-Méry, *Loix et constitutions*, 4:342–43.

65. *Edit du Roi*, August 1679, F/3/269, CAOM.

66. *Edit du Roi*, February 1723, F/3/271, CAOM. On these attempts in the metropole, see Billacois, *Duel*, 95–111.

67. MS note, *Edit du Roi*, August 1679, F/3/269, CAOM; *Lettre du Ministre au Larnage et Maillart*, 11 May 1746, F/3/271, CAOM; Moreau de Saint-Méry, *Loix et constitutions*, 1:576.

68. Charles Frostin has noted that between 1777 and 1778, eighty fatal duels were fought in the colony. McClellan, *Colonialism and Science*, 321n. For other references to dueling identified as such, see *Lettre du Ministre au Larnage et Maillart*, 11 May 1746, F/3/271, CAOM; *Arrêt du Conseil Supérieur du Port-au-Prince*, 4 September 1786, F/3/277, CAOM; *Arrêt du Conseil Supérieur de Saint-Domingue*, 6 October 1788, F/3/280, CAOM; Moreau de Saint-Méry, *Loix et constitutions*, 1:576; 4:342–43, 413–14; 6:713; Moreau de Saint-Méry, *Description topographique, physique, civile, politique et historique de la partie française de l'isle Saint-Domingue*, ed. Blanche Maurel and Etienne Taillemite, 3 vols. (Paris, 1958 [1797]) 1:230–31; 2:543–44.

69. *Lettre du Ministre au Larnage et Maillart*, 11 May 1746, F/3/271, CAOM.

70. This ambivalence regarding the duel's legitimacy extended to the king and his ministers. For a case in which the minister of the navy approved of the deportation of a duelist instead of having him tried for the crime, see *Lettre du Ministre à Monsieur de Vincent*, 21 October 1787, F/3/279, CAOM. See also Billacois, *Duel*, 179.

71. For a disingenuous use of the "right" to duel as a critique of Saint Domingue's militias, see Hilliard d'Auberteuil, *Considérations*, 2:156.

72. *Arrêt du Conseil Supérieur du Cap François*, 26 January 1787, F/3/278, CAOM.

73. M. L. E. Moreau de Saint-Méry, *Moreau de St. Méry's American Journey [1793–1798]*, trans. and ed. Kenneth Roberts and Anna M. Roberts (Garden City, N.Y., 1947), 182–84.

74. MS note, *Arrêt du Conseil Supérieur de Saint-Domingue*, 6 October 1788, F/3/280, CAOM.

75. *Lettre de Larnage et Maillart au Ministre*, 26 January 1742, E/115, CAOM. Due to the resulting slipperiness of the judicial archive and the fact that detailed descriptions of "proper" duels in Saint Domingue are nearly nonexistent, I treat duels and other individual combats as points within a spectrum of practices, all of which adhered to similar dynamics and involved assumptions of the right of white men to defend their bodies and their honor with physical violence.

76. *Mémoire des habitants demandant brevets de remission et graces des homicides*, 1685, C/9a/1, CAOM.

77. *Lettre de Larnage et Maillart au Ministre*, 26 January 1742, E/115, CAOM; *Arrêt du Conseil Supérieur de Saint-Domingue*, 26 January 1787, F/3/278, CAOM. These conclusions are based upon my examination of fourteen cases of single combats from 1685 to 1788 whose documentation provides information regarding the identity of the combatants and, less often, the motives for and nature of their combat.

78. *Interrogatoire de Cardeneau*, 14 May 1774, E/62, CAOM.

79. *Interrogatoire de Raymond sur la sellette*, 2 March 1775, E/62, CAOM.

80. Pitt-Rivers, "Honour and Social Status," 21–22.

81. Moreau de Saint-Méry, *Description*, 1:70–71.

82. Billacois, *Duel*, 201–2. On the ritual implications, see David Geggus, "Haitian Voodoo in the Eighteenth Century: Language, Culture, Resistance," *Jahrbuch für Geschichte von Staat, Windschaft und Gesellschaft Weinamerikas* 28 (1991), 33–35.

83. Moreau de Saint-Méry, *Description*, 1:71.

84. For a view of Afro-Atlantic dance as military training, see John K. Thornton, "African Dimensions of the Stono Rebellion," *American Historical Review* 96 (1991), 1112 (hereafter *AHR*).

85. M. L. E. Moreau de Saint-Méry, *Recueil des vues des lieux principaux de la colonie françoise de Saint-Domingue, gravées par les soins de M. Ponce* (Paris, 1791). The choice of this engraving was conditioned by the fact that he had an English drawing of the more playful scene available.

86. On trickster traditions in the Anglophone Americas, see Philip D. Morgan, "British Encounters with Africans and African-Americans, Circa 1600–1780," in Bernard Bailyn and Philip D. Morgan, eds., *Strangers Within the Realm: Cultural Margins of the First British Empire* (Chapel Hill, N.C., 1991), 216–19.

87. Jean-Baptiste Labat, *Voyage aux Isles: Chronique aventureuse des Caraïbes, 1693–1705*, ed. and abr. Michel Le Bris (Paris, 1993 [1732]), 232–33.

88. Dubuisson, *Nouvelles considérations*, 1:85.

89. *Sentence définitive et appel*, 2 March 1775, E/62, CAOM.

90. This retrial probably resulted from the fact that the first judge had not properly completed the procedures to convict Cardeneau in absentia.

91. *Interrogatoire de Raymond sur la sellette,* 12 September 1775, E/62, CAOM; *Sentence définitive et appel,* 12 September 1775, E/62, CAOM.

92. *Arrêt du Conseil Supérieur du Port-au-Prince,* 20 October 1775, F/3/273, CAOM.

93. The comparative literature on single combats is vast. This chapter has benefited from the following: Billacois, *Duel;* Thomas W. Gallant, "Honor, Masculinity and Ritual Knife Fighting in Nineteenth-Century Greece," *AHR* (2000), 359–82; Kenneth S. Greenberg, *Honor and Slavery* (Princeton, N.J., 1996), 3–23; Lyman L. Johnson, "Dangerous Words, Provocative Gestures, and Violent Acts: The Disputed Hierarchies of Plebeian Life in Colonial Buenos Aires," in Lyman L. Johnson and Sonya Lipsett-Rivera, eds., *The Faces of Honor: Sex, Shame, and Violence in Colonial Latin America* (Albuquerque, 1998), 127–51; Robert A. Nye, *Masculinity and Male Codes of Honor in Modern France* (Berkeley, 1993), 15–30, 148–215; Bertram Wyatt-Brown, *Southern Honor: Ethics and Behavior in the Old South* (Oxford, 1982), 327–61.

94. *Avis des Administrateurs et Procureur-Générale du Roi du Conseil Supérieur du Port-au-Prince,* 10 November 1775, E/62, CAOM.

95. Yvan Debbasch, "Au coeur du 'gouvernement des esclaves': la souveraineté domestique aux Antilles françaises (XVIIe-XVIIIe siècles)," *Revue française d'Histoire d'Outre-Mer* 72 (1985), 31–53; Malick W. Ghachem, "Sovereignty and Slavery in the Age of Revolution: Haitian Variants on a Metropolitan Theme" (Ph.D. diss., Stanford University, 2001).

96. *Arrêts du Conseil Supérieur du Port-au-Prince,* 22 May 1777 and 12 June 1777; *Lettre du Ministre aux Administrateurs,* 10 April 1779, F/3/274, CAOM.

97. Charles Frostin, *Les Révoltes blanches à Saint-Domingue aux XVIIe et XVIIIe siècles* (Paris, 1975).

Chapter 11. Racial Passing

1. See Ann Twinam, *Public Lives, Private Secrets: Gender, Honor, Sexuality, and Illegitimacy in Colonial Spanish America* (Stanford, Calif., 1999), 51–55, for background on *gracias al sacar.* The Cámara was a sub council staffed by officials of the Council of the Indies that, among its other duties, made decisions on *gracias al sacar.* It was the full body of the Council of the Indies that issued royal decrees to successful applicants. Sometimes both groups are referred to as the Council and Cámara of the Indies.

2. One reprint can be found in Santos Rodulfo Cortés, *El regimen de "las gracias al sacar" en Venezuela durante el periodo hispánico* (Caracas, 1978), vol. 2:doc. 7.

3. Ann Stoler and Frederick Cooper, "Between Metropole and Colony: Rethinking a Research Agenda," in Stoler and Cooper, eds., *Tensions of Empire: Colonial Cultures in a Bourgeois World* (Berkeley, 1997), 7.

4. Ann Stoler, "Sexual Affronts and Racial Frontiers: European Identities and the Cultural Politics of Exclusion in Colonial Southeast Asia," in Stoler and Cooper, *Tensions of Empire,* 202.

5. To understand how they were located, see Twinam, *Public Lives,* app. 1.

6. The Crown approved 8, rejected 2, and tabled 5 applications submitted after 1795. There also were 11 precursor applications prior to 1795 (5 approved, 4

rejected, 2 tabled). Of the 26 total applications, 12 came from Venezuela, 6 from Cuba, 5 from Panama, and one each from Mexico, Guatemala, and Santa Fe. Also see Twinam, "Is Race a Defect?" Official and Popular Debates over Whitening in Late Colonial Spanish America" (paper presented at the annual meeting of the American Historical Association, Chicago, January 2003).

7. After the Venezuelan elites declared independence in 1810, the Spanish regent issued a decree in 1812 trying to win the loyalty of pardos and mulattoes for the monarchy, preparatory to peninsular attempts to retake the colony. That decree permitted pardos with the "necessary qualifications" to be admitted to the university and the seminary. Rodulfo Cortés, *El regimen de "las gracias al sacar,"* vol. 2, doc. 34, 1812.

8. Much of the following discussion is based on the five-volume collection of documents by Richard Konetzke, the classic source for colonial social history and the Rodulfo Cortes document collection on Venezuelan *gracias al sacar* themes. To be complete, this research still needs to be augmented by further consultation of the *cédularios*—lists of royal decrees issued in the colonial era—to fill in any gaps before eighteenth-century archival documents become accessible.

9. Richard Konetzke, *Colección de documentos para la historia de la formación social de hispanoamérica, 1493–1810* (hereafter *CD*) (Madrid, 1958–62), vol. 1, doc. 228, 1553.

10. Konetzke, *CD*, vol. 1, doc. 259, 1560; doc. 296, 1568.

11. Konetzke, *CD*, vol. 1, doc. 427, 1586.

12. Konetzke, *CD*, vol. 2–1, doc. 85, 1607.

13. Konetzke, *CD*, vol. 2–1, doc. 86, 1607.

14. Konetzke, *CD*, vol. 2–1, doc. 94, 1608.

15. Officially castas were intermediary groups (between the superior social status of Spaniards and inferior Natives) the product of combinations of sexual relationships between Spaniards, Africans, and Natives. While the castas were racially mixed, eighteenth-century popular custom rarely used the Spanish word for "race" to identify them. This was because Hispanic concepts of mixture were more fluid than Anglo counterparts so that casta status could include literally tens of words to identify supposedly precise variations of mixtures. An individual's caste status might vary according to circumstance: appearance, economic status, marital state, and social relationships might lead to upward or downward mobility during a lifetime. Nor, interestingly enough, was the Spanish word for race considered in whitening petitions. Rather Spanish officials invariably classified the status of being a pardo or quinterón as possessing a "defect"—an absence of whiteness that could be remedied as other absences (e.g. nobility or legitimate birth) by state action. See Twinam, "Is Race a Defect?"; also Douglas Cope, *The Limits of Racial Domination: Plebeian Society in Colonial Mexico City, 1660–1720* (Madison, Wis., 1994), 4–7.

16. Konetzke, *CD*, vol. 1, doc. 205, 1551.

17. Konetzke, *CD*, vol. 1, doc. 392, 1580; doc. 421, 1584; doc. 427, 1586.

18. Konetzke, *CD*, vol. 1, doc. 442, 1587.

19. Konetzke, *CD*, vol. 2–1, doc. 78, 1605; doc. 85, 1607; doc. 263, 1646; doc. 364, 1666; vol. 2–2, doc. 390, 1671; doc. 494, 1681; vol. 3–1, doc. 44, 1697.

20. Konetzke, *CD*, vol. 3–2, doc. 288, 1785.

21. Konetzke, *CD*, vol. 1, doc. 346, 1574.

22. Konetzke, *CD*, vol. 1, doc. 367, 1577; doc. 442, 1587; doc. 478, 1592; vol. 3–1, doc. 60, 1703.

23. Konetzke, *CD*, vol. 1, doc. 208, 1552; vol. 1, doc. 259, 1560; vol. 2–1, doc. 120, 1612.

24. Konetzke, *CD*, vol. 2–1, doc. 120, 1612; vol. 3–1, doc. 114, 1725.

25. There was a hierarchical component of *limpieza*, as the "commoner" was also excluded. However in the Indies this was usually not applicable, for once someone left a low-status occupation, they could pass out of that category.

26. Martínez traces a complicated seventeenth-century discourse concerning *limpieza de sangre* noting contradictory interpretations by legalists, the Inquisition, royal officials, and colonists as to the *limpieza* of Natives and Africans. She concludes that religious origin remained a fundamental definer of who did or who did not have *limpieza* through the seventeenth century. This differentiated Natives (who, in the official if historically inaccurate discourse, had fully accepted Catholicism and met *Limpieza* standards) from Africans, who (according to an also dubious historical reading) had been forcibly converted and did not fit under the cleanliness guidelines. See María Elena Martínez, "Religion, Purity, and 'Race': The Spanish Concept of Limpieza de Sangre in Seventeenth-Century Mexico and the Broader Atlantic World" (paper presented at the International Seminar on the History of the Atlantic World, Harvard University, 2000).

27. Archivo General de Indias (hereafter AGI), Santo Domingo 1474, n. 11, 1789, contains a traditional American rendering.

28. Albert A. Sicroff, *Los estatutos de limpieza de sangre: controversias entre los siglos XV XVII* (Madrid, 1985 [1979]), 293, quotes from Fray Gerónimo de la Cruz, who wrote a 1637 treatise on problems of proofs of nobility and *limpieza*.

29. Sicroff, *Los estatutos de limpieza de sangre*, 119–20, notes that *converso*s might enter but could not graduate from the Universities of Salamanca, Valladolid, and Toledo.

30. Konetzke, *CD*, vol. 3–1, doc. 205, 1768 reprints a royal order requiring that those enrolled in *colegios* and universities prove their *limpieza de sangre* and legitimacy before graduation.

31. Twinam, *Public Lives*, 11, 12, reviews some of the demography.

32. Plebeians also constructed their own versions of honor. See Lyman Johnson and Sonya Lipsett-Rivera, eds., *The Faces of Honor: Essays on Colonial Latin America* (Albuquerque, 1998).

33. For a larger discussion of private and public, see Twinam, *Public Lives*, 26–29. A number of Latin American colonial historians have noted the significance of the private/public divide: they include Richard Cicerchia, "Via familiar y prácticas conyugales, clases populares en una ciudad colonial Buenos Aires: 1800–1810," *Boletín del Instituto de Historia Argentina y Americana "Dr. E. Ravigani,"* 3rd ser., 2 (1990), 95 (for Argentina); María Emma Mannarelli, *Pecados Públicos: La ilegitimidad en Lima, siglo XVII* (Lima, 1994), 125 (for Peru); Alexandra Cook and Noble David Cook, *Good Faith and Truthful Ignorance, A Case of Transatlantic Bigamy* (Durham, N.C., 1991), 97 (for Peru); María Beatriz Nizza da Silva, "Filhos ilegítimos no brasil colonial," *Sociedade Brasileira de Pesquisa Histórica, Anais da XV Reuniao*

(1995), 123 (for Brazil); Pablo Rodrígues Jiménez, "Casa y orden cotidiano en el Nuevo Reino de Granada, s. XVIII," in Beatriz Castro Carvajal, ed., *Historia de la vida cotidiana en Colombia* (Bogotá, 1996), 125, 135–39 (for Colombia).

34. See Twinam, *Public Lives,* 66–73, 147–57, 185–99, 204–17, 228–31, for examples of passing in relation to birth. For sodomy, see Geoffry Spurling, "Honor, Sexuality, and the Colonial Church," in Lyman L. Johnson and Sonya Lipsett-Rivera, eds., *The Faces of Honor: Sex, Shame, and Violence in Colonial Latin America* (Albuquerque, 1998).

35. Barbara J. Fields, "Of Rogues and Geldings: AHR Forum," *American Historical Review* (hereafter *AHR*) 108 (2003), 1404.

36. Vélez de Guevara, quoted in José Antonio Maravall, *Poder, honor, y élites en el siglo XVII* (Madrid, 1989), 84.

37. Stoler "Sexual Affronts," 225.

38. I thank John Smolenski for pointing out this most important distinction.

39. Konetzke, *CD,* vol. 1, doc. 377, 1578.

40. Konetzke, *CD,* vol. 2–1, doc. 215; doc. 248, 1641.

41. See Ben Vinson III, *Bearing Arms for His Majesty: The Free-Colored Militia in Colonial Mexico* (Stanford, Calif., 2001), 132–72, for Mexican pardo militias and Konetzke, *CD,* vol. 2–2, doc. 387, 1670; doc. 402, 1672.

42. Konetzke, *CD,* vol. 2–1, doc. 313, 1657.

43. Vinson (*Bearing Arms,* 200) notes the change in terminology from mulatto to *moreno* as another example of the more favorable Crown attitude toward pardo military service.

44. Konetzke, *CD,* vol. 3–1, doc. 79, 1708; doc 98, 1717.

45. While pardos/mulattoes at lower levels of rank might not welcome identification with their caste by admission to a militia unit (Vinson, *Bearing Arms,* 85–86, 96, 224), the individuals who applied for *gracias al sacar* whitening belonged to the higher ranks of such militias and were willing to admit their designation, to provide royal service, and to be eligible to petition for full white status.

46. This was one way that wives and daughters might benefit from a husband's or father's service to the Crown. See Ann Twinam, "Playing the 'Gender Card': Imperial Bureaucrats, Petitioners, and *Gracias al Sacar* Legitimations and Whitenings" (paper presented at the Rocky Mountain Council of Latin American Studies, Phoenix, February 2003).

47. Konetzke, *CD,* vol. 2–2, doc. 546, 1687.

48. See Twinam *Public Lives,* 259–60.

49. See Twinam, "Playing the 'Gender Card.'"

50. Konetzke, *CD,* vol. 1, doc. 422, 1584; vol. 2–1, doc. 160, 1621; doc 231, 1636.

51. Konetzke, *CD,* vol. 2–1, doc. 180, 1623; vol. 3–1, doc. 84, 1713.

52. Konetzke, *CD,* vol. 2–1, doc. 154, 1620; vol. 3–1, doc. 96, 1717.

53. See Twinam, "Playing the 'Gender Card,'" for gendered differentials in passing.

54. Konetzke, *CD,* vol. 3–2, doc. 294, 1784, p. 604.

55. Konetzke, *CD,* vol. 3–1, doc. 196, 1765, p. 325.

56. Konetzke, *CD,* vol. 3–1, doc. 186, 1763, p. 307.

57. See Twinam, *Public Lives,* 204–7, for regional variations on discrimination.

58. Konetzke, *CD,* vol. 3–1, doc. 196, 1765.

59. See John Tate Lanning and John Jay TePaske, eds., *The Royal Protomedicato: The Regulation of the Medical Professions in the Spanish Empire* (Durham, N.C., 1985).

60. AGI, Santo Domingo 1455, n. 10, 1760.

61. Of course, this case illustrates female passing as well, given that both of his grandmothers were pardos.

62. The full case is in AGI, Santo Domingo 1457, n. 7, 1763; an extract is in Konetzke, *CD*, vol. 3–1, doc. 189, 1763.

63. Konetzke, *CD*, vol. 3–1, doc. 163, 1752.

64. Konetzke, *CD*, vol. 3–1, doc. 177. 1760.

65. See Twinam, "Playing the 'Gender Card,'" for analysis of how gender influenced petitions of pardos/mulattoes and judgments by royal officials. While some petitioners argued that descent from white fathers who were noble (*nobleza*) overrode the negative inheritance from a caste mother, the more usual interpretation was that such "defects" were gender neutral (*naturaleza*) and were invariably inherited from both the father and from the mother.

66. Konetzke, *CD*, vol. 3–1, doc. 191, 1764; doc. 192, 1764.

67. Konetzke, *CD*, vol. 3–1, doc. 336, 1793.

68. Konetzke, *CD*, vol. 3–1, doc. 199, 1765. Pardos, however, could use the ruling for their own ends by suggesting that the exemption granted Polo should serve as a precedent for university graduation. See Ann Twinam, "Pedro de Ayarza—The Purchase of Whiteness," in Kenneth Andrien, *Social Order and Disorder in Colonial Latin America* (Wilmington, 2002) where the Ayarza family successfully used the Polo precedent to graduate a son from university.

69. AGI, Panama 276, n. 3, 1767.

70. AGI, Panama, 286, n. 4, 1786.

71. The three examples were Borbua and two other Panamanian notaries (Hypolito Correoso and Francisco Homboni) whose depositions need to be located on a future research trip. Actually, both men also needed to be decreed legitimate to be notaries, but royal officials inexplicably overlooked the issue in these cases.

72. AGI, Guatemala 411, no n. 1783; sections of the case appear in Konetzke, *CD*, vol. 3–2, doc. 272, 1783.

73. AGI, Buenos Aires 280, n. 6, 1792, also contains a classic statement: "If a *mestizo* marries with a Spaniard it produces a *quarterón*, if this [latter] also marries with a Spaniard it leads to a *puchuelo*, and if this [latter] marries with a Spaniard it creates a pure Spaniard in the common understanding of the people and of those authors that deal with this material."

74. See Twinam, "Is Race a Defect?" for a comparison of how Cámara officials treated "defects" of birth (illegitimacy) and those of caste (pardo, mulatto) in evaluating *gracias al sacar* exemptions. Essentially they conceived of the "defects" themselves as fundamentally similar (in terms of their ability to remedy, the absolute and intergenerational effects if granted, and the reasons [service to the state] for dispensation.) The key difference was that legitimation caused fewer "inconveniences" in local societies compared to whitenings, a variable that led to the Venezuelan protests and the tabling of decisions on whitening in 1803.

75. There were also particular issues in the Ramírez case that led to negative comments. The *fiscal* read between the lines, a practice common to Bourbon officials,

many who had served in the colonies and were meticulous in squeezing nuances from letters or recommendations. In this case, he felt that even though the President of Guatemala had supported Ramírez petition "one can understand the [negative] in the clauses and style of the letter." Nor was he impressed with Ramírez genealogy, noting that when he was married, Ramírez and his wife were given the classification of "free mulattoes." The implication was that Ramirez was not passing socially or interacting with whites. Cope has suggested that race was as much a socially as a somatically or genealogically determined attribute, 49–67.

76. See other comments in Twinam, *Public Lives,* 291–97, 310.

77. Rodulfo Cortés, *El regimen de "las gracias al sacar,"* vol. 2, doc. 7.

78. The 1767 case of Juan Evaristo de Jesus Borbua from Panama refers to a 1758 precedent for a Bartolomé de Salazar, *quinterón,* granted in 1758. This is the earliest quinterón precedent to date. See AGI, Panama 276, no. 3, 1767. No doubt the Borbua and Paz cases were precedents, but other cases need to be located. Also, officials may well have added a price increase to sums originally charged, as this was the aim of the decree.

Afterword

1. My summary of these events comes from Oscar Handlin and Irving Mark, "Daniel Nimham v. Roger Morris, Beverly Robinson, and Philip Philipse—An Indian Case in Colonial New York, 1765–1767," *Ethnohistory* 2 (1964), 193–246. This is a reprint of "A geographic, historical Narrative or Summary of the present Controversy between Dan Nimham a native Indian; King or Sachem of the Wappinger Tribe of Indians so called in behalf of himself and the whole Tribe aforesaid, on the one Part; and Messrs. Roger Morris, Beverly Robinson, and Philip Philipse, all of the City and Province of New York, Heirs and Legal Representatives of Col. Frederick Philipse late of said New York." The author, who remains unknown, indicated who said what, providing a rough transcript of the proceedings. See also Irving Mark, *Agrarian Conflicts in Colonial New York, 1711–1775* (New York, 1965 [1940]); Sung Bok Kim, *Landlord and Tenant in Colonial New York: Manorial Society, 1664–1775* (Chapel Hill, N.C., 1978); Edward Countryman, "'Out of bounds of the Law': Northern Land Rioters in the Eighteenth Century," in Alfred F. Young, ed., *Explorations in the History of American Radicalism: The American Revolution* (DeKalb, Ill., 1976), 40–49; Countryman, *A People in Revolution: The American Revolution and Political Society in New York, 1760–1790* (New York, 1988); Thomas J. Humphrey, *Land and Liberty: Hudson Valley Riots in the Age of Revolution* (DeKalb, Ill., 2004). Simon Newman and Susan Branson helped me refine my thinking on these issues.

2. John Morrin Scott quoted in "Nimham v. Morris, Robinson, and Philipse," 240.

3. Daniel K. Richter makes this point in *Facing East from Indian Country: A Native History of Early America* (Cambridge, Mass., 2001), 8.

4. Here I am paraphrasing some language John Smolenski used in personal correspondence. His turn of phrase is far more explicit and illuminating than mine.

5. Daniel K. Richter, "Whose Indian History?" *William and Mary Quarterly*

3rd ser., 50 (April 1993), 379–93, and his footnotes for others. For the persistence of American exceptionalism, see Deborah L. Madsen, *American Exceptionalism* (Jackson, Miss., 1998).

6. For some examples of this approach, see, among others, Gary B. Nash, *Red, White, and Black: The Peoples of Early North America* (Upper Saddle River, N.J., 2000 [1974]); Richter, *Facing East from Indian Country*; and Geoffrey Plank, *An Unsettled Conquest: The British Campaign Against the Peoples of Acadia* (Philadelphia, 2000). See also White, *The Middle Ground*; Richter, "Whose Indian History?" 379–93; James H. Merrell, *Into the American Woods: Negotiators on the Pennsylvania Frontier* (New York, 1999); and Merritt, *At the Crossroads*. One textbook that follows a more inclusive path is Gary B. Nash and Julie Roy Jeffrey, eds., *The American People: Creating a Nation and a Society* (New York, 2000).

7. The literature on this subject is rich and deep. See, for example, Brian Stock, *The Implications of Literacy: Written Language and Models of Interpretation in the Eleventh and Twelfth Centuries* (Princeton, N.J., 1983); and Matthew Innes, "Memory, Orality and Literacy in an Early Medieval Society," *Past and Present* 158 (1998), 3–36. See also Patricia Seed, *Ceremonies of Possession in Europe's Conquest of the New World, 1492–1640* (New York, 1995).

8. See Thomas J. Humphrey, "Crowd and Court: Rough Music and Popular Justice in Colonial New York," in William Pencak, Matthew Dennis, and Simon P. Newman, eds., *Riot and Revelry in Early America* (University Park, Pa., 2002), 107–24; and Michel Foucault, *Power/Knowledge: Selected Interviews and Other Writings, 1972–1977* (New York, 1980), ch. 1.

Contributors

SHARON BLOCK is a member of the History Department at the University of California, Irvine. Her published essays include "Rape Without Women: Print Culture and the Politicization of Rape, 1765–1815," in the *Journal of American History* and "Lines of Color, Sex, and Service: Comparative Sexual Coercion in Early America," in *Sex, Love, Race: Crossing Boundaries in North American History*. She is the author of *Rape and Sexual Power in Early America* (Chapel Hill: University of North Carolina Press for the Omohundro Institute of Early American History and Culture, 2006).

MATTHEW DENNIS teaches history at the University of Oregon. He is the author of *Cultivating a Landscape of Peace: Iroquois-European Encounters in Seventeenth-Century America* (1993), and *Red, White, and Blue Letter Days: An American Calendar* (2002), and co-editor with William Pencak and Simon P. Newman of *Riot and Revelry in Early America* (2002). This volume's chapter is part of a work in progress, *Seneca Possessed: Witchcraft, Gender, and Colonialism on the Frontiers of the Early American Republic*. He is also at work on another book, *Bones: A Cultural and Political History of Death, Memory, and Mortal Remains in America*.

KIMBERLY GAUDERMAN is a member of the History Department at the University of New Mexico. She is the author of *Women's Lives in Colonial Quito: Gender, Law, and Economy in Spanish America* (2003).

TAMAR HERZOG teaches early modern Spanish and Latin American history at the University of Chicago. She is the author of *Upholding Justice: State, Law and the Penal System in Quito* (2004) and *Defining Nations: Immigrants and Citizens in Early Modern Spain and Spanish America* (2003), as well as other books published in Spanish and concerned with the relationships between Madrid and its overseas colonies. She is also the co-editor of *The Collective and the Public in Latin America: Cultural Identities and Political Order* (2000) and *Observation and Communication: The Construction of Realities in the Hispanic World* (1997).

THOMAS J. HUMPHREY teaches in the History Department at Cleveland State University. A former fellow of the Philadelphia (now McNeil) Center for Early American Studies, Tom is the author of several articles on eighteenth-century New York and of *Land and Liberty: Hudson Valley Riots in the Age of Revolution* (2004).

MARK MEUWESE is a member of the History Department at the University of Winnipeg, where he teaches courses on the history of the aboriginal peoples of the Americas. He is working on a book project dealing with native-Dutch interactions in the Americas.

GENE E. OGLE is Lecturer in History at John Cabot University in Rome. The author of articles in *French Colonial History* and *Historical Reflections/Réflexions Historiques*, he is currently completing a book entitled *Policing Saint Domingue: Race, Violence, and Honor in an Old Regime Colony*.

RICHARD PRICE divides his time between Virginia, where he is Dittman Professor of Anthropology, American Studies, and History at the College of William and Mary, and rural Martinique, which is his base for research and writing. His many books include *Maroon Societies* (Johns Hopkins University Press), *First-Time* (Johns Hopkins University Press), *Alabi's World* (Johns Hopkins University Press), and *The Convict and the Colonel* (Beacon Press). His latest, written with Sally Price, is *Romare Bearden: The Caribbean Dimension* (University of Pennsylvania Press).

CYNTHIA RADDING is the director of the Latin American and Iberian Institute of the University of New Mexico and professor of istory. Her research focuses on the cultural and environmental history of frontier regions of the Spanish-American empire and their development during the early republic. She published *Wandering Peoples. Colonialism, Ethnic Spaces, and Ecological Frontiers in Northwestern Mexico* (1997), and her recent comparative history is titled *Landscapes of Power and Identity: Comparative Borderlands in the Sonoran Desert and the Forests of Amazonia from Colony to Republic* (2005).

JOHN SMOLENSKI is a member of the History Department at the University of California, Davis. The author of articles on legal culture, Indian history, and print culture in colonial Pennsylvania, he is currently completing a book manuscript titled *Friends and Strangers: The Evolution of a Creole Civic Culture in Colonial Pennsylvania*.

CHRISTOPHER TOMLINS is a Senior Research Fellow at the American Bar Foundation in Chicago and the author or editor of several books, including *The Supreme Court of the United States* (2005), *The Many Legalities of Early America* (2001), *Law, Labor and Ideology in the Early American Republic* (1993, 2002), *Labor Law in America: Historical and Critical Essays* (1992), and *The State and the Unions: Labor Relations, Law and the Organized Labor Movement in America, 1880–1960* (1985). His current research addresses the interrelationship of work, colonization, and law in early Anglo-America and the historiography of legal history.

ANN TWINAM is a member of the History Department at the University of Texas at Austin. She is the author of *Public Lives, Private Secrets: Gender, Honor, Sexuality and Illegitimacy in Colonial Spanish America* (1999), which won the Thomas F. McGann Book Prize from the Rocky Mountain Council for Latin American Studies, and *Miners, Merchants, and Farmers in Colonial Colombia* (1982). She is currently completing a manuscript titled "Purchasing Whiteness: Official and Unofficial Passing in Colonial Spanish America" and researching a project titled "Sexuality, Illegitimacy, and Family in the Hispanic World: 1476–1800."

CÉCILE VIDAL is Lecturer in Modern History at University Pierre Mendes-France. The author of over a dozen articles on colonial New France, she is co-author (with Gilles Havard) of *Histoire de l'Amérique Française* (2003) and author of *Au pays des Illinois, Français et Indiens en Haute-Louisiane* (forthcoming).

Index

Acknowledgments

The editors would like to thank the Library Company of Philadelphia, the Ethnohistory and Latin American Cultures Programs at the University of Pennsylvania, the Legal History Colloquium at the University of Pennsylvania Law School, and especially the McNeil Center for Early American Studies for their generosity in funding the conference that gave rise to this volume. We would also like to thank Bob Lockhart, our editor at the University of Pennsylvania Press, two anonymous referees who gave valuable feedback, and especially Dan Richter, director of the McNeil Center, for all of their support and assistance during the production of this volume.